Sara Levy's World

Eastman Studies in Music

Ralph P. Locke, Senior Editor
Eastman School of Music

Additional Titles of Interest

The Art of Musical Phrasing in the Eighteenth Century:
Punctuating the Classical "Period"
Stephanie D. Vial

Bach and the Pedal Clavichord: An Organist's Guide
Joel Speerstra

Bach's Changing World: Voices in the Community
Edited by Carol K. Baron

Marianna Martines: A Woman Composer in the Vienna of Mozart and Haydn
Irving Godt
Edited by John A. Rice

The Music of Carl Philipp Emanuel Bach
David Schulenberg

The Music of the Moravian Church in America
Edited by Nola Reed Knouse

The Music of Wilhelm Friedemann Bach
David Schulenberg

Ruth Crawford Seeger's Worlds:
Innovation and Tradition in Twentieth-Century American Music
Edited by Ray Allen and Ellie M. Hisama

Sacred Song and the Pennsylvania Dutch
Daniel Jay Grimminger

Songs without Words:
Keyboard Arrangements of Vocal Music in England, 1560–1760
Sandra Mangsen

A complete list of titles in the Eastman Studies in Music series may be found
on the University of Rochester Press website, www.urpress.com

Sara Levy's World

Gender, Judaism, and the Bach Tradition in Enlightenment Berlin

Edited by Rebecca Cypess and Nancy Sinkoff

UNIVERSITY OF ROCHESTER PRESS

The University of Rochester Press gratefully acknowledges generous support from the Office of the Dean, Mason Gross School of the Arts, Rutgers University.

First published 2018

University of Rochester Press
668 Mt. Hope Avenue, Rochester, NY 14620, USA
www.urpress.com
and Boydell & Brewer Limited
PO Box 9, Woodbridge, Suffolk IP12 3DF, UK
www.boydellandbrewer.com

ISBN-13: 978-1-58046-921-0
ISSN: 1071-9989

Library of Congress Cataloging-in-Publication Data

Names: Cypess, Rebecca, editor. | Sinkoff, Nancy, 1959– editor.
Title: Sara Levy's world : gender, Judaism, and the Bach tradition in
    enlightenment Berlin / edited by Rebecca Cypess and Nancy Sinkoff.
Other titles: Eastman studies in music ; v. 145.
Description: Rochester : University of Rochester Press, 2018. | Series:
    Eastman studies in music, 1071-9989 ; v. 145 | Includes bibliographical
    references and index.
Identifiers: LCCN 2018006241 | ISBN 9781580469210 (hardcover : alk. paper)
Subjects: LCSH: Levy, Sara, 1761–1854. | Jewish musicians—Germany—Berlin. |
    Jewish women—Germany—Berlin. | Bach
    family—Appreciation—Germany—Berlin. | Music—Social
    aspects—Germany—Berlin—History.
Classification: LCC ML417.L645 S37 2018 | DDC 780.92 [B] —dc23 LC record
    available at https://lccn.loc.gov/2018006241

For Josh, Ben, Joey, and Sally, with thanks for
making a place for Sara Levy in our family.
—R. C.
For Gary, my inspiration and guide from Bach to Bird.
—N. S.

Contents

Part Three: Studies in Sara Levy's Collection

Acknowledgments

The publication of this book would not have been possible without the generosity and support of numerous institutions and individuals. The seeds for this volume were planted at the conference "Sara Levy's World: Music, Gender, and Judaism in Enlightenment Berlin," held at Rutgers University, which received funding from the New Jersey Council for the Humanities and the German Academic Exchange Service (DAAD), as well as the following schools and units at Rutgers: the Center for European Studies, the Dean's Office of the Mason Gross School of the Arts, the Dean's Office of the School of Arts and Sciences, the Bildner Center for the Study of Jewish Life, the Department of Music, the Department of Jewish Studies, and the Department of German, Russian, and East European Languages and Literatures.

This book took root in the rich interdisciplinary environment at Rutgers, for which we are most grateful. A subvention for the publication has been generously provided by the Dean's Office of the Mason Gross School of the Arts at Rutgers, and we thank Dean George B. Stauffer for his gracious and indispensable support—both material and otherwise—throughout our work on this project. Susanna Treesh, Administrator of the Center for European Studies, has been of invaluable help, and we are indebted to her for her patience and her meticulous attention to detail. We thank the librarians at Rutgers University as well as the libraries throughout the United States, Europe, and Israel that have assisted the authors in obtaining and reproducing primary material, especially the staff of the Staatsbibliothek zu Berlin, now the home of the *Sing-Akademie* archive, which includes the vast majority of Sara Levy's collection.

It has been a great pleasure to work with the editors and staff of the University of Rochester Press and the Eastman Studies in Music series. We thank Ralph Locke for his faith in this project, as well as Julia Cook, Tracey Engel, Sonia Kane, and Ryan Peterson for shepherding the book through every aspect of its conceptual and mechanical evolution. We are especially pleased with Steve Kress's creative design for the book's jacket. Thanks are due, too, to Lynette Bowring for her generous editorial assistance.

We are delighted that this project led to the audio recording *In Sara Levy's Salon* (Acis Productions, 2017), with Rebecca Cypess and The Raritan Players: Dongmyung Ahn, Christine Gummere, Rebecca Harris, Benjamin Shute,

Yi-heng Yang, and Steven Zohn. (The recording may be heard at www.acis productions.com/saralevyaudio.) Bringing the sounds of Sara Levy's salon to life in tandem with her intellectual and cultural context has been an illuminating and joyful experience, and we are grateful to these musicians for their contributions to this project.

The anonymous peer reviewers for the press provided extremely helpful comments and suggestions that have improved the book at every level, and we thank them for their time and intellectual generosity. Finally, we extend our heartfelt gratitude to our families for their constant encouragement and their limitless investment in our work.

Rebecca Cypess
Highland Park, New Jersey

Nancy Sinkoff
New York, New York

August, 2017

Introduction

Experiencing Sara Levy's World

Nancy Sinkoff

In the opening scene of Aaron Halle Wolfssohn's hilarious and biting satirical play *Laykhtzin und fremelay* (Yid./Ger., Silliness and Sanctimony, 1796), aesthetics and Jewish tradition are pitted against one another, with Jewish women the leading culprits in a headlong rush into excessive and ruinous modernization through music—both instrumental and vocal.[1] Wolfssohn (1756–1835) was a *maskil*, an enlightened Jew, and a member of the first generation of Prussian Jews to attempt to live as modern Europeans. In 1785, he arrived in Berlin, the capital of both the Prussian *Aufklärung* (Enlightenment) and the *Haskalah* (Heb., Jewish Enlightenment), an ideological movement dedicated to the modernization of Ashkenazic Jewish culture and society.[2] A gifted author in three languages, Wolfssohn soon became part of the circle around the renowned philosopher Moses Mendelssohn, and began to write for the Hebrew *Haskalah* journal, *Ha-me'asef* (The Gatherer), becoming its sole editor from 1794 to 1797. Dedicated to the early *Haskalah*'s moderate pathway of modernization, which sought to encourage Ashkenazic Jewry to shed what *maskilim* (Heb., plural of *maskil*) believed was obscurantist piety and reform it in the spirit of "reasonable" religion without succumbing to the blandishments of the pseudo-Enlightenment, Wolfssohn found himself—with other *maskilim*—in a state of despair toward the century's end.[3] The audience for their enlightened works beyond their own circle of Jewish intelligentsia was the sons and daughters of the Jewish bourgeoisie. Yet this group seemed to be headed solely toward becoming modern Germans, abandoning the world of their ancestors almost as quickly as they discarded the Yiddish vernacular for High German.[4] They—and especially their headstrong daughters—were the primary targets of his satire.[5]

The plot of *Laykhtzin und fremelay*, inspired by Moliere's *Tartuffe*, unfolds in the home of a Prussian Court Jew, Reb Henoch, a recent returnee to devout religious practice who has hired a certain Reb Yoysefkhe from Poland to tutor his son, Shmuel, in traditional Jewish subjects, such as the Talmud and biblical commentaries.[6] The Polish-Jewish tutor, however, is a sanctimonious and hypocritical charlatan who has designs on the hand of Reb Henoch's spoiled daughter, Yetkhen, whom he tries to woo—all the while chasing the household maid and being a regular client at a working-class brothel.[7] The other characters in the play are likewise flawed. Yetkhen herself is depicted as beautiful, intellectually and musically gifted, but superficial; her mother Teltse, as mildly hysterical and oblivious; and her gentile suitor, Herr von Schnapps, who kidnaps Yetkhen (a pun on his name) for ransom money, as criminal.[8] The play's only hero is Uncle Markus, the prototypical *maskil*: sage, calm, and reasonable.

Wolfssohn not only deployed ideological and linguistic markers to express his dismay at the wrongheaded approaches to modernity undertaken by both the rigidly pious and the licentious freethinking, but also directly addressed the ways in which the arts, especially music, functioned as part of the aspirational culture of modernizing elite Prussian Jews in the eighteenth century. In act 2, scene 4 of *Laykhtzin und fremelay*, Reb Yoysefkhe interrupts Yetkhen as she is playing on a keyboard instrument—likely a pianoforte or harpsichord—to declare his marital intentions. Although his bourgeois patron, Yetkhen's father, has approved the match, Yoysefkhe is soundly rebuffed by the imperious girl, who asserts her will—that distinctive feature of the Enlightenment self—to set him straight. The scene ends, presaging Yoysefkhe's failure, with his striking the piano in frustration. Yetkhen cries out, "Mein schönes Klavier ist ganz kaput" ("My beautiful piano is completely destroyed").[9]

Why did Wolfssohn focus on Yetkhen's engagement with music, in this scene highlighting her skill as a keyboardist and in earlier scenes emphasizing her vocal prowess?[10] Because music—its individual study and performance, its patronage through financial support of a composer's domicile as well as the commissioning of pieces, singing, and the hosting of private and semipublic concerts—formed an indispensable part of the lives of the Berlin Court Jews in the last quarter of the eighteenth century.[11] For enlightened eighteenth-century Europeans, music was an essential component of *Bildung*, the broad ideal of individual moral improvement, ethical cultivation, and aesthetic refinement that would foster a more capacious civic sphere.[12] Ardent proponents of *Bildung*, Jewish modernizers, the ideologically motivated *maskilim*, and the acculturating members of the social elite considered engagement with aesthetics and practice of the arts crucial to their negotiations with European culture. Both men and women were deeply engaged with the cultural, social, and linguistic transformations of Prussian Jewish society.

Gender mattered in these transformations. Elite Jewish men and women partook of European culture differently, and there was different symbolic value in the ways in which their participation was interpreted. Although the *maskilim* sought to transform "the Jews" generally, they focused their efforts on Jewish men. Prussian *maskilim* viewed traditional Jewish education, whose goal was to form *talmidei ḥakhamim,* male Torah scholars, not members of the *Gebildetebürgertum* (the educated and cultivated middle class), as an obstacle to *Bildung,* and waged a full-throated assault on traditional rabbinic pedagogy. They attacked it for its lack of standardized curriculum and trained teachers, its almost-exclusive focus on study of the Talmud, and its dependence upon Yiddish—a language considered a shameful "jargon" or bastardized dialect of German by modernizing Jews—as the oral conduit for sacred Hebrew scripture.[13] Prussian *maskilim* sought to transform young Jewish men into modern Jews capable of mastering mathematics, grammar, and geography, among other subjects vital to integration, *and* of learning Hebrew grammar to help revitalize Jewish society.[14]

Daughters were another matter entirely. In traditional homes, girls in Ashkenazic Jewish society learned religious essentials mimetically through their domestic relationships with their mothers, aunts, cousins, and sisters. *Maskilim* were slow to include Jewish daughters in their modern pedagogical efforts.[15] Yet the elite court Jewish families of Berlin supplemented their daughters' education, in order to rear them to be cultivated bourgeois housewives, with instruction in what can only be called the "gentile" arts: writing, speaking, and reading in German and French; dancing; singing; and studying, commissioning, enjoying, and performing music.[16] Keyboard lessons were a required part of the bourgeois training of such young women.[17]

Benefiting from royal patronage under Frederick the Great and bourgeois economic development, the arts and sciences grew among Berlin's cultural and intellectual elite, which included Huguenots, German Protestants, Catholics, and Jews. This dynamic cosmopolitan environment proved fateful for Jewish history. In contrast to the rest of Prussian Jewry, Berlin's wealthiest Jews enjoyed royal privileges after the Seven Years' War that allowed them to participate broadly in the stimulating environment of the capital.[18] Music played a pivotal role in the social gatherings—generally referred to as "salons"—created by German-Jewish women.[19] It was performed, listened to, and discussed by the *salonnières* and their guests, carefully chosen cultured individuals who could appreciate what was being played.[20]

Born in Berlin in 1761 just as the city was becoming a center of the Prussian Enlightenment, Sara Levy was among the select and highly visible cohort of Jewish women actively engaged in becoming modern Europeans and for whom music was a critical vehicle in that process.[21]

Empowered by his wealth and connections to the court as the principal supplier of the Prussian mint, her father, Daniel Itzig, was able to create a lifestyle for his family commensurate with that of elite gentiles of his period. Striving to integrate into non-Jewish society, Itzig adopted the mores, values, and social practices of the surrounding culture, building an extraordinary home, collecting art, becoming a patron of music, and insisting that his children, including his daughters, become proficient musicians.[22] He hired Johann Philipp Kirnberger, a student of Johann Sebastian Bach, to teach Hanna and Bella, the family's two eldest daughters. Sara's younger sister Fanny, later a prominent Viennese *salonnière* in her own right, was an instrumentalist who helped establish the *Gesellschaft der Musikfreunde*, and later created the music hall that became home to the Vienna Philharmonic Orchestra.[23] She and her husband Nathan von Arnstein hosted Mozart in their home in 1781, and entertained numerous other important composers and performers in Vienna.[24] Sara, who studied music with Wilhelm Friedemann Bach, was a gifted keyboardist, cited by both Jewish and non-Jewish writers for her skill. Levy played the harpsichord and the fortepiano, and owned instruments made by the famous Strasbourg craftsman Friedrich Silbermann.[25]

Sara played music at gatherings in her home and in the more public setting of the *Sing-Akademie zu Berlin*. She would become a patron of Friedemann Bach and, later, of his brother Carl Philipp Emanuel. Her patronage extended to numerous Jewish causes as well, including the Jewish orphanage in Berlin. She was also an avid collector, acquiring an enormous number of music manuscripts and printed editions by composers of her own day and from the previous generation.

Being a "young lady at music" did not necessarily mean playing solely for oneself.[26] Music making allowed elite women to blur the boundaries between the private, domestic female sphere and the public, male one. The eighteenth-century salon, though domestic, was not completely private; as Christoph Wolff notes, an orchestra of the size common in the eighteenth century could easily have fit into Levy's music rooms.[27] Levy often performed for an audience at home and—stretching the boundaries of expected female behavior—she also played for friends and acquaintances in the public venue of the *Sing-Akademie zu Berlin*, which had been founded in 1791 by Carl Fasch, a harpsichordist to the Prussian court.

Levy's relationship with the *Sing-Akademie* illustrates the central role that Jews played in the creation of German musical history and in laying the groundwork for Felix Mendelssohn's later initiation of a public Bach revival. After her husband Samuel Levy's death in 1806, Sara became particularly active in the *Sing-Akademie* and later donated her collection of music—which included instrumental pieces, solo works, chamber music, symphonies, and keyboard concertos, many by the Bach family—to the institution in the care of Carl Friedrich Zelter, who had been appointed to the directorship of the *Sing-Akademie* in 1800. Zelter, in turn, became particularly committed to the works of J. S. Bach, performing excerpts from his Passions, Masses, and cantatas at a time when it was not common practice among the general public to revisit the music of the past century. Zelter would become the music teacher of Felix Mendelssohn in 1811, when Abraham and Lea Mendelssohn moved their family to Berlin from Hamburg, and would pass on his ardor for Bach to his remarkable student, ensuring continued interest in Bach's music. We may assume that some of Mendelssohn's zeal for the Bach tradition came from his maternal grandmother and great-aunts, including Sara Levy.[28]

In 1823, Abraham and Lea Mendelssohn formally converted to Protestantism, having baptized Felix and his siblings at birth, and added Bartholdy to their surname to distinguish themselves from their Jewish family. Sara Levy, along with her sister Fanny and some other members of the family, remained faithful to her origins. Sara and her husband had no children, and she left a large proportion of her considerable fortune to the Jewish orphanage mentioned above.[29] Natalie Naimark-Goldberg, in her contribution to the present volume, contends that Sara Levy's active participation in the Jewish community of Berlin was quite unusual within her circle, apparently reflecting a conscious decision to adhere to her family's religious traditions. She combined her participation in and dedication to German and European culture with her uninterrupted commitment to Jewish affairs in a way that other women, including some of her relatives and most of her friends, did not. Levy's deep engagement with music—even with a tradition dominated by Christian motifs—did not threaten her Jewishness.

Though Sara Levy's life intersected with the major social, ideological, political, and musical issues in the history of the European, German, and Jewish Enlightenments, she has been largely ignored. In the not-so-distant past, most scholars focused on the *salonnières* as examples of radical assimilation. The Jewish women of Berlin were seen as a litmus test of Jewish continuity in the face of rapid modernization. For Heinrich Graetz (1817–91) and Shimon Dubnow (1860–1941), master historians, respectively, of the nineteenth and twentieth centuries who wrote Jewish history as part of a spiritual and national commitment to modern Jewish existence, the *salonnières* were traitors who severed their ties to their religion and people.[30] In contrast to the traditionalist and nationalist views, pioneering feminist historians, seeking role models for independent women, praised the Jewish women of late-eighteenth-century Berlin as proto-feminists who successfully challenged the patriarchal conventions of traditional Jewish life.[31] Only recently has scholarship on the circle of modernizing Jewish women in Enlightenment Berlin shifted away from a preoccupation with those who chose to assimilate radically by converting to

Christianity. As we will see, Sara Levy stands out among other Berlin *salonnières* for her resolute commitment to Jewish life. Viewing her choices within a spectrum of complex, distinctive paths to modernization helps us to understand the entangled relationships among the Enlightenment, the *Haskalah*, acculturation, and secularization in the lives of late-eighteenth-century German Jews, both men and women.

Sara Levy's life also appertains to the field of music history generally and to German music history specifically. Examining her life allows scholars to probe how elite German Jews participated in the arts to construct and respond to late-eighteenth-century ideas, including philosophy and aesthetics, as part of their acculturation. The engagement with the arts among the Itzigs, Mendelssohns, Levys, von Arnsteins, and other late-eighteenth-century Jews played a decisive role in German culture, a role that has not always been recognized by musicologists and scholars of German musical history. Levy's passion for Bach and his legacy engages questions of musical historicism and its relationship to the processes of canonization of German and European art music in the eighteenth and nineteenth centuries. Levy's involvement with the *Sing-Akademie* and its archive illuminates the role Jews played in creating, protecting, and preserving the German musical heritage. The musical commitments of elite Jews in Sara Levy's circle also stand in dialogue with the male, textual Hebraist *Haskalah*. Indeed, as recent scholarship has emphasized, music played an important role in the modernizing ideology of the first *maskil*, Moses Mendelssohn, who viewed aesthetics as a key vehicle for uplifting his fellow Jews.[32]

Because Jews were central to the formation of the German middle class in the nineteenth century and music making was key to their aspirations, it behooves scholars to take more seriously the role of women like Sara Levy—and of the music she performed and patronized—in social class formation, as Marion Kaplan did in her pioneering study of the nineteenth century, *The Making of the Jewish Middle Class: Women, Family, and Identity in Imperial Germany*.[33] Fortunately, historians of Jewish modernity have begun to recognize how music making—as much as the acquisition of a literary European education—was a component of *Bildung*. Playing and listening to music could lead to refinement and the development of character. And obviously, Sara Levy's life is fertile ground for women's historians who seek to understand how gender informed Enlightenment ideals, the creation of a civic sphere, educational prescriptions, and every other aspect of German culture at the turn of the nineteenth century.[34]

Finally, reexamining the ways in which Jews in Sara Levy's world interacted with Christian musicians and music reopens the debate about the Prussian Enlightenment's tolerance of Jews. Decades ago, in his *Tradition and Crisis: Jewish Society at the End of the Middle Ages*—first published in Hebrew in 1958—Jacob Katz argued that eighteenth-century Berlin had successfully become a "neutral society," one that offered the possibility of full Jewish participation in and integration into German society.[35] He reevaluated this term in 1973, concluding that modern German nationalism, born in the late eighteenth century, had not been able to expunge the Christological bias against Judaism, even in the heady days of the sympathetic friendship and intellectual camaraderie between Moses Mendelssohn and Gottfried Ephraim Lessing.[36] In his revised view, Katz concluded that late-eighteenth-century Prussia had only created a "semi-neutral society."[37]

Katz's reconsideration of the degree to which modernizing German Jews could be accepted into non-Jewish society at the end of the eighteenth century speaks to the vast issue of the historiographic reassessments of the Enlightenment that continue to this day.[38] Our volume grapples with the role of aesthetics in the Prussian Enlightenment in that reassessment, particularly with the legacy of negotiations of Jews and Christians over the "universality" of the music so beloved by both. Ruth HaCohen defined "the music libel against the Jews" as "the historical categorization of the Jew as a producer of noise in a Christian universe conceived of as dominated by harmonious sounds." She observed that many of the key texts of the Prussian Enlightenment, including Bach's Passions and Handel's oratorios *Samson, Israel in Egypt,* and *Judas Maccabeus,* "exemplify and anticipate artistic articulations of 'communal modes' of sympathy, solidarity, and redemption in the centuries to come. [Yet], concomitantly, they also harbor latent modes of alienation and discrimination."[39] The European Enlightenment unquestionably contained paradoxical, at times contradictory messages about Jews and their Europeanness; even the individuals who have come to be regarded as the most sympathetic to Jewish inclusion were skeptical of the success of Jewish integration.[40] This ambivalence played out musically, producing both harmony and dissonance.[41] Our volume does not shy away from that ambivalence.

On her own terms, Sara Levy was a fascinating and unusual person, whose legacy as a gifted musician allows us to experience her world and musical passions with all of our senses. She crossed cultural and intellectual boundaries of the early modern period, negotiating a variety of environments while maintaining her own religious identity. Levy did so while participating actively in and contributing to a broader cultural context in which secularization, modernization, and interfaith sociability, issues that are still relevant today, were central if contested subjects of discussion.

This volume is the result of an international symposium, "Sara Levy's World: Music, Gender, and Judaism in Enlightenment Berlin," held at Rutgers University in September 2014. It seeks to explore anew the role of gender, music, aesthetics, modernity, anti-Judaism, and Jewish identity in Sara Levy's world. It strives to interpret the experience of the Jewish women of Berlin through their own subjectivity and not through the lens of a maskilic parody or through either German or Jewish nationalist historiography, and to allow scholarship from a multidisciplinary perspective to enrich our understanding of the historical, musical, and philosophical contexts that shaped Sara Levy's role in German musical history—particularly in her family's commitment to preserving the legacy of the Bach family's corpus—and Jewish modernity. We have included articles by musicologists, intellectual and social historians, and scholars of modern Jewish thought and philosophy to create a polyphonic perspective on Sara Levy's world.

Our book is divided into three sections. Part 1, "Portrait of a Jewish Female Artist: Music, Identity, Image," treats Sara Levy the person, analyzing her place within the Jewish Enlightenment as well as her roles as patron, collector, keyboardist, and active participant in the preservation of the Bach musical legacy in late-eighteenth- and early-nineteenth-century Berlin. In some ways, this section could be considered "compensatory," ensuring that Sara Levy gets her rightful place in history and, in so doing, expanding the canvas on which German musical history has been written. Yet this is not a case of "add women and stir."[42] The neglect of Sara Levy's role has also distorted the significance of the Court Jewish phenomenon and extends to issues as broad as the relationship between aesthetics and social class formation, the role of Jews in cultivating musical historicism in late-eighteenth- and early-nineteenth-century Prussia, and the engagement of *maskilim* in what musicologist Ruth HaCohen has called the project of "sonic" integration.[43]

Chapter 1, Marjanne E. Goozé's "What Was the Berlin Jewish Salon around 1800?," looks carefully at the genesis, high point, and demise of the female-hosted salon in late-eighteenth-century Prussia. Despite the paucity of sources generated by the *salonnières* themselves, historians have nonetheless projected their own visions onto these women. Goozé emphasizes that the salons, which she considers liminal or extrasocial spaces, primarily allowed elite Jewish women to attain an education in German secular culture. Growing out of and functioning simultaneously with male-led reading circles, they featured discussions of books read privately as well as reading aloud, play acting, card playing, social interaction, and music. These intimate environments included Jews and Christians until the Napoleonic occupation of Berlin in 1806, which radically changed the political atmosphere that had encouraged the development of the salon.

In chapter 2, "Sara Levy's Musical Salon and Her Bach Collection," Christoph Wolff examines the history of Sara Levy's collection and the archive of the *Sing-Akademie zu Berlin*. It builds on the archival evidence uncovered in 2001 with the rediscovery of the collection of the *Sing-Akademie* in Kiev, and places the archive within the context of Sara Levy's musical and cultural worlds. The chapter also explores Levy's participation and lasting impact upon the musical culture of the *Sing-Akademie* as an institution, with special reference to members of Levy's extended family who contributed to it—especially Felix Mendelssohn. The "Bach Cult" that Levy cultivated in the late eighteenth century reached its full expression in the Bach revival that Mendelssohn and his contemporaries initiated, beginning in the 1820s.

Chapter 3, Natalie Naimark-Goldberg's "Remaining within the Fold: The Cultural and Social World of Sara Levy," examines to what extent Sara Levy was an intrinsic part of the circle of elite female Jews in late-eighteenth-century Berlin whose embrace of modernization led to radical assimilation, including conversion. Naimark-Goldberg argues that Levy was a committed Jew who remained involved in Jewish causes and institutions, including her support of the *Haskalah* and Jewish education, throughout her life. This engagement was matched by her involvement in elite musical circles of her time. Naimark-Goldberg demonstrates that Levy combined her participation in and dedication to German and European culture with her continuous commitment to Jewish life.

In chapter 4, "Women's Voices in Bach's Musical World: Christiane Mariane von Ziegler and Faustina Bordoni," George B. Stauffer continues the examination of gender in eighteenth-century German musical history, illustrating that women played a crucial role in shaping the work of one of the most important composers of the preceding generation, Johann Sebastian Bach. His chapter focuses especially on the Leipzig poetess Christiane Mariane von Ziegler, who wrote texts for nine of Sebastian's cantatas, and on Faustina Bordoni, who appears to have sung the "Laudamus te" at the first performance of the *Missa* of the B-Minor Mass in Dresden in 1733. In their gender, if not their religion, these women foreshadow the significant role that Sara Levy would play in the transmission and reception of the venerable Bach's music.

Part 2, "Music, Aesthetics, and Philosophy: Jews and Christians in Sara Levy's World," treats the social and ideological implications of Sara Levy's world, specifically focusing on Christian–Jewish relations as they affected social interactions, musical commentary, religious polemic, and the role of Jews and Judaism in nineteenth-century German national culture, components of which became virulently anti-Jewish. These chapters explore anew the legacy of Lutheran anti-Judaism; the social meaning of conversion; the question of the "universality" of Christian music performed, commissioned, and preserved by Jews; and the personal negotiations of Sara Levy, who remained part of the Jewish community until her death, when many of those most dear to her had adopted Christianity.

Chapter 5, "Lessing and the Limits of Enlightenment," is reprinted from Martha B. Helfer's full study, *The Word Unheard: Legacies of Anti-Semitism in German Literature and Culture*, about latent anti-Semitism in the classical German literary canon.[44] This chapter reconsiders the literary legacy of the great Enlightenment author Gotthold Ephraim Lessing (1729–81), Germany's most famous advocate of religious tolerance and an icon of interfaith friendship. Reexamining Lessing's three major works promoting tolerance toward Jews and Judaism—the theological treatise *The Education of the Human Race* (1780) and the two plays, *The Jews* (1749) and *Nathan the Wise* (1779)—Helfer finds a persistent tension running throughout this oeuvre, which helped to shape the rhetoric of anti-Semitism that subsequently informed German culture's views of Jews and Judaism.

Elias Sacks turns back to the "first" modern German Jew, the philosopher, intercessor, and biblical translator and commentator Moses Mendelssohn, to draw our attention to his important but little-studied translation of the Psalms and treatment of biblical music. In chapter 6, "Poetry, Music, and the Limits of Harmony: Mendelssohn's Aesthetic Critique of Christianity," Sacks presents a Mendelssohn who deploys his aesthetic commitments not merely to defend Judaism, but also to critique Christianity. He shows that one of Mendelssohn's strategies for insisting on the suitability of extending civic rights to the Jews was to showcase the aesthetic richness of the Jewish tradition, especially through the sonority of biblical poetry. Even more subversively, Sacks claims that Mendelssohn also believed that fundamental theological and ethical problems plagued Christianity. Without a tradition of reciting the biblical text musically through a system of vocalized cantillation, Christians could not hear God's word and were thus deprived of the biblical text's essential meaning. Sacks's chapter complicates the view that Mendelssohn read the Psalms as a proof text for his belief in a common universalist ethos shared by enlightened Christians and Jews.

Chapter 7, Yael Sela's "Longing for the Sublime: Jewish Self-Consciousness and the *St. Matthew Passion* in Biedermeier Berlin" investigates the ways in which commitment to music and the aesthetic intimately shaped the lives—both internal and external—of the elite daughters of the Jewish bourgeoisie in late-eighteenth- and early-nineteenth-century Prussia. Sela explores how Rahel Levin Varnhagen (1771–1833), a Jewish woman in Sara Levy's circle, responded to the most dramatic musical event of her lifetime: the revival of Johann Sebastian Bach's *St. Matthew Passion* in 1829 at the *Sing-Akademie*, a venture initiated, organized, and conducted by Felix Mendelssohn Bartholdy, Levy's great-nephew. Sela claims that Varnhagen's engagement with the aesthetics of the sublime—as well as her understanding of the function of music and poetry in modern music—help to explicate the vexing issue of Jewish reception of the Lutheran ideology embedded in Bach's work among the members of Sara Levy's circle.

Part 3, "Studies in Sara Levy's Collection," turns directly to the music collected and preserved by Sara Levy and her family, examining how music collecting can be interpreted as a social practice, one that gives insight into identity formation and ideological commitment.[45] In chapter 8, "Duets in the Collection of Sara Levy and the Ideal of 'Unity in Multiplicity,'" Rebecca Cypess turns to the collections of Sara Levy and her sisters Fanny von Arnstein and Tzippora Wulff (later Cäcilie von Eskeles), arguing that the sisters had a special interest in music for like instruments: duets for two flutes and two violas, and, especially, keyboard duos and double concertos that could be played on two harpsichords, two fortepianos, or a harpsichord and fortepiano together. Cypess's chapter explores the theoretical underpinnings of the duos in Sara Levy's collection through descriptions of performance and aesthetics by both Jewish and non-Jewish writers with whom Levy was likely familiar. She also adduces Moses Mendelssohn's writings to suggest that shared musical experiences could help to cultivate a sense of *Einheit in der Mannigfaltigkeit*—"unity in multiplicity." Cypess claims that the musical duo may thus be understood as a metaphor for—and enactment of—an ideal of a social and religious sphere in which Jews and non-Jews could maintain their individual identities even as they built a common culture.

Chapter 9, Steven Zohn's "The Sociability of Salon Culture and Carl Philipp Emanuel Bach's Quartets," also interprets musical compositions, in this case the three late quartets for flute, viola, and keyboard, Wq. 93–95, composed by Carl Philipp Emanuel Bach for the Berlin salon of Sara Levy, as a reflection of social practice. These pieces' unique scoring and progressive style set them apart from Bach's earlier chamber music. Building on Christoph Wolff's observation that the music displays "an evenly balanced instrumental discourse that permits the composer to engage in a lively, intense, and witty musical dialogue" and that it served as "a fitting interlude to the verbal conversations" at Levy's salon,[46] Zohn argues that it is precisely this conversational quality that marks Bach's quartets as exceptional within his oeuvre. In their alternating gestures of reciprocity, concession, and subversion, Bach's quartets represent a shift away from the aesthetic of inward self-expression, seen most clearly in his solo keyboard music, and toward an "outward" aesthetic emphasizing the type of human deportment and sociability characteristic of Levy's literary-musical gatherings.

Barbara Hahn's appendix, "The *Salonnière* and the Diplomat: Letters from Sara Levy to Karl Gustav von Brinckmann," gives new documentary evidence of Sara Levy's interfaith sociability. Roughly twenty letters to and from Sara Levy, written between 1796 and 1819 in French and German, found in the archive of Swedish diplomat Karl Gustav von Brinckmann (1764–1847), attest to the active avenues for atypical friendships and interfaith sociability afforded by salon culture. Sara Levy met Brinckmann, the son of Secretary Hans Gustaf von Brinckmann and Countess Beata Kristina Leijon Manor, at the close of the eighteenth century, when his professional duties brought him to Berlin. He had received a strict Protestant religious education as a child. The letters between Sara Levy and Brinckmann cover a broad range of shared cultural interests, including music and literature. Reproducing four complete letters, together with excerpts from others, in their original language and in English translation, the appendix allows readers to enter the intimate world of interfaith friendship at the turn of the nineteenth century.

In addition to the text of these chapters, we are pleased to provide readers with access to a newly released recording of music for solo keyboard or for small chamber groups played, collected, commissioned, or underwritten by Sara Levy (The Raritan Players and Rebecca Cypess, *In Sara Levy's Salon*, Acis Productions B06ZYP8SRN). Readers may access this recording by going to the website www.acisproductions.com/saralevyaudio and entering the password shown in the front cover of this volume. The website includes ample program notes to supplement the multisensory experience of Sara Levy's World.

Immanuel Kant's iconic Enlightenment salvo, "Sapere aude!" (Dare to know!), charged his fellow Europeans to possess fully their own rationality and apply it to understanding and shaping the world. In her own time, Sara Levy did not hesitate to know herself and the world around her. This volume is our effort to explore all the facets of Sara Levy's complex world. In so doing, we also hope to give Sara Levy her historical due, honoring her selfhood as a woman, a musician, a Jew, and an enlightened person.

Notes

1. Wolfssohn wrote the play in a mixture of Judeo-German and Yiddish—with both languages using Hebrew orthography—which allowed the playwright to tailor his characters' speech to their cultural and social positions. A Hebrew version was published the same year. On the play, see Joel Berkowitz and Jeremy Dauber, ed. and trans., *Landmark Yiddish Plays: A Critical Anthology* (Albany: SUNY Press, 2006), 10–18, and Shmuel Feiner, *The Origins of Jewish Secularization in Eighteenth-Century Europe*, trans. Chaya Naor (Philadelphia: University of Pennsylvania Press, 2010), 219–20. On Wolfssohn, see Jutta Strauss, "Aaron Halle-Wolfson: Ein Leben in drei Sprachen," in *Musik und Ästhetik in Berlin Moses Mendelssohns*, ed. Anselm Gerhard (Tübingen: Max Neimeyer Verlag, 1999), 57–76. See 72n86 on his characters' languages.
2. The literature on the *Haskalah* in Prussia is vast. See, for example, Steven M. Lowenstein, *The Berlin Jewish Community: Enlightenment, Family, and Crisis, 1770–1830* (New York: Oxford University Press, 1994); Shmuel Feiner, *The Jewish Enlightenment*, trans. Chaya Naor (Philadelphia: University of Pennsylvania Press, 2004); Michael A. Meyer, *The Origins of the Modern Jew: Jewish Identity and European Culture in Germany 1749–1824* (Detroit, MI: Wayne State University Press, 1979); Nancy Sinkoff, "Haskalah," in *Europe 1450 to 1789: Encyclopedia of the Early Modern World*, ed. Jonathan Dewald (New York: Charles Scribner's

Sons, 2004), 3:141–43; David Sorkin, *The Transformation of German Jewry, 1780–1840* (New York: Oxford University Press, 1987); Shmuel Feiner and David Sorkin, ed., *New Perspectives on the Haskalah* (Oxford: Littman Library of Jewish Civilization, 2001).

3. For an interpretation of the moderate ethos of the Jewish Enlightenment, see David Sorkin, *Moses Mendelssohn and the Religious Enlightenment* (Berkeley: University of California Press, 1996); on the phenomenon of the *falsche Aufklärung* in its various national forms, see Shmuel Feiner, "The Pseudo-Enlightenment and the Question of Jewish Modernization," *Jewish Social Studies* (new series) 3, no. 1 (1996): 62–86.

4. Language—especially the relationship among Yiddish, ancient Hebrew-Aramaic, modernizing Hebrew, and German—played a crucial role in the symbolic world of the Jewish Enlightenment and in the practical world of acculturating Prussian Jews. Wolfssohn's play, as well as a similar parody penned by the *maskil* Isaac Euchel, *Reb Henokh, oder vos tut men damit?* (Reb Henokh, or What's to Be Done with It?), made use of all of these languages. As Berkowitz and Dauber have noted, both Wolfssohn and Euchel placed their characters along a linguistic spectrum that was simultaneously an ideological one. See Berkowitz and Dauber, "Introduction," in *Landmark Yiddish Plays*, 1–23; Isaac Euchel, *Reb Henoch, oder: Woß tut me damit: Eine jüdische Komödie der Aufklärungszeit*, in *Jidische schtudies* 11, ed. Marion Aptroot and Roland Gruschka (Hamburg: H. Buske, 2004). On the language polemics in the *Haskalah*, see Shmuel Werses, "Inter-Lingual Tensions in the Maskilic Periodical '*Hame'asef* and Its Time in Germany," *Dappim: Research in Literature* 11 (1997–98): 29–69; Dan Miron, *A Traveler Disguised: A Study in the Rise of Modern Yiddish Fiction in the Nineteenth Century* (New York: Schocken Books, 1973); Nancy Sinkoff, *Out of the* Shtetl*: Making Jews Modern in the Polish Borderlands.* Brown Judaic Studies 336 (Providence, RI: Brown University Press, 2004), ch. 4; and John M. Efron, *German Jewry and the Allure of the Sephardic* (Princeton, NJ: Princeton University Press, 2016), ch. 1.

5. On Jewish women in late-eighteenth-century Berlin, see Deborah Hertz, *Jewish High Society in Old Regime Berlin* (New Haven, CT: Yale University Press, 1988); Deborah Hertz, *How Jews Became Germans: The History of Conversion and Assimilation in Berlin* (New Haven, CT: Yale University Press, 2007); Natalie Naimark-Goldberg, *Jewish Women in Enlightenment Berlin* (Oxford: Littman Library of Jewish Civilization, 2013); and Lowenstein, *The Berlin Jewish Community.*

6. On the Court Jews, see Steven M. Lowenstein, "Court Jews, Tradition and Modernity," in *Hofjuden: Ökonomie und Interkulturalität die jüdische Wirtshaftselite im 18. Jahrhundert*, ed. Rotraud Ries and J. Friedrich Battenberg (Hamburg: Christians Verlag, 2002), 369–81.

7. The plausibility of Wolfssohn's characterization of Reb Yoysefkhe's lasciviousness is echoed in Henriette Herz's memoirs: "My teacher in this as well as in other subjects was one of the most immoral men that my mother could have selected—my good mother believed she had chosen well, and only later did I come to realize how bad her choice had been." Henriette Herz, "Memoirs of

a Jewish Girlhood," in *Bitter Healing: German Women Writers from 1700 to 1830: An Anthology*, ed. Jeannine Blackwell and Susanne Zantop, trans. Marjanne E. Goozé with Jeannine Blackwell (Lincoln, NE: University of Nebraska Press, 1990), 306.

8. On Schnapps's name, see Berkowitz and Dauber, *Landmark Yiddish Plays*, 93n33.

9. Aaron Halle Wolfssohn, "Leichtsinn und Frömmelei: Ein Familien Gemälde in Drei Aufzügen," in *Lustspiele zur Unterhaltung beim Purim-Feste* (Breslau: s.n. 1796), 1:33–111. In *Landmark Yiddish Plays*, 97, Berkowitz and Dauber leave the phrase untranslated. I have translated *Klavier* as "piano," but this term would have to include a variety of keyboard instruments, including fortepianos and harpsichords, in use in the eighteenth century. Further discussion of keyboard terminology may be found in Rebecca Cypess's contribution to this volume.

10. Reb Henokh: "(Mocking her) . . . 'I'd be willing to bet you that the Rebbe isn't so happy with her! What does she do all day long? Does she say blessings? Does she pray? Does she open a Yiddish Bible or a prayer book? All you hear around her, all day long, *is singing and music, music and singing*, enough to drive a person crazy. And when the beloved Sabbath finally comes around, you wouldn't remember it's holy. God forbid! This is the sin that I'm getting more and more concerned about.'" (Emphasis is mine). Berkowitz and Dauber, *Landmark Yiddish Plays*, 84; see, too, pp. 90 and 94.

11. Alexander Altmann, *Moses Mendelssohn: A Biographical Study* (Tuscaloosa: University of Alabama Press, 1973); Feiner, *The Origins of Jewish Secularization*; Lowenstein, *The Berlin Jewish Community*; and Ruth HaCohen, *The Music Libel Against the Jews* (New Haven, CT: Yale University Press, 2011), 5.

12. David Sorkin, "Wilhelm von Humboldt: The Theory and Practice of Self-Formation (Bildung), 1791–1810," *Journal of the History of Ideas* 44 (1983): 55–73.

13. The language polemics of this period also took on a gendered edge, with Yiddish portrayed as a language "for women or for men who are like women" and Hebrew and High German identified with men. See Naomi Seidman, *A Marriage Made in Heaven: The Sexual Politics of Hebrew and Yiddish* (Berkeley: University of California Press, 1997). Yet acculturating German Jewish women also considered Yiddish shameful and unaesthetic. Rahel Levin—later Varnhagen—referred to Yiddish as "howling" in a letter to her siblings penned in 1794. See Barbara Hahn, *The Jewess Pallas Athena: This Too a Theory of Modernity*, trans. James McFarland (Princeton, NJ: Princeton University Press, 2005), 28.

14. The key text calling for the revitalization of Ashkenazic education by redirecting its emphasis away from the Talmud and including secular subjects is Naftali Herz Wessely, *Divrei Shalom Ve'emet* (Berlin: Ḥevrat Ḥinuch Ne'arim, 1782). *Maskilim* in Berlin created the first modern Jewish school, the *Jüdische Freischule* (1778). A *Haskalah* press called "Society for the Education of the Youth" (1784) published the first modern textbook for children, the *Lesebuch für jüdische Kinder* (1779) and the Hebrew journal mentioned above. Simha Assaf, *Mekorot Le-toldot Ha-Ḥinukh Be-yisra'el* (Tel Aviv: Devir, 1954) and Zohar

Shavit, "From Friedländer's Lesebuch to the Jewish Campe—The Beginning of Hebrew Children's Literature in Germany," *LBIYA* 33 (1988): 385–415. In Russian lands, Isaac Baer Levinsohn picked up the baton to transform Jewish education in *Te'udah Be-Yisra'el: Kolel Gidrei ha-Torah veha-ḥokhmah* (Vilna-Horodno: Menachem Man and Simcha Zimel Publishers, 1828).

15. Only boys studied at the *Jüdische Freischule* in its early years. After some thirty years, in 1812, the *maskil* Joseph Perl's modern Jewish school opened in Tarnopol, Austrian Galicia, with a class of sixteen, of whom five were girls. The girls were expected to study German, Russian, religion, ethics, reading and writing Yiddish, and the "important principles of the skill of homemaking," including agriculture, accounting, and other domestic topics. See Philip Friedman, "Joseph Perl as an Educational Activist and His School in Tarnopol," *YIVO bleter* 31–32 (1948): 148.

16. It would take another half century and an eastward geographic shift for the emergence of *maskilot*, ideologically self-conscious modernizing Jewish women literate in Hebrew and familiar with traditional Jewish texts. See Carole Balin, *"To Reveal Our Hearts": Jewish Women Writers in Tsarist Russia* (Cincinnati, OH: Hebrew Union College Press, 2000); and Iris Parush, *Reading Jewish Women: Marginality and Modernization in Nineteenth-Century Eastern European Jewish Society*, trans. Saadya Sternberg. Brandeis Series on Jewish Women, Tauber Institute for the Study of European Jewry series (Hanover, NH: University Press of New England, 2004).

17. Ezra Mendelsohn, "On the Jewish Presence in Nineteenth-Century European Musical Life," *Studies in Contemporary Jewry, An Annual: Modern Jews and Their Musical Agendas*, 9 (1993): 3–16.

18. Lowenstein, *The Berlin Jewish Community*, 30–32.

19. As Barbara Hahn has noted, the term "salon" was not used until the 1840s, and generally referred to exclusive, highly formal, high-society gatherings. Yet visitors to the Itzig and Levy homes could hear music in a variety of settings ranging from small, intimate gatherings to larger, formal performances. See Hahn, *The Jewess Pallas Athena*, 42–55 and Rebecca Cypess, "Ancient Poetry, Modern Music, and the *Wechselgesang der Mirjam und Debora*: The Meanings of Song in the Itzig Circle," *Bach: Journal of the Riemenschneider Bach Institute* 47, no. 1 (2016): 63.

20. Although the word "*salonnière*"—like the term "*salon*"—is problematic, we have chosen to retain it throughout the volume because it is so widespread in the literature on elite Jewish women in late-eighteenth-century Prussia and because there is no suitable alternative. The word "hostess," while arguably more accurate, connotes a quality of passive domesticity that does not reflect the agency of the women in Sara Levy's circle.

21. On Sara Levy's biography, see Thekla Keuck, *Hofjuden und Kulturbürger: Die Geschichte der Familie Itzig in Berlin* (Göttingen: Vandenhoeck & Ruprecht, 2011).

22. David Conway, *Jewry in Music: Entry to the Profession from the Enlightenment to Richard Wagner* (Cambridge: Cambridge University Press, 2012), ch. 3, particularly pp. 144–48 and 171.

23. Throughout this volume, authors refer to Sara Levy as "Sara Itzig," "Sara Levy," "Madame Levy," and "Sara." Although the use of a first name for a woman could be construed pejoratively, this is certainly not the case in this book. Readers will also note that the physician Markus Herz is referred to as "Markus" and not by his surname in certain passages. The choice to use a forename or a surname was simply stylistic.

24. Hilde Spiel, *Fanny von Arnstein: A Daughter of the Enlightenment, 1758–1818*, trans. Christine Shuttleworth (New York: Berg, 1991). On Mozart's relationship to Sara Levy and Fanny von Arnstein, see Christoph Wolff, *Mozart at the Gateway to His Fortune: Serving the Emperor, 1788–1791* (New York: W. W. Norton, 2012), 57–63.

25. Christoph Wolff, "The Bach Tradition among the Mendelssohn Ancestry," in *Mendelssohn, the Organ, and the Music of the Past: Constructing Historical Legacies*, ed. Jürgen Thym (Rochester, NY: University of Rochester Press, 2014), 213–23. See also Peter Wollny, *"Ein förmlicher Sebastian und Philipp Emanuel Bach Kultus": Sara Levy und ihr musikalisches Wirken, mit einer Dokumentensammlung zur musikalischen Familiengeschichte der Vorfahren von Felix Mendelssohn Bartholdy* (Wiesbaden: Breitkopf & Härtel, 2010); Peter Wollny, "Sara Levy and the Making of Musical Taste in Berlin," *Musical Quarterly* 77, no. 4 (1993): 651–88; Christoph Wolff, "A Bach Cult in Late-Eighteenth-Century Berlin: Sara Levy's Musical Salon," *Bulletin of the American Academy of Arts and Sciences* 58, no. 3 (2005): 26–39. On Levy's circle and the *Sing-Akademie*, see Celia Applegate, *Bach in Berlin: Nation and Culture in Mendelssohn's Revival of the* St. Matthew Passion (Ithaca, NY: Cornell University Press, 2005), ch. 4, "Musical Amateurism and the Exercise of Taste."

26. The phrase "young lady at music" is borrowed from Matthew Head, "'If the Pretty Little Hand Won't Stretch': Music for the Fair Sex in Eighteenth-Century Germany," *Journal of the American Musicological Society* 52, no. 2 (1999): 203–54.

27. See Wolff's contribution to this volume.

28. Wolff, "A Bach Cult." For a brief history of the establishment of the *Sing-Akademie*'s archive, its disappearance after World War II, and its restitution after the end of the Cold War, see Christoph Wolff, "Recovered in Kiev: Bach et al. A Preliminary Report on the Music Collection of the Berlin Sing-Akademie," *Notes*, 2nd series, 58, no. 2 (2001): 259–71; and Joachim Jaenecke, "Das Archiv der Sing-Akademie zu Berlin," *Fontes Artis Musicae* 51, no. 3–4 (2004): 373–78. The introductory essays in the catalogue of the *Sing-Akademie* provide overviews of its holdings and history; see Axel Fischer and Matthias Kornemann, eds., *The Archive of the Sing-Akademie zu Berlin: Catalogue / Das Archiv der Sing-Akademie zu Berlin: Katalog* (Berlin: de Gruyter, 2010).

29. Levy's last will and testament is reproduced in Wollny, *"Ein förmlicher Sebastian und Philipp Emanuel Bach Kultus,"* 57–60.

30. Heinrich Graetz, *History of the Jews*, vol. 5, trans. Bella Löwy (Philadelphia, PA: The Jewish Publication Society of America, 1891–98), 413, and Shimon Dubnow, *History of the Jews* vol. 4, trans. Moshe Spiegel (South Brunswick, NJ: T. Yoseloff, 1971), 641–43.

31. Hertz, *Jewish High Society in Old Regime Berlin*, 13. Naimark-Goldberg also argues that the Berlin women adopted "early feminist positions on the role of women and society." See Naimark-Goldberg, *Jewish Women in Enlightenment Berlin*, 1; on her use of the term "feminist," see 7n17.

32. Jonathan Karp, "The Aesthetic Difference: Moses Mendelssohn's *Kohelet Musar* and the Inception of the Berlin Haskalah," in *Renewing the Past, Reconfiguring Jewish Culture: From al-Andalus to the Haskalah*, ed. Ross Brann and Adam Sutcliffe (Philadelphia: University of Pennsylvania Press, 2003), 93–120. The German-language *Haskalah* journal *Sulamith* published sheet music from 1810 forward. Efron, *German Jewry and the Allure of the Sephardic*, 35–37, and 248n59.

33. Marion Kaplan, *The Making of the Jewish Middle Class: Women, Family, and Identity in Imperial Germany* (Oxford: Oxford University Press, 1991).

34. For a study of French women's participation in the Enlightenment and the revolutionary impact of print culture on their self-creation as modern Europeans, see Carla Hesse, *The Other Enlightenment: How French Women Became Modern* (Princeton, NJ: Princeton University Press, 2001).

35. Jacob Katz, *Masoret u-Mashber: Ha-Ḥevrah Ha-yehudit Be-motsa'ei Yemei Ha-benayim* (Jerusalem: Mossad Bialik, 1957–58) and Jacob Katz, *Tradition and Crisis: Jewish Society at the End of the Middle Ages*, trans. Bernard Dov Cooperman (New York: New York University Press, 1993), chapter 23, "The Emergence of the Neutral Society," 213–25.

36. Altmann, *Moses Mendelssohn*, 27, 36–50. See, too, Klaus L. Berghahn, "On Friendship: The Beginnings of a Christian-Jewish Dialogue in the 18th Century," in *The German-Jewish Dialogue Reconsidered: A Symposium in Honor of George L. Mosse*, ed. Klaus L. Berghahn (New York: Peter Lang, 1996), 5–23; Peter Svare Valeur, "Notes on Friendship: Moses Mendelssohn and Gotthold Ephraim Lessing," *Oxford German Studies* 45, no. 2 (2016): 142–56; and Martha Helfer's contribution to this volume.

37. Jacob Katz, *Out of the Ghetto: The Social Background of Jewish Emancipation, 1770–1870* (Cambridge, MA: Harvard University Press, 1973), 54. David Sorkin expanded upon the idea that acculturating German Jews created a Jewish subculture in the nineteenth century that functioned distinctly from general German culture and, in his words, "remained invisible to its members." Sorkin, *The Transformation of German Jewry*, 3–9.

38. Annelien De Dijn, "The Politics of Enlightenment: From Peter Gay to Jonathan Israel," *Historical Journal* 55 (2012): 785–805.

39. HaCohen, *The Music Libel Against the Jews*, 80–81.

40. For the French case outlining skepticism—and even hostility—to Jewish integration, see the classic work by Arthur Hertzberg, *The French Enlightenment and the Jews* (New York: Columbia University Press, 1968). See, too, Adam Sutcliffe, "Can a Jew Be a Philosophe? Isaac de Pinto, Voltaire, and Jewish Participation in the European Enlightenment," *Jewish Social Studies* (new series) 6, no. 3 (2000): 31–51.

41. For a recent exposition of Bach's Lutheran anti-Judaism, see Michael Marissen, *Bach & God* (Oxford: Oxford University Press, 2016). The novel *And After the Fire* places Sara Levy's fictional inheritance of an anti-Jewish cantata scored by

Bach at the center of its drama. Lauren Belfer, *And After the Fire* (New York: Harper Collins, 2016).

42. By asking questions about women and gender, historians have challenged and transformed whole historical narratives. Commented the American and feminist historian Linda Gordon regarding this revolution in historiography, writing women's history "does not simply add women to the picture we already have of the past, like painting additional figures into the spaces of an already completed canvas. It requires repainting the earlier pictures, because some of what was previously on the canvas was inaccurate and more of it was misleading." Linda Gordon, *U.S. Women's History* (Washington: American Historical Association, 2nd edition, 1997), 2. See, too, the discussion of gender—rather than women—as a category of historical analysis in Joan Wallach Scott, *Gender and the Politics of History* (New York: Columbia University Press, 1988). On the particular challenge of writing premodern Ashkenazic Jewish women's history, in which the over-arching binary and hierarchical framework of the traditional religious context defined gender relations, see Moshe Rosman, "The History of Jewish Women in Early Modern Poland: An Assessment," in *Polin: Studies in Polish-Jewry* 18: Jewish Women in Eastern Europe, ed. ChaeRan Freeze, Paula Hyman, and Antony Polonsky (Oxford: Littman Library of Jewish Civilization, 2005), 25–56.

43. HaCohen, *The Music Libel Against the Jews*, 80.

44. Martha B. Helfer, *The Word Unheard: Legacies of Anti-Semitism in German Literature and Culture* (Evanston, IL: Northwestern University Press, 2011).

45. Aspects of music collecting in the age of Sara Levy are discussed in Matthias Kornemann, "Zelter's Archive: Portrait of a Collector," in *The Archive of the Sing-Akademie zu Berlin*, 19–25; and in Annette Richards, "Carl Philipp Emanuel Bach, Portraits, and the Physiognomy of Music History," *Journal of the American Musicological Society* 66, no. 2 (2013): 337–96.

46. Wolff, "A Bach Cult," 30.

Part One

Portrait of a Jewish Female Artist: Music, Identity, Image

Chapter One

What Was the Berlin Jewish Salon around 1800?

Marjanne E. Goozé

Since the mid-nineteenth century, historians, literary theorists, and cultural critics have written about the Berlin Jewish salons and *salonnières* in the period from roughly 1780 to 1840. Most authors have made assumptions about the nature of the salon and the lives of the *salonnières* based on their own time and interests, generally envisioning this short-lived social phenomenon as a precursor of Jewish and female emancipation or as a kind of idyll of Jewish-German social integration. The salon easily became a site of projection because it was a largely undocumented social activity. Few participants wrote accounts of what occurred on any specific afternoon or evening. The two memoirs by Henriette Herz (1764–1847)[1] and posthumously published letters and diaries by Rahel Varnhagen (1771–1832),[2] as well as some reports written by *salonnières* and guests form the corpus of documents upon which salon historians rely. Scholars such as Deborah Hertz, Petra Wilhelmy-Dollinger, Liliane Weissberg, Barbara Hahn, and I have worked in the last decades both to engage with the activities of the salons and the *salonnières* in greater detail and to demystify the projections of previous writers.[3]

Based on our work and that of other salon historians, as well as on original sources, this essay traces the genesis, high points, and demise of the Berlin Jewish salon, offers a comprehensive overview of salon practices and organization, and addresses some of the complexities of its reception.[4] Although there were other salons in the German-speaking world, those discussed here are the ones hosted by Jewish women in Berlin. In tracing the origins of the salon, this essay concentrates on what are known as the literary salons, although, as this book shows, salons in which musical performance was a central activity were also important. After the occupation of Berlin in 1806 and for the generation that followed Rahel Varnhagen and Henriette Herz, musical salons increased in influence.

The development of salon culture in Berlin can be attributed to a confluence of influences and activities. The single most significant was the desire of a very small group of Jewish women to attain an education in German secular culture.[5] As a result of the influence of their male relatives, who immersed themselves in the philosophy and literature of the German Enlightenment, these women undertook serious reading and study. Secular reading was essential for Jewish women who wished to join the wider educated society in Germany.[6] Rahel Varnhagen read, as Deborah Hertz notes, Voltaire, Rousseau, Kant, and Fichte, and was also a devotee of Goethe,[7] whose language was a revelation and influenced Rahel's own speech and writing.[8] Sara Levy read French literature and philosophy. Reading aloud was a frequent home activity; sometimes plays were read, with the roles divided among the participants. At Henriette Herz's home, Jewish Sabbath observance was followed by the secular practice of reading aloud.[9] Henriette's husband, Markus, a physician at the Jewish hospital and a respected Enlightenment figure in Berlin, had studied with Immanuel Kant.[10] After their engagement, when Henriette was just twelve and a half years old, Markus began to guide her reading and educate her more consistently than she had been before.[11]

Self-education formed the foundation of the *salonnières'* efforts to engage with others in the intellectual pursuits that underpinned the activities of the salons, taking these social gatherings beyond general socializing with family and friends. Henriette Herz's two memoirs offer a history of the development of the salon as it evolved from other social and intellectual practices. Three key activities were: the scientific experiments and lectures conducted by her husband at their home; her *Tugendbund* (Society of Virtue), formed with some of those who came to see these experiments; and the formation of reading groups by Jews and non-Jews alike. While Rahel Varnhagen, several years younger than Henriette Herz, decided not join the *Tugendbund*, she participated in the wave of self-education that occurred during the late eighteenth century.

Beginning in about 1777, Markus Herz offered lectures in philosophy and performed physics experiments at his home.[12] As Henriette Herz states in her first memoir, she assisted him, and in the course of these educational activities met young men such as the Crown Prince and the brothers Wilhelm and Alexander von Humboldt.[13] The Herz home quickly acquired a reputation as an important gathering place for Enlightenment education and social activities. Henriette Herz reflected: "Under such auspicious circumstances, our house grew, and I can say without exaggerating that it became one of the more pleasant and sought-after houses in Berlin. If Herz was attractive because of his brilliant mind and his fame as a physician, I attracted—much time has passed since—because of my beauty."[14] Though she was indeed admired as a beauty, she also made a point to emphasize her knowledge of the sciences and languages.[15] Like Rahel Varnhagen, Herz and the younger generation became avid devotees of the works of Johann Wolfgang von Goethe and the other Romantics such as Novalis, whom Markus and his older friends did not understand.[16] For this reason, people later spoke of the Herz salon as a "double salon,"[17] where Markus met with older friends apart from Henriette's contemporaries.

Her friendship with the Humboldt brothers, in particular with Wilhelm, continued throughout their lives.[18] During Christmas of 1787 they formed a *Tugendbund* that was influenced by the ideals of pietism and freemasonry. Members included Herz's sister Brenna, the Humboldt brothers, Carl von LaRoche (the son of the famous writer Sophie von LaRoche), and Dorothea Mendelssohn-Veit and her sister Henriette, as well as additional "corresponding" members, including Wilhelm's future wife, Caroline von Dacheröden, Therese Heyne, and Caroline von Wollzogen. This group of friends, some still teenagers, formed a club devoted to mutual moral and intellectual improvement, as well as charitable works.[19] They wrote statutes and developed a secret code for their letters.[20] All letters were shared, and they used the familiar form of address with one another.[21] The club was short-lived and began to fall apart after Wilhelm von Humboldt went to university and began to establish a private relationship with Caroline von Dacheröden. The importance of the *Tugendbund* for the development of the salon, which reached its heyday in the 1790s, lies in the intention to engage in goal-directed socializing that would promote self-education. Rahel Varnhagen was also devoted to broadening her horizons, especially through reading and letter writing. In her correspondence with her friend David Veit, she engaged in serious discussion of significant works of philosophy, moral treatises, and other works of nonfiction.[22]

The third contributor to the development of the Jewish salon in Berlin was reading circles of various types. The groups varied in composition from exclusively male and Christian to completely mixed.[23] The reading groups served in part as centers for intellectual discourse before the founding of a university in Berlin in 1811. Just as with Markus Herz's lectures and physics experiments, the reading groups were a part of an Enlightenment-driven urge for self-education. These reading societies offered Jewish women like Henriette Herz and Dorothea Mendelssohn-Veit a significant opportunity to read and discuss important literary and philosophical texts not only with one another, but also with highly educated men.

A key element of the reading groups was discussion, and this took place in more regularized and formalized settings. The inclusion of women's voices in these intellectual exchanges, however limited that inclusion sometimes was, was a radical development in a world where higher education was closed to women. Dorothea Mendelssohn-Veit organized a reading society at her home that met weekly on Thursdays and was primarily, but not exclusively, attended by Jews.[24] Begun in the early 1780s, it continued for fifteen years. Around 1785 Hofrat Bauer, who worked at the palace, formed a group that met inside the palace in winter and in the gardens in summer. It included many of Berlin's prominent men and women. Participants engaged in other social activities together, as well.[25] A circle that formed around friends of the Humboldt brothers and *Tugendbund* members like Carl von LaRoche included noblemen and temporary visitors to Berlin.[26] This was known as the *Theekränzchen* (tea circle) and did not have a set meeting place.[27] Another group of note was the *Mittwochgesellschaft* (Wednesday group) formed by Ignaz Feßler at the end of the eighteenth century.[28] Rahel Varnhagen was, however, dissatisfied with the reading groups because they centered on the male participants; she preferred to set up a form of sociability in her own home where, as Natalie Naimark-Goldberg concludes, "the gender hierarchy, while not completely obliterated, was at least blurred."[29]

Reading groups were both precursors to the salons and continued alongside them. Each had its own degree of formality in combining reading aloud and discussion with other forms of socializing. They differed from what can be considered a salon primarily in that they were organized by men. The reading groups brought people together to read and pursue self-improvement, while the salons provided space for the *salonnières* and their guests to display and share their acquired knowledge, wit, and erudition.

So what exactly was the phenomenon that we now call a Berlin salon? In short, it was a gathering of family, friends, acquaintances, and visitors on a regular basis at the home of a Jewish woman. Among the guests were people of varying professions and classes, men and women, Jews and Christians. They came together to socialize in conversation on significant topics and ideas of the day. The conversations in the salons were a continuation of the process of self-improvement and education in which the participants engaged. Sometimes short literary or musical works were presented.

The following provides a composite outline of salon practices. This cannot apply universally to all aspects of the salons, but can aid us when considering individual *salonnières*. Some cultural historians characterize the salon as an international phenomenon, with French salons serving as a universal model.[30] More recently, Ulrike Weckel has asked: "Is it really true, however, that these gatherings in the Prussian capital had more in common with those of Enlightenment society in pre-Revolutionary Paris than with the contemporary culture of visiting among educated people in other German cities?"[31] She contends that while there was an attempt at imitation, there was a "big difference" between the two.[32] This difference is significant and assists in explaining the Berlin Jewish salon.

We should be cautious when attributing French origins to Jewish salon practices in Berlin in the years 1780 to about 1840. The Revolution brought exiled French nobles and French manners to Berlin. French influence on the court of King Frederick the Great and the general importance of French thought and culture in Germany certainly influenced Berlin salons. And it is indisputable that some of the Berlin salon women were acquainted with French *salonnières* and familiar with their published works. But, as we have seen, multiple factors contributed to the development of the salon and its activities.[33]

When speaking about these social gatherings, two aspects must be clarified. First, the salons were not static social institutions. They developed and changed over time. Second, the term "salon" as a description of a social event rather than a room postdates most French and German gatherings, which used terms such as "assembly" or "tea circle."[34] In the 1830s Henriette Herz bemoaned that the word "salon" had replaced the German term "Gesellschaftszimmer" (parlor).[35] The word "*salonnière*," referring to the hostess, first appeared about 1890.[36]

The primary and most historically significant aspect of the Berlin Jewish salon is that it was hosted by Jewish women who had no social or even legal status in Prussia. In spite of numerous efforts by Jews and their allies to acquire civil rights, especially during the era of the salons, very little was achieved. As women, the *salonnières* possessed even fewer rights than their male counterparts.[37] Steven Lowenstein elaborates on the different paths to modernization often taken by Jewish men and women:

> The difference between men's and women's backgrounds is therefore not merely a matter of the women's lack of Jewish education and men's lack of secular knowledge. Although the difference in education of the two sexes probably had some effect, it was far from the whole story. The contrast is not simply between prematurely modernized women and backward men. Rather it is a contrast between two different forms of modernization. Whereas men's modernization seemed to be directed in institutionalized form in clubs, publications and the reform movement, women's modernization was focused on individual and informal activity and changes in personal lifestyle. . . . The very conspicuousness of the social activities of prominent Jewish women is, however, a reflection of their very limited organizational outlets for sociability.[38]

These Jewish women were successful in attracting to their homes young noblemen, including members of the royal family, who rejected dull and formal court life and who possessed a desire to discuss German literature and culture away from the French-oriented Prussian court. Rahel Varnhagen and Henriette Herz came from a privileged Jewish elite—they were the daughters of a banker and a physician, respectively—and received some secular education. Herz, although known for her beauty, knew many languages and had a strong interest in science.[39] Rahel Varnhagen was an eager learner, and was highly regarded for her intelligence, as evidenced in the thousands of letters she wrote. As previously discussed, both women were influenced by Enlightenment ideals and vigorously pursued self-education. They were skilled conversationalists who encouraged the self-improvement of their guests.

The Berlin salons have been both praised and criticized for their guest lists, which included a mix of genders, classes, religious affiliations, and professions from among the nobility, upper-bourgeoisie, artists, intellectuals, and Jews. The philosopher Moses Mendelssohn had opened the way by inviting important Enlightenment thinkers and writers, such as the famous playwright and Enlightenment thinker Gotthold Ephraim Lessing, to his home. Wealthy Jews hosted amateur theatricals and formed reading groups. As noted above, Markus and Henriette Herz had their "double salon"[40] that brought different generations together, as well.

Salons stood in contrast to other kinds of socializing exclusive to males, such as the clubs that formed in the eighteenth century. There were *Tischgesellschaften* (table societies) and clubs, most of which excluded Jews and women. These were attended by salon guests, officials, and intellectuals, and may be seen as a rejection of female-dominated salon sociability.[41] *Salonnières* did not send formal invitations, but one needed an introduction in order to attend.[42] In the early nineteenth century, *salonnières* in Berlin such as Sara Levy, Amalie Beer (mother of the composer Giacomo Meyerbeer), and the composer Fanny Mendelssohn Hensel (sister of Felix Mendelssohn Bartholdy) conducted musical gatherings that required tickets. These concerts, however, were different from the earlier salons, where musical performance was just one of a variety of activities.[43] During the heyday of the salons, it became *de rigueur* for visitors to Berlin to attend. Salons met on *jours fixes*—at a set day and time each week or several times a week. Herz asserted that their home became "one of the most pleasant and most visited in Berlin."[44] A common saying was: "Whoever has not seen the Gendarmenmarkt and Madame Herz has not seen Berlin."[45]

Salonnières offered their guests more than mere socializing. Most pursued literary and philosophical interests. The *salonnières* and their guests often read aloud and discussed new works. Having emerged in part from the reading groups in Berlin, many German salons focused on new literature, as evidenced in their correspondences and those of their guests.[46] Herz's salon read Goethe and entertained writers and philosophers such as Schiller, Friedrich Schlegel, and her good friend Friedrich Schleiermacher. Musical performances, amateur theatricals, and presentation of works of art were also salon activities.[47] Rahel hosted actresses and commented in her letters on visits to the opera and theater.

The art of conversation dominated the salons, but other pursuits were also included. The Berlin salons set themselves apart from those in other cities by not emphasizing games, particularly card games, although these were not entirely absent. Card games, *tableaux vivants*, play-acting, and music were popular entertainments.[48] Friederike Helene Unger bewailed the general obsession with cards in Berlin society and observed, along with Schleiermacher, that the homes of the Jews offered more high-minded pursuits.[49] The French *salonnières* often served elaborate meals, but this was not the case for the Berlin women.[50] There is little evidence that most Berlin hostesses offered much more than tea to their guests. Guests came to converse with the hostess and interact with one another.

While the salons did not advocate a specific political point of view, the French Revolution, the terror, and Napoleon were topics of conversation in Berlin.[51] The heyday of the Berlin Jewish salons ended with Napoleon's occupation of the city in 1806. During the Wars of Liberation, the German *salonnières* and their guests became increasingly nationalistic and patriotic.[52] After 1815 political allegiances tended to divide guests, and the salons became less diverse.

Much of the contemporary and later criticism of the salons stemmed from their reputation as sites of romantic encounters. The Berlin salons promoted both the ideal and practice of romantic love—perhaps an example of literature influencing life. *Salonnières* and their guests fell in love and even later married, but these social gatherings were more than mere parties. Herz stayed with her husband and after his death in 1803 refused later offers of marriage. Rahel's love affairs with Count von Finkenstein and the Spanish diplomat Rafael d'Urquijo prompted criticism, as did her marriage to Karl August Varnhagen von Ense. Their characterization as dens of iniquity came from both Jews and Christian anti-Semites such as Karl Wilhelm Grattenauer.[53] Salon sociability and *salonnières* prompted critiques and satires by outsiders and guests alike. Anti-Semitic satires mocked the perceived romance between Herz and Schleiermacher and the real one between Dorothea Mendelssohn-Veit and Friedrich Schlegel. Aside from romantic liaisons, satires mocking the *salonnières* were also included within the Berlin salons, composed and read aloud in them by guests such as Wilhelm and Alexander von Humboldt and Karl Gustav von Brinckmann. While these prominent Christian men enjoyed the sociability of the Jewish salons, their attendance had limited mitigating impact on their prejudices. The reception of the Jewish salons will be discussed at greater length at the end of this essay.

Unlike some French *salonnières*, Rahel Varnhagen, Henriette Herz, and the other Berlin hostesses were not published authors during their lifetimes; it was only later that Herz's memoirs and thousands of letters by Rahel appeared. Herz burned much of her correspondence and her diaries; her memoir—an "as told to" autobiography—was published after her death.[54] In 1834 Rahel's husband Karl August Varnhagen von Ense published some of the letters, diaries, and observations that she had arranged for publication as *Rahel: Ein Buch des Andenkens für ihre Freunde* (Rahel: A Book of Remembrance for Her Friends). Through these publications the *salonnières* achieved their reputations, and the short-lived salon phenomenon was documented.

While letter writing was not an activity generally pursued within the salons themselves, the *salonnières* participated in the vast epistolary culture of the time. Through letter writing both Henriette Herz and Rahel Varnhagen strove to improve their German style and sharpen their thinking. Although many of Herz's letters are no longer extant, a good number of her letters have been published, as well as her correspondents' responses. Rahel Varnhagen's papers are still being published. Although most of the letters from Sara Levy's pen have been lost, a handful of the extant letters are transcribed and translated in the appendix to this volume. Collections of letters written *to* Levy are also extant.

To the defining characteristics of the salon listed above, one more must be added: the concept of *Zwangslosigkeit* (unrestraint) as a principle of social interaction.[55] The principle, paired with that of *Zwecklosigkeit* (purposelessness), was put forth in Schleiermacher's 1799 essay, "On a Theory of Social Behavior," in which he advocated for an ideal social interaction for the mutual benefit of the participants free of all secondary aims such as romance, business, and personal promotion.[56] Schleiermacher developed his theory based on his salon experiences, but it should not be seen as a direct description of them. The contemporaneous satires indicate that there was a good deal of networking and social climbing at the salons. Cultural historians, however, have frequently idealized salon interactions based on Schleiermacher's theory, as will be seen in the discussion of salon reception.

Recent scholarship has assessed the impact of salon socializing on the larger society, mostly concurring that salons and *salonnières* had little discernible influence on either women's or Jewish emancipation.[57] The most direct line can be traced to Wilhelm von Humboldt's efforts to include civil emancipation in his drafts for a German constitution at the Congress of Vienna.[58] Most *salonnières* pursued self-education, erudition, and a degree of independent thought and action, yet these did not generally translate into wider efforts for political or social change. The question of Jewish *salonnières*' contributions to Jewish emancipation is also contentious.[59]

Because salon sociability seems to situate itself along the divide between public and private spheres, salon historians almost all engage with the German critic Jürgen Habermas's book, *The Structural Transformation of the Bourgeois Public Sphere*.[60] Habermas located the salon within the emerging public sphere, along with coffeehouses and clubs. All these promoted, according to Habermas, "a kind of social intercourse that . . . disregarded status altogether."[61] Since salons met at private homes, "the line between private and public sphere extended right through the home. The privatized individuals stepped out of the intimacy of their living rooms into the public sphere of the salon, but the one was strictly complementary to the other."[62] His book fails to consider gender and yet makes assumptions about family and gender.[63] Joan Landes vehemently disputes his inclusion of the salon in the public sphere[64] and notes his failure to consider the *"gendering* of the public sphere" as male dominated.[65] Dena Goodman and others still rely on his analysis of the development of bourgeois society.[66] American feminists further challenge the entire ideology of separate spheres in the nineteenth century as a false dichotomy based on binary assumptions.[67] The reception and practices of French and German salons contends with this false division: they have been characterized as creating a "liminal space,"[68] "a hybrid space,"[69] or an "extrasocial space."[70]

The above outline describes the most common practices of Berlin Jewish salons in their heyday around 1800. The unusual set of circumstances that allowed Jewish women like Henriette Herz and Rahel Varnhagen to hold salons was particular to social life in the Prussian capital at the end of the eighteenth century. During the occupation of Berlin by the French, musical salons like Sara Levy's continued, but Rahel Varnhagen's and Henriette Herz's regular evenings ceased, as hostesses and participants scattered. Socializing continued after the Wars of Liberation. Rahel Varnhagen's return to Berlin marked the beginning of her so-called second salon, but the heady mix of Enlightenment ideals; the vibrant contemporary literature of Goethe, Schiller, and the Romantics; promising young male guests; and talented Jewish female conversationalists could not be reassembled after 1815. The political climate had also changed, as Herz noted: participants were separated by politics and personal philosophy where male interests superseded women's.[71] There was a "salon-style socializing" where noblewomen were hostesses.[72] Due to the fame of Rahel Varnhagen's first salon, the second attracted guests from the professions and academia, but its character was different. Sometimes music was played and dinners were served, where before, conversation had been the main focus.[73] By the 1820s, the important musical salons of Amalie Beer and Lea Mendelssohn Bartholdy had also arisen.

When examining the Berlin Jewish salons and their impact upon German and Jewish-German culture, it is important to consider their reception, since the aspirations and projections of these writers have shaped readers' interest in the salons and *salonnières*. The salons have been characterized by both their admirers and their detractors as harbingers of women's and Jewish emancipation. Beginning in the 1830s, a group of writers called the "Young Germans" looked to Rahel Varnhagen in particular as embodying the ideal of feminine intellect. But a number of Jewish historians such as Heinrich Graetz, who lived and wrote in the nineteenth century, emphasized the spiritual and intellectual values of the Jews in order to support their political emancipation and condemned the influence of salons and *salonnières*. Graetz criticized Herz's salon as a "Midianite tent."[74] Others, writing before 1933, blamed the women for converting to Christianity and saw the salons as a causal factor for conversion.[75] Remy-Lazarus names the chapter of her book about these women *Abtrünnige* (heretics).[76] But even if the authors sometimes criticize the *salonnières'* conversions to Christianity, positive portrayals frequently appeared in German and in English during the first decades of the twentieth century, reflecting the first women's movement's identification with these historic figures.[77] Hannah Arendt's biography of Rahel Varnhagen, which included some of her letters, avoids over-assessing the impact of the salons while advocating for Rahel Varnhagen as an intellectual. Arendt places the salons outside of social conventions, claiming a "neutral territory" for them, and emphasizing their precarious existence.[78]

Historians and literary critics in the second half of the twentieth century did not agree in their assessments of the salons as examples of female or Jewish emancipation and questioned whether the salons had any influence at all on either. After 1945, German writers yearned to locate a moment in time and a space where Christian and Jewish Germans had come together without prejudice. Some choose to idealize, quite mistakenly, the salons. They envisioned a "threefold transgression" that momentarily suspended the divisions between faiths, religions, and classes.[79] This was supposedly accomplished as the salons became "enclaves" for experiments in lifestyle and communications.[80] Hannelore Scholz even goes so far as to call them "a brief utopia."[81] Exactly what this utopia might have achieved is assessed by several writers. Konrad Feilchenfeldt, who has written more than one article on this topic, takes varying positions. In one essay, he praises what he sees as the apolitical sociability of the salon, relying upon Friedrich Schleiermacher's theory of sociability.[82] But in a different one, he idealizes Rahel Varnhagen as emblematic of the formation of a new society, the emancipation of women, and the freeing of Jews from Prussian oppression.[83] He situates this unique synthesis of women's and Jewish emancipation within the embodied experience of the *salonnières*.[84] The projection of a symbiosis or synthesis has numerous advocates, such as Horst Meixner, who speaks even of a double symbiosis of Jews and Germans.[85] There remains a predominant tendency among salon critics after 1945 to identify some point during its history when it could have been a zone free of anti-Semitism. Heinz Härtl and Wolfgang Frühwald excuse the early Romantics until about 1810–15.[86] Through their idealization of the salon, they tend to ignore or minimize the anti-Semitic views held by salon guests and gloss over the absence of civil rights for Jews.

Not all writers are so idealistic. More recent salon historians perceive it as a social anomaly that highlighted the contradictions and discrepancies between the social, scientific, and intellectual contributions of Jews to Berlin life and their lack of civil rights. Peter Gradenwitz warns of overestimating the significance of the salons for Jewish integration.[87] Steven Lowenstein agrees that "the salon's relationship to the wider events in Berlin Jewry was more that of a reflection than a direct influence."[88] Deborah Hertz's social history, *Jewish High Society in Old Regime Berlin* (1988), one of the first post-1945 works on the *salonnières*, addresses both the prejudices encountered by them and the resentments of the early twentieth-century writers. She asserts that the salons had a significant impact on German-Jewish society: "Thus the salonières [*sic*] made a distinct contribution to Jewish political emancipation."[89] In her second book, *How Jews Became Germans*, Hertz concerns herself more with the efforts made by German Jews to assimilate. In fact, she debunks utopian notions of mixed socializing: "Yet from many sources we can learn that the volatile social mix of salon society led to hurt feelings, anger, humiliation, and self-deception on the Jewish side, and arrogance, condescension, and sometimes explicit anti-semitism on the Christian side. For there were definite limits on how many and which Jews could succeed in the salons."[90]

Barbara Hahn and Liliane Weissberg are the sharpest critics of any utopian imaginings. Hahn insists that the salon was itself a myth propagated to prove that there was at least once a good relationship between Germans and Jews.[91] Weissberg confronts the admirers of the salon in our time, asking: "Can their wish for a manifestation of a German-Jewish symbiosis be regarded . . . as a wish to heal and unify a body of German and Jewish culture, as a post-Holocaust revival effort with the help of tea?"[92] While I would dispute that the salons were a myth or merely later idealistic constructions by German historians and literary scholars, I do agree that their reception has frequently posited a utopic space separate from the politics and ideologies of their day that demands closer interrogation. The Berlin Jewish salons call for careful historical attention that does not overestimate or minimize their impact on women's strivings for self-education or on efforts for Jewish civil emancipation.

Henriette Herz, Rahel Varnhagen, Sara Levy, and others established salons by combining elements from a German-Jewish culture that was undergoing its own Enlightenment-influenced secularization and from their knowledge of the French salon traditions. They extended and adopted practices from the reading groups and their personal associations among Jews and Christians in Berlin before the founding of the university. The short-lived form of sociability called the "salon" has become a legendary phenomenon in German-Jewish cultural history, but, as this essay suggests, the Berlin Jewish salon has often been misconstrued by its interpreters. Studies of specific *salonnières* like Sara Levy will provide a much-needed nuanced and detailed history that can engage with all of the complex aspects of salon sociability and Jewish life in Berlin around 1800.

Notes

1. Henriette Herz began an autobiography in 1823 and left it unfinished in 1829. This short manuscript was not published until the end of the nineteenth century, when 100 copies were issued as Henriette Herz, "Jugenderinnerungen von Henriette Herz," ed. Heinrich Hahn, *Mittheilungen aus dem Litteraturarchive in Berlin* 1 (1896): 139–84. I translated this memoir into English with Jeannine Blackwell and published it, along with some additions, as "Memoirs of a Jewish Girlhood," trans. Marjanne Goozé with Jeannine Blackwell, in *Bitter Healing: German Women Writers 1700–1830*, ed. Jeannine Blackwell and Susanne Zantop (Lincoln: University of Nebraska Press, 1990), 303–47. Beginning in the late 1830s, in the light of publications such as Karl August Varnhagen von Ense's book containing some of Rahel Varnhagen's letters, friends encouraged her to publish letters and memoirs, but Herz refused. Instead, she gave a young man with journalistic aspirations, J. Fürst, access to her existent letters, diaries, and the unfinished memoir, and spoke to him about her life. Upon the condition that he not publish until after her death, he composed an "as-told-to" autobiography, which included his own biography of her, that appeared in two editions after her death. Relying on this book, salon historians have formulated their definitions of the Berlin salon. See Henriette Herz, *Henriette Herz. Ihr Leben und ihre Erinnerungen*, ed. J. Fürst. Zweite Auflage (Berlin: Besser, 1858).

2. Rahel Varnhagen, *Rahel: Ein Buch des Andenkens für ihre Freunde*, 3 vols. (Berlin: Duncker & Humblot, 1834). There have been numerous editions and additional papers published. Rahel Varnhagen, who came to be known as "Rahel," was born Rahel Levin and married Karl August Varnhagen von Ense. For purposes of clarity here, I have chosen to call her Rahel Varnhagen. Brendel Mendelssohn, the daughter of Moses Mendelssohn, married Simon Veit, and then later Friedrich Schlegel. She was called most often Dorothea. Since the period discussed in this essay comports with the time before she married Schlegel, I have decided to refer to her as Dorothea Mendelssohn-Veit. Henriette de Lemos married Markus Herz and used the name Henriette Herz.

3. See Deborah Hertz, *Jewish High Society in Old Regime Berlin* (New Haven, CT: Yale University Press, 1988); Deborah Hertz, *How Jews Became Germans: The History of Conversion and Assimilation in Berlin* (New Haven, CT: Yale University Press, 2007); Petra Wilhelmy, *Der Berliner Salon im 19. Jahrhundert (1780–1914)* (Berlin: de Gruyter, 1989); Petra Wilhelmy-Dollinger, "Emanzipation durch Geselligkeit: Die Salons jüdischer Frauen in Berlin zwischen 1780 und 1830," in *Bild und Selbstbild der Juden Berlins zwischen Aufklärung und Romantik*, ed. Marianne Awerbuch and Stefi Jersch-Wenzel (Berlin: Colloquium, 1992), 121–38; Petra Dollinger, "Die internationale Vernetzung der deutschen Salons (1750–1914)," in *Europa Ein Salon? Beiträge zur Internationalität des literarischen Salons*, ed. Roberto Simanowski, Horst Turk, and Thomas Schmidt (Göttingen: Wallstein, 1999), 40–65; Liliane Weissberg, "Weibliche Körperschaften: Bild und Wort bei Henriette Herz," in *Von einer Welt in die andere: Jüdinnen im 19. und 20. Jahrhundert*, ed. Jutta Dick and Barbara Hahn (Vienna: Christian Brandstätter, 1993), 71–92; Barbara Hahn, *Die Jüdin Pallas Athene: Auch eine*

Theorie der Moderne (Berlin: Berliner Taschenbuch Verlag, 2002); Marjanne E. Goozé, "Mimicry and Influence: The French Connection and the Berlin Jewish Salon," in *Readers, Writers, Salonnières: Female Networks in Europe 1700–1900*, ed. Hilary Brown and Gillian Dow (Oxford: Peter Lang, 2011), 49–71; Marjanne E. Goozé, "Utopische Räume und idealisierte Geselligkeit: Die Rezeption des Berliner Salons im Vormärz," in *Romantik und Vormärz: Differenzen und Kontinuitäten*, ed. Wolfgang Bunzel, Peter Stein, and Florian Vaßen (Bielefeld: Aisthesis, 2003), 363–90.

4. I derive my definition of the German salon from my own research, as well as engaging with definitions offered by Deborah Hertz (*Jewish High Society*, 15–17, 112–13), Petra Wilhelmy's seven-point detailed outline of Berlin salon ideals and activities (Wilhelmy, *Der Berliner Salon*, 25–26), and Peter Seibert, *Der literarische Salon: Literatur und Geselligkeit zwischen Aufklärung und Vormärz* (Stuttgart: Metzler, 1993). This outline of salon practices draws on my essay "Mimicry and Influence."

5. Natalie Naimark-Goldberg's book concentrates on how Jewish women educated themselves to participate in the secular culture of the German Englightenment; see Natalie Naimark-Goldberg, *Jewish Women in Enlightenment Berlin* (Oxford: Littman Library of Jewish Civilization, 2013).

6. Naimark-Goldberg, *Jewish Women*, 93.

7. Hertz, *Jewish High Society*, 189.

8. Hannah Arendt, *Rahel Varnhagen: Lebensgeschichte einer deutschen Jüdin aus der Romantik* (Munich: Piper, 1981), 113.

9. Peter Gradenwitz, *Literatur und Musik im gesselligem Kreise: Geschmacksbildung, Gesprächsstoff und musikalische Unterhaltung in der bügerlichen Salongesellschaft* (Stuttgart: Franz Steiner, 1991), 84.

10. Martin L. Davies, *Identity or History? Marcus Herz and the End of the Enlightenment* (Detroit, MI: Wayne State University Press, 1995), 7.

11. Herz, *Memoirs*, 314–16.

12. Ibid., 321; Davies, *Identity*, 91.

13. Herz, *Memoirs*, 321.

14. Ibid.

15. Ibid.

16. Ibid., 322–23.

17. Hertz, *Jewish High Society*, 99.

18. Herz, *Memoirs*, 321.

19. Herz, *Ihr Leben*, 157.

20. Ibid., 159–60.

21. For more extensive information on the *Tugendbund*, see Paul Schwenke, "Aus Wilhelm von Humboldts Studienjahren. Mit ungedruckten Briefen," *Deutsche Rundschau* 66 (1891): 228–51.

22. Naimark-Goldberg, *Jewish Women*, 31–35.

23. These are outlined in Barbara Becker-Cantarino, "Die 'andere Akademie': Juden, Frauen und Berliner literarische Gesellschaften 1770–1806," in *Europäische Sozietätsbewegung und demokratische Tradition: Die europäischen Akademien der Frühen Neuzeit zwischen Frührenaissance und Spätaufklärung,*

ed. Klaus Garber and Heinz Wismann, 2 vols. (Tübingen: Niemeyer, 1996). 2:1478–1505.

24. In a chapter of Herz's *Ihr Leben* titled, "Lesegesellschaften," she discusses several of these meetings (102–9). See also Selma Stern, "Die Entwicklung des jüdischen Frauentypus seit dem Mittelalter," *Der Morgen* (Berlin) 1 (1925): 506; Hertz, *Jewish High Society*, 2; Bertha Meyer, *Salon Sketches: Biographical Studies of Berlin Salons of the Emancipation* (New York: Bloch, 1938), 138–39.

25. Herz, *Ihr Leben*, 106.

26. Ibid.

27. Seibert, *Der literarische Salon*, 184.

28. Herz, *Ihr Leben*, 107; Wilhelmy, *Der Berliner Salon*, 52.

29. Naimark-Goldberg, *Jewish Women*, 186.

30. Twentieth-century salon histories have portrayed the salon as an international social practice. See Valerian Tornius, *The Salon: Its Rise and Fall: Pictures of Society through Five Centuries*, trans. Anges Platt (London: Thornton Butterworth, 1929); and Verena von der Heyden-Rynsch *Europäische Salons: Höhepunkte einer versunkenen weiblichen Kultur* (Munich: Artemis & Winkler, 1992). See also Roberto Simanowski, "Einleitung: Der Salon als dreifache Vermittlungsinstanz," in *Europa—Ein Salon? Beiträge zur Internationalität des literarischen Salons*, ed. Roberto Simanowski, Horst Turk, and Thomas Schmidt (Göttingen: Wallstein, 1999).

31. Ulrike Weckel, "A Lost Paradise of Female Culture? Some Critical Questions regarding the Scholarship on Late Eighteenth- and Early Nineteenth-Century German Salons," *German History* 18, no. 3 (2000): 318.

32. Ibid., 319.

33. Scholars propose that there were several factors contributing to the development of the Berlin salon. Many contend that the French salon and its ideals were of greatest influence. Hertz writes: "The leading Jewish salonières [*sic*] founded their salons in conscious imitation of the French noble salon tradition in order to synthesize the best of Gallic intellectual form and German intellectual content" (Hertz, *Jewish High* Society, 115). Gradenwitz and Isselstein concur. Gradenwitz, *Literatur und Musik*, 70; Ursula Isselstein. "Die Titel der Dinge sind das Fürchterlichste! Rahel Levins Erster Salon," in *Salons der Romantik: Beiträge eines Wiepersdorfer Kolloquiums zu Theorie und Geschichte des Salons*, ed. Hartwig Schulz (Berlin: de Gruyter, 1997), 195. Peter Seibert emphasizes the influence of French books on gallantry and the *honnête homme* (*Der literarische Salon*, 48, 69). Nicole Pohl observes how Berlin salon practice grew increasingly French over time. Nicole Pohl, "'Perfect Reciprocity': Salon Culture and Epistolary Conversations," *Women's Writing*, 13, no. 1 (2006): 144–50. The second primary factor that scholars identify is the enlightened reading groups and the response of the younger generation to new, Romantic literature. See, for example, Ingeborg Drewitz, *Berliner Salons: Gesellschaft und Literatur zwischen Aufklärung und Industriezeitalter* (Berlin: Haude & Spener, 1979), 7–11, and Detlef Gaus, *Geselligkeit und Gesellige: Bildung, Bürgertum und bildungsbürgerliche Kultur um 1800* (Stuttgart: J. B. Metzler, 1998), 174. Barbara Hahn asserts that German and Jewish family structures and habits of socializing and visiting

were the formative factor among these Berlin women (*Die Jüdin*, 75–76). Petra Wilhelmy suggests two formative factors—the French tradition and reading groups. Petra Wilhelmy, *Der Berliner Salon* 36–48.

34. Herz referred to her "Theezirkel" (*Ihr Leben*, 134). Seibert elaborates on the development of the word from its Italian roots to the Parisian art exhibitions (*Der literarische Salon*, 8–10).

35. Herz, *Ihr Leben*, 263–64.

36. Wilhelmy, *Der Berliner Salon*, 24–25.

37. Lowenstein lists three stages of efforts to reform the status of Jews in Prussia from 1786 to 1815. In the end, complete emancipation was not achieved. Steven M. Lowenstein, *The Berlin Jewish Community: Enlightenment, Family, and Crisis 1770–1830* (New York: Oxford University Press, 1994), 77–87.

38. Lowenstein, *The Berlin Jewish Community*, 172.

39. Herz, *Ihr Leben*, 97–98.

40. Ibid., 91–97.

41. See Hertz, *How Jews Became Germans*, 79 and Stefan Nienhaus, "Aufklärerische Emanzipation und romantischer Antisemitismus in Preußen im frühen neunzehnten Jahrhundert," *Studia theodisca* 2: (1995): 9–27.

42. Carolyn C. Lougee, *Le Paradis des femmes: Women, Salons, and Social Stratification in Seventeenth-Century France* (Princeton, NJ: Princeton University Press, 1976), 115; Joan B. Landes, *Women and the Public Sphere in the Age of the French Revolution* (Ithaca, NY: Cornell University Press, 1988). 24; James van Horn Melton, *The Rise of the Public in Enlightenment Europe* (Cambridge: Cambridge University Press, 2001), 197.

43. Deborah Hertz analyzes in detail the musical salons of the Mendelssohns and the Beers in *How Jews Became Germans*, 165–216.

44. Herz, *Ihr Leben*, 93.

45. Karl August Böttiger, *Literarische Zustände und Zeitgenossen*, ed. K. W. Böttiger, 2 vols. (Leipzig: Brockhaus, 1838; repr. Frankfurt am Main: Athenäum, 1972), 2:105.

46. Classical and Romantic authors, especially Goethe, had an enormous impact on the literary and educational development of Berlin salon women. See Marjanne E. Goozé, "'Ja ja, ich bet' ihn an': Nineteenth-Century Women and Goethe," in *The Age of Goethe Today: Critical Reexamination and Literary Reflection*, ed. Gertrud Pickar and Sabine Cramer (Munich: Fink, 1990), 39–49.

47. Landes, *Women and the Public Sphere*, 25.

48. Claudia Schmölders, "Einleitung," in *Die Kunst des Gesprächs: Texte zur Geschichte der europäischen Konversationstheorie*, ed. Claudia Schmölders (Munich: DTV, 1979), 59.

49. Friederike Helene Unger, "Briefe einer reisenden Dame über Berlin," *Jahrbücher der preussischen Monarchie unter der Regierung Friedrich Wilhelms des Dritten* 2 (1798): 21; Friedrich Daniel Ernst Schleiermacher, *Kritische Gesamtausgabe*, part 5 (Briefe), ed. Andreas Arendt and Wolfgang Virmond (Berlin: de Gruyter, 1992), 3:66.

50. Steven Kale, *French Salons: High Society and Political Sociability from the Old Regime to the Revolution of 1848* (Baltimore, MD: Johns Hopkins University Press, 2004),

6, 19–20; Dena Goodman, *The Republic of Letters: A Cultural History of the French Enlightenment* (Ithaca, NY: Cornell University Press, 1994), 91; Melton, *The Rise of the Public*, 206.

51. Herz, *Ihr Leben*, 266–74.

52. Ibid., 318–19.

53. Karl Wilhelm Grattenauer wrote numerous anti-Semitic pamphlets. One of his most well-known is *Wider die Juden: Ein Wort der Warnung an alle unsere christliche Mitbürger* (Berlin: Schmidt, 1803).

54. See note 1 above.

55. Herz, *Ihr Leben*, 201, 253.

56. Friedrich Daniel Ernst Schleiermacher, "Versuch einer Theorie des geselligen Betragens" (1799), in Schleiermacher, *Kritische Gesamtausgabe*, part 1 (Schriften und Entwürfe), ed. Günter Meckenstock (Berlin: de Gruyter, 2011), 2:163–84. For a discussion of Schleiermacher's theory, see William Rasch, "Ideal Sociability: Friedrich Schleiermacher and the Ambivalence of Extrasocial Spaces," in *Gender in Transition: Discourse and Practice in German-Speaking Europe, 1750–1830*, ed. Ulrike Gleixner and Marion W. Gray (Ann Arbor: University of Michigan Press, 2006), 328–32; and Goozé, "Utopische," which cites numerous other sources on the relationship between his theory and salon practices (385).

57. The failure of these efforts has been notably outlined in several books that have considered salons and women but not focused on them. See, for example, Michael Meyer, *The Origins of the Modern Jew: Jewish Identity and European Culture in Germany 1749–1824* (Detroit, MI: Wayne State University Press, 1967); and Jonathan M. Hess, *Germans, Jews and the Claims of Modernity* (New Haven, CT: Yale University Press, 2002).

58. See Marjanne E. Goozé, "Wilhelm von Humboldt und die Judenemanzipation: Leistungen und Widersprüche," *Seminar* 48, no. 3 (2012): 317–32.

59. In the 1970s and 80s, writers such as Julius Carlebach attempted to compare Jewish and women's emancipation with a positive outlook. See Julius Carlebach, "The Forgotten Connection: Women and Jews in the Conflict between Enlightenment and Romanticism," *Yearbook of the Leo Baeck Institute* 24 (1979): 107–39. By the 1990s assessments of progress and influence were more tempered, as can be seen in this 1993 edited volume by Jutta Dick and Barbara Hahn, *Von einer Welt in die andere: Jüdinnen im 19. und 20. Jahrhundert* (Vienna: C. Brandstätter, 1993).

60. Jürgen Habermas, *The Structural Transformation of the Public Sphere: An Inquiry into a Category of Bourgeois Society*, trans. Thomas Burger (Cambridge, MA: MIT Press, 1991).

61. Habermas, *The Structural Transformation*, 36.

62. Ibid., 46. The spheres increasingly separated, and the private sphere became more commodified (151–52).

63. Simon Richter, "The Ins and Outs of Intimacy: Gender, Epistolary Culture, and the Public Sphere," *German Quarterly* 69, no. 2 (1996): 111–13.

64. Landes, *Women and the Public Sphere*, 23.

65. Ibid., 2.

66. See: Goodman, *Republic of Letters*; Kale, *French Salons*, 11; Melton, *The Rise of the Public*, 4–15.

67. See Monika M. Elbert, "Introduction," in *Separate Spheres No More: Gender Convergence in American Literature 1830–1930*, ed. Monika M. Elbert (Tuscaloosa: University of Alabama Press, 2000), 3; Cathy N. Davidson and Jessamyn Hatcher, "Introduction," in *No More Separate Spheres!* ed. Cathy N. Davidson and Jessamyn Hatcher (Durham, NC: Duke University Press, 2002), 7–11; Linda K. Kerber, "Separate Spheres, Female Worlds, Woman's Place: The Rhetoric of Women's History," in *No More Separate Spheres!*, 42; and Marjanne E. Goozé, "Challenging Separate Spheres: Female *Bildung* in Eighteenth- and Nineteenth-Century Germany—An Introduction," in *Challenging Separate Spheres: Female* Bildung *in Late Eighteenth- and Nineteenth-Century Germany*, ed. Marjanne E. Goozé. North American Studies in Nineteenth-Century German Literature (Oxford: Peter Lang, 2007), 13–15.

68. Melton, *The Rise of the Public*, 223.

69. Richter, "The Ins and Outs of Intimacy," 111.

70. Rasch, "Ideal Sociability," 323. See also Weckel's term "semi-public" ("A Lost Paradise," 315) and Seibert's "space between" (Zwischenbereich) in *Der literarische Salon*, 4.

71. Herz, *Ihr Leben*, 263–64.

72. Hertz, *How Jews Became Germans*, 168.

73. Heidi Thomann Tewarson, *Rahel Levin Varnhagen: The Life and Work of a German Jewish Intellectual* (Lincoln: University of Nebraska Press, 1998), 181.

74. Heinrich Graetz, *Volkstümliche Geschichte der Juden in drei Bänden*, 3 vols. (Leipzig, 1888), 3:606. For an analysis of orthodox reaction to Jewish assimilation, see Lowenstein, *The Berlin Jewish Community*.

75. Ludwig Geiger, *Geschichte der Juden in Berlin. Festschrift zur zweiten Säkulär-Feier* (1871) (Berlin: Arani, 1988), 110; Nahida Ruth Remy-Lazarus, *Das jüdische Weib*, 4th edition (Berlin: Cronbach, 1922), 147; Selma Stern, "Die Entwicklung," 496–516; Bertha Badt-Strauss, *Jüdinnen* (Berlin: Joachim Goldstein, Jüdischer Buchverlag, 1937), 69.

76. Remy-Lazarus, *Das jüdische Weib*, 139–53.

77. See Badt-Strauss, *Jüdinnen*; Bertha Meyer, *Salon Sketches*; Mary Hargrave, *Some German Women and Their Salons* (London: T. Werner Laurie, 1912).

78. Arendt, *Rahel Varnhagen*, 62–63.

79. Isselstein, "Die Titel der Dinge," 192.

80. Gerda Heinrich, "Die Berliner Salons in der literarischen Kommunikation zwischen 1790 und 1800. Ein Beitrag zur geschichtlichen Funktionsbestimmung," *Zeitschrift für Germanistik* 3, no. 2 (1993): 310.

81. Hannelore Scholz, "Geselligkeit als Utopie: Weiblicher Dialog in den Privatvorlesungen von A. W. Schlegel," in *Salons der Romantik*, 136.

82. Konrad Feilchenfeldt, "'Berlin Salon' und Briefkultur um 1800," *Der Deutschunterricht* 36 (1984): 82–83.

83. Konrad Feilchenfeldt, "Die Anfänge des Kults um Rahel Varnhagen und seine Kritiker," in *Juden im Vormärz und in der Revolution von 1848*, ed. Walter Grab and Julius Schoeps (Stuttgart: Burg, 1983), 215.

84. Konrad Feilchenfeldt, "Die Berliner Salons der Romantik," in *Rahel Levin Varnhagen: Die Wiederentdeckung einer Schriftstellerin*, ed. Barbara Hahn and Ursula Isselstein, *LiLi Beiheft* 14 (1987): 154.

85. Horst Meixner, "Berliner Salons als Ort Deutsch-Jüdischer Symbiose," in *Gegenseitige Einflüsse deutscher und jüdischer Kultur: Von der Epoche der Aufklärung bis zur Weimarer Republik*, Jahrbuch des Instituts für Deutsche Geschichte, Beiheft 4, ed. Walter Grab (Tel Aviv: Tel Aviv University, 1982): 99.

86. Härtl Heinz, "Romantischer Antisemitismus: Arnim und die 'Tischgesellschaft,'" *Weimarer Beiträge* 33, no. 7 (1987): 1159; Wolfgang Frühwald, "Antijudaismus in der Zeit der deutschen Romantik," in *Conditio Judaica: Judentum, Antisemitismus und deutschsprachige Literatur vom 18. Jahrhundert bis zum Ersten Weltkrieg*, part 2, ed. Hans Otto Horch and Horst Denkler (Tübingen: Niemeyer, 1989), 83.

87. Gradenwitz, *Literatur und Musik*, 81.

88. Lowenstein, *The Berlin Jewish Community*, 104.

89. Hertz, *Jewish High Society*, 279.

90. Hertz, *How Jews Became Germans*, 53.

91. Barbara Hahn, "Der Mythos vom Salon: 'Rahels Dachstube' als historische Fiktion," in *Salons der Romantik*, 212.

92. Liliane Weissberg, "Bodies in Pain: Reflections on the Berlin Jewish Salon," in *The German-Jewish Dialogue Reconsidered: A Symposium in Honor of George L. Mosse*, ed. Klaus L. Berghahn (New York: Peter Lang, 1996), 77.

Chapter Two

Sara Levy's Musical Salon and Her Bach Collection

Christoph Wolff

The Bach Family in the Musical Life of Eighteenth-Century Berlin

In a letter of January 9, 1742, to his cousin Johann Ernst Bach in Eisenach, Johann Sebastian Bach wrote that "now in Berlin a musical epoch has begun" (*in Berlin ist ia nunmehro das musicalische seculum angegangen*).[1] This statement apparently reflects what he had observed and experienced the previous summer when visiting Berlin and his son Carl Philipp Emanuel, who in 1740 had been appointed harpsichordist of the Royal Prussian court Capelle. The musical atmosphere in the Prussian capital of the 1740s was being revitalized and indeed completely revamped by the young, powerful, and musically active King Friedrich II ("the Great"). In its broad spectrum, ranging from opera—with a brand-new opera house—to chamber music, there could be found no parallel elsewhere in Europe. Hence, the 57-year-old Bach seems to have been proud that his second son and a number of his former students were part of, and played important roles in, this remarkable scene.

Nobody could have foreseen, however, that the Seven Years' War (1756–63) would soon change all this and bring the abounding musical life at the royal court to a near standstill. Nor could anyone have imagined that the sharply curtailed musical life would have the beneficial side effect of an unprecedented growth of musical activities outside the court proper, notably among the Berlin aristocracy and affluent bourgeois circles, a phenomenon prompted and aided by the availability of idle court musicians. Least of all could it have been anticipated that the later decades of the eighteenth century would establish Berlin as a major center for the performance and reception of music by the Bach family.

Berlin became the city where three of Johann Sebastian's sons would live and work, at least for certain periods: Carl Philipp Emanuel (1740–68), Johann Christian (1750–55) and Wilhelm Friedemann (1774–84). Even Johann Christoph Friedrich, concertmaster in Bückeburg, maintained regular connections in Berlin, since the principality of Schaumburg-Lippe was a kind of Prussian satellite state; his son Wilhelm Friedrich Ernst—the last musician in the family—was in 1789 appointed harpsichordist to Queen Friederike of Prussia and spent the bulk of his professional life in Berlin. In addition, two of Bach's most distinguished Leipzig pupils worked there: Johann Friedrich Agricola, eventual successor to Carl Heinrich Graun as Royal Prussian Capellmeister; and Johann Philipp Kirnberger, employed in the service of Princess Anna Amalia, the younger sister of Friedrich II. The latter exercised particular influence through his authoritative two-volume *Die Kunst des reinen Satzes in der Musik* (Berlin, 1771–79), a composition treatise that largely codified Bach's teachings. Furthermore, Princess Anna Amalia owned one of the largest private manuscript collections, rivaled only by the extensive music library of the noble von Voß family in Berlin.[2] Additionally, Berlin was the home of Friedrich Wilhelm Marpurg, a versatile composer, writer, and author of the two-volume *Abhandlung von der Fuge* (Berlin, 1753), a theoretical companion to Bach's *Kunst der Fuge*. Finally, the bustling music publisher and organizer of public concerts Johann Carl Friedrich Rellstab helped to establish a continuing Bach tradition in Berlin as did, on a larger scale and institutional basis, the *Sing-Akademie,* an organization founded in 1791 on the model of the Academy of Ancient Music in London by Carl Friedrich Fasch, former assistant to C. P. E. Bach.

This all formed the significant background to what is generally known as the nineteenth-century Bach Renaissance and its notable point of origin, the 1829 performance of the *St. Matthew Passion* by the Berlin *Sing-Akademie* under the direction of the young Felix Mendelssohn Bartholdy.[3] The nineteen-year old musician certainly deserves primary credit as the inspiring musical leader of this performance of historic significance. Moreover, the event received unusual publicity because of the attendance of King Friedrich Wilhelm III and the royal family, the aristocracy, and the intellectual elite of the Prussian capital including such luminaries as the theologian Friedrich Schleiermacher, the philosopher Georg Friedrich Wilhelm Hegel, the historian Johann Gustav Droysen, the poet Heinrich Heine, and the writer and salon hostess Rahel Varnhagen. The performance had a nationwide impact and launched a revival of J. S. Bach's music on a much broader scale than anything that had previously occurred in Berlin, with a greater focus on the younger Bach generation.

A second milestone was again set by Mendelssohn Bartholdy, this time during his first season as music director of the Leipzig Gewandhaus. In 1835 he established so-called "historical concerts" (*Historische Concerte*) with programs

designed to feature instrumental compositions of the past. The idea of historical programs was of seminal importance for the further advancement of musical historicism, a phenomenon that first arose in eighteenth-century England
and that had a growing impact on the public taste. It contributed significantly
to an increasing interest in music of the past and eventually led to an apparently irreversible paradigm shift. Up to the early decades of the nineteenth
century, it was contemporary music that overwhelmingly dominated the scene.
However, Mendelssohn's "historical concerts" initiated a reversal that in the
long run changed forever the contents, and eventually the proportions, of public concert programs at the expense of contemporary music. Again J. S. Bach—
but now with his larger instrumental works—played a major role.[4] The very first
such program at the Leipzig Gewandhaus included the Concerto in D Minor
for three claviers and strings (BWV 1063), with Mendelssohn, Franz Liszt, and
Ignaz Moscheles playing the solo parts.[5] A little later, Mendelssohn conducted
and played the solo part of the Keyboard Concerto in D Minor (BWV 1052).
Like virtually all of Bach's orchestral works, which were completely unknown
to contemporaneous audiences since they had fallen out of the active repertoire, this composition spontaneously received great praise from the general
public, but was hailed also by the music critic Robert Schumann as "a sublime
work" (*ein erhabenes Werk*).[6] Nobody, however, including Mendelssohn himself,
knew that this very concerto had actually been played in public in Berlin a full
generation earlier, even before he was born. On New Year's Eve 1807, a concert given by the *Ripienschule*, the orchestral subdivision of the *Sing-Akademie*
(since 1800 under direction of Carl Friedrich Zelter) included Bach's D-Minor
Keyboard Concerto, and the soloist was a certain Sara Levy.[7]

A "Bach Cult" in the Extended
Mendelssohn Family prior to 1800

Madame Levy (1761–1854)[8] was none other than Mendelssohn's great-aunt—the
younger sister of his maternal grandmother, Bella Salomon. It was the latter who
had most likely set things in motion by giving her grandson a most special gift,
perhaps for Christmas in 1823: a manuscript copy of the unpublished autograph
score of Bach's *St. Matthew Passion*.[9] In the final analysis, only this unusual gift to
the fourteen-year-old Felix Mendelssohn made the famous and influential 1829
performance possible. However, the true origins must be sought even further
back, namely in the remarkable musical traditions of Mendelssohn's extended
family—traditions underemphasized, under-researched, and neglected, if not
deliberately suppressed, by earlier scholarship.

In the Mendelssohn family, Bach had been a household name ever since
Felix's grandfather Moses Mendelssohn, a successful businessman and eminent

philosopher of both the German Enlightenment and Jewish *Haskalah* move-ment, took keyboard lessons and instruction in music theory from the Bach student J. P. Kirnberger. Even more important in this respect, however, were the musically well-educated children of Felix's great-grandfather on his moth-er's side, Daniel Itzig. Johann Friedrich Reichardt, last Capellmeister in the service of King Friedrich II, mentioned in his autobiography of 1813 "a veri-table Sebastian and Philipp Emanuel Bach cult" (*einen förmlichen Sebastian und Philipp Emanuel Bach Kultus*)[10] at the house of Daniel Itzig, the king's banker and at the time the most privileged and highest-ranking Jew in all of Prussia. This astonishing reference is in no way remarkable as far as C. P. E. Bach is concerned. He was then a living musician and ranked among the most widely published German composers. On the other hand, Reichardt's statement defi-nitely refers to a surprising interest in the music of J. S. Bach after his death in 1750, something not traceable elsewhere within amateur circles and private homes. Reichardt's phrase also suggests that he did not learn of this "Bach cult" merely from hearsay. Rather, he seems to have personally experienced, perhaps even participated in, performances that took place at the Itzig man-sion in the center of Berlin.

While it is conceivable that Daniel Itzig may have heard of J. S. Bach, per-haps on the occasion of the latter's well-publicized visit to Potsdam and Berlin in 1747, he certainly would have known about Bach's second son, Carl Philipp Emanuel, a longtime prominent member of the king's court Capelle through 1768. Be that as it may, Itzig had a great interest in music, found the best pos-sible music instructors for his children, and paid them well. For his two oldest daughters, Hanna and Bella, he hired the former J. S. Bach student Kirnberger. Hanna Itzig (1748–1801) later married the Prussian privy councillor Joseph Fließ, and they established a weekly semipublic concert series, known as the "Fließische Konzert," in their home. Although the teachers of Itzig's middle daughters Fanny and Zippora are not known, both sisters became musically active. Fanny Itzig (1757–1818) married the Viennese banker Nathan von Arnstein and established a musical salon in Vienna. In 1781–82 she became Mozart's landlady and provided him with Bach scores.[11] As for the sons, the musical interests of Isaac Daniel Itzig (1750–1806) can be documented only indirectly, as it is his wife's name that appears on the subscription list for J. C. F. Bach's *Sechs leichte Sonaten* (Leipzig, 1785). Benjamin Itzig (1756–1831?) is known to have owned an extensive music collection, some of which has sur-vived. In general, the names of Itzig family members regularly appear on the subscription lists for published works by the various Bach sons.

Bella Itzig (1749–1824), who married the banker Levin Jacob Salomon, became Felix Mendelssohn's maternal grandmother. She had shared Kirnberger as keyboard instructor with Moses Mendelssohn, but the latter's second son Abraham received no particular musical training. Nevertheless, in 1793 he joined the newly established *Sing-Akademie,* three years before his future wife, Lea Salomon, joined the same organization. Lea, Bella's daughter and an accomplished pianist, is known to have regularly played preludes and fugues from Bach's *Well-Tempered Clavier.*

The newlywed Mendelssohns moved to Hamburg in 1804, the year in which C. P. E. Bach's daughter Anna Carolina died, the last custodian of the Bach family estate. When the estate came up for auction in 1805, Abraham Mendelssohn acquired a major share of it and, after his return to Berlin in 1811, donated it to the *Sing-Akademie.* He had developed a warm relationship with its director, Zelter. Mendelssohn's acquisition of the Bach estate, which included not only the works of C. P. E. Bach but also a significant portion of the surviving works of J. S. Bach, represented a genuine rescue operation. Its importance for the survival of J. S. Bach's music, contained in more than a hundred unique autograph scores, cannot be overestimated, and it is safe to say that without Abraham Mendelssohn's efforts, the number of lost Bach scores would be considerably greater than the present count.

The acquisition of the Bach estate for the Berlin *Sing-Akademie* forms the immediate salient background for the 1829 performance of the *St. Matthew Passion* under Felix Mendelssohn. Soon after 1811, Carl Friedrich Zelter began performing excerpts from the Passions, Masses, and cantatas of J. S. Bach based on the saved materials. At age ten, Felix joined the *Sing-Akademie* and, more importantly, was put under Zelter's private tutelage. He could have had no better teacher who, among other things, exposed him to Bach's vocal works, but almost exclusively in the form of excerpts. Zelter did not consider the *St. Matthew Passion* performable, for musical-technical reasons as much as for its "wretched texts," referring to the Baroque-style poetry, but the boy Felix eagerly wanted to see and study the whole piece. His grandmother Bella Salomon finally fulfilled his wish, and in 1823 had a professional copy made from the manuscript of the unpublished work.[12]

The gift to Felix was made apparently made a few months after Abraham and Lea Mendelssohn had converted to Protestant Christianity and added "Bartholdy" to their name in order to be distinguished from the Jewish Mendelssohns. The baptism took place in Frankfurt because Abraham wanted to avoid a public rift with his in-laws, especially since Bella Salomon had disowned her son Jacob upon his conversion.[13] Intermarriage and conversion had become major trends among Jews in Prussia, for they opened up new social, commercial, political, and educational opportunities. Bella Salomon, like her father Daniel Itzig, was seriously opposed to what was happening in the younger generation. Details of the internal family disputes are unknown, but seen in this context the present of the Bach score to Felix around the time of his baptism seems a particularly remarkable gesture, perhaps even as a sign of reconciliation: a work of undeniably Christian art handed down by a faithful

Jewess, with Bach's music standing above doctrinal and confessional traditions. Bella Salomon came to tolerate, if not accept, the notion expressed by Abraham Mendelssohn that true Christianity "contains nothing that can lead you away from what is good."[14]

Sara Levy's Salon and Music Collection

Bella's younger sister Sara held similar, probably even stronger, views about conversion. When she died childless at age ninety-four, she left her considerable fortune to charity by establishing a foundation for a Jewish orphanage in Berlin. On the other hand, she fit perfectly into the environment of intellectual, cultural, and to some extent political liberalism of a period quite unique in German history. The quarter-century from 1780 to 1806, the year in which Napoleon conquered Prussia, was also a period in which a group of wealthy Jewish women in Berlin "achieved social glory by entertaining the cream of gentile society."[15] The literary and philosophical salons of Rahel Varnhagen, Henriette Herz, Rebecca Friedländer, and Dorothea Schlegel were among the most prominent and best known. The success of these Jewish *salonnières*, in one view, "was based on defiance of the traditional boundaries separating noble from commoner, gentile from Jew, male from female. The public happiness achieved in these salons was a real-life enactment of the ideal of 'Bildung'—encompassing education, refinement, and the development of character."[16]

Sara Itzig, after her marriage in 1783 to the banker Samuel Levy, established a salon with a strong focus on music at her stately home in old Berlin's poshest neighborhood, occupying a substantial section of what later became the Museum Island in the city center. For about ten years, from 1774 to 1784, she had taken lessons from Wilhelm Friedemann Bach, the oldest of the Leipzig cantor's sons, and had become a keyboard virtuoso in her own right. She regularly performed at the afternoon gatherings in her house and elsewhere. After the death of her husband in 1806, she became more and more engaged in the public concerts of the *Sing-Akademie*, where she regularly appeared as a soloist with the orchestra of the *Ripienschule*, performing concertos by Bach and his sons as well as those of other composers. Sometime after 1831, however, when she was in her early seventies, she stopped performing in public. Her last documented performance took place in 1831, when she played the keyboard solo in Bach's Triple Concerto in A Minor (BWV 1044).[17]

Madame Levy's music collection was quite comprehensive, consisting almost exclusively of instrumental music by major composers active in the second half of the eighteenth century. The works of J. S. Bach and his four sons represent a significant portion of her music library, and they show a scope and character without parallel elsewhere. Moreover, her collection formed a library for practical use; that is, the collection contained not only scores but also performing parts. The music room in her mansion could easily accommodate an orchestra of eighteenth-century proportions. She apparently employed at least one professional music copyist, and the individual manuscripts in the collection invariably bear the stamp *SSLev*[i], identifying them as the property of Samuel and Sara Levy (see fig. 2.1). What today has survived of her music collection represents the principal source of information about her musical salon and the repertoire performed by herself and her husband as well as by other members of her family, friends, and guest musicians.[18] Beyond the rich music collection, Levy owned many keyboard instruments of various kinds, and took an interest in instruments by Friedrich Silbermann of Strasbourg.

Sara Levy not only arranged for musical performances; she and her flute-playing husband also commissioned works and became major patrons for the two elder Bach sons. Peter Wollny has suggested that W. F. Bach wrote the Cantilena Nuptiarum "Herz, mein Herz, sei ruhig" (Fk 97) for the Itzig–Levy wedding in 1783.[19] The Levys apparently supported him financially for the last ten years of his life and he, in turn, provided them with music. It remains unknown when Sara Levy established direct contact with Friedemann's younger brother Carl Philipp Emanuel, who had left Berlin for Hamburg when Sara was just seven years old. It may well have happened only after Friedemann's death on July 1, 1784. Nevertheless, the Levy collection already contained sixteen keyboard concertos by the Hamburg Bach when in 1788 Sara commissioned the seventy-four-year-old composer to write for her two very different types of works.

First, she seems to have ordered three chamber works for fortepiano, flute, and viola. With its unusual combination of instruments the set (Wq. 93–95) must be considered specifically designed for performance in her salon, perhaps with Salomon Levy on flute, a friend playing viola, and Sara at the keyboard.[20] In the last year of his life, C. P. E. Bach took an innovative approach and focused on a well-adjusted distribution of the instrumental voices and clear distinctions between them. The integration of a woodwind and a string instrument adds different colors to the homogeneous keyboard parts. Moreover, using a viola instead of a violin puts emphasis on the middle ground of the score, that is, on the center of the sound spectrum. The result constitutes an evenly balanced instrumental discourse that permits the composer to engage in a lively, intense, and witty musical dialogue—in all likelihood a fitting interlude to the verbal conversations invariably conducted among the cultured guests of Levy's literary-musical salon.[21]

The autograph score of 1788 and sole surviving source of the three works shows the unstable and trembling hand of the seventy-four-year-old composer who suffered from gout and wrote with considerable difficulty. All three pieces are headed "Quartet fürs Clavier, Flöte u. Bratsche" (quartet for clavier, flute,

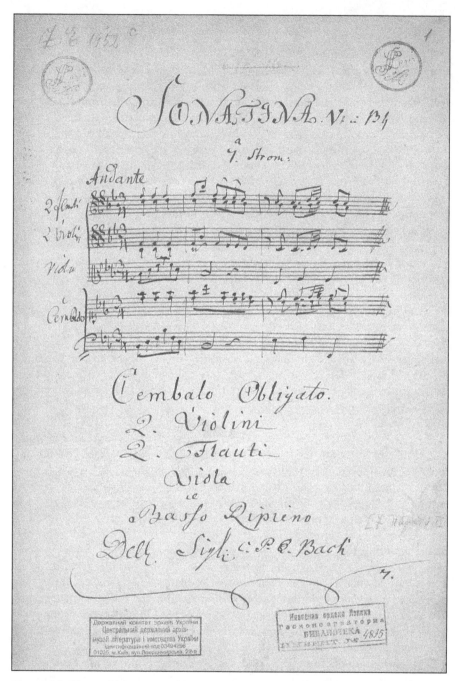

Figure 2.1. The *ex libris* stamp of Sara and Samuel Levy. From the title page of Carl Philipp Emanuel Bach, Sonatina for cembalo and orchestra, Wq. 110 / H. 459, D-Bsa SA 4835. Reproduced by permission of the Staatsbibliothek zu Berlin and the Sing-Akademie zu Berlin.

Figure 2.2. Opening page of Carl Philipp Emanuel Bach, Quartet in D Major for flute, viola, and keyboard, Wq. 94 / H. 538. Autograph manuscript, D-Bsa SA 3328 (1). Reproduced by permission of the Staatsbibliothek zu Berlin and the Sing-Akademie zu Berlin.

and viola), and the layout of the score indicates Bach's definition of quartet: rather than referring to four different instruments, he stresses four independent contrapuntal lines of music, one each for flute, viola, fortepiano right hand, and fortepiano left hand (fig. 2.2). Haydn or Mozart would have called it a piano trio, but their standard scoring would be for violin, cello, and piano.

Second, Sara commissioned a concerto for two keyboards and orchestra, most likely with the intention of sharing the solo parts with her sister Zippora, with whom she frequently played music for two keyboards and for keyboard with four hands.[22] The work that seems to have resulted is the Double Concerto in E-flat (Wq. 47) for harpsichord and fortepiano with large orchestra (two flutes, two horns, and strings), Philipp Emanuel's last composition. The Levy collection contains the autograph score of this most special piece, too. It deliberately juxtaposes two different types of keyboard instruments—the older harpsichord and the more recently invented fortepiano. Whether the idea of making use of the two contrasting instruments was Bach's or Levy's remains unknown.

After C. P. E. Bach's death, the widow Johanna Maria Bach kept in touch with Madame Levy.[23] It was probably after the Hamburg Bach's death that Sara appears to have turned to the youngest living son of the Leipzig cantor, Johann Christoph Friedrich Bach in Bückeburg, for another commission, the Double Concerto in E-flat for fortepiano and viola with large orchestra (two oboes, two horns, and strings), BR-JCFB: C 44, originating from around 1790.[24] In its overall design and scoring, J. C. F. Bach's piece is just as unorthodox as those by his half-brother and might have encouraged continuing discussions among the salon guests, which included the Humboldt brothers and other members of Berlin's intellectual elite. Even though their conversation is not recorded, their listening to the music of different Bach generations would have invited them to compare stylistic dialects of the past with the best of what was new in the contemporary scene of music—like the works of Mozart, who performed in Berlin in the spring of 1789. This experience undoubtedly would have given them a clear idea of a historical dimension in music together with a sense of urgency in preserving the musical past for the future. That aim was ultimately realized when in 1809 Wilhelm von Humboldt expanded the Prussian Academy of Arts by introducing a music professorship. He appointed Carl Friedrich Zelter, director of the Berlin *Sing-Akademie*, Felix Mendelssohn Bartholdy's principal teacher, and the one who consciously started an archive of music that eventually came to incorporate also Sara Levy's collection.

Sara Levy's Library in the Music Archive of the Berlin *Sing-Akademie*

After giving up public performance, Sara Levy donated the bulk of her large music collection to the library of the Berlin *Sing-Akademie*. However, neither on the occasion of the acquisition in the early nineteenth century nor at any other point before the year 1999 was her substantial donation ever catalogued, properly evaluated, or actively studied. Moreover, because of the political and military turmoil of the 1940s, the music archive (*Notenarchiv*) of the *Sing-Akademie* disappeared after 1945 and for more than half a century was believed to have been lost, until it re-emerged largely intact in Kiev, Ukraine, in 1999. The unexpected breakthrough resulted from many years of intensive research and persistent efforts during the 1980s and 1990s, at the end of which the Harvard Ukrainian Research Institute became a most helpful partner.[25]

Toward the conclusion of World War II, many museum, library, and archival holdings were evacuated from German cities and sheltered in remote rural areas. The historical music collections of the Berlin *Sing-Akademie* were transferred in August 1943 to the castle in the remote village of Ullersdorf, near Glatz in Upper Silesia. However, after the Red Army invaded the eastern parts of Germany almost all of the materials located there were seized as trophies and removed, mostly to Moscow. The Red Army cultural officers kept the most significant trophies there and sent those of lesser importance to provincial capitals of the former Soviet Union, but virtually no information was available about the location of these materials.

The trophy materials captured and distributed were invariably held, like most archival possessions in the former socialist states, under the jurisdiction of state security services, the former KGB. Hence, inquiries ordinarily remained unanswered. After the collapse of the Soviet Union, however, a classified document of the Red Army, commissioned in 1957 by the Central Committee of the Communist Party of the Soviet Union and published 1996 by an official German library commission, finally provided a first clue.[26] It cited a document which indicated that 5,170 items of music (including first editions and manuscripts) had been deposited in the Kiev State Conservatory shortly after the war. Listed without provenance references or any descriptive information, the size of the collection corresponded roughly to that of the *Sing-Akademie*'s music collection. Upon inquiry, however, the Tchaikovsky National Music Academy, formerly the State Conservatory in Kiev, claimed to have no wartime-deposited music materials. Further research revealed, however, that the restricted music deposits in the conservatory had been transferred to an undisclosed location in 1973. Eventually, the materials were traced to the Archive-Museum of Literature and Art in Kiev, a division of the Central National Archives of Ukraine. Finally, in July 1999, at the end of a complicated search process and much frustrating experience, Fond 441, an unspecified collection under the name of "European Music from the Seventeenth to the Nineteenth Centuries" in the Archive-Museum of Literature and Art, Kiev, was located and identified as the missing music collection of the *Sing-Akademie*.

Relatively soon after the rediscovery of the materials, which had suffered surprisingly few losses, another unexpected development arose when joint efforts by Harvard University, the Packard Humanities Institute, and German government agencies led to the repatriation of the large collection to Germany. Since December 2001, the large collection, 85 percent of it in manuscripts, is housed and accessible as a permanent deposit of the *Sing-Akademie* in the music division of the Staatsbibliothek zu Berlin. As the Bach sources make up a substantial part of the collection and are of particular importance, they were by 2006 fully catalogued.[27] In the meantime, they are also available online in digitized format via the digital Bach Library of the Bach-Archiv in Leipzig (www.bachdigital.de). Now that the Levy collection can now be fully assessed, it is clear how prominently this extraordinary woman figured in the early reception of the music of the Bach family and in the larger history of German music.

Notes

1. Evelin Odrich and Peter Wollny, eds., *Die Briefentwürfe des Johann Elias Bach (1705–1755)*. Leipziger Beiträge zur Bach-Forschung 3 (Hildesheim: Olms, 2005), 181.

2. See Eva Renate Blechschmidt, *Die Amalien-Bibliothek. Musikbibliothek der Prinzessin Anna Amalia von Preußen (172–787)*, Berliner Studien zur Musikwissenschaft 8 (Berlin: Merseburger, 1965); and Bettina Faulstich, *Die Musikaliensammlung der Familie von Voß. Ein Beitrag zur Berliner Musikgeschichte um 1800*, Catalogus Musicus (Kassel: Bärenreiter, 1997).

3. See Yael Sela's contribution to the present volume.

4. Mendelssohn together with Ferdinand David, concertmaster of the Gewandhaus, played a major role in publicizing also Bach's instrumental chamber works; see R. Larry Todd, *Mendelssohn: A Life in Music* (Oxford: Oxford University Press, 2003), 389.

5. The abbreviation BWV refers to the standard catalogue of the works of Johann Sebastian Bach, the *Bach Werke Verzeichnis*.

6. Robert Schumann, *Gesammelte Schriften über Musik und Musiker*, ed. Martin Kreisig (Leipzig: Breitkopf & Härtel, 1914), 1:314.

7. Georg Schünemann, "Die Bachpflege der Berliner Singakademie," *Bach-Jahrbuch*, 25 (1928): 144.

8. For more detailed discussions of Sara Levy's musical salon, see Christoph Wolff, "A Bach Cult in Late-Eighteenth-Century Berlin: Sara Levy's Musical Salon," *Bulletin of the American Academy of Arts and Sciences* 58, no. 3 (2005): 26–31, and Christoph Wolff, "The Bach Tradition among the Mendelssohn Ancestry," in *Mendelssohn, the Organ, and the Music of the Past: Constructing Musical Legacies*, ed. Jürgen Thym (Rochester, NY: University of Rochester Press, 2014), 213–23, as well as Peter Wollny, *"Ein förmlicher Sebastian und Philipp Emanuel Bach-Kultus": Sara Levy und ihr musikalisches Wirken. Mit einer Dokumentensammlung zur musikalischen Familiengeschichte der Vorfahren von Felix Mendelssohn Bartholdy* (Wiesbaden: Breitkopf & Härtel, 2010), hereafter Wollny, 2010.

9. For the most recent research on the score copied for Bella Salomon by Johann Friedrich Rietz (1767–1828) and given to the young Mendelssohn, see Peter Ward Jones, "Mendelssohn's Performances of the 'Matthäus-Passion': Considerations of the Documentary Evidence," *Music & Letters*, 97 (2016), 409–64. Jones argues that the manuscript was given to Mendelssohn for his birthday in February 1824.

10. Quoted after Adolf Weissmann, *Berlin als Musikstadt. Geschichte der Oper und des Konzerts von 1740 bis 1911* (Berlin: Schuster & Löffler, 1911), 36.

11. See Christoph Wolff, "Mozart 1782, Fanny Arnstein und viermal Bach," *Mozart-Jahrbuch* 10 (2009): 141–49.

12. See note 8 above.

13. After his conversion, Jacob Salomon adopted the name Bartholdy and therewith provided the model for Abraham and Lea Mendelssohn's name change.

14. For Abraham Mendelssohn's views on conversion, see Wulf Konold, *Felix Mendelssohn Bartholdy und seine Zeit* (Laaber: Laaber, 1984), 69–80; see also Natalie Naimark-Goldberg's contribution to this volume.

15. Deborah Hertz, *Jewish High Society in Old Regime Berlin* (New Haven, CT: Yale University Press, 1988), 3.

16. Hertz, *Jewish High Society*, 3–4.

17. Wollny, *"Ein förmlicher Sebastian und Philipp Emanuel Bach-Kultus,"* 39.

18. For a complete listing of her Bach holdings, see Wollny, *"Ein förmlicher Sebastian und Philipp Emanuel Bach-Kultus,"* 69–87.

19. "Fk." is the abbreviation for one of two standard catalogues of the works of Wilhelm Friedemann Bach, the Falck catalogue: Martin Falck, "Thematisches Verzeichnis der Kompositionen Wilhelm Friedemann Bachs," in *Wilhelm Friedemann Bach: Sein Leben und seine Werke* (Leipzig: C. I. Kahnt, 1913).

20. "Wq." is the abbreviation for one of two standard catalogues of the works of Carl Philipp Emanuel Bach, the Wotquenne catalogue.

21. See Steven Zohn's contribution to the present volume.

22. See Rebecca Cypess's contribution to the present volume.

23. Letter of September 5, 1789, quoted in Wollny, 2010, 49–51.

24. "BR-JCFB" refers to the catalogue of works of Johann Christoph Friedrich Bach, now in progress, to be published by the Bach-Repertorium series.

25. For a detailed discussion of the recovery of the *Sing-Akademie* archive, see Christoph Wolff, "Recovered in Kiev: Bach et al. A Preliminary Report on the Musical Archive of the Berlin Sing-Akademie," *Notes*, 2nd series, 58, no. 2 (2001): 259–71.

26. Klaus-Dieter Lehmann and Ingo Kolasa, eds., *Die Trophäenkommissionen der Roten Armee. Eine Dokumentensammlung zur Verschleppung von Büchern aus deutschen Bibliotheken* (Frankfurt/Main: Klostermann, 1996), 245.

27. Wolfram Enßlin, ed., *Die Bach-Quellen der Sing-Akademie zu Berlin: Katalog* (Hildesheim: Olms, 2006), 2 vols. For the complete holdings of the collection, see Axel Fischer and Matthias Kornemann, ed., *The Archive of the Sing-Akademie zu Berlin: Catalogue / Das Archiv der Sing-Akademie zu Berlin: Katalog* (Berlin: de Gruyter, 2010).

Chapter Three

Remaining within the Fold

The Cultural and Social World of Sara Levy

Natalie Naimark-Goldberg

Sara Levy, a fascinating woman by all accounts, was for many years a rather minor figure in historical writing. Only in recent decades has her image gradually emerged. Scholars who include Sara Levy in their accounts typically present her as part of a remarkable group of educated Jewish women who were influenced by secularizing trends and led an acculturated lifestyle, deeply involved in the intellectual, cultural and social scene of their time.[1] The prevalent assumption is that, with few exceptions, these women's acculturation came at the expense of their identification with Judaism: with their increasing participation in European culture and their deepening integration into German society, they purportedly became more and more estranged from the Jewish world.[2]

In this chapter, I delve more deeply into the case of Sara Levy, examining untapped sources and reassessing her affiliation to this group of women. My goal is to reconsider to what extent she was an intrinsic part of this circle—how similar were her lifestyle and her way of thinking and acting to that of other women in this group. Examining the distinctive features of her life in comparison with the whole group yields, I believe, interesting results. It reveals the unexpectedly strong Jewish identity of this acculturated woman and illuminates the ways in which she maintained a solid bond with the Jewish community while integrating into German society and culture. Levy's case as depicted below provides a corrective not only to the strong emphasis often placed on the acculturation of this generation of modernizing women but also to the

heavy attention given to the domestic sphere, especially when discussing manifestations of Jewishness among acculturating women in Germany. A particular
aspect of Levy's obstinate allegiance to Judaism that emerges from the sources
explored in this chapter is that hers was not merely a privatized Jewishness,
confined to practices carried out at home, but involved aspects of a more public character. Born in Berlin in 1761 to the wealthy Itzig family, Sara Levy has
been, for historians, exceptional indeed even at first sight as one of the few
salonnières who remained within the Jewish community. Whereas better-known
Jewish women from her milieu—notably Rahel Levin Varnhagen, Dorothea
Mendelssohn, and Henriette Herz—embraced Christianity at some point in
their lives, Sara Levy never left the fold; when she died in old age, she was laid
to rest in the Schönhauser Allee cemetery that served the Berlin Jewish community at the time.

Of course, Sara Levy was not alone in her lifelong allegiance to Judaism.
Her more famous sister, Fanny von Arnstein, who lived in Vienna after her marriage, also died as a Jew, as did all of their numerous siblings.[3] Also steadfast
in their Judaism were Amalie Beer, another wealthy and acculturated Jewish
woman in Berlin, who hosted (along with her husband) early Reform services
in her home, and Recha Mendelssohn, a daughter of Moses Mendelssohn,
who condemned the conversion of her sisters Dorothea and Henriette to
Catholicism and never considered baptism. But many other women changed
their faith, and those who did not may be seen, in a way, as the exception.

Yet, aside from this undeniably crucial difference, Sara Levy's social and cultural world appears similar to that of women who eventually took the step of
baptism. And this is what allowed scholars to include her without any hesitation in the group of "*salonnières*," or "enlightened Jewish women."[4]

Socially, Sara Levy had much in common with the women who had converted or would eventually follow the path of baptism. Like them, she had
close relations with gentile friends, many of whom frequented the home she
shared with her husband Samuel Levy.[5] These friends kept coming after she
was widowed in 1806. The long list of non-Jewish friends includes notable
intellectuals, young students, learned women, and, of course, musicians. The
Swedish diplomat Gustav von Brinckmann and the German political journal-
ist and statesman Friedrich von Gentz, for instance, attended social occasions
with "Madame Levy" and her husband in Berlin and Vienna.[6] The Protestant
theologian Friedrich Schleiermacher, too, mentioned his friendly acquaintance with Sara Levy in his letters.[7] Sara Levy also counted the geographer and
explorer Alexander von Humboldt as a friend; he frequented her house and
attended her funeral in 1854.[8] He reportedly mediated between her and the
Prussian King concerning her large estate on the Museum Island in Berlin,
which the king coveted for building a new museum but Levy refused to cede
until her death.[9]

Of special interest is Levy's friendship with Elise Reimarus, an enlightened woman from Hamburg. Reimarus, who corresponded with Moses Mendelssohn during his lifetime and considered other Jews among her close contacts, maintained a lively connection with Sara Levy and felt deep appreciation for her. Their missives give evidence to the social—and trans-regional—networking that resulted from this friendship and the cultural exchange that took place between these two enlightened women—one of them a Christian living in Hamburg, the other a Jew living in Berlin.[10] Another notable woman with whom Sara Levy interacted was the French writer Germaine de Staël, a literary figure of international renown, who was her guest in Berlin.[11]

Moreover, just like Jews who displayed a more tenuous connection to Jewish culture, Sara Levy participated in Enlightenment societies that allowed Jews and non-Jews to socialize and discuss cultural matters. In these associations, the borders between Jewish and Christian societies were blurred—at least to a certain extent, for antipathies and hostility towards Jews had not totally disappeared. One of the associations she joined, the new Feßler Wednesday Society (*Feßlersche Mittwochgesellschaft*), an enlightened association founded in 1795 in Berlin, was among the few that accepted Jews *and* women as regular members.[12] At its meetings Levy could interact with dozens of "very educated, meritorious men," among them government officials, scholars, composers, artists, publishers and merchants, as well as "talented, gracious women." The list of members included other Jews, such as Isaac Euchel, a leading *maskil*, playwright, and staunch defender of Hebrew literature, and Henriette Herz, who would choose Christianity in her later years.[13]

A second, related feature that Sara Levy shared with the Jewish *salonnières* was her intense involvement in the German and European cultural world. Many of these women were active in the literary field, some even accomplished authors (notably Dorothea Mendelssohn and Esther Gad). Music was Sara Levy's métier. She was a skilled harpsichordist and very well versed in the world of music. A patron, close friend, and admirer of the Bach family, Levy collected their works and commissioned pieces of music from them to be later performed in various circles. A peculiar piece from the Bach family that may have been in her possession was a "Cantinela [*sic*] Nuptiarum Consolatoria," an adaptation made by Wilhelm Friedemann Bach of one of his keyboard works with text added and copied out in the composer's hand, perhaps for her wedding.[14] Friedemann Bach had been her teacher and she supported him financially for the last decade of his life.[15] Such a nuptial song was obviously a luxury that only a member of a wealthy family could afford. Not by chance, it contains no overt Christian text, though it does reveal some religious imagery.[16] To this set of music-related activities we may add the fact that Levy subscribed to numerous German music publications and that she supported a noteworthy institution in Berlin, the *Sing-Akademie*.[17]

Concerning her intense participation in German culture, and specifically in music, Levy's affiliation with the *Sing-Akademie* is especially revealing. This choral society, established in 1791, began as a circle of music lovers who gathered in the tradition of contemporaneous reading societies and salons and soon developed a public profile, presenting public choral concerts.[18] The society offered a formal framework for Levy's musical activities. The fact that she was given the opportunity to take part in its concerts, performing as a soloist for a German audience,[19] was significant for her as a member of the Jewish community.[20] It was also meaningful for her as a woman, as it offered the possibility to fulfill a public role that was then elusive for members of her sex. Her connection with the *Sing-Akademie* was so strong that she would later donate a significant part of her invaluable music collection to its library.

In her affiliation with the *Sing-Akademie*, she was no different from Jews who would later convert. Members of the Academy, since its early years of existence, included future converts such as Fradchen Liebmann (later Friederike Liman), a close friend of Rahel Levin; Sara's niece Lea Salomon; and Lea's future husband Abraham Mendelssohn. Famously, their son Felix would also join the choral society in later decades, as would their oldest daughter Fanny. Even though the Academy was a Christian society, Sara Levy was not deterred from participating in it any more than other Jews with more tenuous bonds to their religion. It is true that the pieces performed by the Academy, despite the sacred motifs pervading most of them, were, by the Enlightenment era, considered works of art more than religious creations. It is also true that unlike Fradchen Liebmann, for instance, Sara did not *sing*, but "only" *played* music, meaning that she was not pronouncing Christian texts, which often included anti-Semitic elements and stereotypes. However, there is no point in denying that all the same Jews who played—or sang—these pieces were participating in music with origins in Christian practice that propagated negative images of the Jews, or that such activity was controversial, if not outright prohibited, from the point of view of traditional Ashkenazic Jewish society.

And indeed, an important aspect that Sara Levy shared with less committed Jews is the fact that she embraced Christian elements from German and European culture. Although associated with Christianity, these practices and cultural forms had lost, to some extent, their religious significance as they propagated among Jews of this generation. Among those Jews who embraced Christian art forms, some would later convert, but there were others who would never leave the Jewish faith.

One prominent feature worth stressing in this regard is the taste that modernizing Jews acquired for church music. The pleasure Jews derived from this cultural form, which was very popular at the time and engaged the most prominent composers, often led them within the church walls—not in order to participate in Christian worship, but as spectators attracted to an edifying performance. The letters of the young Ludwig Börne reveal that in 1803, while living in Berlin as a student and having just left the Frankfurt ghetto, he attended a performance of the famous—and at the time extremely popular—oratorio *Der Tod Jesu* (The Death of Jesus), composed by Carl Heinrich Graun in 1755. When he arrived at the Nicholas Church, Börne met none other than Henriette Herz, his landlady and the wife of his tutor.[21] Herz apparently attended a performance of this devotional work every year, as did other Jews, and perhaps Sara Levy. What is in any case certain is that Levy was fond of this type of music and it did not bother her that the compositions she admired most had deep Christian roots and typical Christian motifs, including discomfiting characterizations of the Jews.

The inclination of acculturated Jews for church music could encompass more than mere aesthetic appreciation; it could involve actual participation in its performance. Jewish members of the *Sing-Akademie*, including Sara Levy, felt free to perform Christian music, and their Jewishness never prevented them from appearing in concerts at unmistakably Christian places, such as cathedrals and churches. The irony of this involvement did not pass unnoticed, and one contemporary observer, the German writer Jean Paul, wittily remarked that Jewish singers taking part in Graun's oratorio on the death of Jesus were in fact singing "against themselves."[22]

The affinity of acculturated Jews for Christian motifs was not limited to the public or semipublic sphere: Christian elements penetrated the confines of family life, as well. This trend had begun before Sara Levy's generation among Jews of the economic elite, as demonstrated in their art collections. Although Daniel and Miriam Itzig, Sara Levy's parents, led an observant Jewish life, and their elegant house boasted a private synagogue and a special place for building a sukkah,[23] "at least two items with Christian themes"—"pictures of St Jerome in the desert and of Mary Magdalene"—graced their walls. The Ephraim and Fließ mansions displayed similar Christian objects.[24]

Much more consequential was the entry of Christmas into Jewish households, which began in the early 1800s. The celebration of this holiday as a private event in the family bosom, with the brightly adorned tree at its center, was a new custom spreading then in non-Jewish society, not by chance parallel to the rise of the bourgeoisie and the expansion of secularization. In its modern garb, Christmas was perceived as a secular, private festivity—the celebration *par excellence* of the bourgeois family—more than as a Christian religious holiday. Thus, Jewish men and women, not only those who eventually converted but also acculturated Jews in general, could adopt it without serious drawbacks.[25]

The house of Fanny and Nathan von Arnstein, for instance, was apparently the first to boast a Christmas tree in Vienna. This Jewish mansion had been for decades home to one of the most glamorous salons in the Habsburg capital. During the Congress of Vienna, when diplomats from all over Europe gathered in this city to reshape the continent after the Napoleonic wars, they found the Arnsteins' home a hospitable place to meet on social terms. On Christmas Eve in 1814, the Arnsteins hosted a party for distinguished guests, and no one left without a special gift from the hostess. Fanny, born in Berlin in 1758, is said to have brought from her native city the new custom of celebrating Christmas Eve with a decorated tree and presents, a custom that was beginning to expand at about that time from northern Germany into other areas. The Arnstein couple was never baptized; moreover, at the time they celebrated Christmas, Fanny was using her contacts to promote Jewish causes. The Christian celebration and the sense of Jewish commitment obviously did not exclude each other.

The Arnstein case was by no means exceptional. Christmas was celebrated by other lifelong Jews, such as Henriette Mendelssohn (neé Meyer, 1776–1862), and her husband Joseph, the only son of Moses Mendelssohn to remain Jewish. This couple celebrated Christmas in a more confined family circle, together with their son Alexander (who was among the last descendants of Moses Mendelssohn to die as a Jew), his wife Marianne, neé Seligmann, and their children, apparently without granting the event a particularly religious significance. The house of Chaie Levin, Rahel Levin Varnhagen's mother, was likewise the venue of a family celebration at Christmastime, complete with a decorated Christmas tree, the exchange of gifts, and a festive meal. Again here, as in the case of the Arnsteins, this practice did not jeopardize Jewish affiliation: we know that during those same years, in the first decade of the nineteenth century, Chaie Levin, who remained attached to Jewish tradition until her death, took care to celebrate Jewish holidays in the company of all of her family members.

The vexed story of Felix Mendelssohn's manuscript of the *St. Matthew Passion* provides further evidence concerning the observance of Christmas in Sara Levy's circle. Eduard Devrient, an actor and a friend of Felix Mendelssohn who collaborated with him in the revival of this work at the *Sing-Akademie* in 1829, claimed that the manuscript was a Christmas gift from Felix's grandmother and Sara's sister, Bella Salomon, a lifelong Jew; but R. Larry Todd dismisses this claim as implausible, favoring instead Peter Ward Jones's suggestion that it was probably a birthday gift for Felix's fifteenth birthday in February 1824, just a month before Bella's death.[26] Todd puts forward two grounds for his reasoning. First, the Mendelssohn family music library inventory shows that Felix received his copy of the *Passion* in 1824, and since Bella died in March 1824, she could not have given her grandchild a present on that year's Christmas.[27] Moreover, Todd writes: "How are we to understand Bella—an orthodox Jew who had cursed the Protestant Jacob Bartholdy [her converted son] in 1805 and was unaware in 1823 that her children and grandchildren had converted—presenting Bach's Passion as a Christmas present?"[28] Whatever the truth about the date of the gift, the idea that Bella's orthodoxy would have prevented her from giving a gift at Christmas does not hold up. Not only were converted Jews celebrating Christmas; even lifelong adherents to Judaism commemorated the holiday in its modern style, and could certainly have been involved in the practice of giving Christmas gifts. This possibility is supported by Nahida Remy, a late-nineteenth-century writer who sought to extol the virtues of Jewish women who remained faithful to their religion. Remy reported that during Christmastime, Sara Levy displayed items in her salon produced by a poor student she wished to help financially; it is likely that she made these items available for purchase by friends who visited her and needed Christmas gifts.[29]

In light of Sara Levy's strong connection with German culture and society, it is legitimate to ask whether her lifelong affiliation to Judaism had concrete implications at all. Jewish women often converted to Christianity for pragmatic reasons—to marry a non-Jew, or to give their own children better social and economic opportunities. Sara Levy lacked any such motivation to convert, yet she might have been less than passionately attached to her own religion.

However, an additional set of sources indicates that it is wrong to downplay Sara Levy's Jewishness. Unlike most Jewish *salonnières*, Levy—parallel to her intense participation in German culture and music—was strongly involved in Jewish causes and institutions throughout her life and took an especially deep interest in Jewish education. Jewish identification and the promotion of specifically Jewish goals were in fact central dimensions of her life, even though they have received little emphasis in research, with attention usually focused on processes of acculturation and assimilation that help present Sara Levy as an integral part of German culture.

Of special interest is Levy's connection with the *Haskalah*, the Jewish Enlightenment. It is a peculiar thing to say about a woman that she was associated with this movement. First of all, the *Haskalah*—especially in the eighteenth century and the first half of the nineteenth century—is known to have excluded women from its ranks. It was a male movement, whose writings and institutions were created primarily by and for men.[30] Moreover, most Jewish women of Sara Levy's generation—despite their involvement in Enlightenment culture, expressed no interest whatsoever in bringing their knowledge and their critical attitude to bear upon Jewish society. Yet Levy clearly did, advancing maskilic projects and goals throughout her life.

Admittedly, Sara Levy's connection to the *Haskalah* was not as strong as that of the male members of her family, notably her father Daniel Itzig, her brother Isaac, and her own husband Samuel Levy. Not every couple that married had the honor of having a special Hebrew poem written for the occasion, but Sara Itzig and Samuel Levy did, and this was certainly due to her father's or perhaps her husband's solid links with the *maskilim*. Wedding poems in Hebrew were a form of occasional literature that had been widespread among Italian Jewry for quite some time and was taken up by the *maskilim* in the eighteenth

Figure 3.1. Image of one of the nuptial poems for Sara Itzig and Samuel Levy. Staatsbibliothek zu Berlin, Handschriftenabteilung, Ms.or.fol.1267, No. 12. Used with permission.

century, who wrote these poems either for friends and colleagues or for wealthy patrons. At least two Hebrew poems were composed in honor of Sara Itzig and Samuel Levy's wedding in 1783.[31] The author of one poem was Josel Pick, the tutor of Moses Mendelssohn's children and a very active *maskil* at the time.[32] The author of the second poem, beautifully illustrated, is anonymous, but was certainly one of the *maskilim* active in Berlin, and presumably close to either Sara's father or the bridegroom.

However, beyond her male relatives' connection with the *Haskalah*, which is well documented in Jewish historiography, Sara was also personally involved in this movement, as were other female members of the Itzig clan. Her father was a famous patron of leading *maskilim*; her brother co-founded the modern Jewish school in Berlin and co-directed its printing house, which specialized in the publication of maskilic books. Sara's support was unquestionably more modest, but coming from a woman, it was highly significant and rather unexpected.

This support became tangible through her endorsement of maskilic literature; her name figures among the subscribers of several Hebrew books. Although Sara's connection to the German world of music, including her subscription to various works of music, has been discussed in detail, her subscription to Hebrew books, which illuminates a less-known facet of her cultural profile, is seldom mentioned. And although subscribing to a modern Hebrew book did not necessarily mean that she read it, it does indicate a level of interest in and ideological support of the movement.

One outstanding work she subscribed to was *Zemirot Yisra'el*, a maskilic edition of the Book of Psalms published between 1785 and 1791 in five volumes, which was perhaps the *Haskalah*'s best seller. *Zemirot Yisra'el* featured Moses Mendelssohn's German translation of the biblical text and was the result of combined efforts by at least three leading *maskilim*. One was Joel Brill, who wrote a long introduction and the commentary accompanying Mendelssohn's translation; he was an educator and a prolific author in Berlin, and would soon be invited to head the new modern Jewish school in Breslau.[33] Another *maskil* involved in this publication was Shabbetai of Yanov, manager of the *Orientalische Buchdruckerei*, the maskilic printing house in Berlin, and perhaps the leading force behind this specific publication; the third, of course, was Moses Mendelssohn himself, who wrote the German translation and gave his blessing to this initiative (he died several years before the project was completed).[34]

Zemirot Yisra'el was a very interesting publication in the *Haskalah* landscape. Mendelssohn's translation of the Book of Psalms had already been published in 1781,[35] but this new edition was definitely different. Whereas the first edition appeared in German font and was aimed mainly at a non-Jewish public, in the new edition the German translation was printed in Hebrew characters, side by side with the original Hebrew text and along with a modern commentary

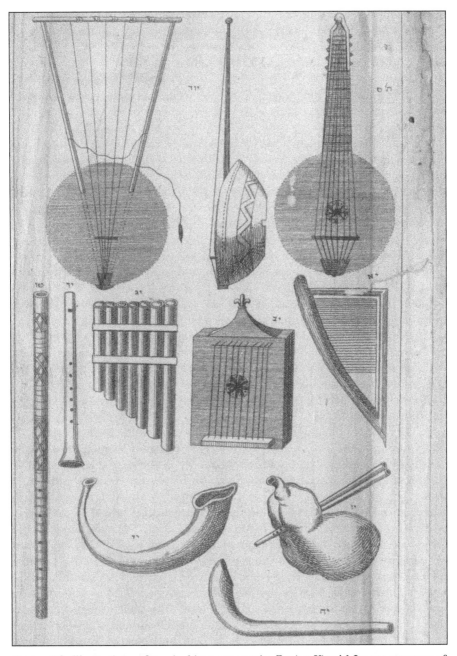

Figure 3.2. Illustrations of musical instruments in *Zemirot Yisra'el*. Image courtesy of the National Library of Jerusalem.

of the biblical text. Moreover, the new edition also differed from the earlier German edition in that its first volume—actually printed last, in 1791—consisted of several long "introductions," with sections dedicated to the history of music and a discussion of musical instruments in Biblical times, including illustrations.

All these features made *Zemirot Yisra'el*, from one perspective, a typical maskilic book. Indeed, it shared prominent characteristics and goals with other maskilic publications—for example, in favoring the study of the Bible rather than the Talmud, placing emphasis on learning proper Hebrew and High German, and providing modern commentaries to biblical texts that took into consideration contemporary non-Jewish exegesis. From another perspective, though, *Zemirot Yisra'el* was a maskilic book unlike any other. One important peculiarity, which may help explain Sara Levy's special interest in it, was its focus on music. Music rarely appeared in *Haskalah* literature, and *Zemirot Yisra'el*—a relatively early engagement with music, at least on a theoretical-historical level, on the part of leading *maskilim*—is clearly an important exception.[36] This is not to say that one may not find individual *maskilim* versed in music. Moses Mendelssohn was considered a music expert and he treated music in his writings.[37] He did so, however, mainly as part of his involvement with the German Enlightenment and not when participating in *Haskalah* culture. Given the purported lack of interest of *maskilim* in music, the contents of *Zemirot Yisra'el* prompt us to reconsider this assumption. This project—a best seller of the *Haskalah*, printed at the *Orientalische Buchdruckerei*, the leading maskilic printing house in Berlin—devotes considerable attention to music, and declared as one of its explicit goals to raise the interest of young Jews in this cultural field.[38]

As noted above, the long list of subscribers includes the name of מ]רת[סערלי לעוו, i.e., Sara Levy, our protagonist. It was not typical of women to subscribe to maskilic books. Female names rarely appear in these lists, and when they do, it is often as widows. In fact, it is Sara's husband's name that is mentioned in many books, not hers.[39] But we see that, though unusual, female participation and support of maskilic literature was possible, and if it was important for a woman (and she had the means), she could leave testimony of her allegiance and have her own name printed. In the case of *Zemirot Yisra'el*, out of approximately 700 subscribers, a noteworthy number were women: a total of thirty-three, including twenty-one from Berlin.[40] A reason for their interest in this book may be the fact that reading the Psalms was common practice among Jewish women, and this edition, with the German translation printed in the Hebrew characters they were familiar with, may have been very attractive to them.[41] In the case of Sara Levy, and perhaps other subscribers, we may assert that the book's focus on music and its goal of expanding knowledge in this field among the Jews was another important reason for their support. In this connection it is quite interesting to find the name of another contemporary Jew who was extremely active in the German world of music, several years before he joined the Church: "Herr Musik-Director Ber Wessely" (ה' מזויק דירעקטר בער ועסלי), that is, Carl Bernhard Wessely, the composer and director of the Berlin National Theatre.[42] Sara Levy most likely had no intention of reading the Hebrew discussions of music themes in the introductions—she probably was unable to do so, as most Jewish women were illiterate in the Hebrew language—but may have been glad to support a project that propagated precisely this type of knowledge and promoted this kind of activity among fellow Jews.

Some two decades later, when she was a widow and many of her friends and close relatives had left or were about to leave Judaism, Levy still supported the goals of Jewish, and even Hebrew education, as we learn from her subscription to another publication called *Modah le'yaldei b'nei Yisra'el* ("Friend to the children of Israel," *Israelitischer Kinderfreund*). This textbook from 1812, mainly aimed at youngsters, included passages from fields as varied as geography, history, ethics, Jewish religion and prayers, Hebrew language, and the sciences.[43] It was printed simultaneously in three languages—German, Hebrew, and French—with Sara Levy's name figuring as a *Pränumerantin* for the Hebrew edition. She is one of only three women, two of them from Berlin, who gave this enterprise financial support. Sara had no children of her own who could have used the book; nevertheless, she cared for orphaned children and she may have purchased it for their sake. More likely, though, she subscribed to this publication either as a way to personally assist the author, Moses Hirsch Bock, who headed a private modern school that he established in Berlin in 1807, or to advance maskilic goals, mainly Hebrew and modern education among Jewish children.

That Sara considered the promotion of Jewish modern education a central goal is also apparent from her strong involvement with the *Freischule*, the maskilic school established by family members in Berlin in 1778. At least since the death of her husband in 1806, Levy took an interest in its curriculum and contributed funds to the school. Lazarus Bendavid, director of this institution, knew he could count on her unconditional support (and that of her sisters) and could always address her in case of need.[44] The fact that Sara's name appeared year after year in Bendavid's school reports as one of the main donors is clear proof of her commitment. In fact, it was to a large extent thanks to her constant funding that the school existed until 1825.[45]

One could assume that her longstanding dedication to the *Freischule* was due to the fact that it was a family enterprise, which she strove to keep alive. But this does not seem to be the only reason. When the *Freischule* eventually closed, she continued supporting new projects aimed at fostering Jewish education—for instance, the Jewish community school *Talmud Torah* in Berlin, established in 1826. This school, headed first by Leopold Zunz and then by Baruch

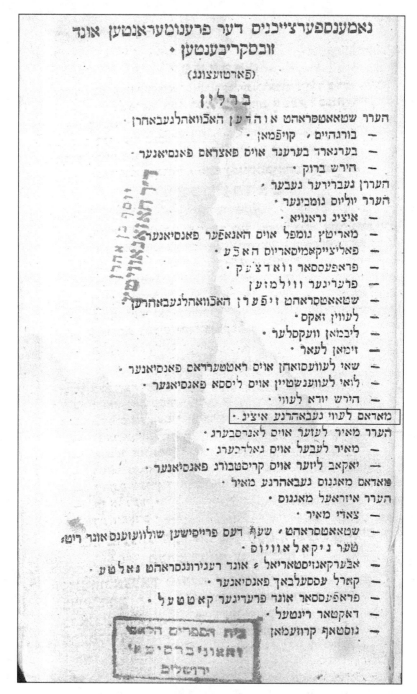

Figure 3.3. Sara Levy's name in the *Pränumeranten* list, *Modah le-yaldei b'nei Yisra'el*. Image courtesy of the National Library of Jerusalem.

Baruch Auerbach, put greater emphasis than the *Freischule* on Jewish education, and Sara Levy was one of its notable patrons. In addition to a sum of
money, a *parochet* (curtain covering the Torah Ark), and educational instruments (a celestial globe and a compass), Levy donated no less than "141 volumes of valuable works" to its library, per one of its reports, perhaps the largest
donation of books to this new institution.[46] In other words, she strove to enrich
not only the stacks of the music-oriented *Sing-Akademie*, but also the book-
shelves of a Jewish educational institution.

Still deeper was Sara Levy's involvement in the Jewish orphanage that was
annexed to this school some years later. Levy not only donated considerable
funds for this home, established in Berlin in 1832 by Baruch Auerbach, but
also sought contributions from her acquaintances, helping create the initial financial basis that would support the boys' orphanage for many years
to come.[47] Besides providing financial support, she did practical work for
the orphanage, even at an advanced age. From the establishment of the
orphanage until her death, she served as chairwoman of the institution's
"Ehrenmütter" (mothers of honor), a group of "honorable women from the
community" considered essential for managing this home.[48] This was by no
means just an honorific title; it entailed significant responsibilities in running the institution, work that was done, of course, on a volunteer basis. The
position of "Ehrenmütter" was undoubtedly conceived to help fulfill the
home's guiding aspiration to grant the orphans "devoted parental love" (*treue
Elternliebe*).[49] Thus, in addition to extensive administrative responsibilities, as
a "mother of honor" Levy undertook practical roles that put her in direct
contact with the pupils. For instance, a "mother of honor" was responsible
for a number of boys and had to be present at least once a week at lunch time
to accompany them. The institute took its parental role with such seriousness
that it continued to care for the pupils even after they left the orphanage.
Graduates were expected to keep in touch with the institution especially at
the beginning of their independent life, and report at least once a month to
the principal or to one of the "mothers of honor."[50]

It is important to stress that this was primarily a Jewish cultural institution.
Although secular goals such as educating the orphans to become upright citizens of the country and imparting practical skills to prepare them for earning
a living were an important part of its curriculum, a main objective was to incul-
cate in these children knowledge of and love for the Jewish religion. According
to its statutes, its religious observance should be that of a pious Jewish family; the orphanage should follow Jewish law, celebrating the Sabbath and the
Jewish holidays according to tradition, as well as strictly adhering to the Jewish
dietary laws.[51] Sales of a book used for the recitation of the *kaddish*, the traditional Jewish memorial prayer, served as a source of income.[52] As chairwoman
of the group of "mothers of honor," Sara Levy obviously dedicated great efforts

to this institution; although she herself did not necessarily lead a religiously stringent way of life, Jewish continuity and tradition were important to her. Having been reared in a religiously observant home, Levy may have felt, consistently with maskilic ideals, that a traditional Jewish education was necessary for the youth, who would then be able to encounter the modern world as Jews.

Parallel to these activities in the field of education, Levy also remained affiliated with Jewish associational life, joining, for instance, the *Brüderverein*, a society of mutual help established in 1815 by Jewish merchants. Unlike the more famous "Society of Friends," this association accepted married men and widows.[53]

Sara Levy's commitment to Judaism remained strong until her last day, as her testament clearly indicates.[54] A wealthy and childless woman, she bequeathed two-thirds of her fortune to charity,[55] with enormous funds going to Jewish causes via philanthropies—from the traditional *Malbish Arumim*, a society for providing garments to the poor and the care to the sick, to modern institutions, including various educational establishments for children and youth. To be sure, donations went to Christian foundations, as well—for instance, to the *Christliche Hausarme für Holz* and the German Wadzeck institution for infants—but these donations were relatively modest compared to the larger amounts bequeathed to institutions that specifically cared for Jewish co-religionists. Notable among these donations are the huge sums of 32,000 thaler bestowed to the Jewish community (as specified, preferably to be spent on the care of the sick); 10,000 thaler to Auerbach's boys' orphanage and a similar amount to Auerbach's girls' orphanage; and 5,000 thaler to a distinctive institution: the *Gesellschaft zur Beförderung der Industrie unter den Juden* (later the *Gesellschaft zur Verbreitung der Handwerke und des Ackerbaues unter dem Juden*), a society for fostering manual labor and technical occupations among Jewish youngsters. The amount of this bequest was so large as to deserve mention almost half a century later in a chronicle of this establishment.[56] Founded in 1812, following the Edict of Emancipation, which urged Jews to expand their fields of occupation beyond commerce and finance to include crafts and agriculture, the society sought to achieve this target by providing appropriate training to young Jews from low economic classes and granting them the means to embark on a profession. This goal was central to the emancipatory discourse in Germany that evolved during the Enlightenment among government officials and was widespread in *Haskalah* writings as well. The society highlighted its lineage with the Enlightenment, presenting itself as following Moses Mendelssohn's advocacy of the productivization of the Jews.[57] Sara Levy's substantial support of this particular institution constituted yet another way for her to endorse the goals of both the *Haskalah* and the *Aufklärung*.

The fact that Levy favored Jewish causes in her testament does not mean she disregarded the welfare of the general population. As a matter of fact, during her lifetime she had "supported not only Jewish but also numerous Christian educational institutions with great humanity and enjoyed the general esteem and admiration even in the highest circles."[58] Yet, when drafting her last will, she may have reasoned, as her sister Fanny von Arnstein did when writing one of her own testaments, that "the poor Jew finds support only among his fellow-believers, while the poor Christian is supported and helped by both nations."[59] Baruch Auerbach, who knew Sara Levy personally and benefitted from her generous contributions toward the institutions he headed, affirmed in one of the eulogies that he wrote for her that she had once expressed her wish to bring Jewish care for its orphans to the same level reached by Christian society, so that the Jewish community would "not be inferior" to the Christian population in any area of welfare.[60] It was thus her keen interest in the well-being of the indigent Jewish population, as well as a clear sense of Jewish pride and the wish to uplift the image of the Jewish community in the eyes of the world, that led her to grant generous support to Jewish philanthropies.

To the long list of Levy's Jewish affiliations, we could add one more, namely her support of Jewish intellectuals, which is parallel to her well-attested support of German musicians. The most famous Jew whom she assisted was Salomon Maimon (1753–1800). Samuel Levy was one of his main patrons, and during the time he lived in Berlin, he was a welcome guest at the Levys' house. As his friend and biographer Sabbatia Joseph Wolff reports, Maimon had a special rapport with the housewife, for whom he felt deep appreciation and trust; he considered Madame Levy a "very intelligent woman" and a source of support in times of need.[61] Shortly before his early death in 1800, Maimon's situation was precarious, and he seems to have trusted that some comfort could come from Sara Levy's side. In a letter he sent to Lazarus Bendavid from Siegersdorf, where he would die later that year, Maimon urged his friend to address her on his behalf:

> You ask me, my friend, what am I doing here. Unfortunately: almost nothing. Why?—Because I do not get any encouragement and am deprived of all correspondence with scholars and publishers. Do something that I might come back to Berlin; what this does depend on you will easily figure out by yourself. Maybe we can undertake something together. Speak about it with Mr. Levi, *or even better, with Madame Levi.*[62]

Maimon was probably the most notable but by no means the only intellectual among her co-religionists to benefit from Sara Levy's support. She personally intervened, for instance, in the life of Moses Wessely, Hartwig Wessely's brother, a merchant and writer who lived in Hamburg but belonged to her social network, trying to ameliorate his poor financial condition after he went bankrupt. When Wessely died leaving his family unprovided for, she wielded her influence to have a posthumous volume of his writings printed for their economic benefit.[63] This collection of essays became a tribute to Moses Wessely's intellectual endeavors, as well.

Thus, although some of her contacts with Jewish intellectuals were initiated by her husband, who turned their home into a "meeting point for the *maskilim*,"[64] Sara Levy was hardly the back-shadowed figure of German-Jewish womanhood made famous by Moritz Daniel Oppenheim's portrayal of Fromet Mendelssohn (1856), holding a tray and standing behind her husband and his intellectual partners. Levy's place was definitively downstage, as a main actor in the world of German *and* Jewish Enlightenment. To be sure, Sara Levy did not become a *maskilah*, a full member of the Jewish Enlightenment. Nevertheless, Sara Levy, and perhaps other contemporary women, found ways to identify with and support maskilic goals and projects. In any event, Levy's case challenges the assumption of dichotomous fields of action for men and women, as if each gender moved exclusively in different orbits—as if women had everything to do with assimilation and nothing to do with Jewish concerns.

The evidence above points to Sara Levy's conscious Jewishness. She combined her activity in the non-Jewish world with her uninterrupted commitment to Jewish causes in a way that many other women of her generation and her class, including some of her relatives and most of her friends, did not. Like many contemporary Jewish women, she was deeply immersed in German and European culture and society; but unlike them, she chose to remain connected to the Jewish community for almost ninety-three years and died as a Jew. The Friedemann Bach song and the Hebrew poems celebrating her wedding, two different types of artistic creations coming respectively from the German and the Jewish realms, were an early sign of the parallel dimensions that would coexist throughout Levy's life.

Notes

1. Deborah Hertz, *Jewish High Society in Old Regime Berlin* (New Haven, CT: Yale University Press, 1988); Petra Wilhelmy, *Der Berliner Salon im 19. Jahrhundert (1780–1914)* (Berlin: de Gruyter, 1989). This is also how I presented her in my study on Enlightenment Jewish women living in Berlin in the last decades of the eighteenth century and the first decades of the nineteenth century; see Natalie Naimark-Goldberg, *Jewish Women in Enlightenment Berlin* (Oxford: Littman Library of Jewish Civilization, 2013).
2. For one of these exceptions, see for instance: Deborah Hertz, "Ihr offenes Haus—Amalia Beer und die Berliner Reform," *Kalonymos* 2, no. 1 (1999): 1–4.
3. According to Steven Lowenstein, all of Daniel Itzig's sons and daughters "died at least as nominal Jews," although some of his sons-in-law converted. Lowenstein, "Jewish Upper Crust and Berlin Jewish Enlightenment: The

Family of Daniel Itzig," in *From East and West: Jews in a Changing Europe, 1750–1870*, ed. Frances Malino and David Sorkin (Oxford: Blackwell, 1990), 195.

4. Hertz, *Jewish High Society*; Wilhelmy, *Der Berliner Salon*; Naimark-Goldberg, *Jewish Women in Enlightenment Berlin*.

5. Samuel Levy was Isaac Daniel Itzig's great-grandson, and Sara was his granddaughter. Jacob Jacobson, *Jüdische Trauungen in Berlin, 1759–1813* (Berlin: de Gruyter, 1968), 284.

6. On Brinckmann's friendship with Sara Levy and her husband, see Hannah Lotte Lund, *Der Berliner 'jüdische Salon' um 1800: Emanzipation in der Debatte* (Berlin: de Gruyter, 2012) 28, 380, 400, 472–73, as well as the appendix by Barbara Hahn in the present volume. Gentz appreciated his sociability with Sara Levy, an "incomparable and unforgettable" friend whom he "always loved and esteemed," as quoted in Hilde Spiel, *Fanny von Arnstein: A Daughter of the Enlightenment, 1758–1818*, trans. Christine Shuttleworth (New York: New Vessel Press, 1991), 182–83. See also Lund, *Der Berliner 'jüdische Salon,'* 426.

7. Heinrich Meisner, ed., *Friedrich Schleiermachers Briefwechsel mit seiner Braut* (Gotha: Klotz, 1919), 284, 331–32, 389. "The Levi" recurs in other cases in this publication, but as in other contemporary sources, it is not completely clear whether the person referred to is Rahel Levin or Sara Levy.

8. In a letter to Alexander Mendelssohn from May 12, 1854, Humboldt inquired about the time of Sara Levy's funeral, which he did "not want to miss." Sebastian Panwitz and Ingo Schwarz, eds., *Alexander von Humboldt / Familie Mendelssohn, Briefwechsel* (Berlin: de Gruyter, 2011), 274.

9. Fanny Lewald, *Meine Lebensgeschichte*, vol. 3, *Befreiung und Wanderleben*, part 1 (Berlin: Janke, 1862), 162.

10. Part of their correspondence has survived until today. On their friendship and cooperation, see Thekla Keuck, *Hofjuden und Kulturbürger: Die Geschichte der Familie Itzig in Berlin* (Göttingen: Vandenhoeck & Ruprecht, 2011), 349–51. On Reimarus's contacts with other Jews, see Almut Spalding, *Elise Reimarus (1735–1805), The Muse of Hamburg: A Woman of the German Enlightenment* (Würzburg: Koenigshausen & Neumann, 2003), 259–79.

11. Spiel, *Fanny von Arnstein*, 208.

12. Sebastian Panwitz, "Die Berliner Vereine 1786–1815," in *Berliner Klassik. Eine Großstadtkultur um 1800 / Online-Dokumente* (Berlin-Brandenburgische Akademie des Wissenschaften, 2001 [http://www.berliner-klassik.de/forschung/dateien/panwitz_vereine.pdf]), 21–24; Keuck, *Hofjuden und Kulturbürger*, 338–39.

13. [Wolf Davidson,] *Briefe ueber Berlin* (Landau: Francini, 1798), quotation from p. 18.

14. The name as it appears on the manuscript is "Cantinela" and not "Cantilena," as it is often cited. Its catalogue number is BR-WFB H 1 / Fk 97. David Schulenberg raises doubts concerning the assertion that this work was written for Sara and Samuel Levy's wedding, since the autograph lacks Levy's distinctive stamp. However, Peter Wollny indicates that omitting the stamp was not unusual for this type of source. David Schulenberg, *The Music of Wilhelm Friedemann Bach* (Rochester, NY: University of Rochester Press, 2010), 321n71; Peter Wollny, "Sara Levy and the Making of Musical Taste in Berlin," *Musical*

Quarterly 77, no. 4 (1993): 683n40. This composition, part of the archive of the *Sing-Akademie*, was believed lost after World War II; see the chapter by Christoph Wolff in the present volume.

15. Christoph Wolff, "A Bach Cult in Late-Eighteenth-Century Berlin: Sara Levy's Musical Salon," *Bulletin of the American Academy* 58, no. 3 (2005): 30; and Peter Wollny, *"Ein förmlicher Sebastian und Philipp Emanuel Bach-Kultus": Sara Levy und ihr musikalisches Wirken. Mit einer Dokumentensammlung zur musikalischen Familiengeschichte der Vorfahren von Felix Mendelssohn Bartholdy* (Wiesbaden: Breitkopf & Härtel, 2010), 25.

16. Michael Marissen, in private correspondence, has recognized the image of the "Crown of Life" in this poem as an "idiosyncratic expression used in the New Testament" to refer to "something Jesus is said to give to those who love him and are faithful to him." The recognition of this imagery has been incorporated into Lauren Belfer's novel featuring Sara Levy, *And After the Fire* (New York: Harper Collins, 2016), but it has not yet made its way into the scholarly literature.

17. Wollny, "Sara Levy and the Making of Musical Taste," 654. See Wollny's catalogue of the music by the Bach family that Levy and her family owned, as well as publications to which they subscribed, in Wollny, *"Ein förmlicher Sebastian und Philipp Emanuel Bach-Kultus,"* 63–107.

18. Karen Ahlquist, "Men and Women of the Chorus: Music, Governance, and Social Models in Nineteenth-Century German-Speaking Europe," in *Chorus and Community*, ed. Karen Ahlquist (Urbana: University of Illinois Press, 2006), 268.

19. Wolff, "A Bach Cult," 29; Wollny, "Sara Levy and the Making of Musical Taste," 653. Sara Levy also performed in other public frameworks. The *Berlinische Musikalische Zeitung*, Fünftes Stück (March 9, 1793), 18, mentions her appearance as harpsichordist in a concert that took place at the house of "Mr. Fliess, from the Jewish colony." She played there along with "Mad. Wulf," "Mr. Dr. Fliess," and other singers. As this source indicates, since admission was paid (though at low price), it is to be considered a public event. See Peter Wollny, "'Ein förmlicher Sebastian und Philipp Emanuel Bach-Kultus': Sara Levy, geb. Itzig und ihr musikalisch-literarischer Salon," in *Musik und Ästhetik im Berlin Moses Mendelssohns*, ed. Anselm Gerhard (Tübingen: Max Niemeyer, 1999), 221.

20. As Wollny notes, "a good deal of Sara Levy's musical activities [appear] to have taken place within this institution, despite its noticeable anti-Semitic tendencies." Nevertheless, "her name never appeared in the institute's official publications." Wollny, "Sara Levy and the Making of Musical Taste," 653 and 680n10.

21. Ludwig Geiger, ed., *Briefwechsel des jungen Börne und der Henriette Herz* (Oldenburg: Schulzesche Hof-Buchhandlung und Hof-Buchdruckerei Rudolf Schwartz, 1905), 64.

22. This remark appears in a letter from December 5, 1797 sent to a Jewish merchant, Emanuel Osmund, who was a close friend of Jean Paul. Jean Paul [Richter], *Jean Paul's Briefwechsel mit seinen Freunden Emanuel Osmund, Friedrich von Oertel und Paul Thieriot* (Munich: Fleischmann's Buchhandlung, 1865), 73.

See Gunnar Och, "'Eß- und Teetisch': Die Polemik gegen das akkulturierte Berliner Judentum im ausgehenden 18. und 19. Jahrhundert," in *Musik und Ästhetik im Berlin Moses Mendelssohns*, 81.

23. Friedrich Nicolai, *Beschreibung der Königlichen Residenzstädte Berlin und Potsdam und aller daselbst befindlicher Merkwürdigkeiten* (Berlin: F. Nicolai, 1779), 2:628.

24. Quotation from Steven M. Lowenstein, "Jewish Upper Crust," 186.

25. Monika Richarz, "Der jüdische Weihnachtsbaum: Familie und Säkularisierung im deutschen Judentum des 19. Jahrhunderts," in *"Und so zogen sie aus: Ein jeder bei seiner Familie und seinen Vaterhaus" (4. Moses 2, 34)*, ed. Miriam Gillis-Carlebach and Barbara Vogel (Hamburg: Dölling & Galitz, 2000), 63–78; Martina Eberspächer, "Wie Weihnachten deutsch wurde: Die Erfolgsgeschichte der modernen Weihnacht," in *Weihnukka: Geschichten von Weihnachten und Chanukka*, ed. Cilly Kugelmann (Berlin: Nicolai, 2005), 33–39.

26. Christoph Wolff's chapter in the present volume favors the theory that this manuscript was indeed a Christmas gift in 1823.

27. R. Larry Todd, "Echoes of the St. Matthew Passion in the Music of Mendelssohn," in *Mendelssohn Essays*, ed. R. Larry Todd (New York: Routledge, 2008), 118.

28. R. Larry Todd, *Mendelssohn: A Life in Music* (Oxford: Oxford University Press, 2003), 123.

29. Nahida Remy, *Das jüdische Weib*, 3rd ed. (Leipzig: Verlag von G. Laudien, 1892), 253.

30. Shmuel Feiner, "The Modern Jewish Woman: A Test Case in the Relationship between Haskalah and Modernity" (Hebrew), in *Sexuality and the Family in History: Collected Essays*, ed. Israel Bartal and Isaiah Gafni (Jerusalem: Zalman Shazar Center for Jewish History, 1998), 253–303; Naimark-Goldberg, *Jewish Women in Enlightenment Berlin*, 11–17, 294–302. In later decades, when the *Haskalah* moved to Eastern Europe, Jewish women were somewhat more involved in this movement; see Tova Cohen and Shmuel Feiner, eds., *Voice of a Hebrew Maiden: Women's Writings of the Nineteenth-Century Haskalah Movement* (Hebrew) (Tel Aviv: Hakibbutz Hameuchad, 2006); Carole B. Balin, *To Reveal Our Hearts: Jewish Women Writers in Tsarist Russia* (Cincinnati, OH: Hebrew Union College Press, 2000), 13–50.

31. The poems were preserved in a manuscript collection, now at the Staatsbibliothek zu Berlin–Preussischer Kulturbesitz, Orientabteilung (ms.or.fol. 1267, no. 12 fol. a and no. 12 fol. c). This collection contains other wedding poems, including two for Sara's brothers Isaac and Bonem. See, too, the interesting poem dedicated to the wedding of Sara Meyer, another enlightened Jewish woman from Berlin, and Jacob Isaac Wulff in 1778. Meyer would divorce her Jewish husband after a decade, convert to Christianity, and marry a German nobleman. On the manuscript collection see Tal Kogman, "From Press to Manuscript: Leaflets in the Jewish Republic of Letters" (Hebrew), in Shmuel Feiner, Zohar Shavit, Natalie Naimark-Goldberg, and Tal Kogman, eds., *The Library of the Haskalah: The Creation of a Modern Republic of Letters in Jewish Society in the German-Speaking Sphere* (Tel Aviv: Am Oved, 2014), 81–101.

32. Josel Pick of Reichenau also wrote a wedding poem for Brendl Mendelssohn and Simon Veit. See Mordechai (Markus) Brann, "Aleh nidaf" (Hebrew), *Magazin für hebräische Literatur und Wissenschaft* 2 (1888): 435–36. On Josel Pick as a *maskil*, see Shmuel Feiner, *The Jewish Enlightenment*, trans. Chaya Naor (Philadelphia: University of Pennsylvania Press, 2003).

33. On Joel Brill, see Natalie Naimark-Goldberg, "The Entrance of Maskilim in Breslau into the German Literary Sphere" (Hebrew), in Feiner et al., *The Library of the Haskalah*, 409–16.

34. For a detailed discussion of *Zemirot Yisra'el* and its publication, see Natalie Naimark-Goldberg, "Entrepreneurs in the Library of the Haskalah: Editors and the Production of Maskilic Books" (Hebrew), in Feiner et al., *The Library of the Haskalah*, 112–16.

35. Moses Mendelssohn, *Die Psalmen, uebersetzt von Moses Mendelssohn* (Berlin: Friedrich Maurer, 1781). See Elias Sacks's contribution to this volume.

36. *Sulamith und Eusebia*, a cantata commemorating Moses Mendelssohn's death, is considered an exceptional engagement of the *Haskalah* with music. Notably, it was not written in Hebrew. On this cantata, see Yael Sela-Teichler, "Music, Acculturation, and Haskalah between Berlin and Königsberg in the 1780s," *Jewish Quarterly Review*, 103, no. 3 (2013), 352–84. *Zemirot Yisra'el* constitutes an additional case of such a type of involvement—although unlike *Sulamith und Eusebia*, this engagement was theoretical and not practical. Its publication began a year before the first performance of *Sulamith und Eusebia*, while the volume with the introductions on music appeared five years after this event.

37. Sela-Teichler, "Music, Acculturation, and Haskalah," 375; Laurenz Lütteken, "Zwischen Ohr und Verstand: Moses Mendelssohn, Johann Philipp Kirnberger und die Begründung des 'reinen Satzes' in der Musik," in *Musik und Ästhetik im Berlin Moses Mendelssohns*, ed. Anselm Gerhard (Tübingen: Max Niemeyer Verlag, 1999), 135–63.

38. This goal is made clear, for instance, in the "second introduction," when the author affirms that his efforts will have been worthwhile if the interest in music of one reader in a thousand is raised by his discussion of the subject (*Zemirot Yisra'el*, 1:14v–15r). The introductions, written in Hebrew, include German translations of Hebrew terms that were deemed unknown to readers of traditional Hebrew. This was a common method used in the *Haskalah* in order to acquaint the Jewish public with fields that were not part of the traditional curriculum, e.g., science, philosophy, and, in this case, music.

39. Among the maskilic books including the name of her husband, see for instance: Isaac Euchel, ed. and trans., *Gebete der hochdeutschen und polnischen Juden* (Königsberg: Kanter, 1786), a German translation of the Jewish prayerbook, mainly addressed to women; Isaac Satanow, ed., *Sefer Hag'darim* (Berlin: Ḥevrat Ḥinuch Ne'arim, 1798) (Samuel Levy contributed much more than any other subscriber; the list includes no women's names); Isaac Satanow, ed., *Moreh Nevuchim*, vol. 2 (Berlin: Ḥevrat Ḥinukh Ne'arim, 1795) (in this case he contributed, again, the highest sum, along with one of Sara's brothers; this list includes no women's names, either). Samuel Levy also gave enormous help to the publishers of Hartwig Wessely's biblical epos *Shirei Tif'eret*, who faced dire

financial problems, and Levy provided them with enough funds to publish one or more of its volumes (see "Moda'a," in *Shirei Tif'eret*, vol. 2, [Berlin: Ḥevrat Ḥinuch Ne'arim, 1791]; and also vol. 4).

40. Hagit Cohen and Stefan Litt, "Publication and Marketing in the Haskalah Republic" (Hebrew), in Feiner et al., *The Library of the Haskalah*, 216.

41. Interestingly, Sara Levy's name does not appear in the long list of subscribers in *Netivot Hashalom*, Mendelssohn's Pentateuch translation and commentary better known as the *Bi'ur* and a maskilic best seller as well, although her sister, Fegelche (Fanny) Arnstein, was among the few women who do figure. The reason may be that Sara was still unmarried, living at her parents' household.

42. Wessely had composed the music for *Sulamith und Eusebia*. Its libretto, written by Karl Wilhelm Ramler, included, among other things, verses from the Psalms in Mendelssohn's translation (obviously taken from the German edition).

43. Mordechai Eliav, *Jewish Education in Germany in the Period of Enlightenment and Emancipation* (Hebrew) (Jerusalem: Jewish Agency, 1960), 130; Tal Kogman, *The Maskilim in the Sciences: Jewish Scientific Education in the German-Speaking Sphere in Modern Times* (Hebrew) (Jerusalem: Magnes Press, 2013), 120–23.

44. See Bendavid's 1821 petition to Sara Levy in Uta Lohman and Ingrid Lohman, eds., *Chevrat Chinuch Nearim. Die jüdische Freischule in Berlin (1778–1825) im Umfeld preußischer Bildungspolitik und jüdischer Kultusreform. Eine Quellensammlung* (Münster: Waxmann, 2001), 2: 951. See also: Keuck, *Hofjuden und Kulturbürger*, 304–5.

45. The reports also indicate that Sara Levy procured contributions from her acquaintances. See for instance, Lohman and Lohman, eds., *Chevrat Chinuch Nearim*, 2:872.

46. Baruch Auerbach, *Ueber die gegenwärtige Einrichtung der jüdischen Gemeindeschule* תלמוד תורה *zu Berlin* (Berlin: J. Lewent, 1832), 92. On this school, see Eliav, *Jewish Education in Germany*, 216–18.

47. Baruch Auerbach, *Geschichte des Baruch Auerbach'schen Waisenhauses für jüdische Knaben vom Tage der Stiftung bis zu seinem fünf und zwanzigjährigen Jubiläum* (Berlin: Friedländer, 1858), 21–22. As Auerbach indicates, other distinguished women of the community joined Sara Levy in this mission. Levy also gave full support to the girls' orphanage that Auerbach established several years later.

48. Baruch Auerbach, *Geschichte des Baruch Auerbach'schen Waisenhauses*, 22; *Statuten des von Baruch Auerbach gegründeten jüdischen Waisen-Erziehungs-Instituts zu Berlin* (Berlin: Friedländer, 1839), 28. In the list of "mothers of honor" published in the *Statuten*, Sara Levy's name is mentioned first as chairwoman, then the others follow in alphabetical order. The short list includes, among others, Amalie Beer and her daughter-in-law Betty Beer, *née* Meyer, who was the daughter of Recha Mendelssohn and thus Moses Mendelssohn's granddaughter.

49. *Statuten*, 15.

50. Ibid., 18–19. If they lived outside Berlin, the students were expected to write to the institution every three months about their doings.

51. Ibid., 15, 16.

52. The book was printed by Auerbach, and revenues from sales went to the orphanage. The "mothers of honor" took part in its marketing. See Baruch

Auerbach, ed., *Gesänge und Gebete zur Todtenfeier, wie sie von den Zöglingen der jüdischen Gemeindeschule zu Berlin begangen wird,* 2nd ed. ([Berlin]: Öhmigke, 1835), iii. Another related source of income was the recitation by the pupils of the *kaddish* in the memory of benefactors or their deceased relatives.

53. Keuck, *Hofjuden und Kulturbürger,* 222–23.

54. "Letzter Wille der Frau Sara Levy geb. Itzig," in Jacobson, *Jüdische Trauungen in Berlin,* 641 (based on a handwritten copy of the will).

55. Thus according to Baruch Auerbach in his eulogy after the passing of Sara Levy, published in the yearly report of the boys' orphanage he headed. Baruch Auerbach, *Zwei und Zwanzigster Jahresbericht über die jüdische Waisen-Erziehungs-Anstalt für Knaben zu Berlin* (Berlin: Friedländer, 1855), 72. Auerbach had published a eulogy in the girls' orphanage yearly report the year before: Baruch Auerbach, *Eilfter* [*sic*] *Jahresbericht über die jüdische Waisen-Erziehungs-Anstalt für Mädchen zu Berlin* (Berlin: Friedländer, 1854), 20–28.

56. Marcus Adler, *Chronik der Gesellschaft zur Verbreitung der Handwerke und des Ackerbaues unter den Juden im preussischen Staate* (Berlin: R. Boll, 1899), 17, 24. As indicated there (p. 24), the interests from the fund bestowed by Levy and even the capital itself were to be used "to settle Jewish manual workers [Handwerker]" in their professions.

57. A text written by Moses Mendelssohn in 1779 to this effect was reproduced in facsimile in the chronicle. The connection with Mendelssohn was stressed by presenting the "three Mendelssohn generations" involved in the society and its goals: in addition to Moses, who fostered the idea behind its establishment, his son Joseph was among the society's founders and leaders. He was followed after his death in 1848 by his son Alexander. See Adler, *Chronik der Gesellschaft,* 22.

58. Auerbach, *Eilfter Jahresbericht,* 21.

59. As quoted in Spiel, *Fanny von Arnstein,* 199.

60. Auerbach, *Zwei und Zwanzigster Jahresbericht,* 67–68.

61. Sabbatia Joseph Wolff, *Maimoniana oder Rhapsodien zur Charakteristik Salomon Maimons,* ed. Martin L. Davies and Christoph Schulte (Berlin: Parerga, 2003), 67 (originally published Berlin: Hayn, 1813).

62. Yitzhak Melamed, "Two Letters by Salomon Maimon on Fichte's Philosophy and on Kant's Anthropology and Mathematics," *International Yearbook of German Idealism* 9 (2011): 385–86 (italics added).

63. Jacobson, *Jüdische Trauungen in Berlin,* 72n78; Keuck, *Hofjuden und Kulturbürger,* 350–51.

64. Keuck, *Hofjuden und Kulturbürger,* 349.

Chapter Four

Women's Voices in Bach's Musical World

Christiane Mariane von Ziegler and Faustina Bordoni

George B. Stauffer

Until the recovery of the long-lost Berlin *Sing-Akademie* manuscript collection in Kiev in the summer of 1999, one seldom encountered the name Sara Levy in musicological research. Whether the neglect was due to ignorance, bias against women, or German anti-Semitism, Levy and her role in the promotion and preservation of the music of Johann Sebastian Bach and his sons received little attention until the *Sing-Akademie* manuscripts were examined and assessed anew. Only then did Christoph Wolff, Peter Wollny, and other scholars finally focus on the largely overlooked Berlin *salonnière* who had played an important role in assembling the collection.[1]

Not ignored to the same extent but nevertheless relatively unexplored is the relationship between Bach and the female musicians of his day. Both the women in his family and the women in his professional circle had a not-unimportant influence on his music and music making, especially during the Leipzig years, when his interest in the German church cantata and Italian opera reached its peak.

"I can assure you that I can already form an ensemble, both *vocaliter* and *instrumentaliter*, within my family, particularly since my present wife sings a good, clear soprano, and my eldest daughter, too, joins in not badly."[2] Thus wrote Bach to his former schoolmate Georg Erdmann in 1730, when describing his domestic situation in Leipzig, where he had served as Cantor of the St. Thomas School since 1723. His second wife, Anna Magdalena Bach (1701–60), *née* Wilcke, had served as a professional singer in Weissenfels and Cöthen and continued to take part in professional engagements after her marriage to Bach in 1721.[3] In addition to bearing thirteen children, she became one of her husband's principal copyists, writing out scores and performance parts for dozens of vocal, instrumental, and keyboard works.[4] Of Bach's eldest daughter, Catharina Dorothea Bach (1708–74), we know little, except that she probably took singing lessons with her father and participated with her stepmother in house concerts at the large family apartment within the St. Thomas School. She, too, may have served as a copyist for her father, but her handwriting has not been identified.[5] And we are equally in the dark about the musical activities of Bach's first wife, Maria Barbara Bach, except that she may have served as a copyist of his music in Mühlhausen, Weimar, and Cöthen.[6]

The role of women in public music making was greatly limited in Germany in Bach's time. Women could perform in court ensembles and the opera, but they were banned from choirs and instrumental ensembles in Catholic and Lutheran worship services, excluded from membership in *collegium musicum* ensembles, and discouraged from pursuing any talent they might show in composition. Women with an interest in music were encouraged instead to study voice and instruments (chiefly violin, flute, lute, and clavier) as a means to enriching domestic life, as was the case with Catharina Dorothea Bach and, ultimately, Anna Magdalena Bach, who seems to have stopped performing publicly after 1729 or so.

Yet in his professional endeavors Bach encountered two prominent figures who defied the traditional constraints on women and achieved international fame: the poet and cantata librettist Christiane Mariane von Ziegler and the soprano and opera diva Faustina Bordoni. If one seeks counterparts in Saxony to the path-breaking, publicly engaged Sara Levy, Ziegler and Bordoni are convincing candidates.

Christiane Mariane von Ziegler (1695–1760) was born and raised in Leipzig, the daughter of mayor Franz Conrad Romanus.[7] Although her father was imprisoned for life on corruption charges in 1705, the Romanus family continued to live in the magnificent town palace constructed on the corner of Brühl and St. Catherine's Streets.[8] Married twice and widowed twice, with deceased children, Ziegler returned to the Romanus House in 1722 to pursue her interest in the arts—painting, music, and most importantly, poetry and letters. In the last two endeavors she received great encouragement from Johann Christoph Gottsched, who arrived in Leipzig in 1724 and soon took over the direction

of the recently formed *Deutsche Gesellschaft*, the society dedicated to promoting German literature and poetry. Using a variety of pseudonyms, Ziegler contributed to the *Gesellschaft*'s weekly paper, *Die vernünfftige Tadlerinnen*, before
publishing her own volume of sacred and secular poetry, *Versuch in Gebundener
Schreib-Art*, in 1728.

Part 2 of the *Versuch* appeared in 1729, followed by a volume of letters on
various topics to unnamed recipients, *Moralische und vermischte Send-Schreiben*.[9]
The success of these publications led to Ziegler's induction into the *Deutsche
Gesellschaft* in 1730 as its first female member and to her being named royal
poet by the Philosophy Faculty of Wittenberg University in 1733. The *Deutsche
Gesellschaft* published a Festschrift in her honor the following year,[10] which
included a poem of praise ("Hochwohlgebohrne Frau! Du Wunder unsrer
Zeit") by Luise Adelgunde Gottsched, wife of Johann Christoph Gottsched and
a playwright in her own right. A medal celebrating Ziegler's accomplishments
was cast in Nuremberg in 1737.

Ziegler published a final volume of poetry and prose selections, *Vermischete
Schriften in gebundener und ungebundener Rede*, in 1739. Stating that "this woman
has made her mark in the world through her erudition, so much so that her
fame has spread even to the outer edges of Europe," Johann Heinrich Zedler
devoted nine columns to Ziegler in his *Grosses vollständiges Universal-Lexicon*, the
most important German-language encyclopedia of the eighteenth century.[11]
Bach, by comparison, belatedly received a one-column entry.[12]

If there was a progressive, enlightened female colleague in Bach's world, Ziegler
was it. In addition to being a woman of letters with numerous publications, she
spoke French, played musical instruments and sang, and was adept with pistols,
rifles, and the crossbow. In *Moralische und vermischte Send-Schreiben* she reasoned
that women possessed the same intelligence as men, and if they studied diligently
in their youth, they could obtain the same level of intellectual accomplishment as
men. To support her case, she pointed to three female role models: Anna Maria
van Schurman (1607–78), the Dutch linguist, philosopher, and artist; Madeleine
de Scudéry (1607–1701), the French novelist and *salonnière*; and Anne Dacier
(1651–1720), the French author, editor, and translator. In a *Deutsche Gesellschaft*
contest on the subject of defending the female sex against the accusations of
men, Ziegler submitted the poem "Vertheidigung unsers Geschlechts wider die
Mannspersonen, in Ansehung der Fähigkeit zur Poesie,"[13] arguing not only that
women could write poetry, but also that they could write it better than men. It was
this outspoken woman to whom Bach turned for cantata texts.

In the spring of 1725, Bach faced a crisis. In June of the previous year he
had embarked on the most ambitious project of his career: the composition
of an annual cycle of homogeneous church cantatas, approximately fifty-nine
in number, each based on a seasonal hymn of the ecclesiastical year. The outer
verses of the hymn were to serve as the opening and closing movements of

the cantata, generally set as a chorus and a homophonic chorale, respectively, and the inner verses of the chorale were to be paraphrased or condensed and presented as recitatives, arias, or choruses in the middle movements. The cycle may have been coordinated with the sermons preached that year—a practice that had taken place in Leipzig in the previous century, when pastor Johann Benedikt Carpzov and cantor Johann Schelle collaborated to produce an annual cycle of sermons and cantatas based on chorales.[14] The texts for Bach's cycle were supplied by an anonymous librettist, now believed to have been Andreas Stübel, co-rector emeritus of the St. Thomas School and a writer with appropriate theological training and poetic experience.[15]

On June 11, 1724, the first Sunday after Trinity, Bach began to write the new cycle.[16] All went well until March 25, 1725, the Feast of the Annunciation, when composition suddenly ceased. The most plausible explanation for the cessation is Stübel's sudden and unexpected death on January 27, shortly after the booklet for his cantata texts up to Annunciation would have been printed.[17] Thus Bach would have been supplied with texts through Annunciation, but after, left in the lurch. For the next three Sundays after Annunciation, he composed cantatas based on texts of an unknown origin. But on April 22, Jubilate Sunday, he began a series of nine cantatas with texts by Ziegler—texts that appeared in slightly altered forms three years later in *Versuch in Gebundener Schreib-Art.* Although the works were not composed in the manner of chorale cantatas, they covered the remaining Sundays and feast days in Bach's second cycle:

Jubilate Sunday	Cantata 103, *Ihr werdet weinen und heulen*
Cantate Sunday	Cantata 108, *Es ist euch gut, daß ich hingehe*
Rogate Sunday	Cantata 87, *Bisher habt ihr nichts gebeten in meinem Namen*
Ascension Day	Cantata 128, *Auf Christi Himmelfahrt allein*
Exaudi Sunday	Cantata 183, *Sie werden euch in den Bann tun*
Whitsunday	Cantata 74, *Wer mich liebet, der wird mein Wort halten*
2nd Day of Pentecost	Cantata 68, *Also hat Gott die Welt geliebt*
3rd Day of Pentecost	Cantata 175, *Er rufet seiner Schafen mit Namen*
Trinity Sunday	Cantata 176, *Es ist ein trotzig und verzagt Ding*

It is uncertain how Bach met Ziegler. He may have initially approached Gottsched with the request to write texts. If so, Gottsched may have turned him down and suggested instead his protégé, Ziegler. Maria Elisabeth Taubert, wife of a prominent merchant, has also been proposed as a possible link.[18] Taubert stood as godmother to Bach's son Christian Gottlieb on April 14, 1725,[19] just eight days before Bach began using Ziegler's texts, and the fact that she and

Ziegler later lived in the same house may reflect a friendship of long standing. But a more direct connection would have been the salon that Ziegler hosted in the Romanus House in the 1720s and 1730s. Like the later salon of Sara Levy in Berlin, Ziegler's was patterned on the French model and included dinner, poetry readings and extemporizations, card playing, and music.[20]

In addition, Ziegler was a well-rounded musician: she sang and played transverse flute, recorder, lute, and clavier. In a letter published in the *Moralische und vermischte Send-Schreiben* of 1731, she thanked a Capellmeister in a neighboring town for music he had sent her and promised to have it performed at her house as soon as possible.[21] It may be that Bach participated in Ziegler's salon, presenting his own clavier, lute, or flute pieces as musical offerings to assembled guests in the Romanus house. It was perhaps in this context, in the early spring of 1725, that he turned to the aspiring poet for cantata texts to complete his second cantata cycle. Two of Bach's other Leipzig librettists, Christoph Birkmann and Christian Friedrich Henrici, similarly combined poetry writing with amateur music making, both taking part in *collegium musicum* performances.[22]

The nine cantata librettos that Ziegler produced for Bach adhere to a common template. They begin with a biblical quotation (dictum) or chorale (Cantatas 128 and 68) followed by free-verse commentary and occasionally additional biblical citation. All nine conclude with a chorale. As Philipp Spitta first noted,[23] Ziegler's texts show an unusually heavy reliance on biblical text, both citing it verbatim and using it as a source of key words for thoughts expressed in the free poetry. In Cantata 74, *Wer mich liebet, der wird mein Wort halten*, for instance, the text of three of the eight movements is drawn directly from the Bible: the opening chorus and second aria quote from the Gospel for Whitsunday, John 14:16–23, and the second recitative quotes from a related passage in Romans 8:1. The free poetry picks up themes from the biblical citations, using crucial words as markers, as can be seen in the opening citation from John 14:23 and the aria that follows (crucial words in bold):

Dictum: Wer mich **liebet**, der wird mein **Wort** halten, und mein **Vater** wird
     ihn **lieben**, und wir werden zu ihm **kommen**, und **Wohnung** bei ihm
     machen.

Aria: **Komm, komm**, mein Herze steht dir offen,
      Ach, laß es deine **Wohnung** sein!
    Ich **liebe** dich, so muß ich hoffen:
      Dein **Wort** trifft itzo bei mir ein;
    Denn wer dich sucht, fürcht, **liebt** und ehret,
      Dem ist der **Vater** zugetan.
    Ich zweifle nicht, ich bin erhöret,
      Daß ich mich dein getrösten kann.[24]

Ziegler's poetry, with its expressive, Bible-oriented imagery, seems to have stimulated Bach's creative energies. In the well-known aria "Mein gläubiges Herze, frohlocke, sing, scherze" from Cantata 68, *Also hat Gott die Welt geliebt*, Bach set Ziegler's text as a dance-like Presto for soprano, violoncello piccolo, and continuo, with an oboe and a violin joining in for a lengthy, purely instrumental coda—a very unusual event in Bach's music. The piece works very much like an opera aria, with an arrêt (a partial vocal entry followed by the complete vocal entry), a coloratura soprano line, a virtuoso cello part, and written-out da capo elements. The consonant upward leap of the fourth in the A section, expressing the words "rejoice, sing, and jest" ("frohlocke, sing, scherze") contrasts sharply with the upward and downward leaps of the sixth and seventh in the B section, expressing the words "misery" and "lamentation" ("Weg Jammer, weg Klagen"; ex. 4.1).

Example 4.1. Cantata 68, "Mein gläubiges Herze."

A section

B section

In spite of this, Ziegler's texts have met with criticism by historians due to the variations that occur between the texts as they appear in Bach's cantatas and as they appear in the *Versuch* of 1728.[25] Critics have claimed these changes were made by Bach to remedy deficiencies in Ziegler's poetry. The variations include not only differences of single words or small phrases—changes commonly encountered in Bach's settings of texts by other librettists[26]—but the alteration or deletion of complete lines. Compare, for instance, the two versions of "Mein gläubiges Herze," cited above, or the recitative "Du wirst mich nach der Angst auch Wiederum erquicken" from Cantata 103, *Ihr werdet weinen und heulen*:[27]

Text in Bach's cantata	Text in Ziegler's *Versuch* of 1728
Cantata 68, movement 2, aria:	
Mein gläubiges Herze,	Getröstetes Herze
Frohlocke, sing, scherze,	Frohlocke und scherze,
Dein Jesus ist da!	Dein Jesus ist da.[28]
Cantata 103, movement 4, recitative:	
Du wirst mich nach der Angst	Du wirst, mein Heyland, mich schon
auch wiederum erquicken;	schon nach der Angst erquicken.
So will ich mich zu deiner	Wohlan! Ich will mich auch zu deiner
Ankunfft schicken,	Ankunfft schicken.
Ich traue dem Verheißungswort,	Ich traue dem Verheissungs-Wort,
Daß meine Traurigkeit	Daß meine Traurigkeit,
	Und dies vielleicht in kurzer Zeit,
	Nach bäng und ängstlichen Gebehrden,
In Freude soll verkehret werden.	In Freude soll verkehret werden.[29]

In the case of the first, Bach drew the music from an earlier aria, "Weil die wollenreichen Herden," from Cantata 208, *Was mir behagt, ist nur die muntre Jagd!*, a Weimar work most probably written in 1713 for the birthday of Duke Christian of Saxon-Weißenfels. One of most important changes Bach made in recycling the aria music was to add an upbeat to the vocal line, which is realized on the word "Mein" and then again on the word "sing" (see ex. 4.2). These one-syllable words produce a stronger upbeat effect than the syllable "Ge" of "Getröstetes Herze" and the conjunction "und" of "frohlocke und scherze." One can make the case that "Mein" and "sing" were substituted by Bach as he anticipated altering the vocal line.

But Mark Peters has suggested recently that the cantata texts that Ziegler provided for Bach may have differed from those that she later published in the *Versuch*. Peters cites Ziegler's own statement that she constantly refined her writings over time, to accommodate improvements and new thoughts; as evidence of this, he reproduces a poem she published first in 1738 and then again in 1739 that contains the types of differences one sees in the Bach cantata texts and the *Versuch* versions.[30] Revisiting "Mein gläubiges Herze" from Cantata 68, one can argue that poetically, "Getröstetes Herze" has a richer meaning than "Mein gläubiges Herze" and that "Frohlocke und scherze" has a smoother rhythm than "Frohlocke, sing, scherze," with its "hiccup" on "sing" in the

Example 4.2. Cantata 208, "Weil die wollenreichen Herden" and Cantata 68, "Mein gläubiges Herze."

Cantata 208

Cantata 68

middle. "Getröstetes Herze" and "Frohlocke und scherze" may have been refinements made by Ziegler herself, in contemplating the texts once again for publication in 1728, unencumbered by musical considerations that obtained in 1725.

With regard to the recitative "Du wirst mich nach der Angst" from Cantata 103, it is more difficult to contemplate the two additional lines in Ziegler's *Versuch* text as later additions. They complete the rhyme scheme, which is disrupted in the cantata version by their absence. Deleting them would have made for a more succinct, immediate recitative, and that seems to be a course of action that would have been taken in conjunction with composing cantata music.

It is possible, then, that the differences between the cantata versions of Ziegler's texts and the later printed versions resulted from a collaboration between the poet and the composer. Ziegler may have submitted preliminary versions of her cantata texts to Bach in 1725, versions that she subsequently revised for publication in 1728. At the same time, Bach probably adjusted the 1725 versions somewhat—or had Ziegler make the revisions—as he set the texts to music. An inspection of the surviving composition scores of seven of the nine cantatas in question[31] shows that Bach did not make alterations to the texts during the act of composing the music—that is, he appears to have been working from a manuscript libretto and entered the text cleanly into the scores.[32] Whether the manuscript libretto was fashioned by the poet, the composer, or both is the question. There is no evidence that confirms that it was created by Bach alone.

In the second part of the *Versuch*, published in 1729, Ziegler finished her cantata cycle—the only complete cycle written by a woman during the Baroque era—by providing cantata texts for the sixty-four Sundays and feast days not covered by the nine printed the year before. In the foreword, she stated that her impetus for finishing the cycle was encouragement received from an unnamed government official, who championed her work. Most probably composed in 1728, the additional texts arrived after Bach had turned to Birkmann, Henrici, and others for cantata and parody texts. After that, he moved away from cantata writing, focusing instead, from March 1729 onward, on secular works for the *collegium musicum*. There is no reason to suppose that Bach failed to set Ziegler's texts for aesthetic reasons, as it is sometimes implied. Rather, it was a matter of timing: the moment had passed for Bach to take up once again his collaboration with Leipzig's extraordinary poet, Christiane Mariane von Ziegler.

In a letter to Johann Nikolaus Forkel written in January 1775, Carl Philipp Emanuel Bach confirmed that Johann Adolf Hasse was among the musicians that his father knew personally and esteemed highly in his last years.[33] Drawing on this information and other material provided by Philipp Emanuel and his brother Wilhelm Friedemann Bach, Forkel later expanded upon their father's friendship with Hasse in his seminal biography *Über Johann Sebastian Bachs Leben, Kunst und Kunstwerke* of 1802:

> At the time that Hasse was Capellmeister at Dresden, the orchestra and opera there were very brilliant and excellent. Bach had had there already in his early years many acquaintances, by all of whom he was much honored. Hasse and his wife, the celebrated Faustina, had also come several times to Leipzig and admired his great talents. He was therefore always received in an exceedingly honorable manner at Dresden, and often went thither to hear the opera.[34]

Although no document confirms that Faustina Bordoni performed with Bach, circumstantial evidence raises the possibility.

The particulars of Bordoni's career are familiar to historians.[35] Professionally known as "Faustina," Bordoni (1697–1781) was born in Venice and raised under the protection of Alessandro and Benedetto Marcello. Taught singing by

Michaelangelo Gasparini, she made her debut in Carlo Francesco Pollarolo's *Ariodante* in 1716 in Venice at age nineteen and then went on to an international career as a highly acclaimed mezzo-soprano. She performed in the principal opera houses of Italy and enjoyed great successes in Munich, Vienna, and especially London, where she created leading roles for Handel at the King's Theatre between 1726 and 1728. The celebrated altercation that took place during a performance of Giovanni Bononcini's *Astianatte* on June 6, 1727, with her archrival Francesca Cuzzoni only served to enhance her reputation.[36]

In 1730 Bordoni married Hasse and accompanied him to Dresden the next year, when Saxon Elector Friedrich Augustus I named Hasse Capellmeister and Bordoni Soprano in the Court Capella. As the most illustrious member of the ensemble, Bordoni earned an annual salary of 3,000 thalers (Bach's fixed salary in Leipzig, by comparison, was just over 100 thalers). Between 1731 and 1751, the year of her retirement, she appeared frequently in Hasse's operas as well as the works of many other composers. Flautist and theorist Johann Joachim Quantz, who served as a member of the Dresden Court Capella between 1727 and 1740, summarized Bordoni's vocal qualities in considerable detail:

> Faustina had a *mezzo-soprano* voice that was less clear than penetrating. Her compass was only from B-flat to G in alt; but after this time [1727], she extended its limits downwards. She possessed what the Italians call *un cantar granite*: her execution was articulate and brilliant. She had a fluent tongue for pronouncing words rapidly and distinctly, and a flexible throat for divisions, with so beautiful and quick a shake, that she could put it in motion upon short notice, just when she would. The passages might be smooth, or by leaps, or consist of iterations of the same tone, their execution was equally easy to her as to any instrument whatever. She was doubtless the first who introduced, with success, a swift repetition of the same tone. She sang *adagios* with great passion and expression, but was not equally successful, if such deep sorrow were to be impressed on the hearer, as might require dragging, sliding, or notes of syncopation, and *tempo rubato*.
>
> She had a very happy memory, in arbitrary changes and embellishments, and a clear and quick judgment in giving to words their full power and expression. In her action she was very happy; and as she perfectly possessed that flexibility of muscles and features, which constitutes face-playing, she succeeded equally well in furious, amorous, and tender parts. In short, she was born for singing and for acting.[37]

Charles Burney, who heard Bordoni perform in London, noted that "E was a remarkably powerful note in this singer's voice, and we find most of her capital songs in sharp keys."[38] The arias she performed in Handel's works confirm this: half are in A or E, major or minor, with a range of c' to a".[39] The vocal parts Hasse composed for her display a similar compass, d' to a",[40] and call for greater virtuosity than those he wrote for other famous singers.[41]

Bach probably heard Bordoni for the first time in Dresden, in the performance of Hasse's *Cleofide* that took place on Thursday, September 13, 1731. The event represented the inaugural appearance of Hasse as the court's new opera composer and Bordoni as its new diva. A correspondent writing for the *Curiosa saxonica* ranked the production of *Cleofide* as a new high point in operatic opulence in Dresden, one that eclipsed even the lavish festivities surrounding the marriage of the Electoral Prince Friedrich August to Maria Josepha in 1719:

> [Opera in Dresden] has been lifted to the highest level through the incomparable voice and acting of the greatest singer of her time and the most famous in all of Italy and Germany, Madame Faustina (now through marriage known as Madame Hasse), and through the music of her husband, Mr. Johann Adolf Hasse. This extraordinary couple can in our time stand before the greatest musical virtuosos in all of Europe, the renowned Mr. Hasse in composition and the incomparable Madame Hasse in singing and acting, and find no equal.[42]

Bach presented a recital on the Silbermann organ in St. Sophia's Church on September 14, the day following the *Cleofide* premiere. According to a local report, he came from Leipzig "a few days beforehand,"[43] and it is difficult to imagine that he did not plan his early arrival in order to attend the *Cleofide* premiere, the most important cultural event in Saxony that year. In addition, the opera was repeated three times up to September 26, to "unusually large crowds."[44] This provided Bach with additional opportunities to see the production during his stay, which lasted until September 21.

Bach visited Dresden at least four other times in the 1730s and 1740s: 1733, 1736, 1738, and 1741.[45] The 1733 visit took place in July, when Bach presented the *Missa* of the Mass in B Minor to the new Saxon Elector, Friedrich August II, in the hope of receiving the title of court composer. The dedicatory letter accompanying the *Missa* is dated July 27, and the performance parts, copied seemingly in haste by members of the Bach family, were written on Dresden paper.[46] These factors point to a Dresden performance of the *Missa* either in the court chapel or in St. Sophia's Church, where Wilhelm Friedemann Bach had been named organist on June 23.[47]

The *Missa*, with its virtuoso arias and obbligato instrumental parts that systematically cover the five voices of the chorus and the principal chairs of the orchestra,[48] seems tailored to the star-studded Dresden court ensemble, and it was Arthur Mendel who first proposed that the aria "Laudamus te" of the Gloria, for soprano 2, solo violin, strings, and continuo, was intended as a coloratura display piece for Bordoni.[49] The aria's vocal compass, c♯' to e", would have fit comfortably within her range; the movement is written in A major, one of her favorite sharp keys; and the copious trills and ornate passagework of the vocal line seem designed to display the technical agility for which she was famous (ex. 4.3). Assuming that the court Capella performed the *Missa*, the solo violin part of the "Laudamus te" would have been taken by Johann Georg Pisendel (1687–1755), the virtuoso concertmaster of the orchestra and long-time acquaintance of Bach's.[50]

Example 4.3. *Missa*: "Laudamus te."

Bach's next visit to Dresden took place three years later, in December 1736, when he finally received the much-delayed title of court composer. He responded by playing an organ recital on the new Silbermann organ of the Church of Our Lady before "many persons of rank" and "a large attendance of other persons and artists."[51] His next trip, sometime before May 22, 1738, may have afforded him another opportunity to hear Bordoni on stage, since Hasse's *Alfonso* premiered in the newly rebuilt opera house on May 11, with additional performances on May 17, 19, 21, and 23.[52] Bach's final documented visit took place in November 1741. He stayed with the Russian Ambassador Count Hermann Carl von Keyserling and returned to Leipzig on November 17.[53] Hasse's new opera *Numa Pompilio*, with an especially beautiful scena (recitative and aria) for Faustina featuring an obbligato oboe performed by virtuoso Antonio Besozzi, premiered on the Elector's birthday on October 7 and was repeated seven times up to November 5. The performances took place at the Elector's hunting palace, Hubertusburg, however, rather than in Dresden Court Theater.[54]

As Forkel stated, Faustina Bordoni visited Leipzig with her husband several times during Bach's tenure, and it is mostly likely that the couple would have traveled to the Saxon commercial center during the annual trade fairs, which by 1730s were the largest in Germany. The fairs occurred three times a year: the New Year's Fair in January, the Easter (Jubilate) Fair in spring, and the St. Michael's Fair in autumn. Each lasted up to three weeks and attracted as many as 10,000 visitors, exhibitors, and vendors.[55] Bach and other composers used the fairs as an opportunity to sell printed editions of their music, announcing their availability with published notices.

The fairs also featured a host of special music performances. Bach appears to have presented organ concerts (most probably in the University Church, which housed the best instrument in Leipzig),[56] and the town's two *collegium musicum* ensembles doubled their weekly concerts to accommodate fair guests. From 1729 to 1742 or so Bach served as the director of the *collegium* founded by Telemann around 1702. During the winter months the ensemble performed in Gottfried Zimmermann's coffee house in St. Catherine Street off the town square; during the summer months it moved outdoors to Zimmermann's coffee garden in the Grimmischer Steinweg outside the east gate of the city. The two *collegia* were described by Lorenz Christoph Mizler in 1736:

> Both of the public musical Concerts or Assemblies that are held here weekly are still flourishing steadily. The one is conducted by Mr. Johann Sebastian Bach, Capellmeister to the Court of Weissenfels and Music Director of St. Thomas's and at St. Nicholas's in this city, and is held, except during the Fair, once a week in Zimmermann's coffeehouse in the Catherine Street, on Friday evenings from 8 to 10 o'clock; during the Fair, however, twice a week, on Tuesdays and Fridays, at the same hour. The other is conducted by Mr. Johann Gottlieb Görner, Music Director at St. Paul's and Organist at St. Thomas's. It is also held once weekly, in the Schellhafter Hall in the Closter-Gasse, Thursday evenings from 8 to 10 o'clock; during the Fair, however, twice weekly, namely, Mondays and Thursdays, at the same time.

> The participants in these musical concerts are chiefly students here, and there are always good musicians among them, so that sometimes they become, as is known, famous virtuosos. Any musician is permitted to make himself publicly heard at these musical concerts, and most often, too, there are such listeners as know how to judge the qualities of an able musician.[57]

Membership in the *collegia* was restricted to men, as confirmed in the detailed roster of the Grosses Concert, a third ensemble formed in 1743.[58] But the groups commonly featured visiting artists, such as "Mr. Fischer," apparently a singer from England, who appeared with the Grosses Concert in 1743,[59] and it is possible that the guests included women, given the enlightened bourgeois setting and the paying audience of "cavaliers et dames."[60] Bach biographer Christoph Wolff has speculated not only that Dresden visitors such as Hasse, Bordoni, and the lutenist Silvius Leopold Weiss might have appeared as guests, but also that members of the local academic and intellectual community may have taken part, too, including professor of rhetoric Johann Abraham Birnbaum and Luise Adelgunde Gottsched, who in addition to writing dramas also played clavier and lute and composed modest musical works.[61]

Forkel links Hasse and Bordoni's trips to Leipzig with their admiration of Bach's talents, suggesting that they heard Bach perform there, either in an organ recital or with the *collegium* ensemble. If Bordoni appeared with the *collegium,* perhaps during the fairs when the group met twice a week for special concerts, what would she have performed? Bach's Italian secular cantata, *Non sa che sia dolore,* BWV 209, for soprano, transverse flute, strings, and continuo, has been suggested as a candidate.[62] Composed sometime after 1729, the compass of the vocal part—d' to a"—fits Bordoni's range. But the topic of the work—the return of a scholar to his homeland in order to serve it—suggests that it was written to honor Mizler or another academic, rather than to serve as a display piece for Bordoni.[63]

More likely pieces can be found among the progressive Italian-texted secular works by other composers that have recently been shown to have been a part of the *collegium*'s repertory—cantatas and opera excerpts by composers more accustomed to writing pieces in Italian than Bach.[64] That such music was standard *collegium* fare is underscored by the remark of university student Christoph Birkmann, mentioned above with regard to Christiane Mariane von Ziegler: "Even so, I did not give up music entirely. I diligently followed the great composer Mr. Bach and his choir, and in winter I took part in the collegia musica, and this gave me the opportunity to continue assisting many students with the help of the Italian language."[65] The Italian vocal music that can be linked with Bach's *collegium* includes secular cantatas by Nicola Antonio Porpora, George Frideric Handel, and Alessandro Scarlatti and opera excerpts by Handel:[66]

Italian-texted secular cantatas:
  Nicola Antonio Porpora
    Dal primo foco in cui penai
    Ecco, ecco l'infausto lido
    Sopra un colle fiorito
    D'amor la bella pace
    La viola che languiva
    Tu ten vai cosi fastoso
  Alessandro Scarlatti
    Se amor con un contento
  George Frideric Handel
    Dietro l'orme fuggaci ("Armida abbandonata")

Opera seria excerpts:
  George Frideric Handel
    Alcina (1735): "Mi lustinga il dolce affetto" and "Di', co mio, quanto t'amai"

The Handel works illustrate well the qualities of this repertory. The chamber cantata *Dietro l'orme fuggaci,* HWV 105, better known as "Armida abbandonata," is an early Handel composition, written in Rome in 1707. The Leipzig materials consist of a score.[67] apparently written by Melchior Hoffmann, one of Bach's predecessors as *collegium* director,[68] and a set of performance parts written around 1731 by Bach, his son Carl Philipp Emanuel (who was then 17), and an anonymous scribe.[69] The seven-movement sequence of recitatives and arias is scored for soprano, two violins, and continuo. With a compass of c' to a♭", the soprano part would have fit comfortably into Bordoni's mezzo-soprano range, and the opening aria, "Ah! crudele e pur ten vai," especially, contains the type of delicate passagework associated with her singing style (ex. 4.4). Bach appears to have pulled the Handel score from the *collegium*'s library[70] in the early 1730s and quickly prepared parts for an upcoming performance.[71] It was common practice for Bach and other composers to prepare such materials on short notice. Still, "Armida abbandonata" was an unusual piece in the Leipzig repertory, and it might have been brought to performance in haste for a special visiting artist.

Example 4.4. George Frideric Handel, *Dietro l'orme fuggaci*: "Ah! crudele e pur ten vai."

The two arias from Handel's *Alcina*, for soprano, strings, and continuo, are passed down in manuscript materials in the hand of Carl Gotthelf Gerlach (1704–61). Gerlach studied organ with Bach, beginning in the mid-1720s,[72] and was appointed organist of the New Church in 1729. He seems to have served as librarian of the *collegium* and Bach's assistant, copying out the Porpora and Scarlatti cantatas cited above around 1734 and leading the ensemble between 1737 and 1739, when Bach temporarily stepped down from the directorship. The *Alcina* arias also stem from 1734 or so and are transmitted in an abbreviated score for soprano and harpsichord together with instrumental parts for violin 1, violin 2, viola, and basso (labeled "Cembalo" and containing continuo figures). This arrangement allows for two performance options: soprano and harpsichord alone or soprano with strings and continuo, much in the fashion of the aria "Schlummert ein, ihr matten Augen" from Cantata 82, *Ich habe genug,* which is scored for alto, strings, and continuo in the cantata version and for alto and continuo in the *Clavierbüchlein* for Anna Magdalena Bach of 1725.[73] The soprano and harpsichord version of the *Alcina* excerpts would have enabled the arias to be performed with very small forces, in the fashion of "Schlummert ein," in an intimate space such as Bach's home. This opens still another possibility for a Bordoni appearance—a house concert.

While "Armida abbandonata" is one of Handel's early works, *Alcina* is a mature composition that premiered in London on April 16, 1735, in Covent Garden. It was an immediate popular success and was repeated sixteen times through July 2 of that year.[74] Thus a performance by Bach's *collegium* in the mid-1730s would have represented bringing to Leipzig the very latest in stylish opera music from the London stage—a scene very familiar to Faustina Bordoni. The range of the two excerpts is c′ to a♭″, and Alcina's aria "Di', cor mio, quanto t'amai," in particular, contains the type of vocal flourishes toward the end of the A section (ex. 4.5) that are found in the "Laudamus te" of the B-Minor Mass and "Ah! crudele e pur ten vai" from "Armida abbandonata." It is noteworthy, too, that the passage calls for the "swift repetition of the same tone"—the very gesture described by Quantz as a Bordoni specialty.

Example 4.5. George Frideric Handel, *Alcina:* "Di', cor mio, quanto t'amai."

Whether or not these particular pieces were performed by Faustina Bordoni during her visits to Leipzig, they illustrate the type of fashionable music that was being featured by Bach's *collegium*—music that would have comfortably fit Bordoni's range, displayed to good advantage the qualities of her singing, and allowed her to perform in her native Italian.

It is clear from the essays in the present volume that Sara Levy played a larger role in promoting, performing, and preserving the music of J. S. Bach than previously thought. The time seems ripe, then, to revisit the lives and activities of two equally impressive female predecessors, Christiane Mariane von Ziegler and Faustina Bordoni, and reconsider the degree to which they interacted with Bach and enriched his professional music-making in Leipzig with their distinctively nuanced voices.

Notes

1. See especially Christoph Wolff, "A Bach Cult in Late-Eighteenth-Century Berlin: Sara Levy's Musical Salon," *Bulletin of the American Academy of Arts and Sciences* 58, no. 3 (2005): 26–39, and Peter Wollny, *"Ein förmlicher Sebastian und Philipp Emanuel Bach-Kultus": Sara Levy und ihr musikalisches Wirken. Mit einer Dokumentensammlung zur musikalischen Familiengeschichte der Vorfahren von Felix Mendelssohn Bartholdy* (Wiesbaden: Breitkopf & Härtel, 2010).
2. *The New Bach Reader: A Life of Johann Sebastian Bach in Letters and Documents*, ed. Hans T. David and Arthur Mendel, revised and enlarged by Christoph Wolff (New York: W. W. Norton, 1998), 152.
3. She performed first in Cöthen, where she continued to serve as a court singer until the Bachs' departure for Leipzig, and then in Leipzig as a singer with her husband in out-of-town guest performances in Cöthen (July 1724, December 1725, and March 1729).
4. The most complete, up-to-date account of Anna Magdalena Bach's life and work is Maria Hübner, *Anna Magdalena Bach: Ein Leben in Dokumenten und Bildern* (Leipzig: Evangelische Verlagsanstalt, 2004). A catalog of the works copied by Anna Magdalena can be found on pp. 137–40 of Hübner's study.
5. It has been proposed that Catharina Dorothea was the scribe known as Anonymous L 77 in *Johann Sebastian Bach: Neue Ausgabe sämtlicher Werke* (*Neue Bach-Ausgabe*) (Leipzig and Kassel: Bärenreiter, 1954–2007), vol. 9, no. 3, *Die Kopisten Johann Sebastian Bachs: Katalog und Dokumentation*, 140–41. Anonymous L 77's hand appears in the Dresden parts of the *Missa* of the B-Minor Mass as well as in several other manuscripts from the 1730s in Bach's music library. Peter Wollny has recently identified Anonymous L 77 not as Catharina Dorothea Bach, however, but rather as Heinrich Wilhelm Ludewig (born 1711), in Peter Wollny "Neuerkenntnisse zu einigen Kopisten der 1730er Jahre," *Bach-Jahrbuch* 102 (2016): 73–78.
6. In *Neue Bach-Ausgabe* vol. 9, no. 3, it is proposed that she was either Anonymous M 1 or Anonymous W 18, two unidentified copyists working under Bach's direction in Mühlhausen and Weimar. Anonymous M 1 has since been identified almost certainly as Bach's student Johann Martin Schubart (see the introduction to *Weimarer Orgeltabulatur*, ed. Michael Maul and Peter Wollny. [Kassel: Bärenreiter, 2007], xxiii–xxiv), but it remains possible that Maria Barbara Bach was Anonymous W 18.

7. The principal historical sources of Ziegler's biography are the forewords and texts of her own publications and her biographical entry in Johann Heinrich Zedler's *Grosses vollständige Universal-Lexicon* (Halle: Johann Heinrich Zedler, 1732–54), vol. 61 (1749). The most important modern accounts of Ziegler are Sabine Ehrmann, "Johann Sebastian Bachs Textdicterin Christine Mariane von Ziegler," *Beiträge zur Bach-Forschung* 9–10 (1991): 261–68; Katherine R. Goodman, *Amazons and Apprentices: Women and the German Parnassus in the Early Enlightenment* (Columbia, SC: Camden House, 1999); and Mark Peters, *A Woman's Voice in Baroque Music: Mariane von Ziegler and J. S. Bach* (Aldershot: Ashgate, 2008).

8. The house still stands and is one of the best surviving examples of a Baroque *Durchgangshof* in Leipzig.

9. Christiane Mariane von Ziegler, *Moralische und vermischte Send-Schreiben* (Leipzig: Braun, 1731).

10. *Sammlung der Schriften und Gedichte welche auf die poetische Krönung der hochwohlge-bohrnen Frauen, Frauen Christianen Marianen von Ziegler, gebohrnen Romanus, ver-fertiget worden* (Leipzig: Bernhard Christoph Breitkopf, 1734).

11. Zedler, *Grosses vollständige Universal-Lexicon*, vol. 61.

12. It appeared posthumously in the supplement of 1751 and is reproduced in *Bach-Dokumente*, ed. Bach-Archiv (Leipzig: VEB Deutscher Verlag für Musik and Kassel: Barenreiter, 1963–present), vol. 2, no. 643.

13. Published in *Die vernünfftigen Tadlerinnen, erster Jahr-Theil* (Halle: Johann Adam Spörl, 1725), 412–15.

14. Alfred Dürr, *The Cantatas of J. S. Bach*, trans. Richard Jones (Oxford: Oxford University Press, 2005), 30.

15. Hans-Joachim Schulze, "Texte und Textdichter," in *Die Welt der Bach-Kantaten*, ed. Christoph Wolff (Stuttgart: J. B. Metzler, 1996–99), vol. 3, 115–16.

16. Cantata cycles normally commenced at the beginning of the church year—the first Sunday in Advent. But because Bach arrived in Leipzig in May 1723 and began his first cycle at that time (May 30, 1723), his cantata cycles started with the first Sunday after Trinity.

17. In Leipzig the texts for weekly cantatas were printed in advance, in batches of two months or so, and sold to the congregation for use during the performances, much like opera librettos.

18. Hans-Joachim Schulze, "Neuerkenntnisse zu einigen Kantatentexten Bachs auf Grund neuer biographischer Daten," in *Bach-Interpretationen*, ed. Martin Geck (Göttingen: Vandenhoeck & Ruprecht, 1969), 23–24.

19. Christian Gottlieb Bach was baptized on April 14, 1725, and died September 21, 1728.

20. The salon is described in Peters, *A Woman's Voice in Baroque Music*, 42–45.

21. Ziegler, *Moralische und vermischte Send-Schreiben*, 392.

22. Henrici, known as "Picander," has long been known as one of Bach's librettists. Birkmann has only recently been recognized as a provider of texts, in Christine Blanken, "A Cantata-Text Cycle of 1728 from Nuremberg: a Preliminary Report on a Discovery relating to J. S. Bach's so-called 'Third Annual Cantata Cycle,'" *Understanding Bach* 10 (2015): 9–30.

23. Philipp Spitta, "Mariane von Ziegler und Johann Sebastian Bach," in *Zur Musik. Sechzehn Aufsätze* (Berlin: Gebrüder Paetal, 1892; Hildesheim: Georg Olms, 1976), 97.

24. English:
    > Whosoever **loves** me, he will keep my **word**, and my **Father** will **love** him,
    >   and we will **come** unto him, and make our **dwelling place** with him.
    > Aria (Komm, komm)
    > **Come**, **come**, my heart is open to thee,
    >   Ah, let it now be thy **dwelling place**!
    > I **love** thee, and must be hopeful:
    >   Thy **word** is now fulfilled in me.
    > For whosoever seeks, fears, loves, and honors thee,
    >   With him the **Father** is content.
    > I do not doubt that I am favored,
    > That I can be among thy comforted.

25. See Wolfgang Herbst, "Ein Vergleich zwischen Joh. Seb. Bach und Chr. Mariane v. Ziegler," *Musik und Kirche* 30 (1960): 248–55, or Hans-Joachim Schulze, "Texte und Textdichter," 115, for instance.

26. They occur between the cantata version (Cantata 198, *Laß, Fürstin, laß noch einen Strahl*) and the printed version of Gottsched's *Trauer-Rede*, written for the death of Saxon Electress Christiane Eberhardine in 1727, for example.

27. The Ziegler texts (cantata and *Versuch* versions) can be compared in Werner Neumann, ed. *Sämtliche von Johann Sebastian Bach vertonete Texte* (Leipzig: VEB Deutscher Verlag für Musik, 1974), which presents the cantata texts as well as facsimiles of the *Versuch* versions (on pp. 358–65).

28. English:

My heart ever faithful,	Oh faithful heart
Exults and sings gladly,	Exults and rejoices,
Thy Jesus is here!	Thy Jesus is here!

29. English:

Once my fear is past thou shall	Thou shall ever, my savior,
Also restore me once again;	Ever restore me once my fear is past.
Therefore I will prepare myself	Well now! I will prepare myself
For thy arrival.	For thy arrival.
I trust in the promise of thy word,	I trust in the promise of thy word.
That my sadness	That my sadness,
	And this perhaps in just a short time,
	After fear and anxious endurance,
Shall be transformed into joy.	Shall be transformed into joy.

30. Peters, *A Woman's Voice*, 141–42. Peters also quotes Ziegler's remark from the foreword to the *Versuch* of 1728: "[Since I have] found that each day gives to humans with their endeavors and studies a new addition, I have in the same, by looking over and repeated reading through, altered one and another thing therein after my current taste, and through these lessons, if I may so flatter myself again, given substance to them, wherein they previously should have appeared poor."

31. The scores to Cantatas 74 and 68 are no longer extant. The examination of the other works was carried out via the digitally scanned facsimiles available on the *Bach Digital* website.

32. Similar to the surviving handwritten text sheets for Cantata 208a, *Was mir behagt, ist nur die muntre Jagd*, in the hand of Bach's amanuensis Johann Elias Bach, and Cantata 216a, *Erwählte Pleißenstadt*, in Bach's own hand. Both are reproduced in facsimile in *Sämtliche von Johann Sebastian Bach vertonte Texte*, 456–69.

33. David, Mendel, and Wolff, *New Bach Reader*, 400.

34. Ibid., 461.

35. Faustina Bordoni Hasse's life and activities are described in Pier Francesco Tosi, *Opinioni de' cantori antichi e moderni* (Bologna, 1723), translated into English as *Observations on the Florid Song*, trans. [John Ernst] Galliard (London: J. Wilcox, 1743); Charles Burney, *A General History of Music from the Earliest Ages to the Present Period* (London: printed by author, 1776–89; New York: Dover, 1957); Moritz Fürstenau, *Zur Geschichte der Musik und des Theaters am Hofe zu Dresden* (Dresden: Rudolf Kuntze, 1861–62), vol. 2; and Arnold Niggli, *Faustina Bordoni-Hasse* (Leipzig: Breitkopf & Härtel, 1880). These accounts are summarized by Winton Dean in the entry "Faustina Bordoni" in the *New Grove Dictionary of Music and Musicians*, ed. Stanley Sadie (New York: Macmillan, 2001), 3: 894–95. More recently, Saskia Maria Woyke has surveyed Bordoni's life and accomplishments in Saskia Maria Woyke, "Faustina Bordoni-Hasse— eine Sängerinnenkarriere im 18. Jahrhundert," in *Göttinger Händel-Beiträge* 7, ed. Hans Joachim Marx (Göttingen: Vandenhoeck & Ruprecht, 1998), 218–57, and Saskia Maria Woyke, *Faustina Bordoni: Biographie, Vokalprofil, Rezeption* (Frankfurt: Peter Lang, 2010). Finally, Suzanne Aspden has appraised Bordoni's London activities and competition with Francesca Cuzzoni in Suzanne Aspden, *The Rival Sirens: Performance and Identity on Handel's Operatic Stage* (Cambridge: Cambridge University Press, 2013).

36. Suzanne Aspden has presented convincing evidence that the fistfight between the two singers commonly described by historians did not actually take place. The disturbance that occurred during the performance transpired instead in the audience, between the supporters of Bordoni and the supporters of Cuzzoni. See Aspden, *The Rival Sirens*, 47–50.

37. Johann Joachim Quantz, cited and translated in Burney, *A General History*, 745–46. Other contemporary accounts are cited in Aspden, *The Rival Sirens*, 31–36.

38. Burney, *A General History*, 738.

39. Dean, "Faustina Bordoni," 895.

40. Fürstenau, *Zur Geschichte der Musik*, vol. 2, 210.

41. Woyke, *Faustina Bordoni*, 122.

42. *Curiosa saxonica* 1731, installments 34 and 35, cited in Fürstenau, *Zur Geschichte der Musik*, vol. 2, 173.

43. *Bach-Dokumente*, vol. 2, no. 294.

44. *Hof- und Staatskalender auf 1733*, page H b, cited in Woyke, *Faustina Bordoni*, 65.

45. On Bach's infatuation with Dresden, see George B. Stauffer, "Bach and the Lure of the Big City," in *The Worlds of Johann Sebastian Bach*, ed. Raymond Erickson (New York: Amadeus Press, 2009), 255–61.

46. *Neue Bach-Ausgabe* vol 2, no. 1a, Kritischer Bericht (Uwe Wolf, 2005), 14–21.

47. Peter Wollny, however, has recently proposed that the parts of the *Missa* were copied in Leipzig and that the first performance took place there, in the Nikolaikirche, as proposed by Arnold Schering in 1936. He believes the work was nevertheless composed with the Dresden court singers and instrumentalists in mind. See Wollny, "Neuerkenntnisse zu einigen Kopisten der 1730er Jahre," *Bach-Jahrbuch* 102 (2016): 73–78.

48. This is in strong contrast with the remaining portions of the B-Minor Mass, which were added in 1748–49 to produce a *Missa tota*. The final portions emphasize choral writing, with just a smattering of arias and duets.

49. Robert L. Marshall, *The Music of Johann Sebastian Bach: The Sources, the Style, the Significance* (New York: Schirmer Books, 1989), ch. 2, "Bach the Progressive: Observations on His Later Works," 42.

50. Pisendel took violin lessons from Giuseppe Torelli and appears to have first met Bach in Weimar in 1709 or so.

51. David, Mendel, and Wolff, *New Bach Reader*, 188. The Silbermann organ had been dedicated on the previous Sunday, November 25.

52. Woyke, *Faustina Bordoni*, 198.

53. *Bach-Dokumente* vol. 2, nos. 497, 498, and 502.

54. Fürstenau, *Zur Geschichte der Musik*, 235–36, and Woyke, *Faustina Bordoni*, 198.

55. George B. Stauffer, "Leipzig: Cosmopolitan Trade Centre," in *Music and Society: The Late Baroque*, ed. George J. Buelow (Englewood Cliffs, NJ: Prentice Hall, 1993), 260.

56. To judge from the letter of G. H. L. Schwanenberger, who reported hearing Bach play the organ during the St. Michael's Fair in 1727. See David, Mendel, and Wolff, *New Bach Reader*, no. 320.

57. David, Mendel, and Wolff, *New Bach Reader*, no. 187.

58. Reproduced in *Bach-Dokumente*, vol. 4, no. 392.

59. Werner Neumann, "Das 'Bachische *Collegium musicum*,'" *Bach-Jahrbuch* 47 (1960): 26.

60. Hans-Joachim Schulze, "Johann Friedrich Schweinitz, 'A Disciple of the Famous Herr Bach in Leipzig,'" in *About Bach*, ed. Gregory G. Butler, George B. Stauffer, and Mary Dalton Greer (Urbana: University of Illinois Press, 2008), 82.

61. Christoph Wolff, *Johann Sebastian Bach: The Learned Musician* (New York: W. W. Norton, 2000), 355.

62. Marshall, *The Music of Johann Sebastian Bach*, 38.

63. As proposed by Klaus Hoffmann, "Alte und neue Überlegungen zu der Kantate 'Non sa che sia dolore' BWV 209," in *Bach-Jahrbuch* 76 (1990): 14.

64. The Italian of *Non sa che sia dolore* is faulty.

65. *Bach-Dokumente*, vol. 3, no. 761.

66. See Andreas Glöckner, "Neuerkenntnisse zu J. S. Bachs Aufführungskalender zwischen 1729 und 1735," *Bach-Jahrbuch* 67 (1981): 66–75; and George B. Stauffer, "Music for 'Cavaliers et Dames': Bach and the Repertoire of his Collegium Musicum," in *About Bach*, 135–56.

67. Darmstadt, Hessische Landesbibliothek, Mus. ms. 986.

68. Hans Joachim Marx, *Hallische Händel-Ausgabe*, vol. 3, Kantaten mit Instrumenten II (Kassel: Bärenreiter, 1995), xxiii.
69. The parts were first described by Oswald Bill in "Die Liebesklage der Armida. Händels Kantate HWV 105 in Spiegel Bachscher Aufführungspraxis," in *Ausstellung aus Anlaß der Händel-Festspiele des Badischen Staatstheater Karlsruhe 1985* (Karlsruhe: Badische Landisbibliothek & Badisches Staatstheater, 1985), 25–40. The dating given here is that proposed by Glöckner in "Neuerkenntnisse," 50.
70. The score might have been kept in the New Church, whose music director had served as leader of this *collegium* from Telemann's time to 1729, when Bach broke precedent and, as Cantor of St. Thomas, took over the group himself.
71. J. S. Bach revised the rhythmic notation of the violin 1 and continuo parts, changing a number of eighth notes into sixteenth notes to produce a sharper rhythm. C. P. E. Bach, copying the violin 2 part from the score, retained the original eighth notes. J. S. Bach did not take the time to bring the violin 2 part into line with violin 1, but rather must have relied on the player to match the rhythmic realization of the first violin in performance.
72. Until recently it was only surmised that Gerlach studied with Bach. But the discovery of copies of the Toccata in C Major, BWV 564, and the *Pièce d'orgue*, BWV 572, written by Gerlach between 1723 and 1727 or so, suggests that he took organ lessons with Bach in Leipzig. See Christine Blanken, "Ein wieder zugänglich gemachter Bestand alter Musikalien der Bach-Familie im Verlagsarchiv Breitkopf & Härtel," *Bach-Jahrbuch* 99 (2013): 95–105.
73. Bach reworked Cantata 82 several times between its first performance in 1727 and its last, ca. 1747, shifting the solo voice from bass (version 1) to soprano (version 2) to mezzo-soprano (version 3) and finally back to bass (version 4). See Hans-Joachim Schulze and Christoph Wolff, ed., *Bach-Compendium* (Leipzig: Edition Peters, 1985–89), vol. 2, A 169a–d.
74. In addition, Handel repeated *Alcina* in the 1736 and 1737 seasons with a different castrato taking the role of Ruggiero. This resulted the transposition of the aria "Mi lusinga il dolce affetto" (act 2, scene 3) from E-flat major to F major (*Hallische Händel-Ausgabe* series II, vol. 33 [*Alcina*], ed. Siegfried Flesch [Kassel: Bärenreiter, 2009], xiii). The Leipzig version of "Mi lusinga" is in E-flat major, and thus the two excerpts appear to be drawn from the music used for the 1735 London performance.

Music, Aesthetics, and Philosophy: Jews and Christians in Sara Levy's World

Chapter Five

Lessing and the Limits of Enlightenment

Martha B. Helfer

This chapter is reprinted from Martha Helfer's book, *The Word Unheard: Legacies of Anti-Semitism in German Literature and Culture* (2011), about latent anti-Semitism in the classical German literary canon.[1] Helfer's study treats German literary texts that were produced and read between 1749 to 1850, when the issue of Jewish political emancipation was fiercely debated among German political thinkers, writers, religious figures, and other intellectuals. This chapter reconsiders the literary legacy of the great Enlightenment author Gotthold Ephraim Lessing (1729–81), Germany's most famous advocate of religious tolerance and an icon of interfaith friendship. Reexamining Lessing's three major works promoting tolerance toward Jews and Judaism—his theological treatise, *The Education of the Human Race* (1780), and two plays, *The Jews* (1749) and *Nathan the Wise* (1779)—Helfer claims that there was a persistent tension running throughout this oeuvre, which helped to shape the rhetoric of anti-Semitism that subsequently informed modernizing German culture's views of Jews and Judaism. In shedding new light on the ideals of tolerance for which Lessing stood, Helfer's chapter offers a complex view of crucial aspects of Sara Levy's world.

The Word Unheard begins with a necessary provocation: Lessing and latent anti-Semitism. The great Enlightenment playwright and critic Gotthold Ephraim Lessing was unequivocally a pro-Jewish author and political activist. Lessing was very likely the sponsor of the first published document calling for the full emancipation of the Jews in Germany,[2] and his theological and dramatic writings on Jews and Judaism form the *de facto* benchmark of pro-Jewish discourse in German letters. Lessing's influence on German literature and culture is profound. Just as every Jewish character in Western literature in some sense references Shakespeare's Shylock, every Jewish character in German literature in some sense references Lessing's Nathan the Wise.[3] Lessing's merchant Nathan is a good Jew, a wise Jew, the embodiment of Enlightenment who famously advocates tolerance for the three great monotheistic religions, Judaism, Christianity, and Islam. Lessing's Nathan is so good, so wise, and Lessing's reputation as a pro-Jewish German cultural icon so strong, that the Nazis peremptorily prohibited the production of the play at the beginning of the Third Reich in 1933. After the war, in 1945, many German theaters reopened with *Nathan the Wise*, the symbol of tolerance and Enlightenment humanism, and the play is still one of the most frequently performed on the German stage today.[4]

And yet I begin—and must begin—my study of latent anti-Semitism with Lessing, the paragon of pro-Jewish thought in German literature and culture. I begin with Lessing not only because of his influence on subsequent authors and on German culture in general, but also because of systemic tensions inherent in Lessing's texts themselves. The three major works Lessing wrote promoting tolerance toward Jews and Judaism[5]—the theological treatise on *The Education of the Human Race* and the two plays *The Jews* and *Nathan the Wise*—all question their pro-Jewish and anti-anti-Semitic Enlightenment messages, and hence constitute a pivotal juncture in the formation of the rhetoric of anti-Semitism in German letters.

I want to make very clear from the start that I am *not* arguing that either Lessing or his texts are anti-Semitic. My argument is rather this: Lessing's pro-Jewish agenda turns back on itself and subtly and programmatically questions its own basic premises in true Enlightenment fashion. This is Enlightenment criticism pure and simple, and it is operative in Lessing's works in general. As Friedrich Schlegel incisively noted, Lessing's entire life and oeuvre are defined by criticism.[6] In both form and content, Lessing's writings enact a thoroughgoing questioning of established concepts, definitions, and thought patterns. The goal of Lessing's criticism is to combat dogma, to combat prejudice in the true sense of the word—pre-judging that does not examine its own basic premises. This constant calling into question informs Lessing's writing: it is self-reflexive, self-critical, internally contradictory, intentionally polemical, dialectical, multi-perspectival, and dynamically fluid in nature. The *process* of looking for truth, not truth itself, is at stake in Lessing's epistemology and in his poetic production.[7] This is why it is notoriously difficult to establish Lessing's own views in a given text, and this is why it would be folly to argue that there is only one possible reading of a given Lessing text. The following discussion analyzes the language and structure of Lessing's three major works on Jews and Judaism, and demonstrates that these texts by design set up a dialectical relationship between the rhetoric of philo-Semitism and the rhetoric of anti-Semitism, and hence articulate a self-reflexive, self-critical theory of the discursive construction of the Jew.

We begin somewhat anachronistically with *The Education of the Human Race* (*Die Erziehung des Menschengeschlechts*, 1777–80), since this theological essay in many ways functions as a blueprint for the discursive construction of Jewishness evident in the earlier play *The Jews* (*Die Juden*, 1749) and the roughly contemporaneous play *Nathan the Wise* (*Nathan der Weise*, 1779).[8] In *The Education of the Human Race* Lessing, writing from a Protestant theological vantage, sets out to account for the evolution of Christianity from Judaism; or, more precisely, to explain why, in his view, Christianity must necessarily supersede Judaism, and why Christianity as it is currently practiced likewise must give way to a more Enlightened version of Christianity, to a Christian religion of reason.[9] Lessing's essay, importantly, is cast as a response to Reimarus and Warburton debating the roles of reason versus revelation in recognizing eternal truths, and in fact intends to defend Judaism as a valid religion, as the historical predecessor to Christianity.[10] Neatly, if somewhat arbitrarily, divided into one hundred paragraphs, the essay's rational form reflects its rational Enlightenment agenda, and here, as in Kant's contemporaneous essay "What is Enlightenment?" of 1783, Enlightenment is inextricably tied to the written word. Using a logical argument motored by metaphors and internal inconsistencies,[11] Lessing presents a history of theology—a theology of history—divided into four distinct stages. According to Lessing's fanciful historical schema, the religious development of the human race from polytheism through Judaism and Christianity to an Enlightened Christian "Gospel of Reason" parallels the physical stages of human development from birth through childhood and adolescence to manhood.[12] This phylogenetic maturation metaphor implies that the evolution of Christianity from Judaism is both a theological and a biological necessity. Moreover, Lessing equates religious maturation with sexual maturation, and he explicitly genders this Enlightenment maturation process as male: Jews are unsexed children (*Kinder*); present-day Christians are lads or male adolescents (*Knaben*); and practitioners of Lessing's new Enlightened "Gospel of Reason" are men (*Männer*). According to the metaphoric logic of Lessing's argument, Jews are less than men. *Ex negativo*, and likely unintentionally, Lessing invokes the stock anti-Semitic stereotype of the Jews as an effeminate people in the very framework of his argument.

Disturbingly, Lessing relies on many other anti-Semitic stereotypes and anti-Semitic rhetorical gestures to develop his theological history of the education of the human race. The story Lessing tells is this. In the beginning there was polytheism. The human race, Lessing implies without actually using the metaphor, was in its baby stage at this earliest phase of its development. Then God selected the Jews, "the crudest and wildest of all peoples" (§8:76; das ungeschliffenste, das verwildertste), to reveal Himself to, so as to begin His educational plan with a clean slate, as it were. The Israelites, a people still in its childhood, raw, and clumsily incapable of abstract thought, had to be educated as one educates children, using a doctrine of immediate punishment and reward (§16:78). The Old Testament, a primer for children (§26:81; ein Elementarbuch für Kinder), guided the Jews' pedagogical development. In Persian captivity the Jews began to compare "their Jehovah" to the Being of all Beings, a more rational and more moral being than they themselves had envisioned. The Jews then turned to their long-abandoned Old Testament to blame their own immaturity on the word of God, but had to admit to themselves, ashamed, that they themselves bore the guilt for not having recognized the true nature of God and for not having lived their lives accordingly (§38:85). Remarkably, the Jews themselves are "guilty" of being Jews—children—in Lessing's schema, and the Jews—who must be "ashamed" of their own behavior—need an outside guiding force to set them straight. Using the Persian model as an example, the Jews then became "a completely different people" (§40: 85), and scoured their Bible for evidence of the truths they had seen in other religions. (In particular, Lessing is concerned here with the doctrine of the immortality of the soul.) But for all its richness and its hints at truth, its allegorical allusions to truth, Lessing argues, the Jews' Bible had its limits: "A better pedagogue had to come to tear this tired, worn-out primer from the children's hands: Christ came" (§53:88). Under the tutelage of Jesus, "the first reliable, practical teacher of the doctrine of the immortality of the soul" (§58:89), the "better teacher," the Israelites began to mature. The Jews became Christians; the children became young men (§58:89; Knaben). The New Testament, "the second, better primer" (§64:91; das zweite, beßre Elementarbuch) now directs their development. Guided by a "better" teacher and a "better" primer, the Christians are clearly "better" than the Jews in Lessing's view, but their education is as yet incomplete. The Christian ethos still is motivated by a reward system: the doctrine of eternal salvation. The youths will become men when they act in a moral way not because of a promise of salvation or a fear of damnation, but simply because it's the right thing to do. Goodness for the sake of goodness is the new Gospel of Reason, "the highest stage of Enlightenment and purity" (§81:96; diese höchste Stufen der Aufklärung und Reinigkeit). The metaphors Lessing uses here jarringly introduce an implied impurity, an implied dirtiness, into earlier stages of development; rhetorically, Lessing casts the Jews as an unclean, impure people, excluded from the highest stages of Enlightenment. Lessing reasons that it cannot be fair that those people who were born at the early phases of humankind's development should miss out on this highest level of human perfection. Hence he concludes his essay by speculating on metempsychosis, the transmigration of souls.[13] According to the logic of Lessing's Enlightenment agenda, Jews can and should become—literally—born-again Christians.

Just as each earlier stage of Enlightenment is tied to the written word in Lessing's model—the childlike Jews are guided by the Old Testament, the lad-like Christians by the New Testament—the last stage of Enlightenment, the new "Gospel of Reason" for mature Christian men, is inaugurated by a text: Lessing's own *The Education of the Human Race*. In a telling self-reflexive rhe-torical gesture located at the precise center of the essay's one hundred para-graphs, Lessing draws a pronounced parallel between his own writing and the "clothing" and "style" of the Jews' *Elementarbuch*, the Jews' "primer."[14] With its allegories and instructive examples, its presentation that is at times plain, at times poetic, and full of polyvalent tautologies designed to sharpen its read-er's acumen, *The Education of the Human Race* is explicitly patterned after the Old Testament (§§48–51, 87–88). In drawing this bold connection between the Jews' "primer" and his own, Lessing emphasizes the like education that Jews and Christians must undergo, an education that is to take place in and through language, through the written word: here, through the very text of *The Education of the Human Race* itself.

This is why the essay's anti-Jewish rhetoric is so important. On the one hand, Lessing clearly intends to portray Judaism in a positive light, defending Judaism as a necessary predecessor to Christianity, as a developmentally early stage of Christianity. And of course, historically, this is the case: Jesus was a Jew, and Christianity is an outgrowth of Judaism. On the other hand, Lessing clearly criticizes the Jews in his rhetoric throughout the essay. To be sure, from a Protestant theological perspective Lessing *must* criticize the Jews. To justify the later stages of this religion—the religion of reason, as well as the prevailing state religion of the time—Lessing *must* explain why Judaism, in this view, is superseded by Christianity. Lessing arguably softens his critique of Judaism by casting present-day Christians as likewise immature: the new Gospel of Reason is still to come. Yet there is no sense in which the essay should be read *only* as a critique of present-day Christianity, no sense in which Lessing uses the Jews *only* as a cipher for his critique of present-day Christians.[15] Both the form and the rhetoric of Lessing's essay belie the real object of his critique. Structurally, the bulk of the essay—almost half of the one hundred paragraphs—addresses the Jews as a crude, raw, wild, people clumsily incapable of abstract thought who are themselves to blame for their own ignorance, as children at an imma-ture developmental stage that must be superseded. Fewer than twenty para-graphs are addressed to the present-day Christians, who have yet to develop into mature adult practitioners of Lessing's new Gospel of Reason. Nowhere does Lessing characterize present-day Christians as "crude," "raw," "wild," "clumsy," or "guilty," as he does the Jews. Importantly, the essay contains no rec-ognition of present-day Jews as practicing a reasonable or defensible religion.[16] Unsurprisingly, Lessing's close friend and collaborator Moses Mendelssohn, the great German Jewish Enlightenment philosopher famous for his piercing intellect, blasted Lessing for basing his entire argument on an invalid meta-phor: the human race does not undergo a phylogenetic maturation process through religious stages of development as a baby progresses from childhood through adolescence to adulthood.[17] The motivation for Mendelssohn's cri-tique is clear. There is no place for "grown-up Jews" in Lessing's new Gospel of Reason: "adult" Jews must become Christian. Despite his pro-Jewish intentions, in *The Education of the Human Race* Lessing scripts Enlightenment in its highest form, the new "Gospel of Reason," as anti-Jewish.

A similar dialectic informs *The Jews* of 1749, a comedy (*Lustspiel*) Lessing identi-fied in the preface to the 1754 edition of his works as a serious reflection on the disgraceful repression of the Jewish people, intended to give its Christian audience pause. Irony figures prominently in the play's design: Lessing states that he tried to show virtue on the stage where the audience never would have suspected it, in the figure of the Jew.[18] Yet ironically, and perhaps intentionally, Lessing's Enlightenment defense of the Jews simultaneously contains a veiled but devastating critique of the Jews. Significantly, both form and content of the play turn back on themselves and question their own basic premises; in true Enlightenment fashion, the play stages a self-reflexive critique. On the for-mal level, the level of genre, Lessing's experimental *Lustspiel* defies the then-current comedic convention of making a mockery of its title figure(s).[19] The play likewise defies comedic convention in that it does not end with the requi-site marriage, thereby challenging the entire genre of comedy, itself included, with its lack of a clear resolution. This self-reflexive critique—the challenge to comedic conventions and the lack of a clear resolution—also is evident in the play's content. In short, in both form and content, the text programmatically and self-consciously calls its surface pro-Jewish stance into question.

The Jews picks up on two interrelated social issues current at the time of the play's writing concerning the moral character and the physical identity of Jews in Germany. The first was the popular belief, reflected in published pamphlets and police reports, that Jewish swindlers and bands of Jewish robbers were ter-rorizing the mainstream Christian population, at times shaving their beards and otherwise disguising themselves so as not to be recognized as Jews. There are also records of Christian thieves disguising themselves as Jews. To be sure, there were isolated crimes that had Jewish perpetrators, yet these single cases grew in the public's eyes to a general characterization about the Jews as a peo-ple.[20] According to this line of thinking, a dangerous—and at times disguised or hidden—Jewish element threatened Christian society.

A cognate concern for marking the Jew as "Jew"—for outing the disguised or otherwise unrecognizable, and hence dangerous, Jew in Christian soci-ety—is at stake in the second sociohistorical event motivating Lessing's play. In August 1748 Frederick the Great of Prussia issued a decree prohibiting Jews from shaving their beards completely, precisely so that they would be readily identifiable as Jews. The decree opens with a statement that numerous investigations (*Inquisitionen*) have shown that most robberies are either committed or organized by Jews; that Jews are shaving their beards "in order not to pass as Jews" and then slinking into houses and carrying out their plans with great success; that accordingly the King hereby orders Jews not to shave their beards completely, so that they can be identified as Jews.[21] (Frederick the Great, noted in historical annals for his tolerance toward religious minorities, harbored a pronounced animosity toward the Jews. In eighteenth-century Prussia some Jewish men, in an effort to acculturate into the mainstream population, had started to shave their traditional beards. Fear of the unmarked Jew "passing" in Christian society no doubt prompted Frederick's legislation.)[22] Lessing's *The Jews*, first published in 1754 but prominently dated in its subtitle as having been completed in 1749, arguably references the 1748 beard decree. The play's plot, set in motion by "Jew-beard" disguises, clearly addresses the public's fears about bands of Jewish criminals terrorizing the Christian population, and its central theme resonates strongly with the unspoken fears motivating the 1748 beard decree: how to recognize the Jew, to read the Jew, to identify the unmarked Jew in German society.

The play's pedestrian plot revolves around a good-hearted, upright, clean-shaven traveler who saves a baron from two murderous robbers wearing "Jew-beard" disguises. The robbers in fact are not Jews, but the baron's own servants. The good-hearted traveler discovers their true identity when one of the servants stupidly dumps the "Jew-beard" disguises out of his bag. The traveler warns the baron that his servants have turned against him and intend to kill him. As a reward, the baron wants to give the good man his daughter's hand in marriage. But the good-hearted traveler must decline, since he himself, it turns out, is a Jew.

On its most basic plot level, then, the play is about the discovery and exposure of Jewish identity. Now, the good-hearted clean-shaven traveler's Jewish identity and the beard-clad murderous robbers' non-Jewish identity are clearly evident from the start of the play. In the first lines of the play Martin Krumm and Michel Stich are introduced into the play as the "dumb" robbers whose plot has failed. Their "speaking names," *Krumm* (Crooked) and *Stich* (Stab), draw attention to their criminal nature, and alert the play's readers and viewers to focus on names in this text. In the second scene the "Jewish" robber Krumm condemns the Jews as a godless, murderous people, as deceivers, thieves, and highway robbers who deserve to be poisoned en masse, clearly identifying himself as a non-Jew. Conversely, the good-hearted traveler's protestation of this characterization strongly suggests he is a Jew. The traveler exclaims that he simply cannot understand how Jews possibly can be making the streets unsafe, since there are so few Jews allowed (*geduldet*, or tolerated) in Germany

(2:452).[23] When Krumm warns the traveler to protect himself against the Jews more vigilantly than against the plague, thereby rhetorically linking the Jews *to* the plague, the traveler remarks that he wishes this were only the voice of commoners speaking. Lest there be any doubt that the traveler is a Jew at this early point in the play, Lessing heavy-handedly reinforces this identification in the next scenes of the text. The traveler's Enlightenment defense of the Jews in the third scene, and his impassioned reaction to the slew of anti-Jewish comments the baron makes in the sixth scene, unequivocally identify the traveler as a Jew. In the third scene, immediately following the robber's comments that the Jews are a godless, thieving people, the traveler protests that when Jews are deceivers, most of the time it is because Christians have driven them to such behavior, and Christians then wonder that Jews react badly when they have been treated badly. If the two peoples are to treat each other with respect and trust, the traveler continues, both parties must act accordingly. But what if one religion considers the persecution of the other to be virtually a calling (*ein verdienstliches Werk*), the traveler muses, and then breaks off his comments (3:454). With his strong condemnation of "Christian" behavior that is not Christian, as well as his critique of Christian behavior that *is* Christian, the traveler again implicitly identifies himself as a Jew. In the sixth scene the identification is overt. The traveler, crestfallen when the baron exclaims that the Jews are the most malicious, despicable people of all, conspicuously averts his face when the baron states that the Jews' negative character is said to be evident in their physiognomy.[24] At this early point in the text the good-hearted traveler is definitively marked as a Jew, and the bulk of the play works to reinforce his virtuous nature. The play's conclusion, in which the traveler reveals his Jewish identity, may come as a surprise to the other characters, but it comes as no surprise to the text's attentive readers.[25]

The most obvious way to interpret this play about the discovery and exposure of Jewish identity, then, is as a sledgehammer approach to combating anti-Semitic stereotypes: the murderous, deceiving Christian robbers are the "Jews" in this text, and the real Jew in the text, the traveler, is a good-hearted person. According to this reading, *The Jews* is a play that challenges stock anti-Semitic stereotypes and portrays real Jews as virtuous, good people. The deep-rooted prejudice Lessing was attempting to combat is evident in one of the few reviews the play received when it was first published in 1754. The Protestant theologian Johann David Michaelis attacked *The Jews* on the grounds that it presented the entirely improbable characterization of a Jew who was completely good, completely noble, completely concerned for the well-being of others: even a middling virtue and probity are exceedingly rare among Jews, Michaelis argued. Lessing countered this critique by publishing an indignant anonymous letter, authored by Moses Mendelssohn, responding to Michaelis's attack.[26] Lessing clearly had cause to want to educate people about the nature of prejudice, and explicitly set out to portray a virtuous Jew in his play. The play is called *The Jews*, it would seem, precisely to underscore that it is a play about characterizing the Jews as a good people.

Strikingly, however, there is only one real Jew identified as such in this text, a Jew who says he is no fan of general characterizations like "Jews are thieves," or "Jews are good people" (6:461). Given that this a play about the discovery and exposure of Jewish identity, the very fact that the good-hearted traveler's Jewish identity is evident from the start suggests that the point of the play is not merely to combat anti-Semitism and to characterize the Jews as good people. This we know from the opening scenes; so what is the play really about? The play's title in its plural form, *The Jews*, suggests another possible reading: there is another Jewish identity, a hidden Jew, to be discovered and exposed in this text.[27] And in fact the Jew's servant—named, ironically, *Christ*oph—is subtly but repeatedly characterized as being, very possibly, a Jew. The very possibility of this concealed Jewish identity profoundly problematizes the play's surface pro-Jewish and anti-anti-Semitic messages.

Christoph's "speaking name" marks him as a Christian, yet the text is almost overdetermined in calling this Christian identity into question. Christoph is introduced into the play as a character not in his place, as a character found nowhere and everywhere (4:455).[28] He is repeatedly asked about his employer's identity, but the question put to him—"Wer mein Herr ist?" (14:473; Who my master is? / Who my Lord is?)—obliquely asks after Christoph's own religious identity. Significantly, Christoph is characterized as an accomplished, smooth schemer who invents stories and lies to get what he wants—material goods and a woman. Christoph protests bitterly—perhaps too bitterly—when he discovers that he, "an honest Christian," (22:487) has been serving a Jew, the good-hearted traveler. Since the play has established Christoph as anything but an honest Christian, his ensuing harangue against the traveler is suspect. Proclaiming that the Jew has insulted all of Christendom by taking a Christian into his service, and that this is why he had not understood why the traveler did not want to eat pork and did "a hundred" other "silly things" (22:487; *Alfanzereien*), a noun that derives from "Alfanz," a foreign rogue or deceiver,[29] Christoph threatens the traveler with legal action.

This scene subtly illustrates *in nuce* the point of the entire play. Christoph's comment about why he did not understand the Jew's avoidance of pork and his "foolish" behavior does much more than simply mock the traveler's religious practices. Christoph in fact suggests the traveler duped him into not recognizing the signs of Jewishness in his character. This accusation—that the Jew was passing unmarked and had injured all of Christendom by his deceptive actions—resonates with the sociohistorical context motivating the play: the widespread belief that a "hidden" criminal Jewish element threatened Christian society to its very core, and Frederick the Great's beard edict designed to distinguish Jews from Christians. In short, Christoph's rant against the traveler underscores that this is a text about learning to "read" the Jew, the Jew passing unmarked in Christian society. Ironically, of course, the text has *marked* the good-hearted traveler as a Jew from the start. At the same time, Christoph is typecast in the role of "the Jew." This is why it is significant that Christoph, marked by name but not by behavior as Christian, begins his rant with the words: "But now I return from my astonishment back to myself again!" (22:487; Nun komme ich erst von meinem Erstaunen wieder zu mir selber!). Again the text suggests we should read self-reflexively, that we too should return to Christoph again.

As if to underscore the fundamental question surrounding Christoph's identity, the traveler responds to Christoph's harangue in a predictably good-hearted manner, yet intimates that Christoph himself has a shady background. Noting the wretched circumstances from which he had saved Christoph in Hamburg, the traveler dismisses Christoph from his service and gives him his coveted silver tobacco can. In a dramatic volte-face Christoph then praises the traveler's generosity, remarking, "It seems there are also Jews who aren't Jews" (22; Es gibt doch wohl auch Juden, die keine Juden sind).[30] Christoph's words can be interpreted two ways. First, the good-hearted traveler isn't a "Jew" because he would willingly give away the valuable silver tobacco can—something a "Jew" never would do—and the traveler is hence a good person.[31] This reading is substantiated by Christoph's subsequent remark that a Christian, in contrast, would have kicked him in the ribs, and by the baron's ensuing exclamation that all Jews would be worthy of respect if only they were like the traveler. The traveler's rejoinder that all Christians likewise would be worthy of love if they had the baron's traits would seem to suggest that *The Jews* is a simple morality play: not all Jews are bad; not all Christians are good. According to this reading the play ends where it began, with an attack on common prejudices, with a plea for universalism.

Yet Lessing is an author known for nuance and irony, and the very fact that Christoph is the character marked by name as Christian perforce draws attention to his religious identity, especially in a play titled *The Jews*, a play about the discovery and exposure of Jewish identity. Importantly, there is a second way to interpret Christoph's remark that "it seems there are also Jews who aren't Jews" (Es gibt doch wohl auch Juden, die keine Juden sind): there are in fact Jews who are not identified as Jews. The conclusion of the play supports this latter reading. In the final scene, which immediately follows Christoph's comment about Jews who aren't Jews, the servant woman Lisette pointedly asks Christoph a question laden with innuendo: "Are you perhaps also a Jew? You're constantly misrepresenting yourself / you're constantly putting yourself in the wrong place!" (23:488; Ist Er wohl gar auch ein Jude, so sehr Er sich verstellt?). Christoph laughs off Lisette's question with a flip retort; this is too curious a question for a maiden to be asking—that is, a virtuous woman should not be asking him whether he is circumcised. The play ends on a comic note, but Lisette's question—"Are you perhaps also a Jew?"—hangs, unanswered, over the play's resolution.

Subtly, but significantly, in the very last lines of the play Christoph references that ultimate "hidden" sign of the Jew—circumcision—the sign the Jews take as the mark of the covenant between God and the Jews, "the supreme obligatory sign of loyalty and adherence to Judaism."[32] Of course this is no proof that Christoph *is* circumcised, and even if he were circumcised, this would not prove that he is a Jew. The point is rather this: the text underscores the *possibility* that Christoph is perhaps also a Jew. And the very possibility that Christoph, the slippery operator who lies and misrepresents himself to get what he wants—material goods and a woman—is indeed perhaps also a Jew severely compromises the play's surface pro-Jewish message. While the good-hearted Jewish traveler is a virtuous person, Christoph is the stereotypical "Jew" who poses as a Christian but in fact may be a Jew. The implications of this conclusion extend far beyond a simple statement of the play's universalist theme that there are good Christians and bad Christians, good Jews and bad Jews. In scripting Christoph as very possibly a hidden Jew who displays stereotypical "Jewish" traits, Lessing reinforces popular anti-Semitic suspicions about a concealed, dangerous Jewish element that threatens mainstream Christian German society—precisely the threat addressed by Frederick the Great's 1748 beard decree. No wonder, then, that the good-hearted Jewish traveler's library consists of comedies that move one to tears and tragedies that make one laugh (10:467; besteht aus Lustspielen, die zum Weinen, aus Trauerspielen, die zum Lachen bewegen). Again the play marks itself with a self-reflexive gesture. Lessing's pro-Jewish comedy *The Jews*—the comedy that is not really a comedy because it programmatically does not end with the requisite marriage and because it would not seem to mock its title figures—Lessing's pro-Jewish comedy that is not really pro-Jewish and does mock one of its title figures, this too is a comedy that moves one to tears.

The pro-Jewish tolerance message of Lessing's great masterpiece *Nathan the Wise* likewise programmatically calls itself into question, but here the text's self-reflexive Enlightenment critique is much more subtle and much more refined than in *The Jews* or *The Education of the Human Race*. Here, as in the earlier pieces, both form and content underscore the text's self-reflexive criticism, its constantly calling itself into question in true Enlightenment fashion. On the formal level, Lessing identifies the play as a "dramatic poem." This innovative genre aims to call traditional categories into question: it breaks down established boundaries and fuses together disparate genres or categories, ironically creating a new norm, a new standard, a new genre. This aesthetic program is reflected in the play's content. The plot aims to break down established boundaries between the three great monotheistic religions—Judaism, Christianity, and Islam—and to create a new Enlightened Gospel of Reason, as it were.

Set in the holy city of Jerusalem in the twelfth century during a pause in fighting in the Third Crusade, the play revolves around a wise Jewish merchant Nathan, who is cast as *the* Enlightenment figure in the text. One day Nathan returns home from a business trip to find that his house has burned down and that his adoptive daughter Recha has been rescued from the flames by a Christian crusader, the Templar. Predictably, Recha and the Templar fall in love, although the Templar tries to resist the burning desire he feels for Recha, since he assumes—incorrectly—that she is Jewish. Fortuitously, the Templar's own life has been spared by the Sultan Saladin because the Templar looks like Saladin's brother. Following some convoluted plot twists, Recha and the Templar improbably turn out to be brother and sister, niece and nephew to the Sultan Saladin. The play ends with the construction of a natural family that conjoins Christian, Muslim, and Jew: the play ends with the construction of an Enlightened Gospel of Reason in which Christian, Muslim, and Jew are united in one big happy family.

Like *The Education of the Human Race, Nathan the Wise* stages a critique of both Judaism and Christianity as it labors to construct this Enlightened Gospel of Reason. (Islam is bracketed from this self-reflexive critique, presumably because there were very few Muslims in Lessing's target audience in eighteenth-century Germany.) The Jews are criticized for being the first to maintain that they are "the chosen people," the first to maintain that their God is "the right God," and for passing on this false pride to their heirs, the Christians and Muslims (2.5:532).[33] The Christians—Daja, the Templar, and especially the Patriarch of Jerusalem—are taken to task for their belief in being "Christian" at the expense of all else, a belief that frequently leads them to act in an un-Christian, inhuman way. The most extreme example of this inhuman "Christian" behavior is the Patriarch's repeated insistence that Nathan (or, more precisely, "the Jew") should be burned at the stake for raising a Christian girl. This self-reflexive critique of Christianity and Judaism would seem to culminate in act 4 when the Lay Brother (*der Klosterbruder*)—who *is* a good Christian—exclaims that Nathan is Christian, that there never was a better Christian, and Nathan replies that precisely those traits that make him a good Christian make the Lay Brother a good Jew (4.7:597). With this statement the border between Christianity and Judaism is broken down, paving the way for the play's conclusion, the construction of an Enlightened Gospel of Reason in which Christian, Jew, and Muslim are united in one big happy family.

Unsettlingly, however, the staying power of this universalist vision is called into question from the start of the text. The play is set in a pause in fighting during the Third Crusade: Lessing's eighteenth-century audience knows that the religious wars will continue, that this happy end will not last. The play begins with Nathan the Wise, Nathan the Jew, agreeing with his Christian servant Daja that the harmonious conjoining of Jew, Christian, and Muslim is a "sweet illusion" or "sweet delusion" (ein süßer Wahn) that is sweet to him too, but at the same time, Nathan argues that sweet delusions must make way for "sweeter truth" (1.1:490). With this statement, the text underscores its self-reflexive, self-critical, realist agenda. And indeed, the plot's neat resolution is programmatically called into question by a number of troubling details that threaten to undermine the text's central Enlightenment tolerance message.

First, the natural family constructed in the last scene of the play faces a profound Freudian challenge: incest. Throughout the text both Recha and the Templar have been "burning" for each other; now they discover they are brother and sister. On hearing the news of their sibling relationship, Recha seemingly transforms her ardent passion for the Templar into familial love, saying "my brother? . . . Oh! my brother!" and moves toward him, while the Templar says "I? her brother? . . . her brother?" and steps away. Giving voice to the true nature of the burning desire she and the Templar both still feel for each other, Recha then exclaims: "This cannot be! This cannot be! His heart / knows nothing of this!—We're deceivers! God!" (5.8:625). Needless to say, this smoldering sexuality does not bode well for the future of this natural family.

The "blood" problematic also threatens the play's Enlightenment resolution on a second level—that of religion. Throughout the play Nathan has been worried that Recha will disown him because he has not told her she is adopted and has not told her she is Christian. But Recha repeatedly insists that "blood" does not define families: Nathan is her father because he has raised her, not because of biological circumstances. Ironically, however, "blood" does define the natural family constructed at the end of the drama. The play's happy end depends precisely on genealogy, on bloodlines. As if to underscore the fact that the play's resolution is grounded in blood, the Templar exclaims to the Sultan in the play's penultimate lines: "I am of your blood!" (5.8:627; Ich deines Bluts!). Given that the play aims at the construction of a natural family that conjoins the three great monotheistic religions in one big happy family, it is significant that Nathan—the Jew—is not related by blood to any of the other characters.[34] At the end of the play, "Nathan der *Weise*"—Nathan the Wise—becomes "Nathan die *Waise*"—Nathan the orphan.

The Jew's problematic status in this Enlightenment family is further accentuated in the so-called Ring Parable, which forms the structural and thematic core of the text. Here, too, "blood" is the driving force that motivates the text's central religious disquisition. Saladin, in dire financial straits, summons Nathan, but rather than asking the Jew for money, decides to trick him by posing a probing religious question. Only one of the three religions—Judaism, Christianity, and Islam—can be the true religion, and a wise man like Nathan would not stay where the accident of birth, of blood, had thrown him; if he does stay, it must be because of insight, principles, choice of "the better," Saladin asks, so how does Nathan justify his faith? Nathan hesitates before answering, aware that Saladin wants money and is trying to trick him, to "Jew" him: "Who's the Jew here," Nathan asks, "me or him?" (3.6:554; Wer ist denn hier der Jude? / Ich oder er?). The suspicion that the potentate Saladin may be using "truth" as a trap, Nathan reasons, forces him to proceed cautiously in answering the question.

(It is worth noting parenthetically that Nathan is faced here with the same dilemma that tormented his real-life model Moses Mendelssohn, who in 1769 was challenged by the Swiss clergyman Johann Caspar Lavater to defend his Judaism publicly or convert to Christianity.[35] Given the dangers inherent in offending the ruling authorities and the mainstream population, the Jew clearly must proceed cautiously in defending his faith. Likewise, in Lessing's source for the Ring Parable, Boccaccio's *Decameron*, the Jew Melchisedech, by recounting the Tale of the Three Rings to the Sultan Saladin, prevents a great danger that had been prepared for him. It is also worth noting that in Lessing's play, Saladin is correct that Nathan has *chosen* to retain his Judaism: following the murder of his wife and seven sons by Christians, Nathan, at wit's end in a Job-like state of despair, had questioned God and vowed irreconcilable hatred toward all Christians, but then reason returned, and with it his equanimity and his faith in God [4.7:596–97].)

Nathan, by birth and by choice a Jew, is now forced to justify his religion. Aware that Saladin may be trying to trick him, he then considers what kind of Jew he should present himself as, and concludes he should answer Saladin's "Jewing" with "Jewing." Nathan decides to "fob off" a fairy tale on Saladin in lieu of an answer, thereby opting to present himself as an upright Jew who nonetheless engages in stereotypical crafty "Jewish" behavior, deception:

> Being a Jew through and through, won't work. –
> And not being a Jew at all is even worse.
> Since—if not a Jew, he might ask,
> Why not a Muslim?—That's it! That can
> Save me!—It's not just children to whom one feeds
> fairy tales [one fobs off fairy tales on].

>   (So ganz
> Stockjude sein zu wollen, geht schon nicht. –
> Und ganz und gar nicht Jude, geht noch minder.
> Denn, wenn kein Jude, dürft' er mich fragen,
> Warum kein Muselmann?—Das war's! Das kann
> Mich retten!—Nicht die Kinder bloß, speist man
> Mit Märchen ab.) (3.5:554)

Nathan identifies his story as both a *Märchen*—a "fairy tale"—and *a Geschichtchen*—a "little story" or a "little history," a history in miniature that he wishes to tell Saladin *before* he answers his question in complete trust, in complete confidence (3.7:555). Nonetheless, scholars and readers almost uniformly interpret Nathan's tale as *the* answer to Saladin's question, an answer that takes the form of a parable illustrating the equal truth value of the three great monotheistic religions.[36] Certainly there is a great deal of validity to this standard interpretation. Read from a different perspective, however, Nathan's tale tells a very different story: Nathan the Jew in fact defends Judaism as the originary religion.

Structurally, the ring tale is divided into two distinct parts. In the first, Nathan tells of a ring with magic powers that makes its bearer beloved in the eyes of God and his fellow men. The ring is passed on from one generation to the next, from father to son, until one day a father cannot decide which of his three beloved sons should receive the ring. In "pious weakness" he promises each son his ring (3.7:556). On his deathbed, "in embarrassment" (3.7:556), the father devises an aesthetic solution to his problem. He has an artist make two copies of the ring, gives each of his sons a ring, and dies. Now there are three rings, an original ring and two artistic reproductions indistinguishable from the original. If the rings do indeed represent the three great monotheistic religions in this little historical story (*Geschichtchen*), the original would represent Judaism; the reproductions, Christianity and Islam. (Historically, Christianity and Islam are derived from Judaism; elsewhere in the play, Lessing pointedly underscores this genealogy by having the good Christian Lay Brother exclaim emphatically that all of Christianity builds on Judaism, and that Jesus was a Jew [4.7:595], and by having the Templar identify Christianity and Islam as Judaism's heirs [2.5:532].) According to Nathan's tale, the original "Jewish" ring still exists (or perhaps has been lost—but not destroyed), and this indistinguishable "Jewish" ring threatens the integrity of Christian and Islamic societies by virtue of the fact that *is* the original. As Nathan puts it: "The true ring was not / Demonstrable; (*Nathan pauses, waiting for Saladin's answer*) Almost as indemonstrable as / The true religion is to us now. (3.7:557; Der rechte Ring war nicht / Erweislich; [*nach einer Pause, in welcher er des Sultans Antwort erwartet*] *Fast* so unerweislich, als / Uns itzt der rechte Glaube. Emphasis mine.) The stage directions dictating Nathan's dramatic pause emphasize the enormity of the conclusion he is about to draw: the adverb "almost" (*fast*) suggests that the true faith—presumably Judaism—is indeed distinguishable to us today. And at this point, Nathan notes, his story is over (3.7:557).

Nathan, criticized at the start of the scene for being repeatedly "so proudly modest" (3.7:555), carefully does not draw any conclusion from his little historical story. He humbly asserts that the story is not meant as an answer to Saladin's question about the single true religion; it is only meant to excuse him if he does not feel he can distinguish what the father intentionally designed to be indistinguishable. Saladin, taken aback, responds that there are distinct differences among the religions. Nathan replies that the differences are discernible only in the religions' practices, not in their foundations, since each religion is grounded in history, be it written or oral, and history must be accepted on the basis of loyalty and faith. And are we not least likely to question the word of the father, whose blood we share, Nathan asks, are we not least likely to question the father who tests our love, the father who never deceives us except when deception is more healing than truth? (3.7:557–58). The irony here is profound. Nathan has just related a story in which the father—"in pious weakness" and "in embarrassment," but with every good intention—deceives his sons, calling "each especially" to him, giving each son a ring and giving "each especially" his blessing (3.7:557). If this deception is more healing than truth, as Nathan suggests, then truth itself has been jeopardized in the father's well-intentioned act. In short, in Nathan's story, there *is* reason to doubt the word of the father, to question the history that grounds each son's faith. (In a doubly ironic gesture, the status of "the father" is repeatedly called into question in the main body of the play—in Nathan's standing as Recha's father, in the crucial question of the Templar's paternity, and in the distressingly bigoted Patriarch of Jerusalem. The issue of literary paternity—of Lessing's indebtedness to Boccaccio—comes into play on the metatextual level here, as well.)

The question of historical legitimacy, of testing the word of the father, forms the core of the second part of Nathan's tale. Following the death of the father, Nathan relates, all three sons claim to have the true ring, given by the father. Predictably, the sons begin to fight. They go to a judge, who states that the value of each ring is to be proven by the behavior of its bearer. If none of the rings works with its original intent, then all three sons have been deceived: presumably the real ring was lost, and the father made three copies to hide the loss of the original. But, the judge continues, if each son believes he has received the original ring from his father, each should strive to prove its validity through his behavior, and in a thousand years a wiser judge than he might be able to identify the true ring. This suggests, of course, that the adherents of each faith must prove their religion's worth through their actions. If all three rings can prove their worth, the judge continues, perhaps the father no longer wished to tolerate the "tyranny" of a single ring in his own house. This pragmatic proof would surely establish the practical validity of all three rings, of all three religions, but it cannot change the fact that there *is* an original ring in Nathan's historical account—a ring that might be identified in a thousand years. And the existence of this original Jewish ring constitutes a challenge to the other two religions. This is why Nathan is left out of the natural family constructed at the end of the play. The Jew, by virtue of his originary status, represents a threat to the integrity of Christian and

Muslim societies, and hence is excluded from the natural family's bloodline at the drama's conclusion.

As if to confirm this reading, the ring tale ends with a subtle anti-Jewish gesture presented in an entirely positive light. Nathan, aware that Saladin's real motivation in asking him to justify his faith is financial, offers the Sultan money. His magnanimous gesture notwithstanding, the truth of Nathan's tale is thus "Judaized" by that quintessential "Jewish" trait: money. Nathan's ring tale is framed by money: it is introduced by money; it concludes with money; it is grounded in money. "As if truth were a coin," Nathan says in introducing his tale (3.6:554).[37] And indeed, truth *is* a coin in the ring tale, an object presented as having truth value, as having exchange value, when in fact it has none: the tale is presented in lieu of an answer.

The truth of Nathan's tale is Judaized on a second level as well. The tale—introduced as an excuse not to tell the truth, as a deception—tells a "Jewish" truth that is, ironically, the truth of the Jew. The smart Jew Nathan uses stock anti-Semitic stereotypes, craftiness and subterfuge, to defend his own Judaism as the originary religion. And it is precisely this defense of Judaism—the Jews' insistence that they are "the chosen people"—for which the Jews are criticized in the text. It is no accident that Nathan is introduced into the play, in a structurally prominent position in the last lines of act 1, scene 1 as being "so good, and at the same time so bad!" (1.1:490; Ihr seid so gut, und seid zugleich so schlimm!). For all his wisdom, for all his goodness, Nathan remains "the Jew"—with all its stereotypical associations—at the end of the play. In true Enlightenment fashion, *Nathan the Wise*, like *The Education of the Human Race* and *The Jews*, turns back on itself and calls its own pro-Jewish message into question.

This self-reflexive gesture is entirely in keeping with the spirit of Enlightenment criticism, and I do not believe that either Lessing or his writings should be characterized as anti-Semitic. In comparison to the unambiguous anti-Semitism evident elsewhere in Enlightenment letters—Kant's call for the euthanasia of Judaism, Voltaire's attack on the Jews as a barbarous, contemptible people who nonetheless should not be burned, or Fichte's proposal to decapitate the Jews and replace their Jewish heads with Christian ones, to cite but a few famous examples—Lessing clearly intends to promote a pro-Jewish Enlightenment tolerance agenda. It is also the case, I believe, that we simply cannot read Lessing's writings on Jews and Judaism as they were read in the eighteenth century. Our post-Holocaust eyes perforce read the anti-Jewish moments in these texts more critically, and perhaps with an ineluctable implied teleology. Still, these anti-Jewish moments in Lessing's writings must be read, and not simply read over or excused away as not existing. This is precisely the point of the three close readings I have offered here: to demonstrate a structural homology that *must* be accounted for in any study of "Lessing and the Jews." At the limits of his Enlightenment discourse, Lessing's pro-Jewish writings turn back on themselves programmatically and self-critically. Whether Lessing *intentionally* wrote this critique into his texts—as I have proposed— ultimately is a matter of little consequence. Intentional or not, the anti-Jewish moments in these texts constitute an important juncture in the history of the formation of the rhetoric of anti-Semitism.

This essay has exposed systematic blind spots on which our critical understanding of the pro-Jewish author and activist Lessing has been predicated for over two hundred years. It has opened up new dimensions of three foundational works by paying close attention to their language and structure, by pausing to consider troubling features of these works that do not fit neatly into the image of the "pro-Jewish Lessing" that has been the unassailable basis of most scholarship to date. The methodological framework used here has focused instead on structural tensions inherent in Lessing's writing, thereby allowing formative, and heretofore unnoticed, aspects of these texts to come into view. Reading synthetically across these texts, this essay has argued for a new way of analyzing Lessing's discursive construction of "the Jew" in its complexity. In so doing, it has presented a fundamental reevaluation of Lessing's writings on Jews and Judaism. Situating these works within the context of Lessing's entire oeuvre, an oeuvre *defined* by criticism, by a constant calling into question, the preceding analysis has unraveled the myth of the staunchly pro-Jewish Lessing, not so much to discredit it, but rather to complicate it, as Lessing's texts themselves programmatically do. These results are important not only for our critical understanding of Lessing per se, but also because the tensions inherent in Lessing's writings on Jews and Judaism lay the groundwork for, and to some extent inform, the discursive construction of Jewishness in subsequent German letters.

Notes

1. Martha B. Helfer, *The Word Unheard: Legacies of Anti-Semitism in German Literature and Culture* (Evanston, IL: Northwestern University Press, 2011). We are grateful to Northwestern University Press for permission to reprint the essay.
2. In 1753, in the wake of edicts of emancipation in Holland and England, a pamphlet published anonymously in Berlin, "Letter from a Jew to a Philosopher, Together with the Response" (Schreiben eines Juden an einen Philosophen nebst der Antwort), called for the complete equality of the Jews in Germany. The text very likely was authored by Aaron Salomon Gumpertz, possibly with Lessing's encouragement; Lessing may well have been directly involved in its publication. Lessing reviewed the piece very shortly after it appeared in the *Berliner privilegirte Zeitung*, the leading newspaper in Berlin. See Gad

Freudenthal, "Aaron Salomon Gumpertz, Gotthold Ephraim Lessing, and the First Call for an Improvement of the Civil Rights of Jews in Germany," *Association of Jewish Studies Review* 29, no. 2 (2005): 299–353.

3. For readings of *Nathan the Wise* against *The Merchant of Venice*, see Gunnar Och, *Imago judaica Juden und Judentum im Spiegel der deutschen Literatur 1750–1812* (Würzburg: Königshausen & Neumann, 1995), 159–62; and Klaus L. Berghahn, *Grenzen der Toleranz: Juden und Christen im Zeitalter der Aufklärung* (Cologne: Böhlau, 2000), 102–26.

4. Barbara Fischer and Thomas C. Fox, "Lessing's Life and Work," in *A Companion to the Works of Gotthold Ephraim Lessing*, ed. Barbara Fischer and Thomas C. Fox (Rochester, NY: Camden House, 2005), 33. Writing in 1940, Elisabeth Frenzel explained why a production of *Nathan* was simply not possible now: the play was "understood and exploited as philo-Semitic" (quoted in Berghahn, *Grenzen*, 126). As Berghahn notes, Frenzel's scholarship, with its pronounced anti-Semitism, is a prime example of Nazi *Germanistik*. This is the same Elisabeth Frenzel who co-authored one of the standard reference works used in *Germanistik* up through the present, *Daten deutscher Dichtung*. See Herbert A. Frenzel and Elisabeth Frenzel, *Daten deutscher Dichtung. Chronologischer Abriß der deutschen Literaturgeschichte*, 2 vols., 22nd ed. (Munich: Deutscher Taschenbuch Verlag, 1985).

5. Some scholars have questioned whether "tolerance" should be the organizing principle of a study of "Lessing and the Jews" or German–Jewish interactions in the eighteenth century, arguing that this approach in effect misreads Lessing and does not account for the agency of Jews in the emancipation process. I use the term here precisely because of the strong reception of Lessing as a symbol of tolerance. The focus of my own analysis is not on tolerance per se, but on the discursive construction of the figure of the Jew in Lessing's texts. See Jonathan M. Hess, *Germans, Jews and the Claims of Modernity* (New Haven, CT: Yale University Press, 2002), 9–10 and 212n20; and Willi Goetschel, "Lessing and the Jews," in *A Companion to the Works of Gotthold Ephraim Lessing*, 200–201. For fine studies that take "tolerance" as their organizing principle, see Peter R. Erspamer, *The Elusiveness of Tolerance: The "Jewish Question" from Lessing to the Napoleonic Wars* (Chapel Hill: University of North Carolina Press, 1997), and Berghahn, *Grenzen der Toleranz*.

6. See Friedrich Schlegel, "Vom Wesen der Kritik" (1804): "Alles was Lessing getan, gebildet, versucht und gewollt hat, läßt sich am füglichsten unter den Begriff der Kritik zusammenfassen" ("Everything that Lessing did, formed, tried, and wanted is most appropriately summarized by the concept of criticism"). *Kritische Friedrich Schlegel Ausgabe*, vol. 3, *Charakteristiken und Kritiken II*, ed. Hans Eichner (Munich: Schöningh, 1975), 51.

7. Lessing famously makes this argument about truth in *Eine Duplik (A Rejoinder)*, stating that it is not truth, which every person possesses, or presumes to possess, but the sincere effort expended to get behind truth that determines a person's worth: "Nicht die Wahrheit, in deren Besitz irgendein Mensch ist, oder zu sein vermeinet, sondern die aufrichtige Mühe, die er angewandt hat, hinter die Wahrheit zu kommen, macht den Wert des Menschen." Throughout

this chapter, all Lessing citations will reference *Gotthold Ephraim Lessing: Werke und Briefe in zwölf Bänden,* ed. Wilfried Barner (Frankfurt am Main: Deutscher Klassiker Verlag, 1985–2001) as *Lessing: Werke.* Here, 8:61. The translations are my own.

8. The first half of the essay was written in 1776 and published in 1777; Nisbett suggests that Lessing may have written the second half in 1776 as well. The complete text was published for the first time in 1780, anonymously. Lessing's contemporaries and friends—Elise Reimarus, Moses Mendelssohn, Herder, and Friedrich Jacobi—had no doubt that Lessing was the author. Hugh Barr Nisbett, *Lessing: Eine Biographie,* trans. Karl S. Guthke (Munich: Beck, 2008), 746–47.

9. My assertion that Lessing writes from a Protestant theological perspective should of course be qualified by the fact that he very clearly is critical of Protestantism and promotes the development of a new religion of reason in this essay and elsewhere in his oeuvre. That Lessing considers this new religion of reason to be fundamentally Christian is suggested by the framework of his argument, by his rhetoric calling for "a new eternal gospel" ("das neue ewige Evangelium" [§86:96]), and by an earlier fragmentary essay entitled *The Christendom of Reason* (*Das Christentum der Vernnunft,* 1754). Lessing eschewed the label "theologian," arguing that he could not commit to one dogma: "I am a lover of theology," Lessing famously stated, "not a theologian." *Lessing: Werke,* 9:57. Parenthetical references are to *Die Erziehung des Menschengeschlechts,* in *Lessing: Werke,* 10:75–99. I have included the paragraph number, followed by the page number. The translations are my own.

10. For good discussions of the theological context of the essay, see Nisbett, *Lessing,* 745–63; and Arno Schilson, "Lessing and Theology," in *A Companion to the Works of Gotthold Ephraim Lessing,* 157–83.

11. The most famous of these inconsistencies is the contradiction between §4 and §77.

12. Lessing is not particularly original in advancing this model linking the history of religion to the history of human development. See also Nisbett, *Lessing,* 748.

13. Nisbett, *Lessing,* 757–58. Nisbett points out that Lessing's interest in the transmigration of souls was not especially unusual or eccentric in the last few decades of the eighteenth century.

14. Ibid., 752–53. Nisbett also notes the text's self-reflexivity here.

15. In an excellent and informative discussion Willi Goetschel analyzes Lessing's interest in Jews not simply as "a token of good will," but as playing a "crucial role in his critical rethinking of both the claims of Christianity and the groundwork of modern national identity." Goetschel reads Lessing as exposing a mechanism of prejudice independent of its object (i.e., the Jews), and argues that any analysis of the representation of the Jewish characters in Lessing must remain circular, since the Jewish characters "all point back to their origin as Christian constructions." Goetschel, "Lessing and the Jews," 186, 203. In his analysis of the early Lessing, Barner likewise suggests that Lessing's main motivation in depicting Jews is not primarily philo-Semitic, but a critique of the contemporary Christian majority, and that the Jews are representative of discriminated

minorities in general. Wilfried Barner, "Vorurteil, Emperie, Rettung. Der junge Lessing und die Juden," in *Juden und Judentum in der Literatur*, ed. Herbert A. Strauss and Christhard Hoffmann (Munich: Deutscher Taschenbuch Verlag, 1985), 64, 68.

16. Lessing presents a very different argument about the validity of Judaism as a contemporary religion in *Nathan the Wise* (1779), which was written after *The Education of the Human Race*. *The Education of the Human Race* was published in its entirety in 1780, after *Nathan* appeared.

17. The pertinent excerpt of Mendelssohn's critique, which appeared in *Jerusalem*, is reprinted in *Lessing: Werke*, 10:835–36.

18. The pertinent excerpt from the preface to the published edition of *The Jews* is reprinted in *Lessing: Werke*, 1:1152.

19. Before the play was published, Lessing's friend Naumann reported that Lessing was working on a text called *The Jew (Der Jude)*. It is unclear whether Lessing changed the title of the play to *The Jews (Die Juden)*, or whether Naumann erred in his report. *Lessing: Werke*, 1:1152.

20. Och, *Imago judaica*, 73–74.

21. A copy of the decree is reproduced in the article "Prussia," in *Encyclopedia Judaica*, vol. 13 (New York: Macmillan, 1978), 1291.

22. Goetschel offers a differing interpretation of the significance of the beard decree to Lessing's comedy, arguing that Lessing's play demonstrates the "absurdity" of this law and illustrates that this legislation undermines Frederick's aspirations to be an enlightened ruler. Goetschel, "Lessing and the Jews," 190. Horowitz notes that German Jews "had generally been more loyal to their beards than others in Western Europe." Elliott Horowitz, "The Early Eighteenth Century Confronts the Beard: Kabbalah and Jewish Self-Fashioning," *Jewish History* 8, no. 1–2 (1994): 109.

23. Parenthetical references are to *Die Juden*, in *Lessing: Werke*, 1:447–88. I have included scene number, followed by page number. The translations are my own.

24. In scene 16 the traveler—whose Jewish identity is as yet undisclosed to the other characters—returns to the physiognomy argument. Holding a "Jew beard" disguise to his chin, he asks whether he now looks like a Jew.

25. Most scholars read the text from the perspective of its characters and argue that the traveler's Jewish identity is not revealed until the end of the play. See, for example, Karl S. Guthke, "Lessing und das Judentum. Rezeption. Dramatik und Kritik. Krypto-Spinozismus," in *Judentum im Zeitalter der Aufklärung, Wolfenbütteler Studien zur Aufklärung*, vol. 4, ed. Günter Schulz (Wolfenbüttel: Jacobi, 1977), 244; Wilfried Barner, "Lessings *Die Juden* im Zusammenhang seines Frühwerks," in *Humanität und Dialog. Lessing und Mendelssohn in neuer Sicht*, ed. Ehrhard Bahr, Edward P. Harris, and Lawrence G. Lyon (Detroit, MI: Wayne State University Press, 1982), 199; Och, *Imago judaica*, 79; Berghahn, *Grenzen der Toleranz*, 71; Goetschel, "Lessing and the Jews," 190; and Nisbett, *Lessing*, 98.

26. Lessing's response is included in *Lessing: Werke* 1:489–97.

27. This argument is indebted in part to an analysis David Wellbery sketched out in a graduate seminar on Lessing at Stanford University on April 11, 1989.

28. The scene opens with the following exchange: "Der Reisende: 'Daß man Euch doch allezeit eine Stunde suchen muß, wenn man Euch haben will.' Christoph: 'Sie scherzen, mein Herr. Nicht wahr, ich kann nicht mehr, als an einem Ort zugleich sein? Ist es also meine Schuld, daß Sie sich nicht an diesen Ort begeben? Gewiß Sie finden mich allezeit da, wo ich bin'" ("The Traveler: 'I always have to look for you for an hour when I want you.' / Christoph: 'Surely you're joking, sir. Isn't it true that I can't be in more than one place at the same time? Is it my fault that you're not here? You'll certainly always find me where I am'" [4:455]).

29. *Alfanz*, "der aus der Fremde gekommene Schalk, Betrüger." Gerhard Wahrig, *Deutsches Wörterbuch* (Munich: Bertelsman, 1991), 316.

30. The 1754 version of the text does not contain this line; Lessing added it in the revised version of 1767 (second edition 1770). *Lessing: Werke*, 1:1151, 1163.

31. Robertson suggests "on a skeptical reading" that Christoph has "unwittingly blurted out the truth: Jews can be admitted to the society of Enlightenment if they are not Jews, that is, if they have no distinctively Jewish features." Ritchie Robertson, *The "Jewish Question" in German Literature, 1749–1939* (Oxford: Oxford University Press, 1999), 36.

32. "Circumcision," in *The Oxford Dictionary of the Jewish Religion*, ed. R. J. Zwi Werblowsky and Geoffrey Wigodor (New York: Oxford University Press, 1997), http://www.cirp.org/library/cultural/JewishEnc (accessed July 9, 2007).

33. Parenthetical references are to *Nathan der Weise*, in *Lessing: Werke*, 9:483–627. I have included act, scene, and page number. The translations are my own.

34. Other scholars have offered differing interpretations of the fact that Nathan is left out of the natural family constructed at the end of the play. To cite a few recent examples, Robertson argues that Nathan must earn his membership in a community of which the others are already members by merit of blood (Robertson, *The "Jewish Question,"* 45). Berghahn sees this as a "mistake" that draws attention to the dialectic of Enlightenment (Berghahn, *Grenzen*, 123). Garloff suggests that Nathan be viewed not as an outsider here, but as part of a longer historical chain established in the text. Katja Garloff, "Sublimation and Its Discontents: Christian-Jewish Love in Lessing's *Nathan der Weise*," *Lessing Yearbook / Jahrbuch* 36 (2004/2005): 63. Nisbett argues that Nathan is left out because Judiasm, unlike Christianity and Islam, constitutes not just a religious community, but also an ethnic one (Nisbett, *Lessing*, 805).

35. For a good discussion of the Lavatar affair, see Hess, *Germans, Jews and the Claims of Modernity*, 97–105.

36. Atkins is one notable exception, arguing that Nathan tells the parable as an evasive answer to Saladin's question. Stuart Atkins, "The Parable of the Rings in Lessing's *Nathan*," in *Germanic Review* 26, no. 4 (1951): 262. Robertson likewise maintains that Nathan "sidesteps" Saladin's question by telling the tale (Robertson, *The "Jewish Question,"* 42). See also Robert S. Leventhal, "The Parable as Performance: Interpretation, Cultural Transmission and Political Strategy in Lessing's *Nathan der Weise*," *German Quarterly* 61, no. 4 (1988): 507–8. Leventhal reads the parable itself as "in part a rhetorical device, a diversionary tactic" that functions to direct "the focus away from the question of the

one 'true' belief or religion" and to redirect "focus toward the question of the basis for any belief whatsoever." It is worth emphasizing that Nathan himself does not identify the story as a parable, but as a "Märchen," a "fairy tale," or a "Geschichtchen," a "little story" or "little history." This is significant, in that the genre designation to a large extent determines how the text itself should (and will) be read. For a recent interpretation of the ring tale that does analyze the text as a "Märchen," within the context of the theory of experiments in the eighteenth century, see Christine Weder, "Ein manipulierter Versuch: Das Märchen vom Experiment in Lessings *Nathan* und die naturwissenschaftliche Methodenlehre der 'durch Fleiß hervorgebrachten Erfahrung,'" *Deutsche Vierteljarhsschrift für Literaturwissenschaft und Geistesgeschichte* 2 (2008): 237–61.

37. Nathan draws a distinction here between "uralte Münze" and "neue Münze," intimating that coins from time immemorial may still have truth value, while modern coins do not. This distinction arguably is important from a religious point of view as well: the tale he is about to tell positions Judaism as the "uralte" religion, and then calls into question the significance of this originary status.

Chapter Six

Poetry, Music, and the Limits of Harmony

Mendelssohn's Aesthetic Critique of Christianity

Elias Sacks

Barely a week before his sudden death in January 1786, one of the most prominent Jewish figures in Sara Levy's world, the celebrated philosopher Moses Mendelssohn, offered the following thoughts in a letter to his non-Jewish friend Sophie Becker:

> You say that the philosopher does not pray, or at least not out loud, not with singing—but rather, at most, in thoughts. Dearest Sophie! If his hour comes and he is disposed toward prayer, then against his will he will break out into word and song. The most common person, it seems to me, does not sing so that God hears him and finds pleasure in his melodies. We sing for our own sake, and the wise man does this as easily as the fool. Have you ever read the Psalms with this purpose? It seems to me that many Psalms are of such a type that they must be sung with true edification by the most enlightened people [sie von den aufgeklärtesten Menschen mit wahrer Erbauung gesungen werden müssen]. I would once again recommend to you my translation of the Psalms, if this would not betray too much of the frailty of an author. This much is certain: the Psalms have sweetened many a bitter hour for me, and I pray and sing them as often as I feel a need in me to pray and sing.[1]

Appearing in his last extant letter, Mendelssohn's comments invoked two themes that figured prominently in his writings: the value of aesthetic phenomena such as poetry and music, and the existence of common ground between different religious communities. Mendelssohn is remembered today as one of the German Enlightenment's leading theorists of aesthetics, and his remarks to Becker reflected his long-standing concern with that field, casting "song" as irresistible even for a philosopher and describing the biblical Psalms as poems that offer "true edification" and have "sweetened many a bitter hour."[2] And while Mendelssohn famously refused to endorse the creation of a "union of faiths" and claimed, instead, that religious "diversity is evidently the plan and purpose of Providence,"[3] he is widely known for emphasizing the existence of points of agreement between seemingly disparate religious traditions—for insisting, for example, that there are "fundamental principles on which all religions agree."[4] Here, too, his letter to Becker is in keeping with his broader reputation. He presented the Psalms not as the exclusive inheritance of any one religious community, but rather as poetry "that must be sung with true edification by the most enlightened people," and he took a German translation of the Psalms that he had published to be appropriate not only for Jewish readers but also for his Christian correspondent.

That Mendelssohn discussed aesthetics and common ground between religious communities in one and the same paragraph should not be surprising, for scholars have long understood these themes to be deeply intertwined in his thought. More than four decades ago, Alexander Altmann argued that the German-Jewish philosopher took biblical poems such as the Psalms to be important, in part, because they highlight the existence of religious beliefs shared by both Jews and Christians. Mendelssohn, this interpretation suggests, viewed the ideas expressed in the Psalms as "a kind of universal human piety," and he decided to translate these poems "to draw attention to an important legacy shared by the synagogue and the church."[5] More recently, David Sorkin has suggested that Mendelssohn turned to such poetry not only in order to present the Psalms as "a literary document of general religious sentiment," but also in order to foster the creation of a more inclusive society open to members of all religious traditions.[6] On this reading, one of Mendelssohn's goals in translating the Psalms was to make an argument for extending civic rights to Prussian Jews: by showing how aesthetically and religiously sophisticated this ancient poetry was, Sorkin suggests, Mendelssohn hoped to present modern Jews as heirs of an earlier "period of enlightenment which could now inspire them," and thus as worthy of inclusion in German society.[7]

Turning to aesthetics in order to highlight or create common ground between Jews and Christians has come to be seen not simply as a Mendelssohnian move, but rather as a strategy that was widespread among German Jews. Participation in theatrical and artistic life—attendance at plays, for example, or the creation of art collections—has long been recognized as one of the ways in which "Berlin Jews tried to resemble their non-Jewish neighbors."[8] Music served a similar function, with activities such as attending orchestral and operatic performances as well as private musical education and patronage allowing Jews to engage in shared cultural pursuits with their non-Jewish neighbors without abandoning a commitment to the Jewish tradition.[9] Musical performances organized by Jewish groups could even serve as opportunities to press the case for the creation of a society in which Jews would enjoy the same rights as their Christian neighbors, since such performances might highlight the degree to which Jews had come to accept widely shared cultural values, and thus establish this group's suitability for full civic participation.[10] For many scholars, then, aesthetics functioned as a realm in which Mendelssohn and other German Jews sought to build bridges across confessional boundaries—to narrow the gaps between their own cultural practices and those of their Christian neighbors, to highlight the existence of beliefs and values shared by members of both communities, and to forge new, more inclusive forms of civic life open to adherents of both traditions.

This essay seeks to complicate this picture. Drawing on widely read German sources along with lesser-known Hebrew texts, I will recover a crucial yet neglected dimension of late-eighteenth-century aesthetic life and show that poetry and music provided Jews in Enlightenment Berlin not only with opportunities to discover and create common ground between religious communities, but also with opportunities to call attention to problems plaguing other religious traditions. More specifically, I will argue that claims about poetry and music allowed Mendelssohn to cast Christianity as deeply flawed, especially in comparison to Judaism. Mendelssohn developed what we might call an aesthetic critique of Christianity—a critique revolving around what he saw as Christianity's posture toward poetry and music associated with the Bible. He suggested, implicitly but forcefully, that theological and ethical problems plague Christianity because it neglects the substantive content of biblical poetry and the musical recitation of the biblical text. Christianity, he claimed, remains mired in problematic beliefs regarding topics such as divine punishment and loses morally efficacious pedagogic resources because it fails to heed the Book of Psalms and employ the system governing the chanting of the Bible in Jewish liturgical contexts. For one of the leading Jewish figures in Sara Levy's world, we will discover, aesthetics provided an opportunity not only to highlight a constellation of values that Jews and Christians shared, but also to cast doubt upon aspects of the tradition that the latter group cherished. Aesthetics offered not only a path to religious harmony but also a basis for religious critique.

Some background is in order. Mendelssohn was a universalist in two ways that will be important for this essay. First, he affirmed the universal accessibility of core religious principles, insisting that "eternal truths" indispensable for "human felicity" are accessible to all individuals without the assistance of supernatural revelation. Rational reflection, he argued, is capable of providing a sufficient basis for accepting beliefs such as God's existence, divine providence, and the soul's immortality, and there are no truths necessary for the well-being of all human beings that are not accessible simply through reason.[11]

Second, Mendelssohn posited a universal human *telos*, arguing that all human beings are charged with the "vocation" or task of pursuing "flourishing" or "perfection"—a condition, never fully achievable, in which an individual has properly and harmoniously cultivated the faculties of the body and soul.[12] He placed this vocation at the center of his ethics, arguing that acts count as good to the extent that they foster the pursuit of perfection. For instance, charitable giving and other forms of beneficence would count as good, in part, on the grounds that they provide other individuals with the resources they require to address physical needs and cultivate faculties such as the intellect.[13] Mendelssohn also linked this vocation to his theology, arguing that the pursuit of perfection is divinely endorsed because "God cannot want anything but the best" or "have any other intention than the perfection of creatures"—that a God who is all-knowing, and whose will is perfect, will wish for human beings to seek this noble goal. This means, Mendelssohn reasoned, that reflecting on God can spark reflection on ethical issues such as the goodness of our actions, since grasping God's concern with human flourishing will lead us to recognize the importance of ensuring that our behavior promotes this end.[14] Moreover, he continued, reflecting frequently on ethical matters can actually dispose us to act in ways that count as good, since "the more we reflect on certain reasons and the more we derive motives for our actions from them, the livelier the impression is which they leave on the mind and the easier it is for them to include the lower powers of the soul," generating "inclinations and passions that have the same ultimate purpose as the precepts of reason" and allowing "action to become easy for us." In this model, frequent reflection on ethical issues fosters the performance of actions that we identify as good, since our judgments might become so deeply ingrained that they cultivate new "inclinations and passions" and allow certain types of "action to become easy," producing instincts and desires for behaviors we judge to be good and thereby disposing us to act in morally praiseworthy ways.[15]

These views on the accessibility of truth and the nature of ethics will turn out to loom large in Mendelssohn's treatment of poetry and music. It is to this treatment—to his use of the Psalms in one of his best-known writings, the German treatise *Jerusalem, or On Religious Power and Judaism*,[16] and to his discussion of music in the *Bi'ur* or "Elucidation," his much less widely-read Hebrew commentary on, and German translation of, the Pentateuch[17]—that I now turn.

Poetry and Theology

Mendelssohn's interest in the poetry in the Book of Psalms went back to the earliest stages of his career. Already in 1758, one of his German essays held up the Psalms as an example of an aesthetic category—the sublime—appearing in diverse types of literature, ranging from ancient Latin works to Shakespeare's writings to contemporary German poetry.[18] Similarly, in the early 1770s, Mendelssohn began to translate the Psalms into German for Jewish and Christian readers, casting this project as an attempt to present these poems as a source of universal religious principles that transcend confessional boundaries. He described the Psalms to Becker as a source of "edification" for "the most enlightened people," and he insisted throughout his correspondence that one of his goals in producing his translation was to correct confessionally specific, messianically inflected interpretations by earlier Jewish and Christian exegetes. He offered new readings of poems "which have been taken to be prophecies of the messiah by interpreters from both nations."[19] When the translation was finally published in 1783, Mendelssohn would dedicate this work not to a Jewish reader, but rather to the non-Jewish poet Karl Wilhelm Ramler.[20] It is no wonder, then, that scholars have emphasized the extent to which Mendelssohn saw the Psalms as a source of common ground between Jews and Christians.

While important, this scholarly picture offers an incomplete account of the Psalms' role in Mendelssohn's thought. If we go beyond general statements such as his remarks to Becker and look at his more detailed comments regarding the Psalms' content, and more specifically at comments expressed in the period surrounding his translation's publication, we discover that he repeatedly presented this poetry not only as a source of common ground between Jews and Christians, but also as a particularly strong rebuke to Christianity. In particular, he cast these poems as rejecting what he took to be problematic beliefs associated with Christianity but *not* with Judaism.

The key work is his 1783 *Jerusalem*, published in the same year as the Psalms translation. Consider the following passage, focused on "a great thought which our rabbis discovered":[21]

> *This, too, is a quality of divine love that for man nothing is allowed to go entirely unpunished.* A venerable friend, with whom I once conversed upon religious matters, put the question to me *whether I would not wish to be assured by a direct revelation that I would not be miserable in the future.* We both agreed that I did not have to fear eternal punishment in hell, for God cannot let any of His creatures suffer unceasing misery. Nor can any creature, by his actions, deserve the punishment of being eternally miserable. That the punishment for sin must be proportionate to the offended majesty of God and, therefore, infinite, this hypothesis my friend had given up long ago, as many great men of his church had likewise done. . . . This being assumed, my friend's question

became more precisely defined: *Whether I must not wish to be assured by a revelation that in the future life I should be exempt even from finite misery?*[22]

Mendelssohn described conversations with a "friend" who "had given up" the traditional doctrine of sinners' eternal punishment in hell, but who nevertheless retained the idea of "a revelation" assuring believers that they will be "exempt even from finite misery." Put more simply, his friend continued to affirm the idea that believers will be spared from even a finite period of punishment after death. This latter doctrine, Mendelssohn suggested, represents a point of contention between Judaism and Christianity. While he did not explicitly state that the Christian tradition affirms the notion that believers will be allowed to avoid even finite suffering, he linked the unnamed friend who retained this view to other "great men in his church," and thus seems to be invoking this individual's beliefs as an example of commitments associated with Christianity. Altmann reads this passage in precisely this manner, arguing that the idea in question was not the idiosyncratic proposal of one individual, but rather reflected "the Protestant doctrine of man's justification by faith, which bids the sinner trust in the divine forgiveness as promised in the Christian revelation."[23] Mendelssohn also used nearly identical language regarding a "venerable friend" posing a theological question about salvation and temporary misery in an earlier work concerned with eighteenth-century defenses of Christian theology, further suggesting that he saw this belief in the possibility of avoiding punishment as a key Christian position.[24] By contrast, *Jerusalem* presented this doctrine as foreign to Judaism, stating that "our rabbis" hold that "for man nothing is allowed to go entirely unpunished."[25]

The important point for us is Mendelssohn's account of why he rejected his friend's—meaning Christianity's—position that believers might be "exempt even from finite misery" after death. Mendelssohn's response began as follows: "No, I answered; this misery can be nothing other than a well-deserved chastisement; and, in God's paternal household, I shall gladly suffer the chastisement I deserve . . . God's justice, that is, His all-wise love, seeks to guide me to moral improvement by means of physical misery."[26] Mendelssohn initially rejected his Christian friend's position on purely rational or philosophical grounds, suggesting that finite "misery" after death is merely "a well-deserved chastisement" leading to "moral improvement." Finite punishment after death is simply God's way of acting justly and eliciting repentance, and thus a prospect to be embraced rather than shunned.

Mendelssohn continued, however, by raising additional concerns:

Can I wish that my Father withdraw his chastising hand from me before it has had the effect it was meant to produce? If I request that God let a transgression of mine go entirely unpunished, do I know what I am requesting? Oh, surely this too is a quality of God's infinite love that He allows no transgression of man to go entirely unpunished. Surely "All-power is God's alone; / And love also is Thine, o Lord! / When Thou renderest to everyone according to his deeds." Ps. 62:12–13[27]

Mendelssohn began by elaborating on his rational rejection of the Christian doctrine in question, arguing that if finite punishment after death is God's way of acting justly and eliciting repentance, then such punishment is an expression of divine love.[28] But he then went further and argued that the doctrine deemed problematic on rational grounds is *also* undermined by the Psalms. He used Psalm 62 as a proof text, reading the final stitch quoted above as support for his view rejecting an exemption from finite punishment. What this text teaches, he claimed, is that God's love is evident "when Thou renderest to everyone according to his deeds"—that God's love involves administering, rather than withholding, deserved punishments. Mendelssohn thus presented the Psalms as rejecting a problematic belief that he associated with Christianity. Taking "church" figures to hold that believers will be spared from even a finite period of punishment after death, he suggested not only that this posture differs from the teachings of "our rabbis" and is rationally untenable, but also that such a doctrinal position ignores the message of Psalm 62.[29]

Mendelssohn made a similar move in *Jerusalem*'s very next passage. Recall his insistence that indispensable eternal truths are accessible to all individuals without the assistance of divine revelation. As is well known, *Jerusalem* portrayed this idea both as a view held by Judaism and as a rejection of Christian doctrine, arguing that while the former tradition affirms the universal accessibility of truths through rational reflection, the latter posits the existence of principles, such as Jesus's divinity, that are necessary for salvation but accessible only through revelation. Declaring that he recognized "*no eternal truths other than those that are not merely comprehensible to human reason but can also be demonstrated and verified by human powers*," Mendelssohn claimed to "consider this an essential point of the Jewish religion and believe that this doctrine constitutes a characteristic difference between it and the Christian one," since "Judaism boasts of no *exclusive* revelation of eternal truths that are indispensable to salvation."[30]

Now, *Jerusalem* famously cast the position ascribed to Christianity as problematic on rational or philosophical grounds. According to Mendelssohn, insofar as Christianity's revelation has reached only a portion of humanity (while "the two Indies wait until it pleases the Europeans to send them a few comforters"), and insofar as *any* revelation would have to be given in a particular language to a particular group of recipients and would thus possess only limited intelligibility for other individuals, there would be little reason for God to make indispensable truths accessible exclusively through a medium of such limited availability and intelligibility.[31] Moreover, he argued, Christianity's claim that some indispensable principles are accessible exclusively through revelation is not merely incoherent, but actually insulting:

> I therefore do not believe that the powers of human reason are insufficient to persuade men of the eternal truths which are indispensable to human felicity, and that God had to reveal them in a supernatural manner. Those who hold this view detract from the omnipotence or the goodness of God, on the one hand, what they believe they are adding to his goodness on the other. He was, in their opinion, good enough to reveal to men those truths on which their felicity depends, but not omnipotent, or not good enough to grant them the powers to discover these truths themselves.[32]

For Mendelssohn, if we hold that "the powers of human reason are insufficient to persuade men of the eternal truths which are indispensable to human felicity," then we are inadvertently impugning God's omnipotence or benevolence. Mendelssohn's point was that the ideal state of affairs would be one in which all human beings have access, through their own cognitive capacities, to truths necessary for their felicity, and that if we deny that such a state of affairs exists—if we affirm that there are indispensable truths accessible only by means of supernatural revelation—then the responsibility for this flaw must lie with the Deity: either God was unable to provide this type of universal access to truth (and thus does not possess unlimited power), or God could have provided such access but chose not to do so (and thus is guilty of deliberately depriving humanity of a great good).

Once again, however, Mendelssohn proceeded to describe Christianity's posture not only as rationally or philosophically problematic, but also as objectionable on poetic grounds. The crucial passage, appearing after his discussion of punishment and the Psalms, reads as follows:

> Religious doctrines and propositions or *eternal truths* about God and His government and providence, without which man cannot be enlightened and happy . . . did not have to be given by direct revelation, or made known through *word* and *script*, which are intelligible only *here* and *now*. The Supreme Being has revealed them to all rational creatures through *things* and *concepts* and inscribed them in the soul with a script that is legible and comprehensible at all times and in all places. For this reason our much-quoted poet sings: "The heavens declare the majesty of God, / And the firmament announceth the work of His hands; / From one day this doctrine floweth into another / And night giveth instruction to night. / *No teaching, no words, / Without their voice being heard. / Their choral resoundeth over all the earth, / Their message goeth forth to the ends of the world, / To the place where He hath set a tent for the sun, etc.*" [Ps. 19:2–5][33]

By citing Psalm 19, Mendelssohn now presented what he took to be Christianity's problematic position—that some principles necessary for salvation are accessible only by means of divine revelation—as likewise a failure to attend to the teachings of the Psalms. On this reading of Psalm 19, by taking a recognition of God's "majesty" to extend "over all the earth" and emerge from contemplating nature rather than from "words," this poem presents a view diametrically opposed to the one ascribed to Christianity, suggesting, instead, that essential principles are universally accessible without verbal revelation.[34]

Indeed, Mendelssohn continued, Psalm 19 is not the only poetic text to adopt this view of eternal truths. His discussion of such truths continued as follows: "Their effect is as universal as the beneficent influence of the sun, which, as it hurries through its orbit, sheds light and warmth over the whole globe. As the same poet explains still more clearly in another place: 'From sunrise to sundown / The name of the Eternal is praised' [Ps. 113:3]."[35] Like Psalm 19, Psalm 113 was presented here as emphasizing the universal accessibility of core truths. On this interpretation, Psalm 113 stresses that God's existence and providence are recognized "from sunrise to sundown," and thus "over the whole globe."[36] Mendelssohn thereby framed the Book of Psalms as a source that affirms a sound belief associated with Judaism and, by implication, rejects a problematic commitment associated with Christianity. Holding that beliefs regarding access to indispensable truths constitute "a characteristic difference between [the Jewish tradition] and the Christian one," Mendelssohn suggested that Christianity's approach to this issue is not only conceptually problematic, but also ignores the teachings of the Psalms.

None of this is to deny that there are ways in which Mendelssohn saw the Psalms as a source of religious truths shared by Jews and Christians. He translated this poetry for both Jewish and Christian readers and recommended this material to Becker as a source of "true edification" for "enlightened people." There is also an important sense in which the arguments reconstructed above presented the Psalms as a source of universal religious truths. Insofar as *Jerusalem* claimed that the beliefs rejected by the Psalms are flawed on purely rational grounds, it implied that the Psalms echo conclusions derived through human reason. For Mendelssohn, then, the Psalms point to religious commitments that are, in principle, accessible to anyone. They articulate universal religious truths that all individuals *should* be able to reach. Indeed, as we have seen, he presented Psalms 19 and 113 not only as echoing universally derivable conclusions, but also as declaring that key truths possess this status—as insisting that ideas such as God's existence and providence are accessible to all individuals.

At the same time, my analysis suggests that the widespread scholarly emphasis on the universalistic thrust of Mendelssohn's engagement with the Psalms fails to capture an important dimension of his position. During the same period in which he published a German translation that made this material accessible to both Jewish and Christian readers, he composed an additional treatise that presented these poems as rejecting theological commitments that he associated with Christianity, but not with Judaism. He may have seen the Psalms as reflecting what Altmann called "a kind of universal human piety," but *Jerusalem*'s arguments also implied that this "piety" is a theological posture that Christianity has failed to realize. That is, while Mendelssohn may have seen the Psalms as a source of universal principles, he also presented these texts as a particularly strong rebuke to Christianity, suggesting that not only rational reflection, but also these beloved poems, cast doubt on Christian theology—that Christianity can maintain key doctrinal claims only by ignoring *both* the results of rational inquiry *and* the content of the Psalms. Even though his decision to publish a translation of the Psalms for Jews and Christians invites—even begs for—a universalistic reading, then, it turns out that this biblical poetry functioned far more subversively in his thought, highlighting not only an inheritance shared by Judaism and Christianity, but also flaws plaguing the latter tradition.

Mendelssohn was understandably cautious about the manner in which he made this claim. Aware of how perilous it would be for a Jew in late-eighteenth-century Prussia to criticize Christianity too explicitly,[37] he advanced his argument by placing biblical citations alongside problematic doctrines rather than by explicitly characterizing Christianity in harsh terms. Nevertheless, his repeated, striking juxtapositions of verses from the Psalms with Christian beliefs leave little doubt about his convictions. Rather than recognizing that the substantive content of the Psalms cautions against affirming rationally problematic beliefs, Christianity fails to heed the message of this poetry and thus remains mired in untenable positions.

Music and Ethics

I wish to suggest that Mendelssohn advanced a similar claim regarding the system of accents or cantillation signs that determine how the Bible is chanted or sung in Jewish liturgical contexts such as synagogue worship.[38] The key text is his introduction to the *Bi'ur*, published in the early 1780s. Written during an era that witnessed the emergence and growing acceptance of historical-critical Bible scholarship, Mendelssohn's introduction was deeply concerned with the tendency of Christian practitioners of such scholarship to dismiss the accents as baseless innovations created long after the Bible's composition.[39] For example, noting that "Christian scholars" and "Christian translators . . . treat the words of the Torah as a broken wall, before which each individual rises and which each individual treats as he desires," he held up these Christian readers' rejection of the cantillation signs as a prime example of what he saw as their cavalier attitude toward the biblical text, lamenting the fact that these individuals "do not even accept the vowels and accents that we possess."[40] What is important for us is that Mendelssohn traced this dismissive attitude not only to these individuals' scholarly commitments but also to their religious background, writing that "I do not condemn these scholars for this, for what compels them to heed the tradition that they have not received from their ancestors?"[41] His point was that it is natural for Christian scholars to reject the cantillation system because they were raised in a religion that, moving away from Jewish textual and liturgical traditions, did not require that the Bible be chanted through cantillation.

While Mendelssohn claimed not to condemn Christians for reproducing the attitude with which they were raised, his comments elsewhere in the *Bi'ur*'s introduction suggested that this attitude is itself problematic. Christian scholars may have understandably replicated a posture inherited from their predecessors, but for Mendelssohn, this long-standing neglect of the cantillation signs has resulted in the loss of a vital resource:

> There is no doubt that Moses our master, peace be upon him, heard all the Torah's words from the mouth of the Almighty with every type of beauty and with the vowels and accents. . . . And people would teach the words to their children and their students in this way, for this is the commandment *and you shall teach them diligently to your children* [Deuteronomy 6:7]—namely, that the words shall be ever ready [*mehudadim*] in one's mouth [Babylonian Talmud Kiddushin 30a and Sifre Deuteronomy 34].[42] They would not give the Holy Scripture to their sons or students, leaving them to read it in written form alone, for then it would be like the words of a sealed book to them. Rather, [teachers] would recite it before [their students] and repeat it with [their students], with the sound of the words and with melody and singing. They would thereby pass along the accents of the Torah and sweeten the honey of their speech, until the words would enter their hearts [*ad shenikhnesu hadevarim belibam*] and be present there, like goads and nails that have been planted.[43]

Mendelssohn's writings took the cantillation system to serve a variety of functions,[44] but he focused here on the idea that one result of employing these accents (of reciting Scripture "with melody and singing") is that the Bible's words "would enter . . . hearts and be present there, like goads and nails that have been planted."[45] He seems here to be invoking an idea familiar to anyone who has had a song stuck in her head: that musically recited statements remain more fixedly in our mind, or are more easily memorized, than spoken words. Moreover, drawing on rabbinic texts, he suggested that these chanted biblical words lodged in our mind will also be *mehudadim*, meaning "ever ready," "well discussed," or "finely honed"[46]—that we will find ourselves frequently discussing and reflecting on these musically recited, easily memorized words. His claim was thus that the musical system neglected by Christianity transforms biblical words into objects of recurring attention: if we are likely to remember words that are sung, then chanting the Bible might lodge its words firmly in our minds, encouraging us to reflect again and again on the content they express.

What is at stake here? What has Christianity lost by neglecting music capable of yielding such reflection? The *Bi'ur*'s introduction did not explicitly address this point, but Mendelssohn's account of biblical poetry in the *Bi'ur* on Exodus 15 offers a basis for clarifying his views. The key lines begin as follows: "The end desired in [biblical poetry is] that the words enter [*sheyikansu*] not only the listener's ear, but also his heart [*belibo*]. They should remain engraved on the tablets [of his heart] . . . firmly establishing within him the virtues and excellent dispositions."[47] Mendelssohn applied to poetry the same language that we have seen him use when he discussed music. Just as the *Bi'ur*'s introduction stated that musically recited words "would enter [*shenikhnesu*] their hearts [*belibam*] and be present there," so too did the *Bi'ur* on Exodus 15 claim that the words of the Bible's poetic passages "enter [*sheyikansu*] not only the listener's ear, but also his heart [*belibo*]." Mendelssohn thus likened the impact of the cantillation signs to the impact of biblical poetry; indeed, he proceeded to emphasize this similarity, stating just a few words later that both "the pleasantness of poetry and pleasing music contribute greatly to meeting this need and promoting this end."[48]

With this connection between music and poetry in mind, let us consider the details of Mendelssohn's reasoning. In the passage cited above, he stated that poetry serves the end of "firmly establishing . . . the virtues and excellent dispositions," described elsewhere in the *Bi'ur* as "dispositions to do . . . good"—to act in ways that promote the pursuit of perfection.[49] His claim was thus that biblical poetry instills dispositions to foster human flourishing, that is to say, dispositions to act in ways that cultivate the faculties—for instance, to engage in acts of charitable giving that provide others with the resources that they need to develop their capacities. He then explained how this process of moral formation occurs:

> So that the poem's words might serve this end, our ancestors would cut every utterance into parts and divide each part into short clauses nearly equal in their quantity. Therefore, you will not find in any one of these clauses more than four or fewer than two words, and most pairs include three words in each clause. . . . This practice aids memory, since when a short clause contains content and meaning that enter the heart, this content easily becomes orally preserved, memorized, and enduringly familiar.[50]

Mendelssohn advanced three claims: (1) that biblical poetry "cut[s] every utterance into parts and divide[s] each part into short clauses nearly equal in their quantity"; (2) that this feature renders the Bible's "content . . . memorized and enduringly familiar"; and (3) that such a structure serves the "end" of cultivating dispositions to promote perfection.[51]

This argument drew from sources such as the sixteenth-century Jewish thinker Azariah de Rossi and the eighteenth-century British scholar Robert Lowth.[52] Mendelssohn's first claim was that biblical poetry is governed by parallelism. According to this view, instead of being structured around the presence of rhymes or specific numbers of long or short syllables in each line, biblical poetry is organized into units consisting of short, parallel clauses.[53] For example, Exodus 15:11 includes two such units:

Unit A	*mi*	*khamokhah*	*ba'elim*	*adonai*
	Who	is-like-you	among-the-powers	O-Eternal?
	mi	*kamokhah*	*nedar*	*bakodesh*
	Who	is-like-you	glorified	in-holiness?

Unit B	*nora*	*tehilot*
	Formidable	in-praise,
	oseh	*fele*
	doer	of-wonders![54]

Units A and B consist of parallel clauses of four and two words, respectively.

We can now turn to Mendelssohn's suggestion that this poetic structure renders biblical "content . . . memorized" and "enduringly familiar." He claimed that short parallel clauses will likely become lodged in our memories, and that these words and their "content" will therefore become "enduringly familiar"—that we will find ourselves reflecting, again and again, on the biblical text and its claims. In the example of Exodus 15:11, short phrases such as "formidable in praise" and "doer of wonders" will naturally stick in our minds, and we will find ourselves thinking, over and over, about the deity such words describe. For the *Bi'ur*, then, the structure of biblical poetry transforms the Bible's content into an object of recurring attention.

Mendelssohn also identified additional ways in which the structure outlined above might produce this effect. For example, he claimed that "with short clauses, the number of caesuras and points of rest increase, which helps considerably to awaken attention to the intended meaning and impress this intended meaning on the heart, as linguists have observed."[55]

What is important for us now, however, is Mendelssohn's third suggestion outlined above—namely, that this capacity of biblical poetry to transform the Bible's content into an object of recurring attention serves the "end" of cultivating a disposition to promote perfection. His meaning becomes clear if we recall his claims regarding perfection: (1) that reflecting on God generates reflection on ethics, since recognizing God's concern for perfection will lead us to recognize the importance of ensuring that our behavior promotes this end; and (2) that reflecting frequently on ethics disposes us to perform actions that count as good, since our judgments might become so ingrained that they generate drives for behavior judged to be morally praiseworthy, producing instincts and desires for such deeds and thereby disposing us to act in those ways. If the structure of biblical poetry encourages recurring reflection on the Bible's content, and if that content includes claims about God, then biblical poetry will produce frequent contemplation of the divine, and this preoccupation with the deity will likewise foster recurring ethical reflection that produces inclinations for the good and disposes us to act in ways that promote perfection. By describing God with short, memorable phrases such as "formidable in praise" and "doer of wonders," Exodus 15:11 will lead us to reflect frequently on those words and the deity they describe, and such reflection will have ethical consequences, motivating us to ask whether our deeds promote the pursuit of perfection God endorses, producing inclinations for behavior judged to meet this standard, and thereby cultivating a disposition to act in accordance with this *telos*. For Mendelssohn, then, insofar as the Bible's words become objects of recurring attention, we will find ourselves assessing the goodness of our actions and yearning for behavior deemed good, and we will thus be disposed to act in ways that foster human flourishing.[56]

The force of his claims regarding music now comes into sharper relief. Discussing the cantillation signs that determine how the Bible is chanted or sung in Jewish liturgical contexts, the *Bi'ur*'s introduction suggested that Christianity neglects such music even though this system transforms biblical words into objects of recurring attention. Mendelssohn's discussion of poetry elsewhere in his commentary then indicated that precisely this type of frequent reflection on biblical words possesses ethical import, directing attention to a deity concerned with human flourishing and thereby inculcating dispositions to pursue this goal. We have seen, in fact, that he used strikingly similar language when discussing poetry and music and even stated that they serve the same "need" and "end," strongly suggesting a connection between his approaches to these aesthetic phenomena.[57] If Mendelssohn thus held that Christianity neglects the system of Jewish oral musical cantillation that encourages frequent reflection on the biblical text, and if he in turn insisted that this type of frequent reflection cultivates ethically praiseworthy dispositions, then his view was that Christianity, with its rejection of this system, has lost a critical tool for moral formation and human flourishing. By failing to employ these signs, Christianity fails to employ a musical system that embeds the Bible's words in our memory and leads us to contemplate the God they describe, motivating us to ask whether our actions foster our divinely sanctioned vocation, generating desires for behavior judged to meet this standard, and thereby disposing us to act in ways that promote human flourishing.[58] Casting aside a system that would ensure that individuals hear biblical words chanted on a regular basis,[59] Christianity abandons a system that allows adherents to reap the ethical benefits that result.

As with his treatment of the Psalms in *Jerusalem*, Mendelssohn left the *Bi'ur*'s critique of Christianity largely implicit.[60] But the thrust of his claims is clear: Christianity's neglect of the accents is the neglect of a system that generates *precisely* the type of reflection that cultivates virtuous dispositions. In both *Jerusalem* and the *Bi'ur*, therefore, we find Mendelssohn developing an aesthetic critique of Christianity. Implicitly but forcefully, these German and Hebrew works suggested that theological and ethical problems plague the Christian tradition because it neglects the substantive content of biblical poetry and the musical recitation of the biblical text. A disregard of the Psalms' claims regarding punishment and knowledge leaves Christianity mired in flawed doctrines, and a failure to employ the cantillation system constitutes the loss of an ethically powerful pedagogic resource.[61] Were the Christian tradition to attend more seriously to poetry and music associated with the Bible, Mendelssohn suggested, this religion would more accurately grasp key truths and more effectively cultivate human virtue.[62]

Sara Levy's World

There are, of course, questions we might raise about Mendelssohn's arguments. We might wonder whether his readings of the Psalms are defensible. He took Psalm 62 to reject the idea of an exemption from posthumous punishment, and Psalms 19 and 113 to insist on the universality of core religious truths, yet we might doubt that he provided sufficient grounds for reading this material in these ways.[63] We might also ask whether his claims about cantillation overlooked the significance of music for his Christian contemporaries. As someone familiar with many developments in eighteenth-century music,[64] he was presumably well aware that Christian composers set biblical material to music, and we might therefore wonder whether he provided adequate grounds for his charge that Christianity neglected the musical recitation of the biblical text.[65] Finally, we might raise questions about the audiences at which Mendelssohn directed his arguments. His claims about music appeared in a Hebrew text largely aimed at Jewish readers: what, we might ask, was he trying to accomplish by attacking Christianity for such an audience? Was he attempting to reassure his co-religionists that Judaism was not only just as sophisticated as, but in fact more sophisticated than, other traditions with respect to aesthetic praxis and moral pedagogy?[66] By contrast, his arguments about the Psalms appeared in a German work directed not only at Jews, but also at a Christian audience. Was he simply attempting to provide his diverse readers with a deeper understanding of Judaism and caution them against dismissing this tradition as inferior to Christianity, or did he have other goals in mind as well? By highlighting what he took to be poetic texts opposed to Christian doctrines, was he encouraging his Christian readers to rethink elements of their own tradition?[67]

More important for us than these questions about the details of Mendelssohn's arguments, however, are the broader implications of his claims for our understanding of aesthetics and religion in the eighteenth century. I began this essay by noting that, in the eyes of many scholars, aesthetics functioned as a realm in which Mendelssohn and other German Jews sought to build bridges across confessional boundaries. A commitment to shared aesthetics ideals could narrow the gaps between Jews' cultural practices and those of their Christian neighbors, highlight the existence of beliefs and values shared by members of both communities, and forge more inclusive forms of civic life open to adherents of both traditions.

Nothing in my analysis implies that we should abandon this picture of German Jewry. I see no reason to deny that participation in musical and theatrical life allowed Jews to pursue the same activities as their non-Jewish neighbors, and even to make the case for the inclusion of Jews as full participants in Prussian society. Similarly, as I argued above, there are ways in which Mendelssohn understood biblical poetry as a source of truths that transcend— or at least should transcend—confessional lines. Even his argument about music and the Bible pointed to the existence of common ground between religious traditions. His position was that the cantillation system employed by Judaism cultivates dispositions to act in ways that promote human flourishing, and that this system thereby directs Jews towards a vocation that is incumbent upon *all* human beings. For the *Bi'ur*, the musical system used exclusively in Jewish contexts fosters the pursuit of a human *telos* that transcends all confessional bounds.[68]

Nevertheless, my interpretation of Mendelssohn suggests that the widespread scholarly narrative outlined above offers only a partial picture of German-Jewish life. Aesthetics may have grounded the possibility of a shared cultural sphere for Jews and Christians and served as an argument for Jewish civic inclusion. My analysis, however, uncovers another, less irenic dimension of late-eighteenth-century aesthetics, revealing that poetry and music provided a German-Jewish philosopher such as Mendelssohn not only with opportunities to discover and create common ground between religious communities, but also with opportunities to call attention to problems plaguing other religious traditions. If my reading of *Jerusalem* and the *Bi'ur* is correct, then claims about aesthetic phenomena allowed Mendelssohn to cast Christianity as deeply flawed, especially in comparison to Judaism.[69] Even as he published a translation of the Psalms for Jewish and Christian readers, he drew on these poems to raise serious concerns about the tradition accepted by the latter group: he identified a series of beliefs which he took to be associated with Christianity rather than with Judaism, and he suggested that these specifically Christian doctrines clash with the teachings of both human reason and biblical poetry. For Mendelssohn, Christian views regarding punishment and truth are not only philosophically untenable but also challenged by the Psalms, and the presence of these problematic beliefs at the heart of Christian theology thus reflects a failure to heed the message of some of the Bible's best-known poetry. Similarly, even as he took Judaism's cantillation system to orient adherents towards a universal human *telos*, he called attention to the failure of Christianity to employ this ethically significant musical scheme, implicitly accusing this tradition and its practitioners of leaving aside a morally efficacious pedagogic tool. For one of the leading Jewish figures in Enlightenment Berlin, then, aesthetics served a dual purpose, providing an opportunity not only to highlight a constellation of values that Jews and Christians shared, but also to cast doubt upon aspects of the tradition that the latter group cherished. Aesthetics offered not only a path to religious harmony, but also a basis for religious critique.

Notes

1. Moses Mendelssohn to Sophie Becker, December 27, 1785, in Mendelssohn, *Gesammelte Schriften Jubiläumsausgabe* (hereafter Mendelssohn, *JubA*), ed. Fritz Bamberger et al., 24 vols. (Stuttgart-Bad Canstatt: Frommann, 1971–), 13:334. All translations are mine unless otherwise noted.

2. Mendelssohn's reputation as an aesthetic thinker was already well established in his own historical context. For some recent treatments of this aspect of his thought, see Jonathan Karp, "The Aesthetic Difference: Moses Mendelssohn's *Kohelet Musar* and the Inception of the Berlin Haskalah," in *Renewing the Past, Reconfiguring Jewish Culture: From Al-Andalus to the Haskalah*, ed. Ross Brann and Adam Sutcliffe (Philadelphia: University of Pennsylvania Press, 2004), 93–120; Frederick Beiser, *Diotima's Children: German Aesthetic Rationalism from Leibniz to Lessing* (Oxford: Oxford University Press, 2009), 196–243; Michah Gottlieb, "Aesthetics and the Infinite: Moses Mendelssohn on the Poetics of Biblical Prophecy," in *New Directions in Jewish Philosophy*, ed. Aaron Hughes and Elliot Wolfson (Bloomington: Indiana University Press, 2010), 326–53; Reiner Munk, ed., *Moses Mendelssohn's Metaphysics and Aesthetics* (New York: Springer, 2011); Grit Schorch, *Moses Mendelssohns Sprachpolitik* (Berlin: de Gruyter, 2012), 96–140; Zachary Braiterman, "The Emergence of Modern Religion: Moses Mendelssohn, Neoclassicism, and Ceremonial Aesthetics," in *German-Jewish Thought Between Religion and Politics: Festschrift in Honor of Paul Mendes-Flohr on the Occasion of His Seventieth Birthday*, ed. Christian Wiese and Martina Urban (Berlin: de Gruyter, 2012), 11–27; and Leah Hochman, *The Ugliness of Moses Mendelssohn: Aesthetics, Religion, and Morality in the Eighteenth Century* (New York: Routledge, 2014).

3. Moses Mendelssohn, *Jerusalem, or On Religious Power and Judaism*, trans. Allan Arkush with intro. and commentary by Alexander Altmann (Hanover, NH:

Brandeis University Press and University Press of New England, 1983), 135–39; for the German, see Mendelssohn, *JubA*, 8:200–204. Further references appear as Mendelssohn, *Jerusalem*, English page numbers / German volume: page numbers (e.g., Mendelssohn, *Jerusalem*, 135–39/8:200–204).

4. Mendelssohn, *Jerusalem*, 63/8:131. On Mendelssohn as both defending religious diversity and positing significant points of commonality among religious traditions, see Michah Gottlieb, "Mendelssohn's Metaphysical Defense of Religious Pluralism," *Journal of Religion* 86, no. 2 (2006): 205–25.

5. Alexander Altmann, *Moses Mendelssohn: A Biographical Study* (Tuscaloosa: University of Alabama Press, 1973), 501.

6. David Sorkin, *Moses Mendelssohn and the Religious Enlightenment* (Berkeley: University of California Press, 1996), 52.

7. Ibid., 117. See also Jonathan Sheehan, *The Enlightenment Bible: Translation, Scholarship, Culture* (Princeton, NJ: Princeton University Press, 2005), 176–81. For other discussions of the role of aesthetics in Mendelssohn's defense of Judaism, see note 69 below. As I indicate there, while other scholars have shown that Mendelssohn drew on aesthetics to make a case for Judaism's inclusion in modern life alongside other religious traditions, my analysis suggests that aesthetics also played a further, significantly less irenic role in his thought—aesthetics also functioned subversively to undermine key elements of Christianity.

8. Steven Lowenstein, *The Berlin Jewish Community: Enlightenment, Family, and Crisis, 1770–1830* (New York: Oxford University Press, 1994), 43–50; the quote appears on p. 46 in a discussion of linguistic dimensions of this acculturation. On the link between this turn to aesthetics and Jews' broader embrace of the German cultural ideal of *Bildung* or "education," see George Mosse, *German Jews Beyond Judaism* (Bloomington: Indiana University Press, 1985), 1–8.

9. A comprehensive survey of scholarship on Jews, music, and modernity lies beyond the scope of this essay. For some recent examples, see Lowenstein, *The Berlin Jewish Community*; Ruth HaCohen, *The Music Libel Against the Jews* (New Haven, CT: Yale University Press, 2011), 1–16, 71–125; Yael Sela-Teichler, "Music, Acculturation, and Haskalah between Berlin and Königsberg in the 1780s," *Jewish Quarterly Review* 103, no. 3 (2013): 352–84. See also Hochman, *The Ugliness of Moses Mendelssohn*, 49–54.

10. See, in particular, Sela-Teichler, "Music, Acculturation, and Haskalah," 372–81.

11. See, for example, Mendelssohn, *Jerusalem*, 89–98/8:156–65. Mendelssohn suggested that there are beliefs—for example, in the historicity of events such as the revelation at Sinai—that Jews should affirm but which are not accessible through reason: see, for example, Mendelssohn, *Jerusalem*, 98–99/8:165, 126–27/8:191–92. He denied, however, that these beliefs are universally indispensable for salvation. See also his *Gegenbetrachtungen über Bonnets Palingenesie*, in Mendelssohn, *JubA*, 7:90–91.

12. See Allan Arkush, *Moses Mendelssohn and the Enlightenment* (Albany: SUNY Press, 1994), 100–11; Anne Pollok, *Facetten des Menschen: Zur Anthropologie Moses Mendelssohns* (Hamburg: Meiner, 2010). Mendelssohn's German writings generally used terms such as *Vollkommenheit* or "perfection," while his Hebrew

writings referred not only to *shlemut* (perfection), but also to *hatzlahah* or "flourishing." Compare, for example, *JubA*, 6.1:19–65 with *JubA*, 15.2:23, 26. (The latter passages appeared in Mendelssohn's Hebrew commentary on the Book of Genesis. While some portions of this commentary were written by his assistants, he was the author of this section; see Altmann, *Moses Mendelssohn*, 400.)

13. On the "good," see Moses Mendelssohn, "On Evidence in Metaphysical Sciences," in *Philosophical Writings*, trans. and ed. Daniel Dahlstrom (Cambridge: Cambridge University Press, 1997), 296–99; for the German, see Mendelssohn, *JubA*, 2:317–20. Further references appear as Mendelssohn, "On Evidence," English page numbers/German volume: page numbers. On charitable giving and other forms of beneficence, see Mendelssohn, *Jerusalem*, 42–48/8:111–16. Mendelssohn took such behavior to be good not only because it contributes to the perfection of those who receive, but also because (on his account) it contributes to the perfection of those who give.

14. This point is developed across a variety of Mendelssohn's German and Hebrew writings. See Elias Sacks, "Law, Ethics, and the Needs of History: Mendelssohn, Krochmal, and Moral Philosophy," *Journal of Religious Ethics* 44, no. 2 (2016): 355–62; and Elias Sacks, *Moses Mendelssohn's Living Script: Philosophy, Practice, History, Judaism* (Bloomington: Indiana University Press, 2017), 93–121. For some key elements of this position, see Mendelssohn's "On Evidence," 297–300/2:318–21 (which includes the lines quoted in the body of my essay), along with his *Rhapsodie*, in *JubA*, 1:420–21.

15. Mendelssohn, "On Evidence," 305/2:327, as well as the sources in the previous note.

16. On *Jerusalem*, see Altmann, *Moses Mendelssohn*, 514–52.

17. See Altmann, *Moses Mendelssohn*, 368–420. Strictly speaking, "*Bi'ur*" denotes the Hebrew commentary, while the entire work—also including the translation—is *Sefer Netivot Hashalom* (The Book of the Paths of Peace). Following widespread practice, I use "*Bi'ur*" for the commentary and translation.

18. Mendelssohn, *Ueber das Erhabene und Naive in den schönen Wissenschaften*, in *JubA*, 1:453–94. For other early works that drew on the Psalms, see Sorkin, *Moses Mendelssohn*, 173n2.

19. The quoted statement appears in Mendelssohn to Johann Georg Zimmerman, November 1771, in Mendelssohn, *JubA*, 12.2:22. See also Mendelssohn to Johann David Michaelis, November 12, 1770, in *JubA*, 12.1:232–35; and Mendelssohn to Elise Reimarus, May 20, 1783, in *JubA*, 13:109. On the background and publication of the Psalms translation, see Altmann, *Moses Mendelssohn*, 242–45, 274–75, 500–501, 718–20; Sorkin, *Moses Mendelssohn*, 46–52; 117–18; Daniel Krochmalnik, "Die Psalmen in Moses Mendelssohns Utopie des Judentums," in *Der Psalter in Judentum und Christentum*, ed. Erich Zenger (Freiburg: Herder, 1998), 235–67.

20. See Mendelssohn, *Die Psalmen*, in *JubA*, 10.1:3–6.

21. Mendelssohn stated that the rabbis "discovered" this "thought" in Exodus (*Jerusalem*, 122–23/8:187–88), but we will see that he went on to emphasize the idea's presence in the Psalms.

22. Mendelssohn, *Jerusalem*, 123–24/8:188–89. The italics appear in the original.
23. See Alexander Altmann, "Commentary," in Mendelssohn, *Jerusalem*, 228.
24. See Mendelssohn, *Gegenbetrachtungen*, in *JubA*, 7:72. According to Altmann, the friend invoked here is Johann August Eberhard, a philosopher and member of the Christian clergy: see Altmann, "Commentary," in Mendelssohn, *Jerusalem*, 228.
25. For a similar claim in an earlier work, see Mendelssohn, *Gegenbetrachtungen*, in *JubA*, 7:96.
26. Mendelssohn, *Jerusalem*, 124/8:190.
27. Ibid., 125/8:190. *Jerusalem*'s German rendering of these lines is: "Allmacht ist nur Gottes: / Und Dein ist auch die Liebe, Herr! / Wenn jedem Du nach seinem Thun vergöltest."
28. In addition to echoing the position that he has just ascribed to "our rabbis," Mendelssohn may have been drawing on a Leibnizian definition of justice that he used elsewhere in his writings—namely, the view that justice is "benevolence administered with wisdom" (Mendelssohn, "On Evidence," 274/2:292). If justice involves benevolence, it might be said to involve love—implying, in turn, that if divine punishments reflect a degree of justice, such punishments also reflect a degree of love.
29. Mendelssohn's German rendering of this poem in his Psalms edition also insisted that God "recompenses everyone according to his works," although this divine behavior was cast there as an expression of "grace" or "favor" (*Gnade*), rather than of love. See Mendelssohn, *Die Psalmen*, in *JubA*, 10.1:94.
30. Mendelssohn, *Jerusalem*, 89/8:156–57, 97/8:164. The italics appear in the original. For Mendelssohn's account of the beliefs which Christianity takes to be indispensable but accessible only through revelation, see his *Gegenbetrachtungen*, in *JubA*, 7:90–93. On the ways in which Mendelssohn did take Judaism to involve some beliefs inaccessible through reason, see note 11 above.
31. See Mendelssohn, *Jerusalem*, 93–94/8:160–61; see also 97/8:165.
32. Ibid., 94/8:160–61.
33. Ibid., 126/8:191–92. The italics are in the original. *Jerusalem*'s rendering of these lines is: "Die Himmel erzählen die Majestät Gottes, / Und seiner Hände Werk verkündet die Veste / Ein Tag strömt diese Lehr dem andern zu; / Und Nacht giebt Unterricht der Nacht. / Keine Lehre, keine Worte, / Deren Stimme nicht vernommen werde. / Ueber den ganzen Erdball tönet ihre Saite: / Ihr Vortrag dringet bis an der Erden Ende, / Dorthin, wo er der Sonn' ihr Zelt aufschlug." For the similar rendering in Mendelssohn's Psalms edition, see Mendelssohn, *Die Psalmen*, in *JubA*, 10.1:31.
34. Mendelssohn read this poem in a similar manner in his Hebrew commentary on the Pentateuch: see *Bi'ur* on Exodus 20:2 (in *JubA*, 16:186). On Mendelssohn as the author of the commentary on Exodus, see Altmann, *Moses Mendelssohn*, 405.
35. Mendelssohn, *Jerusalem*, 126/8:192. *Jerusalem*'s rendering of these lines is: "Von Sonnenaufgang bis zum Niedergange / Preist man des Ewgen Namen." For the similar rendering in Mendelssohn's Psalms edition, see Mendelssohn, *Die Psalmen*, in *JubA*, 10.1:176.

36. Mendelssohn also took this idea to be echoed by Malachi 1:11. See Mendelssohn, *Jerusalem*, 127/8:192.

37. Lacking civic rights, Mendelssohn referred in a 1769 text to these "domestic circumstances" as a reason for "carefully avoiding religious disputes": "I am a member of an oppressed people," he wrote, "who must beg for protection by appealing to the benevolence of the dominant nation." See Mendelssohn, "Open Letter to Lavater," trans. Curtis Bowman, in *Moses Mendelssohn: Writings on Judaism, Christianity, and the Bible*, trans. Allan Arkush, Curtis Bowman, and Elias Sacks, ed. Michah Gottlieb (Waltham, MA: Brandeis University Press, 2011), 12; for the German, see *JubA*, 7:14.

38. On Mendelssohn and this system, see, for example, Edward Levenson, "Moses Mendelssohn's Understanding of Logico-Grammatical and Literary Construction in the Pentateuch: A Study of His German Translation and Hebrew Commentary (the Bi'ur)" (PhD diss., Brandeis University, 1972); Raphael Jospe, "The Superiority of Oral over Written Communication: Judah Halevi's *Kuzari* and Modern Jewish Thought," in *From Ancient Israel to Modern Judaism: Intellect in Quest of Understanding: Essays in Honor of Marvin Fox*, ed. Jacob Neusner, Ernest Frerichs, and Nahum Sarna, 4 vols. (Atlanta, GA: Scholars Press, 1989), 3:138–41; Andrea Schatz, *Sprache in der Zerstreuung: Die Säkularisierung des Hebräischen im 18. Jahrhundert* (Göttingen: Vandenhoeck & Ruprecht, 2009), 244–55; Avi Lifschitz, "A Natural yet Providential Tongue: Moses Mendelssohn on Hebrew as a Language of Action," in *Language as Bridge and Border: Linguistic, Cultural, and Political Constellations in 18th to 20th Century German-Jewish Thought*, ed. Sabine Sander (Berlin: Hentrich & Hentrich, 2015), 31–50. Mendelssohn's discussion of the cantillation signs was linked to a broader emphasis on orality that was crucial to his defense of Judaism. See the sources cited above, along with, for example, Sorkin, *Moses Mendelssohn*; Edward Breuer, "Rabbinic Law and Spirituality in Mendelssohn's *Jerusalem*," *Jewish Quarterly Review* 86, no. 3/4 (1996): 299–321; Gideon Freudenthal, *No Religion without Idolatry: Mendelssohn's Jewish Enlightenment* (Notre Dame, IN: University of Notre Dame Press, 2012), 90–92. This concern with orality may also have shaped Mendelssohn's turn to the Psalms in *Jerusalem*. As indicated in the letter quoted at the beginning of this essay, he saw these poems as literature that deserves to be *sung*; perhaps, then, his emphasis on these poems reflected, in part, a belief in the importance of texts that receive oral expression.

39. See Edward Breuer, *The Limits of Enlightenment: Jews, Germans, and the Eighteenth-Century Study of Scripture* (Cambridge, MA: Harvard University Press, 1996).

40. Mendelssohn's introduction is entitled *Or Lanetivah* ("Light for the Path"). For the lines that I quote, see *Or Lanetivah*, in Mendelssohn, *JubA*, 14:242; I slightly alter my translation in Mendelssohn's "From *Light for the Path*," in *Moses Mendelssohn: Writings on Judaism, Christianity, and the Bible*, 196. The "vowels" invoked here are vowels that are added to the Bible's consonantal text and, like the accents, were attacked by scholars in Mendelssohn's era as post-biblical innovations. Mendelssohn also identified other Jewish textual traditions that he took to be rejected by Christian scholars, including determinations regarding the Bible's consonantal text and rabbinic interpretation.

41. Mendelssohn, *Or Lanetivah*, in *JubA*, 14:243; I follow my translation in "From *Light for the Path*," 196.
42. These are rabbinic works from late antiquity.
43. Mendelssohn, *Or Lanetivah*, in *JubA*, 14:218.
44. For example, Mendelssohn took the cantillation system to clarify the Bible's meaning through devices such as changes in intonation and pitch. He took this system to be so vital, in fact, that it was actually employed by God when revealing the Torah to Moses: "There is no doubt," we saw Mendelssohn write in the passage quoted in the body of my essay, "that Moses . . . heard all the Torah's words from the mouth of the Almighty . . . with the vocalizations and accents" (*Or Lanetivah*, in *JubA*, 14:218). On this view, God *sang* the Torah to Moses, providing subsequent generations with a vital resource. See also the sources in note 38 above.
45. Mendelssohn borrowed this language from Ecclesiastes 12:11.
46. On this term, see Marcus Jastrow, *A Dictionary of the Targumim, the Talmud Babli and Yerushalmi, and the Midrashic Literature*, 2 vols. (New York: Judaica Press, 1996), 1:425. See also the translation of this term in a modern English edition of one of the rabbinic texts from which Mendelssohn borrows this language: *Sifre: A Tannaitic Commentary on the Book of Deuteronomy*, trans. Reuven Hammer (New Haven, CT: Yale University Press, 1986), 63.
47. Mendelssohn, introduction to *Bi'ur* on Exodus 15 (in *JubA*, 16:126); I follow my translation in Mendelssohn, "On Biblical Poetry," in *Moses Mendelssohn: Writings on Judaism, Christianity, and the Bible*, 212. On Mendelssohn as the author of this section of *Bi'ur*, see note 34 above. Mendelssohn's use of the word "tablets," or *luhot*, was perhaps intended to bring to mind the tablets on which the Ten Commandments will be engraved later in Exodus: I thank the editors for calling attention to this point. In the clause that I omit, Mendelssohn suggested that biblical poetry also produces various emotions in its audience.
48. Mendelssohn, introduction to *Bi'ur* on Exodus 15 (in *JubA*, 16:126); I follow my translation in Mendelssohn, "On Biblical Poetry," 213.
49. See Mendelssohn, *Bi'ur* on Genesis 2:9 (in *JubA*, 15.2:23); I follow my translation in Mendelssohn, "On Adam's Sin," in *Moses Mendelssohn: Writings on Judaism, Christianity, and the Bible*, 209. On Mendelssohn as the author of this section of the *Bi'ur*, see note 12 above. On Mendelssohn's use of "good" for actions that promote the pursuit of perfection, see the first section of my essay.
50. Mendelssohn, introduction to *Bi'ur* on Exodus 15 (in *JubA*, 16:126); I follow my English translation in Mendelssohn, "On Biblical Poetry," 214.
51. The context clarifies that "this end" is the "end" outlined above: the cultivation of virtues.
52. On the background of Mendelssohn's position, see Altmann, *Moses Mendelssohn*, 409–13; Sorkin, *Moses Mendelssohn*, 76–77; Gottlieb, "Aesthetics and the Infinite," 337.
53. On different types of parallelism that Mendelssohn identified, see Gottlieb, "Aesthetics and the Infinite," 337.
54. I follow Mendelssohn's German translation of this verse in the *Bi'ur*: see Mendelssohn, *JubA*, 16:141.

55. Mendelssohn, introduction to *Bi'ur* on Exodus 15 (in *JubA*, 16:126); I follow my English translation in Mendelssohn, "On Biblical Poetry," 214. Mendelssohn also suggested that this poetic structure makes it easier for biblical poetry to be sung without obscuring its meaning, which for him would have a similar effect, since as we have seen, one of the benefits he associated with music is a capacity to lodge words in our memories and thereby transform such content into an object of ongoing contemplation.

56. For Mendelssohn, these behaviors that foster human flourishing might also be understood as a form of divine service. As noted above, he took the pursuit of perfection to be divinely endorsed, arguing that God will recognize that human beings are charged with pursuing perfection and wish for them to seek this goal. Acting in ways that promote this pursuit would thus involve acting in ways that accord with divine intentions.

57. At the conference "Sara Levy's World" at Rutgers University in September, 2014, Yael Sela spoke about Mendelssohn's ideas of music as the fullest realization of the biblical text.

58. My analysis suggests that Mendelssohn took biblical poetry and the cantillation signs to have an effect similar to the one he ascribes to Jewish law more generally—the effect of generating ethically significant reflection on religious matters. See the discussions of ethics and Jewish law in the works cited in note 14 above. On connections between Jewish law and aesthetics in Mendelssohn's thought, see also Gottlieb, "Aesthetics and the Infinite," 334–40; Braiterman, "The Emergence of Modern Religion," 19–27; Hochman, *The Ugliness of Moses Mendelssohn*, 54–65.

59. Given Mendelssohn's concern with orality, it may be that both the oral recitation of the words, and the repetition of this oral production, are essential.

60. As with Mendelssohn's claims regarding the Psalms, it would be interesting to consider the question of why he left his point implicit. Is this another case of him exercising caution, given his precarious legal status?

61. As noted above, there may be other problems arising from this failure: if (as Mendelssohn held) God employed this system when revealing the Torah to Moses, then Christianity's neglect of this system is also a neglect of divinely revealed and enacted content.

62. To be sure, Mendelssohn conceded *some* aesthetic advantages to Christianity. See, for example, his praise for the beauty of some aspects of Christian Bible translations in Mendelssohn, *Or Lanetivah*, in *JubA*, 14:242; for my English translation, see Mendelssohn "From *Light for the Path*," 196.

63. Mendelssohn may have planned to compose a volume more fully outlining and defending his approach to the Psalms; see Mendelssohn, *Die Psalmen*, in *JubA*, 10.1:7.

64. For example, Mendelssohn received music lessons from Johann Philipp Kirnberger, a Prussian court musician and student of Johann Sebastian Bach, and composed an essay intervening in eighteenth-century discussions about constructing a well-tempered pianoforte. See Altmann, *Moses Mendelssohn*, 66–67; Henk Visser, "Mendelssohn's Euclidean Treatise on Equal Temperament," in *Moses Mendelssohn's Metaphysics and Aesthetics*, 83–104.

65. Mendelssohn might have attempted to respond to this concern in various ways. Insofar as he expressed reservations about the christological beliefs and text-critical practices informing some Christian Bible translations (despite, as indicated in note 62 above, praising some aesthetic features of these works), he might have argued that musical renderings of the Bible in Christian settings exposed audiences to flawed versions of the biblical text: see, for example, Breuer, *The Limits of Enlightenment*, 115–75, along with the sources in note 19 above. Indeed, Mendelssohn singled out for criticism a German biblical translation—the Psalms translation by Johann Andreas Cramer—used in musical compositions by Carl Philipp Emanuel Bach: see Altmann, *Moses Mendelssohn*, 244. Moreover, insofar as Mendelssohn claimed (as we saw above) that the cantillation system was employed not only whenever Bible was publicly read during worship, but also in educational settings in which teachers "would not give the Holy Scripture to their sons or students" without "the sound of the words and . . . melody and singing" (Mendelssohn, *Or Lanetivah*, in *JubA*, 14:218), he might have attempted to argue that this system is able to have more far-reaching effects on its listeners than Christian songs have on their audience: hearing the Bible chanted musically in multiple worship services every week along with certain types of educational settings, he might have argued, creates numerous, recurring opportunities for its words to become objects of ongoing reflection and instill morally admirable dispositions. Nevertheless, I know of no text in which Mendelssohn developed these potential lines of reasoning—nor would such arguments be without their own difficulties.

66. On the audience of Mendelssohn's Hebrew writings, see Sacks, *Moses Mendelssohn's Living Script*, 13–14. Mendelssohn expressed worries about his co-religionists seeing non-Jewish sources as more aesthetically sophisticated than Jewish ones in, for example, his introduction to *Bi'ur* on Exodus 15 (in *JubA*, 16:134); for my English translation, see Mendelssohn, "On Biblical Poetry," 215.

67. Mendelssohn explicitly described *Jerusalem* as a text read by both Jews and non-Jews: see Mendelssohn to Herz Homberg, June 14, 1783, in Mendelssohn, *JubA*, 13:112–13. The question of why Mendelssohn chose to attack Christianity is also one that might be posed regarding other works in which he sounded universalistic notes yet subtly took aim at his neighbors' religious commitments, such as the "Open Letter to Lavater" discussed in note 37 above. Even as Mendelssohn stressed the universal accessibility of key truths and the afterlife and disavowed any intention of explicitly criticizing the religious errors of his neighbors, he attacked numerous positions often associated with Christianity, including a commitment to missionary activity and the idea that salvation is accessible only through the church. See Mendelssohn, "Open Letter to Lavater," 6–15; for the German, see Mendelssohn, *JubA*, 7:7–17.

68. In this respect, the *Bi'ur* was wrestling with a question that recurred throughout Mendelssohn's writings, especially *Jerusalem*: the question of how to understand the fraught relationship between the particular and the universal. Just as *Jerusalem* famously explored (for instance) the relationship between laws specific to Judaism and truths universally accessible through reason

(Mendelssohn, *Jerusalem*, 89–139/8:156–204), so too was the *Bi'ur* concerned here with the relationship between music specific to the Jewish tradition and the perfection pursued by all human beings.

69. As noted above, other readers have called attention to the role of aesthetics in Mendelssohn's defense of Judaism—to the ways in which he drew on his aesthetics to highlight the strengths of this tradition, thereby making a case for its inclusion in modern life alongside other religions. See, for example, Sorkin, *Moses Mendelssohn*, 117–18; Sheehan, *The Enlightenment Bible*, 176–81; and Hochman, *The Ugliness of Moses Mendelssohn*, 30–73. On the links between Mendelssohn's defense of Judaism and his aesthetics, see also Gottlieb, "Aesthetics and the Infinite," 326–53; and Braiterman, "The Emergence of Modern Religion," 11–29. My claim, by contrast, is that a second, more subversive project was also crucial to Mendelssohn's thought. He drew on aesthetics not simply to win a place for Judaism alongside other religions traditions, but also to call one of those traditions into question—to suggest that profound flaws plague Christianity's doctrinal content and capacity for moral formation. See also Schorch, *Moses Mendelssohns Sprachpolitik*, 96–140. A future essay might further examine the apologetic dimension of Mendelssohn's argument—ways in which his critique of Christianity functioned as a defense of Judaism in response to specific attacks. We might also explore whether his Christian contemporaries responded to his claims about Christianity and aesthetics.

Chapter Seven

Longing for the Sublime

Jewish Self-Consciousness and the
St. Matthew Passion in Biedermeier Berlin

Yael Sela

The extraordinary musical accomplishments of Sara Levy *née* Itzig, which place her as a key figure in the reception and cultivation of the music of Johann Sebastian Bach in Berlin during the last quarter of the eighteenth century, are recorded almost exclusively in her remarkable collection of music manuscripts and prints of the instrumental works of Bach and his sons.[1] Yet apart from a handful of letters written to her by contemporary composers, some billets, and sporadic anecdotal references in letters and memoirs by younger family members and acquaintances,[2] which provide little if any insight into her musical world, Levy's persona largely remains shrouded in mystery.

In contrast to other contemporary women of the enlightened Berlin Jewish elite, Levy left no autobiographical or epistolary writings that could shed light on her ambitions and choices as a female Jewish musician and patron in a male-dominated, non-Jewish cultural universe: What were her aspirations, motivations, and dilemmas? How did she feel about the music she avidly performed and collected, and why did she refrain from pursuing other repertoires? It is particularly tempting to imagine how the sixty-eight-year-old Sara Levy would have reacted upon hearing, in 1829, the revival performance of Bach's *St. Matthew Passion*, the monumental oratorio of the great Lutheran composer, whose instrumental works she had known so intimately; how would she have perceived the extraordinary event that marked a watershed in Bach's public reception? And what would she have thought of the pronounced Lutheran theology imparted by the libretto of the *Passion*, which otherwise lies safely latent in Bach's instrumental music?[3]

We might seek some answers regarding the reception of Bach's music amongst Levy's milieu of music lovers—*Musikkenner und -liebhaber*—in the writings of contemporary enlightened women of the Berlin Jewish elite. Such documents, consisting primarily of letters and memoirs, reveal that while Levy was an exceptional music connoisseur, for daughters of other Jewish families in Berlin born during the third quarter of the eighteenth century, music was from early on in life a vital mode of experiencing the world and of fashioning themselves in relation to it.[4] Moreover, it seems that like the Itzig daughters, other privileged Jewish maidens of their generation obtained musical training marked by an exclusive taste for the instrumental music of the Bach family.[5] Exploring Jewish voices in the reception of the 1829 revival of Bach's *Passion*, the present article locates music as a distinct *topos* in epistolary and autobiographical writings by Jewish women in Sara Levy's circle.

Musical Renderings in Jewish Women's Writings

Recent research on Jewish women in Berlin of the late Enlightenment and early Romanticism has focused on letters and autobiographical writings, exposing the nuances and riches that constituted (if often burdened) those women's lives and the challenges and dilemmas they faced as twofold outsiders.[6] To enlightened Jewish women in Berlin of the late eighteenth and early nineteenth century, the practice of letter writing was often more than a form of sociability, nourishing friendships, and manifesting virtue.[7] Particularly among intellectually exceptional women of that circle, letter writing was also a literary practice, socially sanctioned for a woman and a Jew. Their correspondences comprise a literary genre that is irreducibly heterogeneous, open to those who were excluded from the public sphere, adequately lending itself to addressing "the problem of understanding and existing in the political, social, and cultural ruptures around 1800 in a variety of ways."[8]

However, little attention has been given to what the letters and memoirs of Rahel Levin Varnhagen, Brendel Veit (Dorothea Schlegel), Henriette Herz, Henriette Mendelssohn, Fradchen Liebmann (Friederike Liman), and others reveal about these Jewish (if later converted)[9] women's passion for music and the aesthetic; and, more specifically, to how music functions in their writings as a distinct *topos*, a literary strategy of critical reflection, self-fashioning, and cultural negotiation through learned scrutiny and sensual contemplation.

Growing up in the sociocultural and political atmosphere of the *Berliner Aufklärung* (Enlightenment), which offered unprecedented possibilities for interreligious encounter on many social, cultural, and intellectual levels, these women were raised in a milieu that had come to embrace Enlightenment ethics of *Bildung* and culture while emulating the lifestyle of German aristocracy. For the emerging enlightened Jewish elite, the consumption of European art, literature, theater, music, and opera had become by the last third of the eighteenth century increasingly common as an expression of a new civil self-consciousness and "life feeling."[10] Being the first generation in the Ashkenazic world to obtain a more or less comprehensive liberal education that included music, dance, and languages, next to painting, sewing, and housekeeping, the daughters of often affluent Jewish families such as Itzig, Ephraim, Fließ, Friedländer, Lemos, Mendelssohn, and Levin not only grew up into, but partook in bringing about, a world marked by a growing sense of individualism and religious laxity. In contrast to their mothers, they ceased to wear the traditional headdress after marriage, adorned themselves with fashionable, low-cut dresses, whirled around gaily in the daring waltz, and socialized with non-Jewish aristocrats, artists, and intellectuals in private salons and public theaters, concert halls, and spas.[11] Intoxicated by a world of sensuous, intellectual, and aesthetic stimuli, their liberated sensuality was immortalized in portraits and expressed in their autobiographical, epistolary, and literary writings.[12]

Impressions, critiques, and recollections of musical experiences and events are interwoven into those women's writings in a variety of ways, reflecting a fascination, at first somewhat hesitant, with German musical culture, an eagerness to know and understand music, and a keenness to demonstrate refined taste, aesthetic discernment, and musical knowledge: from one of the earliest extant letters, written in 1792 by Brendel Veit *née* Mendelssohn, eldest daughter of the philosopher Moses Mendelssohn, which inextricably binds music and the politics of social emancipation, through numerous discussions of opera productions in the correspondences of Rahel Levin Varnhagen, including a description of a Sabbath carriage ride to the opera fraught with agitation and guilt; to Henriette Herz's memoirs that recall her bedazzlement upon first attending the royal opera as a child.[13]

Without doubt, the most dramatic musical event in Sara Levy's Berlin would have indeed been the encounter with Johann Sebastian Bach's choral music at the revival of his *St. Matthew Passion* in 1829 at the *Sing-Akademie*—the city's prestigious bourgeois choral society and first mixed-sex amateur choir—a venture initiated, organized, and conducted by Felix Mendelssohn Bartholdy, Sara Levy's young grandnephew (and Brendel Veit's nephew). Bach's music was altogether a novelty for the general public; but even the musicians, connoisseurs, and patrons who had cultivated his instrumental music for decades were mostly unfamiliar with his vocal works. The performance of the *Passion* thus offered a new experience for all.

In contrast to Bach's *St. John Passion,* which overtly accuses Jews for the death of Christ, the focus in the *St. Matthew Passion* is on Christ as "suffering servant" whose death is brought on by the guilt of all. Yet the story of the Passion in general nonetheless poses a fundamental challenge to Jews, those associated in Christian theology with the rejection of Christ as king and Messiah, and accused of responsibility for his crucifixion. After all, the genealogy of Baroque Passion oratorios goes back to the long medieval and early modern tradition of Passion plays, whose performance in German lands during Lent unleashed anti-Jewish sentiments often followed by violent acts.[14] Coupled with the fact that the revival of Bach's *Passion* instantly gained a pivotal place in the formation of German national culture, the cardinal role played by Jews (and converts) in this endeavor and, more generally, in the patronage of the *Sing-Akademie,* raises questions concerning their reception of the piece and of the cultural moment that its performance constituted. Even Felix Mendelssohn himself, largely raised and educated in enlightened Protestantism, sarcastically observed that it took a "Judenjunge" to restore "to the people the greatest Christian musical work."[15] While Mendelssohn's Jewish background has in recent decades been subjected to scrutiny,[16] a consideration of other, less conspicuous contemporary voices might contribute to a more differentiated, more polyphonic view of the cultural, religious, and political sensibilities that played into the negotiation of German Jewish modernity in Berlin of the early nineteenth century.[17]

Nobody articulated the ambivalence inherent in the Jewish encounter with that cultural moment more eloquently than the Berlin *salonnière* and writer Rahel Varnhagen von Ense *née* Levin (fig. 7.1). Her sensitivity, perceptiveness, and above all, her in-betweenness enabled her to capture the cultural and religious dilemmas that the *Passion* stirred in the minds of Germans like her, whose Jewishness continued to loom large in their self-consciousness despite conversion to Christianity. By far the most prolific writer in her circle of Jewish women in Berlin, Rahel Levin Varnhagen,[18] daughter of the diamond merchant and banker Levin Markus (Löb Cohen) and Chaie Levin Markus, became not only one of the most celebrated Jewish *salonnières* of all times, admired for her acute intellect, aesthetic sensibilities, and charm, but also the first Jewish woman to establish herself as a recognized intellectual in a German, Christian-dominated society between the Enlightenment and early Romanticism. Like many Jewish women of her generation in Berlin (but unlike Sara Levy and some of her siblings), she, too, converted to Protestantism in preparation for marriage at the advanced age of forty-three. Over six thousand extant letters and diaries written over four decades by and to Rahel Levin Varnhagen give voice to an entire network of Jewish women (and fewer Jewish men, primarily husbands and brothers) bonded through family ties and friendships. Although she was not the only woman to engage in epistolary writing, she and her correspondents

Figure 7.1. *Rahel (Friederike) Varnhagen von Ense,* by William Hensel, July 27, 1822. Pencil on paper, 18.5cm x 14.9cm. Kupferstichkabinett, Staatliche Museen zu Berlin (Photo: Jörg P. Anders). Used with permission.

gave the practice of letter writing new significance as a common literary enterprise ultimately available for posterity as a literary genre.[19]

In what follows, I draw upon Rahel Varnhagen's impressions from the revival performance of Bach's *St. Matthew Passion* in a letter written shortly after the event in the spring of 1829. I draw upon her commentary as a lens for exploring the reception of Bach's *Passion* through the eyes (and ears) of a German Jewish-Protestant woman. Listening to the different voices that emerge from the letter, we get to hear a universe—by no means a homogeneous one—of Jewish-born women and men engrossed in a non-Jewish world while constantly probing and negotiating a modern German self-consciousness and a new sense of Jewishness. The arena within which they acted was the predominantly Protestant universe that had begun to embrace German music, particularly Bach's music, as national cultural patrimony.

More broadly, I suggest that as daughters, sisters, wives, or friends of *maskilim* (enlightened Jewish intellectuals) on the one hand, and with strong ties to non-Jewish intellectuals, artists, and musicians on the other, freethinking women like Rahel Levin Varnhagen, Henriette Herz, Friederike Liman, and Dorothea Schlegel should be seen as partakers in the negotiation of modern Jewish self-consciousness.[20] The topics they chose to discuss, in German rather than Hebrew, and their ambivalent perspective enable us to consider more nuanced boundaries of Jewish modernity as a simultaneous embrace and critique of Enlightenment. In the lives and personalities of these "Hellenized" Jewesses, enlightened reason and passionate Romanticism, Greekness and Jewishness, past and present intermingled—extremes that would ultimately yield a new, modern "Greekjew,"[21] epitomized in the fashioning of Henriette Herz as a Hellenic goddess (fig. 7.2).

The *St. Matthew Passion* in Berlin

On March 11, 1829, the *Sing-Akademie zu Berlin* performed Johann Sebastian Bach's *St. Matthew Passion* in a grand public concert.[22] Composed in 1727 in Leipzig for the annual cycle of the Lutheran liturgy, the piece was originally intended for performance during Holy Week on Good Friday at the St. Thomas Church, where Bach served as music director (*Thomaskantor*) and educator at the *Thomasschule* from 1723 to his death in 1750. Now, in Berlin, Bach's *Passion* would be performed for the first time since 1742, over a hundred years after its inception. Initiated, organized, and conducted by the twenty-year-old Felix Mendelssohn Bartholdy, the revival of Bach's most complex and challenging choral work was a daring venture even in the eyes of the fervent director of the *Sing-Akademie* and Felix's composition teacher, Carl Friedrich Zelter.

Figure 7.2. *Henriette Herz*, by Anna Dorothea Therbusch, 1778. Oil on canvas, 75cm x 59cm. Alte Nationalgalerie, Staatliche Museen zu Berlin (Photo: Andres Kilger). Used with permission.

In the weeks prior to the concert, the editor of the *Berliner Allgemeine musikalische Zeitung* and Mendelssohn's friend, Adolph Bernhard Marx, had announced with zealous enthusiasm in a series of articles the "important and happy event" that "awaits the musical world, first in Berlin. . . . The greatest and holiest work of the greatest composer comes to life having been concealed for almost a hundred years, a celebration of religion and of art."[23] Having "had to remain muted" for decades, Bach's choral music had become outmoded, and was now perceived as dense, dry, and unintelligible.[24] Now, writes Marx, "with this performance, the gates of a long locked temple open up."[25]

By early morning on the day of the performance, all tickets had sold out (nearly one thousand, not including the royal balconies), and additional seats had to be set up behind the orchestra. In the evening, over a thousand of Berlin's high society—aristocrats, prominent intellectuals, poets, bureaucrats, men and women of the bourgeoisie, Christians and Jews—streamed into the newly built hall of the *Sing-Akademie* on Unter den Linden; another thousand disappointed music lovers had to be turned down at the door. The audience, we are told, was frenzied with enthusiasm for Bach's oratorio, a musical marvel that seemed to embrace "the whole of humanity, the whole of life, the whole world."[26] Subsequent performances in Berlin and throughout the country precipitated similar excitement.[27] To the majority of the public, apart from a handful of Bach connoisseurs and members of the *Sing-Akademie* who had participated in informal readings of excerpts from Bach's choral works,[28] the performance of the *St. Matthew Passion* was no less than a revelatory experience—"a new, hitherto unknown world of artistic creation."[29]

Largely performed by amateur singers and musicians, members of the *Sing-Akademie*, the 1829 performance transfigured Bach's *Passion* not only in time but also in space: from the ecclesiastical St. Thomas in Leipzig to the civic neoclassical hall of the *Sing-Akademie*, a Greek temple of music that the Prussian architect Karl Friedrich Schinkel had erected on Berlin's royal boulevard (fig. 7.3); from the somber piety of Good Friday to the festivity of a historically conscious musical enterprise. In the theological-historical imagination of the organizers, as formulated by Marx with religious no less than aesthetic zeal, and perhaps also in the minds of many in the audience, the New Testament story of Christ's crucifixion celebrated in the hermeneutical marriage of words and music opened up new interpretative paths for imagining Second-Temple Jerusalem in Athens-on-the-River-Spree—"*Spree-Athen.*"[30]

In the historiography of the 1829 performance of the *Passion*, the significance of the event has been primarily located in two aspects: not only was it a turning point in the public reception of Bach's music that heralded his veneration in a nineteenth-century imagined pantheon of German composers; it was also a seminal event in the formation of a national German culture. As Celia Applegate has demonstrated, the 1829 performance of Bach's *Passion*,

Figure 7.3. *Sing-Akademie zu Berlin,* by Eduard Gärtner, 1843. Oil on canvas. In private hands. Image courtesy of the Sing-Akademie zu Berlin.

"more than any other single event . . . made music, *Bach's* music, *German* music, as essential to what it meant to be German as the language itself."[31] Carl Dahlhaus has observed that the significance of the event to the formation of German nationalism was matched perhaps only by the 1882 premiere of Richard Wagner's *Parsifal.*[32] Indeed, it seems that what lent the performance of Bach's monumental Passion oratorio its broad impact and enormous success as a historical moment of national significance, primarily in Prussia, was above all its appeal to sentiments that resonated with a new Protestant theology, coupled with an emergent sense of German nationalism, sentiments that were further enhanced by Felix Mendelssohn's edited score of the piece and his design of the performance.

The 1820s saw the rise of a new Protestant theology in Prussia, engendered, partly in reaction to the recent unification of the Prussian Church, by Friedrich Schleiermacher, the charismatic theology chair at the University of Berlin, and Friedrich Hegel, who advanced a philosophy of religion that sought to unite faith and reason (*Vernunftreligion*).[33] Schleiermacher's idea of a communal the-ology (*Gemeindetheologie*), systematically formulated in his monumental treatise *The Christian Faith*, saw the Christian Church in its entirety as a collective body of its believers; the image of Christ could be achieved only by the community, not by the individual alone.[34]

Congruently, the emergent sense of a national German culture rested upon Johann Gottfried Herder's notion that religion constitutes the most fundamental formative experience of a nation. To him, "the real living cul-ture of a people" starts "with the awakening and cultivation of their lan-guage—and this depends on religion." That is, religion alone introduced the first elements of culture, and the two were inextricable.[35] To Schleiermacher as to Hegel, this new cultural-religious consciousness traversed the confines of ecclesiastical spaces and practices, engaging the arts—above all music, now performed in civic public spaces such as the *Sing-Akademie*—as a richly sensual reiteration of religious experience.[36] Accordingly, German *Kultur* was now bound up with a sense of piety and with specifically Protestant religious and textual traditions, constituting a cultural religion (*Kulturprotestantismus*) that engaged the Luther Bible as a national, more than a theological, text.[37] Whereas the eighteenth-century Enlightenment witnessed a plurality of aes-thetically conscious Bible translations (among them Moses Mendelssohn's translation of the Pentateuch into German in Hebrew characters with Hebrew commentary) that attempted to traverse the distance to ancient Hebrew Scripture through aesthetic modes of hermeneutics, the early nine-teenth century brought the Luther Bible back into fashion, making it an inte-gral part of the German cultural patrimony and a supreme model of German literary language.[38] And, if the Luther Bible was now the one central text of German national culture, Bach would become for the nineteenth century his ultimate musical interpreter.

The educated Protestant bourgeoisie, the *Bildungsbürgertum*, to which the converted members of the Mendelssohn family now belonged, was immersed in this cultural atmosphere. The religious world of the young Felix Mendelssohn and his musical circle, which included his sister Fanny Hensel, his friend the music critic Adolph Bernhard Marx (similarly a converted Jew), and the singer Eduard Devrient, was greatly influenced by Schleiermacher's popular theology. Indeed, as family letters indicate, by the early 1830s, before the theologian's death in 1834, Felix Mendelssohn had developed a close personal relation-ship with Schleiermacher, who had naturally attended the 1829 performance of the *Passion*.[39] Expressions of spiritual sentiments in contemporary accounts of the *Passion* performance similarly reflect Schleiermacher's influence: Fanny Hensel described the "church-like aura" that descended upon the hall of the *Sing-Akademie*.[40] Mendelssohn himself recalled how the choir "sang . . . as if they were in a church," while the audience "felt that this was not merely a matter of music and concert, but of religion and church."[41] The emphatic language used in these and other extant descriptions, as in Marx's reports, invokes sentiments evocative of the specifically Lutheran *Gemeindetheologie* with music's community-building power at its service.

On March 7, four days before the first concert, Marx articulated in his newspaper the spiritual atmosphere that surrounded the event and heralded the effect it would have, not merely as a concert, but as a religious, revelatory calling, a confirmation of the foundational bond of the New Testament:

> And we are summoned not to an art event, but to a solemn religious celebration. The reflection and sensation of the congregation is directed toward the message about the foundation of our religion through the bond of the New Testament and Jesus's self-sacrifice for the salvation of mankind; that is the essence of the celebration, which the art of music alone can capture, only through it can all the abundance and valor, all its blessing be completely revealed.[42]

Considered in this light, we cannot but wonder about the cardinal role played by Jews and Jewish-born converts in the 1829 performance of Bach's *Passion*. After all, it was Felix Mendelssohn's maternal grandmother, Babette (Bella) Salomon *née* Itzig, a devout Jew like her musical sister Sara Levy, who in late 1823 or early 1824 presented him with a copy of the rare score of Bach's *Passion* that he had been longing to possess.[43] Growing up in the 1760s and 1770s, Babette and her siblings, like other children of privileged Jewish families in Berlin, were the first generation of Ashkenazic Jews to obtain musical training as part and parcel of their upbringing, becoming music connoisseurs, collectors, amateur performers, and, since its founding in 1791, patrons of the *Sing-Akademie*.[44] Thus, although by 1829 the presence of Jews in Berlin's musical life might have seemed self-evident, it had in fact barely been three generations since Jews had begun cultivating and co-constituting musical culture as an integral part of a bourgeois and upper-class lifestyle.

Furthermore, if in early nineteenth-century Prussia religion was fundamental to the ideas of culture and of nation, Jews were largely excluded from what it meant to be German through their religion, laws, tradition, language, and history. Whereas in the atmosphere of the Berlin Enlightenment during the second half of the eighteenth century music traversed religious boundaries and seemed to offer an inclusive mode of sociocultural participation hitherto unknown in central and western Europe, the religious-cultural atmosphere of the Biedermeier time—the period between the Congress of Vienna in 1815 and the 1848 revolutions—now underscored the exclusion of those whose religious traditions were based on an ancient, pre-Christian text, the Hebrew Bible, a peculiar and remote historical "archive of ancient humanity."[45]

Varnhagen on Bach

In a letter to her husband, August Varnhagen von Ense, on March 13, 1829, two days after the performance of Bach's *Passion* in Berlin, Rahel Varnhagen reflected upon the event. Her acute observations unveil some of the cultural dilemmas it brought to the surface and the ambivalence of German Jewish cultural experience in Biedermeier Berlin. Born in 1771 to a wealthy Berlin family, Rahel Levin had been raised among the increasingly secularized, enlightened Jewish elite. In her youth and early adulthood, she had witnessed the promises that the Enlightenment project held for Jewish civil betterment and political emancipation, at a time when the practice, consumption, and discourse of music had become a mark of Jewish acculturation, and offered, particularly in instrumental form, a mode of participation even more readily available than literature or visual arts (fig. 7.4). Now in the winter of her life (she would die in 1833, only four years later), Rahel Varnhagen confronted the demise of the project of Enlightenment, having lived through its prime, decline, and the disillusionment that followed the Napoleonic wars and the Congress of Vienna.[46]

Written in her typical style as an intricate stream of reflective contemplation, the letter reveals extraordinary cultural perceptiveness and an unusually learned engagement with music and aesthetic concepts. It offers a retrospective account of Rahel Levin Varnhagen's life experience as a German Jewish "Pallas Athena," a Jewish-Protestant "gift from heaven,"[47] who transformed her own difference and marginality into a source of strength and defiance.

Varnhagen frames her letter as if to draw up an autobiographical perspective: it opens with a gesture toward a temporality of nowness through reference to a newspaper item (imagine an opening shot of a film showing a front-page news headline). It concludes, after intricate excursions into aesthetic scrutiny, childhood memories, and a music-historical discussion, by returning to the present, to the concert she has just heard, this time through a prism of the writer's own autobiographical past, suggesting a temporality of pastness. The remark made before returning, in the final sentence, to the concert recalls Varnhagen's childhood days: "My music lessons consisted entirely of music by Sebastian and all the Bachs and the entire school, so that we, from *that* time, are well familiar with it all."[48] Without explicating who "we" are or what "that time" was (words underlined in the original hand), this interjection articulates, somewhat apologetically, a sense of the cultural distinction enjoyed by an implied social milieu in their role as elite music connoisseurs of Bach's music. The newspaper entry mentioned at the outset of the letter is a poem by the Jewish poet Michael Beer, brother of the composer Giacomo Meyerbeer; the two were sons of Amalie Beer, a revered Berlin *salonnière* and music patron, and Jacob Herz Beer, a wealthy entrepreneur and pioneering proponent of reformist Judaism in Berlin. In other words, Varnhagen positions herself within a

Figure 7.4. *Rahel and* [brother] *Marcus Levin,* by Johann Christoph Frisch, ca. 1783. Oil on canvas, 22.5cm x 29.6cm. Staatsbibliothek zu Berlin, PK (Photo: Dietmar Katz). Used with permission. Marcus was Rahel's brother.

loosely demarcated, musically privileged Jewish social circle, where the instrumental music of the Bach family had long been known—in opposition to most of the general public, to whom Bach's music was a discovery. We shall encounter this underlying collective voice again later.

In her letter, Varnhagen not only distances herself from the spiritual sentiments expressed by the public, she is even deterred by them. Writing to her husband, she rushes to declare that like her young companion, the poet Heinrich Heine, she, too, "was bored by the music" ("Auch ich hatte Langeweile in dieser Musik"). But the impassioned discussion and learned scrutiny in the pages that follow leave no room for doubt that there is more behind this nonchalant remark. Rahel Varnhagen is irritated; she is disturbed by the piece she has just heard and is displeased with its performance. As if to add insult to injury, she endorses the dismissive gesture with which she began by commenting on the choir—"as always [in Berlin], insultingly bad." "Then," she continues, "the most bizarre, frugal text. Christ's last days and death, purely out of the Bible."

What is, then, the source of her irritation, and what is the meaning of her displeasure?

We ought to keep in mind that Felix Mendelssohn conducted an expurgated version of the *Passion* score: he omitted eleven arias (about a third), four recitatives, and seven chorales, and made cuts in most of the remaining arias and especially in the recitative sections of the Evangelist.[49] He also left out many small sections from within the recitatives in part two of the piece, particularly from the arrest and trial scene (but left in place the Turba scene of the Jewish mob crying for Jesus's crucifixion).[50] Celia Applegate notes that these alterations were probably intended to make the demanding and unfamiliar work more easily accessible to the audience, emphasizing "the drama of the *Passion* story and the congregational tradition of the Lutheran chorale at the expense of the reflective and Italianate solo singing."[51] Michael Marissen has compellingly argued that Mendelssohn's editorial decisions may also have had religious motivations, influenced by Schleiermacher's *Gemeindetheologie*, in the emphasis on the second article of the creed ("I believe in God the son") rather than the more universal first ("God the father"), which Enlightenment deism stresses, while attempting to mitigate anti-Jewish elements in the piece. By keeping most of the recitatives, which consist of verbatim biblical account, and the congregational responses in the chorales, largely leaving out expressions of individual religious experience in the form of arias, Mendelssohn's score thus favors Lutheran congregational sentiments over religious individualism.[52]

Varnhagen, "bored by the music," reacts to these sentiments with estrangement, dissociating herself from that imagined community. Her critique rapidly arrives at the heart of the matter: an aesthetic assessment of Bach's choral composition, the affective power of the performance, and the desirable relationship between words and music. Drawing upon the knowledge and skills she had acquired, somewhat eclectically, in her youth,[53] she confidently proceeds to scrutinize Bach's music, comparing the vocal work she had just heard for the first time with the instrumental music that she evidently knew intimately: "Sebastian, I have long been saying, is entirely Kant: with great poetic talent, fantasy; a great architect of prime proportions; a pure soul, inclined toward godly thoughts. Always sublime and entertaining when he follows the impulse of his own inspiration. But not when he sets texts, words, to music."

Did Rahel Varnhagen truly find Bach's vocal music so uninspired and uninspiring, lacking in fantasy, unlike his "sublime" instrumental music? Bach, she assures her reader, "has done *so* much great, rich, sensual, sublime, right, new, that he completely forgot to develop in one area, because it also was not his own. To me, it is clear that vocal music is not, and cannot, be so pure, so heavenly, so sublime, as instrumental music."

What was it, to Varnhagen, that made music "sublime"? German musical culture had begun, at the turn of the nineteenth century, to assert itself through a new metaphysical aesthetic, located in instrumental music;[54] but did Varnhagen indeed believe that instrumental music was superior to vocal music in its potential to arouse sublime sentiments? Reiterating the ethos by which the paramount purpose of music, and utmost task of the artist, was to move the listener to sublime sentiments, her aesthetic expectation, based on her previous experience of Bach's instrumental music, is disappointed upon hearing the oratorio. To her, Bach's greatness is asserted in his instrumental, abstract music, which, like Kant's philosophical writings, is characterized by precision, frugality, lucidity, "prime proportions"—but not when the artistic expression becomes concrete, referential, through words, not in his vocal music. This might explicate the meaning behind Varnhagen's allusion to Kant: To Immanuel Kant, an aesthetic idea constituted a "representation of the imagination" that "occasioned much thought without however any definite thought, any concept, capable of being adequate to it; it consequently cannot be . . . made intelligible by language."[55] However, it would be rather simplistic to assume that Varnhagen regarded vocal music as categorically inferior, as we shall shortly see.[56]

The rhetorical and aesthetic category of the sublime had emerged as a central philosophical *topos* in eighteenth-century English and, subsequently, German thought, in *Empfindsamkeit* culture (sentimentalism) and in the aesthetics of *Sturm und Drang*, and continued to be important (albeit somewhat transformed) in nineteenth-century aesthetics. One of the chief formulators of German aesthetic theory in the third quarter of the eighteenth century was Moses Mendelssohn. His aesthetics of the sublime in particular provides an important context for understanding the reception of the sublime in German thought, and is, moreover, in itself key to the ethical and political implications of his writings on aesthetics and on language.

Varnhagen's musical taste and aesthetic notions had been shaped early in her life in a cultural environment that embraced new aesthetic theories embedded in Enlightenment ethics.[57] She was an avid reader of popular German philosophy, including Kant, a favorite of Jewish women in Berlin and a philosophical mainstay among their maskilic male friends and husbands.[58] Yet her concepts regarding the sublime seem to resonate no less, and possibly more closely, with Moses Mendelssohn's earlier formulations, published in his aesthetic writings between the mid-1750s and 1770, which greatly contributed to the emergence of modern German aesthetics.[59] In her youth, during the 1780s, Rahel Levin would have become familiar with the writings of Mendelssohn, the "German Socrates," an icon of *Aufklärung* and a philosophical authority to Christians no less than to Jews. The north German enlightened Jewish elite, to which the Levin family belonged, devotedly subscribed to and purchased Mendelssohn's writings—not only his Pentateuch translation but also his extensive writings on aesthetics.[60] An intimate friend of Mendelssohn's eldest daughter Brendel, the young Rahel Levin would have frequented the Mendelssohn household, where intellectuals, theologians, and musicians, Christians as well as Jews, regularly gathered to discuss philosophy, music, literature, and politics.

Following and further developing English theories of the sublime, Mendelssohn's discussions herald the aesthetics of *Sturm und Drang*: juxtaposed contrasting affects, dramatic expression, rapidly changing affects, and the concept of the sublime as a mixed sentiment. The sublime, to Mendelssohn, is that which is "intensively enormous in strength and in perfection," God being the most sublime being. "In the fine arts and sciences the sensuously perfect representation of something immense will be *enormous, strong,* or *sublime.*"[61] The sensation associated with the sublime is, as Kant would later reiterate, a mixed sentiment: its immensity "arouses a sweet shudder that rushes through every fiber of our being. . . . All the sentiments blend together in the soul, flowing into one another, and become a single phenomenon which we call *awe.*"[62] It is art's highest purpose, according to Mendelssohn, to arouse in us sublime emotions: "If an artist by his power of enchantment can put us into such a frame of mind, then he has reached the pinnacle of his art and satisfied the worthiest calling of the fine arts."[63]

Subsequent formulations of the sublime in music similarly refer to that "which exceeds the conceptual powers of the imagination: which appears too large and significant, too foreign and strange for the imagination to grasp it easily."[64] Music that features rapidly changing and juxtaposed contrasting affects, metrical and rhythmic irregularity, frequent modulations, free fantasia, and improvisational style was considered sublime. The widely popular keyboard music of Carl Philipp Emanuel Bach, printed in the 1780s and intended for amateurs, is one example of this style, which Rahel Levin would have known in her youth.[65] Some of Johann Sebastian's solo keyboard music, purchased and domestically performed in households of Bach connoisseurs in Berlin following its first publication, in 1801, could similarly be considered sublime in its frugal, repetitive, free fantasia style.[66]

Already in his first essay on aesthetics, "On the Sentiments" (*Über die Empfindungen*, 1755) and in all subsequent writings on language and aesthetics, Mendelssohn links music, which he considers a "divine art,"[67] to the aesthetic, emotional, and ethical experience he associates with the sublime: "The expression of sentiment in music is intense, lively, and moving, but indeterminate." However, the abstract, nonreferential expression in music does not allow for a distinct emotion: "One is pervaded by a certain sentiment but it is obscure, general, and not limited to any individual object. This lack can be remedied by the addition of distinct and arbitrary signs [i.e., words]." Such signs can "make the sentiment into an individual sentiment which breaks out more easily. If this more intimate determination of the sentiment in music takes place by means of poetry and painting or stage design, the result is the modern opera."[68]

Reflecting upon Bach's music and discussing the desirable expressive relationship between words and music, Varnhagen seems to reiterate Mendelssohn in her deployment of the notion of "arbitrary signs."[69] Since instrumental music is so pure, she contends, "the music must be composed *first,* and only then comes the text: first the sentiment (*Empfindung*) . . . the vague perception; and only then comes grammar, logic; the entire structure and the arbitrary signs, from which the languages are not yet free." To Varnhagen, as to Mendelssohn, the best example for the successful marriage between words and music is opera, more precisely operas by Mozart, "the newest revolutionary," as she renders him. Mozart, she explains, has managed to subordinate the singing to the music, and created a coherent whole (*ein Ganzes*). By contrast, she argues somewhat anachronistically, Bach's music has not caught up, as it were, with these aesthetic ideas. "We Germans," she grumbles, "even hear, see, and write entirely declamatory operas! . . . We draw sentiments from grammar and syllable counts; and the more the music is left out, the better we find it!" That is, it is the words, language, which should be subordinate to the music.

Not unlike Mendelssohn and, subsequently, other male Jewish intellectuals, Varnhagen's engagement with aesthetics can be similarly read as an attempt to partake in a culturally and politically constitutive discursive arena. Mendelssohn's choice to embark on aesthetics at the outset of his philosophical career was arguably an attempt to liberate this field of thought from the tutelage of moral philosophy and Christian metaphysics.[70] He thereby participated in the liberation of the ethical function of the arts, particularly of music, from its association with Christian moral virtue toward more neutral and increasingly porous boundaries of aesthetic and ethical experience.[71] Varnhagen may have understood, as some of Mendelssohn's Jewish and non-Jewish contemporaries had, how his distinct conception of the sublime provided a kernel to a critique of the marginalization of "Jerusalem" in an increasingly "Hellenic," Christian-dominated modernity.[72] Mendelssohn's engagement with aesthetics thus marked a transformation of his experience as a Jew excluded from the center of European philosophy into a project of personal emancipation and participation in a Christian-dominated conceptual universe, making him an exemplary model of a modern "Greekjew."

In contrast to the ambivalence toward vocal music intimated by the comment at the outset of Varnhagen's letter, Varnhagen had acknowledged the affective power of vocal music to arouse sublime sentiments in response to the vocal music of another Protestant Baroque composer, Bach's contemporary in mid-eighteenth-century London, George Frideric Handel. Listening to Handel's oratorios, Varnhagen was overwhelmingly moved to sublime sentiments, allowing the music to draw her entirely back to "a primal state of being." Following a performance of Handel's oratorio *Judas Maccabaeus* in the fall of 1824,[73] she wrote to her brother,

> Already last winter I have heard many works by Handel, and every time I immediately felt uplifted and could not comprehend how only three notes set by that man to voice inevitably produce this effect! Literally three notes. He knows how to let them begin, lead them in a sequence, so that every time they pull us away, and transpose us unto a field of wistfulness, of sublimity, and of humility. . . . How does he do it, with such frugal means! . . . Handel's music puts us in the domain of wistfulness: it cries, his music, but *les larmes de la charité*. Not tears of suffering over conditions of our current life situation, but the big tears of being; those of an urgent longing for a primal state [*Urzustand*]; he guides us into the realm of surrendering, of calm reflection, of higher hope, and of a different kind of calmness . . . : into a previous piety, whose atmosphere—life conditions—is innocence, purest will and aspiration, and hence already calmness. . . . He, Handel . . . he is *sublime*.[74]

The sublime that Varnhagen experienced was the overawing effect achieved through minimalist, frugal expressive means ("only three notes"). Similarly, upon hearing Handel's *Joshua*, Varnhagen writes to her sister Rose, "I wept there, too."[75] Enthralled by Handel's music, she admits, "no composer, not even the metaphysical, God-fearing . . . Sebastian Bach elicits in me such violent-gentle elation and uplift."[76]

Varnhagen seems to have found in Handel's oratorios the sublimity she would miss in Bach's *Passion*—the expressive marriage between music and words that brings out the deepest, most primal sentiments of all human existence, a "previous piety." In the final outcry that concludes her letter, her ambivalence toward Bach's *Passion* grows into resentment: "That audience, how sanctimonious they were. They read that piece of Bible as mere text, not in the least moved! No, they studied it, pretentiously, as if it were difficult: as if it were Kant's *Critique of Pure Reason*." Captivated by the arresting operatic style of Handel's oratorios and their rich, overpowering palette of emotional expressions, Varnhagen longed for a performance that stood "in natural connection" with the music, a performance in which the voice "must be [expressive] of sentiments, inclinations, and passions . . . to express the strong, the heroic, the terrifying, the melancholy . . . and the tender by . . . suitable inflictions in the voice."[77] Yet Varnhagen's critique may also reflect her reaction to the literary content of the piece—"purely out of the Bible," that is, the New Testament.

Barbara Hahn has suggested a reading of Varnhagen's account that follows Friedrich Nietzsche's privileging of Handel, rather than Bach, as the musical interpreter of Luther and of Protestantism:[78] "Only in Handel's music did there resound what was best in the souls of Luther and those related to him, the Jewish-heroic trait that gave the Reformation a trait of greatness—the Old Testament become music, *not* the New."[79] Nietzsche marks Handel, not Bach, as the composer who truly realized the spirit of the Reformation in music, and that on the basis of Handel's thematic choices—the Old Testament, not the New; the Jewish element, as it were, within the Reformation.

Notwithstanding the profundity of Nietzsche's thesis, nor of Hahn's interpretation, I suggest a slightly broader and perhaps more complex view of Varnhagen's critique. Unlike Bach's cantatas and oratorios, which emphasize the New Testament, Handel's oratorios epitomize the distinctly mideighteenth-century Protestant affinity for the sublimity of Hebrew Scripture. Handel's oratorio *Judas Maccabaeus*, which aroused in Varnhagen transcendent sentiments, is based on the deuterocanonical 1 Maccabees (2–8) and, more generally, the *Antiquitates Judaicae*, an account of the history of the Jews written in Greek by the great Jewish historian of the Second Temple period, Flavius Josephus.[80] The oratorio tells the story of Judea under the rule of the Hellenic Seleucid Empire in the second century BCE (167–160), and the persecution of the Jews who refused to worship Zeus. To rebel against the subjection to idolatry and save Judea and Judaism from the threat of paganism, the subversive Jewish priest Mattathias led a religious guerilla war against the Hellenic occupier. The oratorio begins when his son, Judas Maccabaeus, assumes the role of his deceased father and leads the people to victory. Handel's music celebrates the jubilation of the Jewish rebels in their revolt against the pagan Hellenes.

By contrast, the Passion of Christ ultimately affirms the typological defeat of Judaism and the Jews' theologically essential fault. As mild a portrayal of the Jews as the *St. Matthew Passion* imparts, especially in Felix Mendelssohn's expurgated version, the story of the crucifixion nonetheless inevitably marks the Jews as those who rejected Christ and were eventually punished for it (if not altogether for their role in sacrificing the son of God) through the destruction of

Jerusalem and exile from their land. Ecclesia thus rose triumphant, leaving the crestfallen Synagoga forever humiliated.

Could Rahel Varnhagen and other "Greekjews" like her in Biedermeier Berlin—a neoclassical, Protestant "Athens"—have felt more comfortable imagining historical Jews as victors conscious of their right to religious freedom in a pre-Christian Hellenic world than as culpable sinners in an anachronistically "Christianized" Second-Temple Jerusalem? Might the lament of Zion and her daughters over the death of the Jewish priest and wise leader, Mattathias, have invoked in such members of the audience more sympathy than the lament of the desolate Daughter of Zion over Christ's crucifixion? A religious liberation leader would have surely had more appeal to Jews who had witnessed the rise of a struggle for civil emancipation than the treacherous chief priests who delivered Christ to Pontius Pilate, a mark of Cain that would forever tarnish Jews in the Christian world and its arts. Handel's oratorios, with their Old Testament and historical themes, would have posed a pre-Christian, and hence more universal and inclusive, alternative to the Christian theological messages of the Passion story.

If Christ's Passion marks a nascent moment of the beginning of civilization, that moment was also a pivotal turning point in human history that would set Jews and Judaism apart through a typological alignment of the Old Testament. Yet now, if the Luther Bible had begun to lose its theological authority, becoming an original German text, which, as Jonathan Sheehan puts it, "simultaneously created a German religion, a German culture, and a German nation,"[81] the Old Testament, too, could be reclaimed to reflect the distinctness of the Hebrew Bible as a source of Jewish cultural and historical consciousness—also in German. "In the bet with the *Neuchristen* [i.e. converts]," Varnhagen writes to her husband in 1817, now that the "Reform Jews . . . say sermons and prayers in German, in special chapels and temples, and follow modern ceremonies," Moses Mendelssohn's German translation of the Pentateuch ought to be printed in German—"but in real German letters . . . like Luther's Bible." Nobody, she contends, "so far nobody writes better German than that true artist; I am sure the translation is a masterpiece. But who can read it in Jewish letters?"[82]

Similarly, when the *maskilim* rediscovered, in the early nineteenth century, Hellenic Jewish literature such as the Book of Maccabees and Flavius Josephus, it was not only a rediscovery of ancient forgotten literature for scholarly use. It enabled modern Jews to sketch "a new portrait of Second Temple Judaism that brought about an intellectual renaissance."[83] Handel's *Judas Maccabaeus* thus offered an alternative to the historical imagination of Second-Temple Jerusalem invoked through Christological theological accounts, without exposing the underlying watershed, the abyss, which had cut Jerusalem off from Athens with the rise of Christianity and determined its fate throughout European modernity.[84]

Thus, in contrast to the Passion of Christ, which ultimately celebrates the triumph of Ecclesia over Synagoga and over her perfidious believers who had rejected Christ, the Maccabean war not only against the Hellenic conqueror but also against fellow Jews who participated in Hellenizing Judaism and paganizing Judea—a war that eventually led to a period of autonomous Jewish rule in Judea—could stimulate in the imagination of Jews in Biedermeier Berlin a different path from, and back to, pre-Christian antiquity, a path of a seldom-told history of Jews among other Hellenes.

Negotiating Second-Temple Jerusalem in Biedermeier "Athens"

Rahel Varnhagen's letter illustrates how inasmuch as the nineteenth-century revival of Bach's choral music was significant in the formation of German (Prussian) national culture, indeed of *Deutschtum*, at least to some Jews it underscored the dilemmas regarding their cultural, aesthetic, and religious identification, and the need to find strategies for mitigating them. Her boldly articulated voice as a twofold outsider—a woman and a Jew—not only offers a nuanced historiographical view of the reception of Bach's *St. Matthew Passion* in Berlin of 1829 but also expands the purview of the discourse we associate with *Haskalah* (Jewish Enlightenment) as an irreducible cultural and historical self-consciousness within European modernity.

A child of the cultural and ideational environment of the *Berliner Aufklärung*, in which Moses Mendelssohn was a towering philosophical lighthouse who laid an ideational foundation for Jewish modernity, Rahel Levin seems to have understood Mendelssohn's attempt to link aesthetic experience and its ethical imports with the quest for religious pluralism, *Bildung*, and enlightenment. While some Berlin *maskilim*, disciples of Mendelssohn and of Kant, produced scholarly essays that drew a nexus between aesthetics and the politics of Jewish civil betterment more explicitly and more systematically in philosophical essays,[85] Rahel Levin Varnhagen, like Brendel Veit and others of their circle, engaged in this discourse in a manner and in genres socially sanctioned and available to them as women.

Varnhagen's expressed ambivalence toward Bach's *Passion* can perhaps be understood precisely in light of the musical intimacy with Bach's instrumental repertoire that had previously gained the Jewish elite—those "we," from "that time"—a privileged position within Berlin's high society. The cultivation of Bach's instrumental music in the latter decades of the eighteenth century had empowered such connoisseurs as the sons and daughters of the Itzig family with weighty cultural agency. The revival of the *Passion*, and with it the popularization of Bach as the great Lutheran composer, threatened to marginalize that cultural distinction.

The estrangement Varnhagen voices in reaction to the ecstatic emotions expressed by the public seems to be directed largely toward the veneration of the texted Bach, Luther's musical interpreter, as a monument of an increasingly exclusive German national patrimony. The transformation of the Luther Bible into a central text of nineteenth-century *Bildungskultur* required a total realignment of values, as Sheehan points out, away from a Judeo-Christian framework, which had been a vital force of Enlightenment culture, particularly in Prussia, and toward one in which Jews were increasingly excluded from the emerging idea of the German nation.[86]

Varnhagen's sensibilities and her ability to articulate the tensions that Bach's *Passion* brought to the surface is striking: early on in her letter, she agrees with her old friend, Friederike Liman, that "it is *important* to *hear* [the *Passion*], just as it is to read the Nibelungen and suchlike." The Germanic mythological saga of the Nibelungen would later provide Richard Wagner a basis for his operas and inform his vision of a united (Christian) German nation. In their references to the Nibelungen, Liman and Varnhagen astutely observe how in 1829 Berlin, Bach's *Passion* constituted a textual-musical construct that struck a chord already vibrating in resonance with Romantic and increasingly national sentiments that saw the roots of the German *Volk* within the new notion of German Protestant *Kultur*. Read from our present-day perspective, Liman's remark seems nearly prophetic, as if anticipating the embodiment of such collective sentiments in music that culminated in the mythological universe of Wagner's operas.

Gazing back at the ruins of eighteenth-century Enlightenment—and perhaps further back at the biblical Rachel weeping for her children, as Heine would immortalize her[87]—Rahel Varnhagen critically links past and future in her attempt to resist both exclusion from, and assimilation into, German modernity. To some extent, Felix Mendelssohn seems to have shared, if further removed, the hybridic consciousness of the previous generation. As Michael P. Steinberg has proposed, the young Mendelssohn "absorbed the German Bach tradition not so much as a way of returning to past tradition but as a way of defining a new cultural identity in music."[88] This observation can be extended to the entire group beyond the Mendelssohn family and their forebears. As Varnhagen and Liman agree, "like Gluck and Mozart, we, too, must *know* the past without dwelling on it, always looking toward the future." But more than Felix Mendelssohn, Rahel Levin Varnhagen and her generation of Berlin Jews straddled two overlapping conceptual universes of Enlightenment and Romanticism, and saw one supplanting the other. The circle that Varnhagen sketches out in light, almost unnoticeable drops of color—the Beer family, Heinrich Heine, Friederike Liman, even the Mendelssohns and doubtlessly also the musical daughters and sons of the Itzig family, all those "*we, from that* time"—who lived simultaneously on the outside and inside of Prussian high culture, continued to grapple with their Jewish self-consciousness despite conversion to Christianity, through European music, poetry, philosophy, and theater.[89]

The view onto the past, both near and ancient, as a reinterpretation of faith, religion, and history was common to both Christians and Jews in the effort to negotiate modernity between Enlightenment and Romanticism.[90] The revival of the *St. Matthew Passion* was one cultural moment that exemplified most potently just how divergent the different investments were: with its multilayered, multitemporal portrayal of Jews, Christ, his church, congregation, and disciples, the Passion of Christ in Second-Temple Jerusalem performed on the stage of the *Sing-Akademie*, a Greek temple of music open to all in a Protestant *Spree-Athen*, not only reflected contemporary Prussian constructs of the relationship between religion, philosophy, and history; it also underscored the tensions inherent in the hybridity of modern German Jewish consciousness, articulating the inevitable simultaneity of religion, culture, and politics. Thus, without touching upon political issues, questions about the status of the Jews, Judaism and Jewishness become transposed in Varnhagen's contemplations about music, aesthetics, history, and the Bible into an abstract formulation of the Hebraism–Hellenism opposition, or the question about the place of "Jerusalem" in a "Hellenic" Christian world, a question that would continue to be at the core of the quest for German Jewish modernity well into the twentieth century.

Notes

This article originated in a colloquium paper presented at the Music Department of the University of Pennsylvania in January 2014, during a Rose and Henry Zifkin Postdoctoral Fellowship at the Herbert D. Katz Center for Advanced Judaic Studies. I am grateful to the colloquium participants for the fruitful discussion, and particularly to Liliane Weissberg and David Rotman for their thoughtful insights on the initial paper. For their indispensable comments on subsequent drafts of the article, I am indebted to Barbara Hahn, Vivian Liska, Yakir Paz, and Elchanan Reiner, as well as to the two editors of this volume, Rebecca Cypess and Nancy Sinkoff.

1. See Peter Wollny, *"Ein förmlicher Sebastian und Philipp Emanuel Bach-Kultus"*: Sara Levy und ihr musikalisches Wirken. Mit einer Dokumentensammlung zur musikalischen Familiengeschichte der Vorfahren von Felix Mendelssohn Bartholdy. (Wiesbaden: Breitkopf & Härtel, 2010).

2. See Peter Wollny, *"Ein förmlicher Sebastian und Philipp Emanuel Bach-Kultus,"* 49–61. In addition, the Karl Gustav von Brinckmann archive holds sixteen letters by Sara Levy, none of which contains substantial information about her musical activity; see Barbara Hahn's essay in this volume. Later references to

Levy include, for instance, letters by contemporary female family members and later memoirs, for instance, those of Fanny Lewald, *Meine Lebensgeschichte*, 2 vols. (Berlin: Janke, 1861/2), 158; and Wilhelm Erman, *Paul Erman, ein Berliner Gelehrtenleben. 1764–1851* (Berlin: Mittler, 1927), 64–98.

3.　To the best of my knowledge, there is no documented evidence of Sara Levy's attendance at any of the three performances of Bach's *Passion* in Berlin in 1829. However, it is safe to assume, based on circumstantial evidence, that like other prominent patrons of the *Sing-Akademie* she, too, attended the first concert.

4.　See Barbara Hahn, "Häuser für die Musik: Akkulturation in Ton und Text um 1800," in *Fanny Hensel. Komponieren zwischen Öffentlichkeit und Privatheit. Symposionsbericht Berlin 1997*, ed. Beatrix Borchard and Monika Schwarz-Danuser (Stuttgart: Metzler, 1999), 3–26. The role of music in Jewish elite women's lives changes slightly in the following generation, with the rise of the music salons after 1819, held in the Berlin households of Amalie Beer, Lea Mendelssohn Bartholdy, and her daughter Fanny Hensel. See also Michael P. Steinberg, "Culture, Gender, and Music: A Forum on the Mendelssohn Family," *Musical Quarterly* 77, no. 4 (1993): 648–50.

5.　The attainment of music lessons by Jewish maidens in Berlin is described, for instance, in Henriette Herz, *Ihr Leben und ihre Zeit*, ed. Hans Landsberg (Weimar: Kiepenheuer, 1913); Hans M. Schletterer, *Johann Friedrich Reichardt: Sein Leben und seine musikalische Thätigkeit* (Augsburg: J. A. Schlosser, 1865), 100; and Carl Friedrich Zelter, *Carl Friedrich Zelters Darstellungen seines Lebens*, ed. Johann Wolfgang Schottlaender (Weimar: Verlag der Goethe-Gesellschaft, 1931), 136–37.

6.　Rahel Levin Varnhagen, *Edition Rahel Levin Varnhagen*, ed. Barbara Hahn and Ursula Isselstein (Munich: Beck Verlag, 1997–), and Rahel Levin Varnhagen, *Rahel: Ein Buch des Andenkens für ihre Freunde*, ed. Barbara Hahn, 6 vols. (Göttingen: Wallstein Verlag, 2011) represent the most substantial achievements of this scholarly effort. Two recent studies in particular shed new light on the subject by richly drawing upon women's letters and autobiographical documents: Hannah Lotte Lund, *Der Berliner "jüdische Salon" um 1800: Emanzipation in der Debatte* (Berlin: de Gruyter, 2012); and Natalie Naimark-Goldberg, *Jewish Women in Enlightenment Berlin* (Oxford: Littman Library of Jewish Civilization, 2013).

7.　See, for instance, Heidi Thomann Tewarson, *Rahel Levin Varnhagen: The Life and Work of a German Jewish Intellectual* (Lincoln: University of Nebraska Press, 1998), 45–48.

8.　Barbara Hahn, *The Jewess Pallas Athena: This Too a Theory of Modernity* (Princeton, NJ: Princeton University Press, 2005), 44.

9.　For most converted Jewish women (and men) in that generation, baptism, which usually occurred late in their lives, did not mark a turning point in terms of social life or worldview. See Naimark-Goldberg, *Jewish Women*, 257–59, as well as Naimark-Goldberg's contribution to the present volume.

10.　See Steven M. Lowenstein, *The Berlin Jewish Community: Enlightenment, Family, and Crisis, 1770–1830* (Oxford: Oxford University Press, 1994); and Miriam

Bodian, "The Jewish Entrepreneurs in Berlin and the 'Civil Improvement of the Jews' in the 1780s and 1790s," *Zion* 49, no. 2 (1984): 159–84 (Hebrew). For contemporary accounts of the Jewish elite of Berlin, see, for instance, Friedrich Nicolai, *Beschreibung der Königlichen Residenzstadt Berlin und Potsdam und aller daselbst befindlicher Merkwürdigkeiten* (Berlin: Nicolai, 1786), 725–849; and Wolf Davidson, *Über die bürgerliche Verbesserung der Juden* (Berlin: Ernst Felisch, 1798).

11. Henriette Herz describes how shortly after her marriage she ceased to cover her hair with the traditional headdress, briefly wearing a wig before fully exposing her natural hair, in Herz, *Ihr Leben und ihre Zeit*, 34–35. Fanny von Arnstein *née* Itzig in Vienna was similarly at ease exposing her natural long hair as a married woman. See Shmuel Feiner, *The Origins of Jewish Secularization in Eighteenth-Century Europe*, trans. Chaya Naor (Philadelphia: University of Pennsylvania Press, 2010), 158. On spas, see Naimark-Goldberg, *Jewish Women*, 146–79.

12. See Liliane Weissberg, *Life as a Goddess: Henriette Herz Writes her Autobiography*, Braun Lectures in the History of the Jews of Prussia 6 (Ramat Gan: Bar-Ilan University, 2001).

13. Brendel Veit in Strelitz to Rahel Levin in Berlin, September 13, 1792. I am grateful to Barbara Hahn for sharing with me her critical edition of the letter prior to its publication. Rahel Varnhagen and David Veit, *Briefwechsel zwischen Rahel und David Veit*, 2 vols. (Leipzig: Brockhaus, 1861), 1:76. Herz, *Ihr Leben und ihre Zeit*, 117.

14. See, for instance, Marshall Blakemore Evans, *The Passion Play of Lucerne: An Historical and Critical Introduction* (New York: Modern Language Association of America, 1943); and James Shapiro, *Oberammergau: The Troubling Story of the World's Most Famous Passion Play* (New York: Pantheon Books, 2000). See also Michael Marissen, *Lutheranism, Anti-Judaism, and Bach's St. John Passion* (New York: Oxford University Press, 1998); and Ruth HaCohen, *The Music Libel Against the Jews* (New Haven, CT: Yale University Press, 2011), chapter 1.

15. Eduard Devrient, *Meine Erinnerungen an Felix Mendelssohn-Bartholdy und seine Briefe an mich* (Leipzig: Weber, 1872), 62. All translations from German texts are mine unless indicated otherwise.

16. See responses to the disputed perspective in Jeffrey S. Sposato, *The Price of Assimilation: Felix Mendelssohn and the Nineteenth-Century Anti-Semitic Tradition* (Oxford: Oxford University Press, 2006); in Leon Botstein, "Mendelssohn, Werner, and the Jews: A Final Word," *Musical Quarterly* 83, no. 1 (1999): 45–50; and Michael P. Steinberg, "Mendelssohn's Music and German-Jewish Culture: An Intervention," *Musical Quarterly* 83, no. 1 (1999): 31–44. See also Michael P. Steinberg, "Mendelssohn and Judaism," in *The Cambridge Companion to Mendelssohn*, ed. Peter Mercer-Taylor (Cambridge: Cambridge University Press, 2011), 26–41.

17. Compare with the discussion about the appeal of Bach's *St. Matthew Passion* across religious boundaries through the different planes of sympathy in the piece in HaCohen, *The Music Libel*, 90–98.

18. Rahel Levin Varnhagen was usually referred to simply as Rahel, both during her lifetime and after her death, in private correspondence as well as in

printed publications. Her name seldom appears in any of its full versions. Unless quoting, I henceforth use either Levin or Varnhagen according to the chronology of the cited text or event.

19. The literary value of Rahel Levin Varnhagen's epistolary writings was recognized by her husband, Karl August Varnhagen von Ense, who edited and published them in the years following her death. See Barbara Hahn, "Rahel Levin Varnhagen," *Jewish Women: A Comprehensive Historical Encyclopedia*, March 1, 2009. Jewish Women's Archive (viewed on July 12, 2015), http://jwa.org/encyclopedia/article/varnhagen-rahel-levin. In addition to her correspondence, which she avidly maintained and carefully preserved for posterity, Rahel Levin Varnhagen also published a series of epistolary essays in different German and Swiss journals.

20. It is seldom stressed that enlightened Jewish women in Berlin socialized not only with non-Jewish intellectuals, but also with *maskilim*, such as Isaac Euchel; see, for example, Naimark-Goldberg, *Jewish Women*, 213–15.

21. After James Joyce, *Ulysses* (New York: Random House, 1990). Joyce characterizes modernity as an ambivalent struggle between "Hellenism" and "Hebraism" through the figure of Leopold Bloom, a "Greekjew" who imagines himself in a long genealogical line of "Hellenized," cosmopolitan non-Jewish Jews, a line that begins with Moses Mendelssohn. See Miriam Leonard, *Socrates and the Jews: Hellenism and Hebraism from Moses Mendelssohn to Sigmund Freud* (Chicago, IL: University of Chicago Press, 2012), 4–6.

22. Bach's Passion oratorio BWV 244 was composed for solo voices, double choir and double orchestra to a libretto by Picander (Christian Friedrich Henrici). A second performance took place in Berlin on March 21, 1829, Bach's birthday, and a third (conducted by Zelter) on April 17, Good Friday, which would henceforth replace the traditional annual performance of Heinrich Graun's popular Passion cantata *Der Tod Jesu*. The most comprehensive studies on the 1829 revival of the piece are Martin Geck, *Die Wiederentdeckung der Matthäuspassion im 19. Jahrhundert* (Regensburg: Gustav Bosse Verlag, 1967); and Celia Applegate, *Bach in Berlin: Nation and Culture in Mendelssohn's Revival of the* St. Matthew Passion (Ithaca, NY: Cornell University Press, 2005).

23. [A. B. Marx], "Bekanntmachung," *Berliner allgemeine musikalische Zeitung* 6, no. 8 (February 21, 1829): 57.

24. [A. B.] Marx, "Bekanntmachung," *Berliner allgemeine musikalische Zeitung* 6, no. 9 (February 28, 1829): 65; and Devrient, *Meine Erinnerungen*, 46.

25. "Erster Bericht über die 'Passionsmusik nach dem Evangelisten Matthäus' von Johann Sebastian Bach," *Berliner allgemeine musikalische Zeitung* 6, no. 10 (March 7, 1829): 73.

26. Joseph Maria von Radowitz, courtier and diplomat, cited after Applegate, *Bach in Berlin*, 223.

27. [A. B.] Marx, "Zweiter Bericht über die Passionsmusik nach dem Evangelium Matthäi von Johann Sebastian Bach," *Berliner allgemeine musikalische Zeitung* 6, no. 11 (March 14, 1829): 82. See also Geck, *Die Wiederentdeckung*, 34–35; and Applegate, *Bach in Berlin*, 37–38.

28. Devrient, *Meine Erinnerungen*, 46; and Georg Schünemann, "Die Bachpflege der Berliner Singakademie," *Bach-Jahrbuch* 25 (1928): 155.

29. Cited after Geck, *Die Wiederentdeckung*, 46–47.

30. An epithet of Berlin coined in 1706; see Christian Scholl, "Normative Anschaulichkeit versus archäologische Pedanterie: Karl Friedrich Schinkels ästhetischer Philhellenismus," in *Graecomania*, ed. Gilbert Heß, Elena Agazzi, and Elisabeth Décultot (Berlin: de Gruyter, 2009), 85–98.

31. Applegate, *Bach in Berlin*, 2.

32. Ibid., 3.

33. See Philip M. Merklinger, *Philosophy, Theology, and Hegel's Berlin Philosophy of Religion, 1821–1827* (Albany: SUNY Press, 1993). For a summary of Friedrich Wilhelm III's Prussian state reform toward a church union in 1817, see Applegate, *Bach in Berlin*, 175–77.

34. Friedrich Schleiermacher, *Der christliche Glaube nach den Grundsätzen der evangelischen Kirche im Zusammenhange dargestellt* (Berlin, 1821/2, rev. ed. 1830/31). See also Sposato, *The Price of Assimilation*, 49.

35. Johann Gottfried Herder, "Ueber National-Religion," in *Adrastea* (1801–3); cited after Jonathan Sheehan, *The Enlightenment Bible: Translation, Scholarship, Culture* (Princeton, NJ: Princeton University Press, 2005), 219.

36. See Applegate, *Bach in Berlin*, 198.

37. See Sheehan, *The Enlightenment Bible*, 224.

38. Ibid., 224–40.

39. See Michael Marissen, "Religious Aims in Mendelssohn's 1829 Berlin Sing-Akademie Performances of Bach's St. Matthew Passion," *Musical Quarterly* 77, no. 4 (1993): 721; and Sposato, *The Price of Assimilation*, 48–49. On Schleiermacher's presence at the concert, see Geck, *Die Wiederentdeckung*, 34.

40. Letter to Karl Klingemann; cited after Geck, *Die Wiederentdeckung*, 43.

41. Letter to Franz Hauser; cited after Susanna Großmann-Vendrey, *Felix Mendelssohn Bartholdy und die Musik der Vergangenheit* (Regensburg: Bosse, 1969), 49.

42. "Erster Bericht," 73.

43. According to one view, it was an 1823 Christmas present; see Geck, *Die Wiederentdeckung*, 18. An alternate view concerning the date of this gift is in Peter Ward Jones, "Mendelssohn's Performances of the 'Matthäus-Passion': Considerations of the Documentary Evidence," *Music & Letters*, 97 (2016): 409–64. See also the discussions of this point in the chapters by Wolff and Naimark-Goldberg in the present volume.

44. See Yael Sela-Teichler, "Music, Acculturation, and Haskalah between Berlin and Königsberg during the 1780s," *Jewish Quarterly Review* 103, no. 3 (2013): 372–75.

45. I borrow the phrase from Sheehan, *The Enlightenment Bible*, 214–15.

46. Efforts to gain Jewish emancipation in Prussia were resisted during this period, as the 1820s saw a rise of German nationalism and an upsurge of anti-Jewish sentiments, which erupted, for instance, in the Hep-Hep riots of 1819. See *German-Jewish History in Modern Times, II: Emancipation and Acculturation,*

1780–1871, ed. Michael A. Meyer, Michael Brenner, Mordechai Breuer, and Michael Graetz (New York: Columbia University Press, 1997), 27–42, 251–76.

47. "Rahel, a marvelous gift from heaven, the German Pallas Athena." Quotation from the article "Rahel," which appeared on the front page of the *Zeitung für die elegante Welt* 147 (July 31, 1834), preceding a review of *Rahel: Ein Buch des Andenkens für ihre Freunde*, cited after Hahn, *The Jewess Pallas Athena*, 8–9. See also Hannah Arendt, *Rahel Varnhagen: The Life of a Jewess*, ed. Liliane Weissberg, trans. Richard and Clara Winston (Baltimore: Johns Hopkins University Press, 1997).

48. Rahel to Karl August Varnhagen von Ense, March 13, 1829, in *Buch des Andenkens*, 5:262–65. Emphasis in the original.

49. Gerald Hendrie, *Mendelssohn's Rediscovery of Bach* (London: Open University, 1971), 91–92. See also R. Larry Todd, *Mendelssohn: A Life in Music* (New York: Oxford University Press, 2005), 196–97.

50. Sposato, *The Price of Assimilation*, 55. Picander's libretto of the *St. Matthew Passion* consists of chapters 26 and 27 of the Gospel of Matthew in Luther's German translation with interspersed chorales and arias.

51. Applegate, *Bach in Berlin*, 39. See also Todd, *Mendelssohn*, 197.

52. Marissen, "Religious Aims," 720–21.

53. The young Rahel Levin received piano lessons and acquired some basic skills in composition and possibly continuo. See Tewarson, *Rahel Levin Varnhagen*, 24–26.

54. See Mary Sue Morrow, *German Music Criticism in the Late Eighteenth Century: Aesthetic Issues in Instrumental Music* (Cambridge: Cambridge University Press, 1997).

55. Immanuel Kant, *Critique of the Power of Judgment* (1790), trans. J. H. Bernard (New York: Hafner, 1951), 157, sec. 49.

56. My view on this matter differs from Beatrix Borchard's claim that Rahel Varnhagen shunned vocal music because of her Jewish upbringing; see Borchard, "Zur Rolle der Instrumentalmusik im jüdischen Akkulturationsprozeß," *Menora Jahrbuch für deutsch-jüdische Geschichte* 16 (1996): 171–202.

57. See Tewarson, *Rahel Levin Varnhagen*, 17–52.

58. Kant's writings were first introduced to Jewish women at the salon of the Kant student and physician Markus Herz and his wife Henriette. Jewish women were among the first to participate in the popular Kant reception, following some of the men with whom they socialized, among them such Kantian *maskilim* as Isaac Euchel. This became an object of anti-Jewish polemic and caricature, including a description of Kant as Jewish women's "Golden Calf," "a sensation so extraordinary that it could not be surpassed even by the appearance of the Messiah." Cited, in my translation, after Christoph Schulte, *Die jüdische Aufklärung* (Munich: C. H. Beck, 2002), 157–71.

59. See Emily Brady, *The Sublime in Modern Philosophy: Aesthetics, Ethics, and Nature* (Cambridge: Cambridge University Press, 2013), 48–49.

60. See Lowenstein, *The Berlin Jewish Community*, 39–40.

61. Moses Mendelssohn, "On the Sublime and Naïve in the Fine Sciences" (1758), in Mendelssohn, *Philosophical Writings*, trans. Daniel O. Dahlstrom (Cambridge: Cambridge University Press, 1997), 194–96. All subsequent citations from Mendelssohn's aesthetic writings are from this edition.

62. Mendelssohn, "On the Sublime and Naïve," 195.

63. Ibid., 199.

64. Christian Friedrich Michaelis, "Einige Bemerkungen über das Erhabene in der Musik," *Berlinische Musikalische Zeitung* 1, no. 40 (1805): 180; cited after *Music and Aesthetics in the Eighteenth and Early Nineteenth Centuries*, ed. Peter le Huray and James Day (Cambridge: Cambridge University Press, 1981), 202–3. See also Annette Richards, "An Enduring Monument: C. P. E. Bach and the Musical Sublime," in *C. P. E. Bach Studies*, ed. Annette Richards (Cambridge: Cambridge University Press, 2009), 149–72.

65. C. P. E. Bach's six collections of sonatas, rondos, and fantasias "für Kenner und Liebhaber" (Wq. 55–9, 61) were published by Breitkopf between 1779 and 1787. Among the subscribers, nearly thirty percent were women, including those of Jewish families in Berlin.

66. Bach's *Inventions and Sinfonias* (BWV 772–801) as well as both books of the *Well-Tempered Clavier* (BWV 846–93), were published in 1801.

67. Moses Mendelssohn, "On the Sentiments" (1755), letter 11, in *Philosophical Writings*, 48.

68. Moses Mendelssohn, "On the Main Principles of Fine Arts" (1761), in *Philosophical Writings*, 187. Kant would later echo these very notions, adding furthermore that the sublime in art "may be combined with beauty in . . . an *oratorio*"; and this, in turn, makes beautiful art "yet more artistic," though not necessarily more beautiful; Kant, *Critique of the Power of Judgment*, 166, sec. 52.

69. Mendelssohn first made the distinction between natural, mimetic, and arbitrary signs in his unpublished 1756 essay "Über die Sprache" (On Language), terms that would continue to feature throughout his discourse on language; see Moses Mendelssohn, *Gesammelte Schriften: Jubiläumsausgabe*, ed. Alexander Altmann et al. (Stuttgart: Frommann-Holzboog, 1983), 6.2:10–16. Immanuel Kant would later adopt the distinction between arbitrary and natural signs in his *Anthropologie in pragmatischer Hinsicht* (Anthropology from a Pragmatic Point of View, 1798). See Immanuel Kant, *Anthropologie in pragmatischer Hinsicht*, ed. Wolfgang Becker (Stuttgart: Reclam, 1983).

70. See Willi Goetschel, *Spinoza's Modernity: Mendelssohn, Lessing, and Heine* (Madison: University of Wisconsin Press, 2004), 87.

71. See, for example, Isabella van Elferen, "'Ihr Augen weint!' Intersubjective Tears in the Sentimental Concert Hall," *Understanding Bach* 2 (2007): 77–94.

72. See Grit Schorch, *Moses Mendelssohns Sprachpolitik* (Berlin: de Gruyter, 2012), 136–40; and Yael Sela, "The Voice of the Psalmist: On the Performative Role of Psalms in Moses Mendelssohn's *Jerusalem*," in *Psalms In and On Jerusalem*, ed. Ilana Pardes and Ophir Münz-Manor (Berlin: de Gruyter, forthcoming, 2018).

73. George Frideric Handel, *Judas Maccabaeus* (HWV 63), an oratorio in three acts composed in 1746, based on a libretto by Thomas Morell.

74. Rahel to Ludwig Robert, November 26, 1824, in *Buch des Andenkens*, 4:502–4.

75. Rahel to Rose, January 12, 1827, in *Familienbriefe*, 963.
76. Rahel to Ludwig Robert, November 26, 1824, in *Buch des Andenkens*, 4:503.
77. Mendelssohn, "On the Main Principles," 185.
78. Hahn, "Häuser für die Musik."
79. Friedrich Nietzsche, "Nietzsche contra Wagner," in *The Portable Nietzsche*, trans. Walter Kaufmann (New York: Viking Press, 1954), 668.
80. See Alexander H. Shapiro, "'Drama of an Infinitely Superior Nature': Handel's Early English Oratorios and the Religious Sublime," *Music & Letters* 74, no. 2 (1993): 215–45; and Ruth Smith, *Handel's Oratorios and Eighteenth-Century Thought* (Cambridge: Cambridge University Press, 1995). In eighteenth-century England, Hebraism was invested with political, no less than religious meanings, as it would later develop also in Germany. The seminal text on biblical Hebrew poetry, whose influence on modern Bible scholarship also in eighteenth-century Germany cannot be overstressed, is Robert Lowth, *Lectures on the Sacred Poetry of the Hebrews* (1753, trans. from Latin 1787). In Germany, Lowth was first introduced through Mendelssohn's review, in "Lowth, R.: De sacra poesi Hebraeorum. Oxford 1753: Rezension," *Bibliothek der schönen Wissenschaften und der freyen Künste* 1, no. 1 (1757): 122–55, and 1, no. 2 (1757): 269–97.
81. Sheehan, *The Enlightenment Bible*, 226.
82. Rahel to August Varnhagen, October 28, 1817, in *Buch des Andenkens*, 3:514. Mendelssohn's German translation of the Pentateuch with Hebrew commentary (*Biur*, 1780–3) was originally printed in Hebrew characters. Rahel Varnhagen was unaware that a transcription in German characters had been published two years earlier.
83. Yaacov Shavit, *Athens in Jerusalem: Classical Antiquity and Hellenism in the Making of the Modern Secular Jew*, trans. Chaya Naor and Niki Werner (Oxford: Littman Library of Jewish Civilization, 1999), 329.
84. My argument regarding the universality and inclusive neutrality of fictional narratives based on Hebrew Scripture applies also to Handel's other Old Testament oratorios, such as *Joshua*.
85. See especially Markus Herz, *Versuch über den Geschmack und die Ursachen seiner Verschiedenheiten* (Leipzig: Voss, 1776); and Lazarus Bendavid, *Versuch einer Geschmackslehre* (Berlin: Belitz & Braun, 1799).
86. Sheehan, *The Enlightenment Bible*, xiv.
87. In the Forward to his *Buch der Lieder* (2nd edition; Hamburg: Hoffmann & Campe, 1827, ca. 1837), Heinrich Heine writes about the publication of Rahel's letters by August Varnhagen in *Buch des Andenkens* (1834): "The book arrived at the right time to give comfort. It is as if Rahel knew what sort of posthumous mission was hers. She believed that things would improve, and waited; but as the waiting knew no end, she shook her head impatiently, glanced at Varnhagen, and quickly died—in order all the more quickly to rise again. She reminds me of the legend of Rahel who climbed from the grave and stood crying in the road as her children were carried off into bondage." Translation cited after Hahn, *The Jewess Pallas Athena*, 9.

88. Michael P. Steinberg, *Listening to Reason: Culture, Subjectivity, and Nineteenth-Century Music* (Princeton. NJ: Princeton University Press, 2006), 103.

89. Henriette Herz responded with some hesitation to her first encounter at the St. Nicholas church in Berlin with Heinrich Graun's Passion cantata *Der Tod Jesu*, a piece that after the founding of the *Sing-Akademie* in 1791, Jewish members of the choir, among them Fradchen Liebmann, would perform every year on Good Friday. Herz, *Ihr Leben und ihre Zeit*, 150. On Jews singing *Der Tod Jesu* at the *Sing-Akademie*, see Davidson, *Über die bürgerliche Verbesserung*, 109. On Liebmann, see Naimark-Goldberg, *Jewish Women*, 268.

90. Compare to Michael P. Steinberg, "The Incidental Politics to Mendelssohn's *Antigone*," in *Mendelssohn and his World*, ed. R. Larry Todd (Princeton, NJ: Princeton University Press, 1991), 137–57.

Part Three

Studies in
Sara Levy's Collection

Chapter Eight

Duets in the Collection of Sara Levy and the Ideal of "Unity in Multiplicity"

Rebecca Cypess

As we begin increasingly to explore Sara Levy and her world from the interdisciplinary perspective that she seems to warrant through her position in both Jewish history and musical history, we test the limits of both fields to accommodate and speak to one another. The complexities of Sara Levy as a subject of interdisciplinary study are clear: very few written documents survive that attest to her views of her religion, her musical activities, or her views on her social and cultural environments, let alone her understanding of the connections among these various aspects of her intellectual, spiritual, and artistic life. And yet we would be mistaken not to consider her as a complete individual, with all of the complexities that her biography connotes. Levy lived, after all, in a pre-disciplinary world, in which the aesthetic, the religious, and the political were deeply intertwined, and in which all of these had tangible ramifications for the lives of enlightened individuals.

In this chapter I propose to explore a test case for an interdisciplinary approach to Sara Levy. I will consider a portion of the music that she is known to have held in her collection and that she likely played or heard in her salon. I will then explicate the social practices upon which this music drew, and read it metaphorically, attempting to understand what it might have meant for the modernizing Jews of Berlin. Through consideration of the ideas of Moses Mendelssohn, whose monumental corpus of writings dealt both with aesthetics and with a political philosophy that he envisioned as allowing Christians and

Jews to coexist within a tolerant society, I argue that Sara Levy's musical activities may be understood as a representation of the ideals—however unrealistic—that Mendelssohn and his followers sought to put into place.

The repertoire that I consider here is that of duets for two identical or similar instruments in manuscripts that Sara Levy collected, some of which she is thought to have commissioned. These include duets for two flutes, for two violas, and for two keyboard instruments. The tradition for all of these types of duet extended to the early eighteenth century, with some theorists reaching back far enough to connect them to the pedagogical *bicinia* of the Renaissance. Yet these pieces took on a distinctive meaning in the second half of the eighteenth century. The special challenge presented by the genre of the duet was to maintain an even balance between the parts, allowing them to play equally important roles even as they supported one another. The analogy to social music making during the Enlightenment is apparent: the equality between the two parts in a musical duet represented a model for the socialization of individuals within an enlightened society.

Such analogies to social music making on a broad scale constitute a well-established means of interpreting chamber music of the period.[1] Yet juxtaposition of Sara Levy's strong adherence to Judaism and her cultivation of the duet for two like instruments within her salon point the way toward an interpretation that extends beyond general ideals of socialization. An understanding of these duets as carrying meaning for *interreligious* socialization is enabled by writings of the Jewish philosopher and aesthetic theorist Moses Mendelssohn, with whose work Sara Levy and other women in her circle were familiar. Mendelssohn valorized the ideal of *Einheit in der Mannigfaltigkeit*—"unity in multiplicity"—as a model for a tolerant society in which both Jews and Christians could coexist in perpetuity. This same ideal in Mendelssohn's social and political philosophies formed the aesthetic category used to describe the musical merits of the duet for two like instruments. Performances of instrumental duets in Sara Levy's salon may thus be understood as articulations of the principle of *Einheit in der Mannigfaltigkeit*; the musical genre serves as a metaphor for the ideal of religious tolerance in an enlightened society.

The Aesthetics of the Duet

Johann Georg Sulzer described the aesthetics of the musical duet in his *Allgemeine Theorie der schönen Künste* (1773). In such works, he wrote,

> both of the featured voices are primary voices, and neither dominates the other; that first one, then the other lets itself be heard for a while, yet afterward, both [sound] together—each, however, in its particular way. From this

stems the requirement, in both types, that the duet should be fugue-like and fully worked out in the manner of double-counterpoint, through which both melodies, *while there is unity of character, contain a beautiful multiplicity* [beyde Melodien bey der Einheit des Charakters eine schöne Mannigfaltigkeit haben].[2]

In situating the duet within the aesthetic dichotomy of *Einheit* and *Mannigfaltigkeit,* Sulzer encapsulated the main challenge posed by the genre: the two instruments must act in concert with one another, constantly responding to each other through counterpoint and imitation, as well as refreshing and varying the material heard, even as they remain equally prominent and retain their individual voices. These various kinds of balance and diversity are evident, for example, in the duets for two violas, Fk. 60–62 / BR B7–9, composed by Wilhelm Friedemann Bach, of which Sara and Samuel Levy owned both autograph and manuscript copies.[3] In the touching "Lamento" of Friedemann's Viola Duet 61 / BR B8, the two instruments intertwine in such a way that they support one another while constantly exchanging roles. The two lines blend until they become nearly indistinguishable; this, indeed, is a purposeful and vital part of the genre. The instruments exchange motifs and gestures, repeating ideas and varying them, and leapfrogging over one another so that they create a continuous stream of the new and the familiar (see ex. 8.1).

Peter Wollny has pointed out the note written by Sara's husband, Samuel Salomon Levy, in the autograph score of the viola duets (D-Bsa SA 3921) directing the copyist ("Herr Kriger") to write the pieces out "as in the original, Primo and Secondo on a single sheet," using "good white paper; I will gladly pay somewhat more for it."[4] (Krieger's copy is preserved as D-Bsa SA 3912). It is unclear who within the Levy circle would have played these duets for viola, though a relatively high proportion of scores in the Levy collection feature the viola prominently. The value that Samuel placed on these pieces—indicated by his willingness to pay extra in order to have them copied on fine paper—suggests that he held both Sara's teacher and his contribution to the genre of the duet in high esteem. A set of six viola duets by a certain "Tartini," uniquely preserved in the Levy collection in two copies (D-Bsa SA 3970 and 3993), indicates further interest in this genre. The duets for violin and viola by the French composer Pancratius Huber (D-Bsa SA 3943) are also in the collection; here, however, the relationship between the two instruments is predictably less than equal. When they were printed, the Huber duets were issued in separate partbooks for violin and viola, indicating a less thorough integration than Samuel Levy was apparently seeking when he requested that the Friedemann duets be copied with both parts on a single page.

Levy's collection of duets for two like instruments included duos for flute, which Samuel probably played himself. As Wollny points out, Samuel made

Example 8.1. Wilhelm Friedemann Bach, "Lamento" from the duet for two violas, Fk. 61 / BR B8, mm. 1–21.

notations in the manuscript of Friedemann's Flute Concerto in D Major (D-Bsa SA 2637) that indicate that he was an accomplished flutist.[5] It is not surprising, therefore, that the Levy collection includes numerous works that employ the flute (some apparently composed with that instrument in mind and others that seem to be alternate versions or arrangements of pieces without flute).[6] Among these are the duets for flute by Georg Philipp Telemann. As Steven Zohn has noted, Levy's collection includes nine duets attributed to Telemann that are not found in any other sources (D-Bsa SA 3903). While Zohn questions the authenticity of the last three of these, he concurs that at least nos. 1–6 of this manuscript are by Telemann; eight of them were excerpted by Johann Joachim Quantz in his *Solfeggi*—a set of pedagogical excerpts for flute—indicating that they were widely known and highly regarded in Berlin.[7] Zohn observes that the preface to the published

Sei duetti for flutes by Quantz cites the flute duets of Telemann as models of the genre. In extracting principles of composition for the duet, Quantz included statements that resonate strongly with Sulzer's definition of the duet, quoted above. As Quantz explained, "The imitations and variations of the designs being more apparent in the duo than in any other pieces . . . the imitations should be very correct and regular, no matter at what interval they are made. . . . The two parts should participate equally by turn in such a way that one always seems to support the design of the other."[8] Telemann's flute duets formed the archetype for the duet as a genre, and Sara and Samuel Levy's collection reflects their interest in this composer and in the genre as a whole.

If the balance between the two instruments was a requirement in duos broadly speaking, it was especially difficult and important in the repertoire for two keyboards. Keyboardists are, after all, required to perform more than just one line of music; multiple voices must be maintained and coordinated on each instrument and combined artfully on the two instruments together. Independent yet intertwined, the two keyboardists must enact this balance between their individual musical personae and their collective identity. I have argued elsewhere that the performance of keyboard duos was more common in Germany in the latter half of the eighteenth century than has previously been recognized.[9] Yet Levy's collection of musical sources reveals a distinctive cultivation of two-keyboard compositions and performances. She and her sisters collected a substantial quantity of music for two keyboards, much of which was difficult to find in the eighteenth century, and she commissioned one of the most significant works for two keyboards from this period: the Concerto for Harpsichord, Fortepiano, and Orchestra, Wq. 47 / H. 479, of Carl Philipp Emanuel Bach—one of only a handful of pieces composed during this period that explicitly prescribes the combination of these two instruments.

In the eighteenth century, the performance of music on two keyboard instruments was essentially linked with the expression of relationships between family members and between teachers and students. This point was articulated as early as 1725, in the introduction to the *Apothéose de Lully* by the French composer François Couperin. There, Couperin suggested that his trios—originally scored for two treble instruments and *basso continuo*—could be performed just as well on two keyboards; as he explained,

> This trio, as well as the *Apothéose de Corelli*, and the complete book of trios that I hope to publish next July, may be executed on two harpsichords, as well as all other types of instruments. I play them [on two harpsichords] with my family and with my students, with a very good result, by playing the first soprano line and the bass line on one of the harpsichords, and the second [soprano line], with the same bass line, on another at the unison.[10]

That Couperin situated his performances of keyboard duos within the contexts of family and the student-teacher relationship finds resonance with the practices of the Bach family. Johann Sebastian Bach is thought to have composed his concertos for two or three keyboards and orchestra for performances that he gave himself, together with one or more of his sons.[11] Wilhelm Friedemann Bach may have prepared the string orchestral parts to accompany his father's Concerto in C Major for two keyboards, BWV 1061, and Sebastian copied a score of Friedemann's Concerto for two keyboards (without orchestra) Fk. 10 / BR A12, and perhaps played it with him in Dresden in the 1740s.[12] For the Couperin family, the Bach family, and others, performance on two keyboards would have served a pedagogical purpose, with the teacher demonstrating proper technique and style of execution, even as it articulated the bonds of family, as both individuals shared a common physical, emotional, and aesthetic experience.

Given the precedent of the Bach family, it is no surprise that Sara Levy, a student of Wilhlem Friedemann Bach, would grow to appreciate the value of keyboard duos, which she probably played with her sisters. The documented collections of music held by these women indicate that keyboard duos were of special interest within the Itzig family.[13] Among the sources known to have been owned by Sara and two of her sisters, Zippora Wulff (later Cäcilie von Eskeles) and Fanny von Arnstein, are concertos for two keyboards by Johann Sebastian Bach (BWV 1060, 1061, and 1062), works which, according to one writer in 1772, "have not been printed, and are rather difficult to find."[14] The sisters owned copies of double concertos by Friedemann Bach, as well as concertos and sonatinas for two keyboards and orchestra by Carl Philipp Emanuel Bach. It is possible that other sources for two keyboards (the Concerto Fk. 10 of Wilhelm Friedemann Bach is a likely candidate) have been lost in the intervening years.[15] Wollny has wondered whether, in addition to playing these keyboard duos with her sisters, Sara might have played them with her husband as well.[16]

Two sources stand out in the collections of the Levy circle as particularly noteworthy for what they reveal about the sisters' keyboard-duo practices. First is a manuscript owned by Fanny von Arnstein containing an arrangement of the organ trios by J. S. Bach, BWV 525–30, for two domestic keyboard instruments—harpsichords, fortepianos, or other keyboard instruments without pedals.[17] That Fanny's score dated to her youth in Berlin, prior to her marriage to Nathan von Arnstein in 1776 and their subsequent move to Vienna, is clear from one of two copies of the Sonata BWV 525 contained in the manuscript; the title page shows both her married name, "F Arnstein," and her maiden name, "Vogelchen Itzig."[18] In taking it to Vienna, Fanny brought with her a taste of what Johann Reichardt dubbed a "veritable Sebastian and Philipp Emanuel Bach cult" active at the Itzig mansion in Berlin.[19] The same copyist who produced this manuscript also copied a number of other musical scores in the Itzig circle, including Sara's copy of the Bach organ trios.[20] In Bach's original version, the organist's two hands are required to play two treble lines, each, apparently, on its own manual of the organ. The bass line was assigned to the pedals performed by the organist's feet. In the keyboard-duo arrangement, these parts are divided in precisely the manner described by Couperin: each keyboardist plays one of the treble lines with her right hand, while both left hands execute a single bass line in unison. One might easily imagine Sara playing one part from her score, extracting the lines she needed as Couperin suggested, while Fanny played her part on another instrument, reading from her copy of the arrangement.

Musically, it is easy to understand how such an arrangement would create a sense of "unity in multiplicity." The players' right hands play the same treble lines as in the original organ trios. Thus, in some cases, they are playing in harmony, while in others, one is clearly subservient to another. But in a manifestation of the principles that Sulzer claimed as integral to the duet as a genre, there are many places where the two right hands intertwine with and respond to each other as equal partners. With identical bass lines, the two keyboardists must enact a process of responding to the same musical stimulus in their own individual manner (see ex. 8.2).

The other source that stands out within this remarkable collection of music for two keyboards is the autograph of Carl Philipp Emanuel Bach's Concerto Wq. 47 for Fortepiano, Harpsichord, and Orchestra, perhaps the last work that he composed before his death.[21] Indeed, as Wollny has demonstrated, it is likely that Sara Levy herself commissioned this double concerto from Philipp Emanuel, perhaps as a "companion piece" to Friedemann's Concerto Fk. 46 / BR C11.[22] Whereas scholars in the past have assessed this work as a curious attempt to synthesize the "old" harpsichord with the "new" fortepiano, it is more likely that this work merely codified a combination of instruments that was already in frequent use in other keyboard duos in the late eighteenth century. The fortepiano did not replace the harpsichord immediately, nor render it obsolete or outdated. Instead, the fusion of these keyboard technologies was itself considered innovative, and the combination of timbres from different keyboard mechanisms was thought to enhance the effect of the whole.

Although the choice of keyboard instruments was usually left to the discretion of the players, rather than prescribed in specific terms by the composers, there were instruments in use in the second half of the eighteenth century—especially in the 1770s through '90s—that fused the mechanisms and sounds of the harpsichord and the fortepiano.[23] Some of these—for example, the so-called *Vis à vis*, designed by the instrument builder Johann Andreas Stein, or the *mechanischer Clavier Flügel* by P. J. Milchmeyer—were made to accommodate two players simultaneously: one player could sit at a keyboard that activated a

Example 8.2. Johann Sebastian Bach, Organ Trio in C Minor, BWV 526, I, mm. 24–29, arranged for two keyboard instruments as in A-Wn Mus.Hs.5008.

harpsichord mechanism, while the other sat at another keyboard that acti-vated a fortepiano mechanism.[24] Combination keyboard instruments of these sorts often enabled the player to apply dozens or even hundreds of different *Veränderungen*—"stops," analogous to those on an organ—that modified the timbres of the instrument even further. These instruments enabled the players to control and alter the sounds they produced to a remarkable degree, over-whelming their listeners with a sense of variety, invention, and innovation with each performance.

Although Sara Levy is not known to have owned one of these combination keyboard instruments, a letter sent to her by a representative of the Silbermann workshop of keyboard builders in 1794 indicates that she was interested in both harpsichords and fortepianos; the letter conveys information about the costs of each and the time required for their preparation.[25] Her relationship to the double concerto by Philipp Emanuel suggests that she used both instru-ments together in other keyboard duos as well. In the case of the organ trios of J. S. Bach, this seems especially suitable: if these arrangements were per-formed on two harpsichords, the distinct sound of each of the three voices on the organ would be lost. Executed on harpsichord and fortepiano together, however, each voice would retain its individual character; the fortepiano-harp-sichord combination would simulate the registration of an organ.[26] As in the organ trios, there are numerous instances in the concerto where the two parts come together to form a greater whole. In the passage shown in example 8.3, the two bass lines of the C. P. E. Bach concerto are identical (as they would be in an arrangement of the sort shown in ex. 8.2). The players' two right hands execute rapid arpeggios that knit together in order to produce a swirling har-monic effect. The individual lines overlap, collaborate, and make way for one another, manifesting, once again, the principle of *Einheit in der Mannigfaltigkeit.*

Taking stock of the interest in duets of various sorts within Sara Levy's cir-cle—the duets for two violas of W. F. Bach, the flute duets of Telemann, the keyboard-duo compositions and arrangements from the Bach family, and oth-ers—we might ask why these individuals displayed such an interest in these genres. How did the compositional principles of the duet—especially the ideal of *Einheit in der Mannigfaltigkeit* as alluded to by Quantz and articulated by Sulzer—resonate with the aesthetic and social concerns of Levy's musical practice? And how did instrumental timbre figure into that aesthetic under-standing—that is, what might it have meant to juxtapose, in some cases, two identical instruments (two flutes or two violas), and in other cases, to prescribe *different* instrumental timbres for the *zwei Claviere* in a keyboard duet?

In order to address these questions, I turn to the writings of Moses Mendelssohn, for whom the principle of *Einheit in der Mannigfaltigkeit* carried considerable import. Mendelssohn applied the terminology of *Einheit* and *Mannigfaltigkeit* to his definition of beauty in his *Letters on Sentiments* (1755),

Example 8.3. Carl Philipp Emanuel Bach, Concerto for Harpsichord and Fortepiano, Wq. 47 / H. 479, mvt. 1, mm. 43–48.

[Flutes and horns tacet]

and he used the same ideal to outline his theories of the coexistence of multiple religions within a single state, in which all people would be allowed to retain their individual identities, beliefs, and practices, even as they came together for the good of society as a whole. Indeed, as recent scholarship has shown, Mendelssohn's writings reflect a clear and constant synthesis of his concerns with aesthetics, politics, and religion. As Willi Goetschel has written, "The issue of Jewish identity is never far away or simply suspended, and by no means is it cordoned off from his philosophical and aesthetic interests.

Instead, the specifically critical impulse of Mendelssohn's thinking thrives on the recognition of the intimate connection of all his concerns—theoretical, practical, intellectual, and political."[27] As I will show, Mendelssohn's advocacy of a social and religious *Einheit in der Mannigfaltigkeit* is intimately related to his aesthetic views, and they provide an opening to understand the meaning of the arts for the Jews of Enlightenment Berlin.

Mendelssohn's *Einheit in der Mannigfaltigkeit* from Aesthetics to Political Theory

Like Sulzer, Moses Mendelssohn regarded the concept of *Einheit in der Mannigfaltigkeit* as a key aesthetic concept, describing it as the source of beauty. He began to articulate his ideas on this subject early in his career, first in the "Letters on Sentiments," the numerous printings of which attest to its importance for a large readership and continued relevance throughout this period.[28] The concept first appears in the fifth letter of this collection, which opens with the heading, "Schönheit sezet Einheit im Mannigfaltigen voraus"—"Beauty presupposes unity in a multiplicity."[29] The interlocutor Theocles explains to his student, Euphranor:

> The sameness, the oneness in a multiplicity of features is a property of the beautiful object. They must exhibit an order or otherwise a perfection which appeals to the senses and, indeed, does so effortlessly. If we want to feel a beauty, then our soul wishes to enjoy with ease. The senses are supposed to be enthralled and from them the gratification ought to extend to idle reason.[30]

However, as he explains in the same letter, the appreciation of beauty among human beings is limited, due to the limitations of human perception. The perception of beauty arises from the mind's inability to harmonize diversity; it thus apprehends what it imagines to be an *Einheit in der Mannigfaltigkeit*, but that aesthetic quality is really an illusion, and does not allow the human mind to approach the Divine. It is the intellect—the seat of reason—that goes beyond beauty and seeks further, yearning to identify the *harmony* in diversity. It is in the intellectual search for harmony, rather than in satisfaction with sameness, that human beings can approach the Divine. Alexander Altmann has explained that this additional layer to the notion of perfection is what set Mendelssohn's theory of the arts apart from Sulzer's. In contrast to Sulzer, Altmann claimed, "Mendelssohn . . . redefined perfection as a unity in diversity that challenged our intellect to understand the reason for the harmonious coexistence of all parts."[31]

Subsequent excerpts from the "Letters on Sentiments" join the fifth in establishing the three sources of pleasure available to the human mind, soul, and body, and these are summarized in the eleventh letter of the collection. As Mendelssohn explained there, the fine arts draw upon these three sources of pleasure: "We have uncovered *sameness in multiplicity* or beauty, *harmony in multiplicity* or intellectual perfection, and final the *improved condition of the state of our body* or sensuous gratification. All the fine arts draw from this sanctuary that refreshing potion by means of which they quench the soul's thirst for pleasure."[32] Music, he continued, was the only one of the fine arts that draws on all three sources of pleasure, engaging with the human intellect, body, and appreciation of beauty, and in that sense it is the most complete—the most perfect—of all the arts.

Mendelssohn repeated his view concerning the limitations of beauty per se to approach Divine truth in his essay *On the Main Principles of the Fine Arts and Sciences*: "Nature has an immeasurable plan. The multiplicity incorporated in that plan extends from the infinitely small to the infinitely large, and its unity is far beyond all astonishment. The beauty of external forms in general is only a very small portion of its purposes."[33] Yet Mendelssohn presumes that the true purpose of the fine arts and sciences, which seek to imitate Nature, is to approach the Divine. This is the foundational concept of his essay "On the Sublime and the Naïve in the Fine Sciences": the artist employs these aesthetic categories to offer human observers or listeners the means to comprehend the scope of God's own creations.[34] Music, by activating the appreciation of beauty, the intellect, and the senses of the listener, brings her closest to the experience of the Divine.

Mendelssohn's understanding of the limits of human perception, which informed his views of aesthetics, also extended to religion. As Michah Gottlieb has shown, Mendelssohn saw religion as a set of signs and principles that led people to reflect on God; because of human epistemological limitations, no single religion or set of religious signs was capable of representing God fully. Human beings could never know God entirely. This understanding of religion was not merely academic, but had concrete implications for the Jews of the Enlightenment. As Gottlieb has suggested, Mendelssohn's formulation of the limitations of religion constituted a justification for the persistence and coexistence of *numerous* religions, including Judaism.[35] As values of tolerance began to take root across western Europe, the nature of the relationship among the various religions under the auspices of territorial governments became an increasingly pressing issue. While Protestants and Catholics sought out means of smoothing over their differences, enabling a religious intermingling and assimilation that would have been unthinkable just a generation earlier, Mendelssohn rejected, and indeed feared, this amalgamation. David Sorkin has explained that "Mendelssohn regarded these efforts with horror. He understood the differences between the religions to be divinely ordained."[36] Mendelssohn eschewed religious syncretism not only because it would dilute the distinctiveness of each faith, but, if applied universally, would eventually result in the complete dissolution of Judaism, which would become entirely subsumed by Christianity. Furthermore, as Gottlieb has observed, Mendelssohn advocated religious pluralism as an *a priori* good: without pluralism, human beings would become too deeply entrenched in their own understandings and representations of God, thus risking the danger that they would come to see God as capable of being fully represented in human terms.[37]

In order to resist the assimilationist tendencies in moral and religious philosophy and in the pressure to convert that he had himself experienced in his public controversy with the theologian Johann Caspar Lavater,[38] Mendelssohn advocated a balance of religious *Einheit* and *Mannigfaltigkeit* within the new, secularizing state. He stated this clearly in his treatise on religion's role in relationship to civil authority, *Jerusalem, oder über religiose Macht und Judentum* (1783): "Brothers, if you care for true piety, let us not feign agreement where diversity is evidently the plan and purpose of Providence."[39] As Gottlieb has noted, Mendelssohn was careful in this case to distinguish between the concepts of "sameness" (*Einerleiheit*) and "unity" (*Einheit*). If "sameness" were considered ideal and were to take hold, the *Mannigfaltigkeit* within humanity would disappear—a circumstance that would, in fact, reduce the perfection of the world.[40] It is worth noting that in this context, Mendelssohn employed a metaphor that was as much musical as social: "In the most complete unity [*Einheit*] is an unending diversity [*Mannigfaltigkeit*]. . . . All natural powers have, at their base, the tendency toward *harmony* of diversity, or toward perfection."[41]

Mendelssohn envisioned his ideal society as one with a government in which all men are granted citizenship and rights, and that allows for the flourishing of diverse religious systems without mandating adherence to any single one. Such a government would allow for a balance between the protection of common interests and the common good (*Einheit*) with the Enlightenment values of liberty, free thought, and diversity among individuals (*Mannigfaltigkeit*). As he wrote, "The members of a state have various wills, manifold powers; and in the union of them, for the common good, consists the perfection of the government. It is from the different shades, in which that multiplicity and unity change each other, that the different forms of government arise."[42] He went on to explicate this relationship in various systems of government: monarchy puts unity above multiplicity, and despotism does away with multiplicity altogether. A republic allows greater multiplicity, while anarchy brings multiplicity to the greatest extreme. The ideal form of government, he proposed, was one that united its citizens for the common good while allowing them to retain their individual beliefs and practices.

Mendelssohn was not alone in applying the concept of *Einheit in der Mannigfaltigkeit* within the political and religious realms; in this he was joined by non-Jewish writers as well. In 1781 Christian Wilhelm von Dohm published his treatise *Über die burgerliche Verbesserung der Juden* (On the Civic Improvement of the Jews); even as he claimed that "Jews may be more morally corrupt than other nations,"[43] he also called for the emancipation and integration of Jews into German society, insisting that "the Jew is more a human being than a Jew,"[44] and he argued for autonomy of the religious community. In the view of Shmuel Feiner, Dohm's work, written with the knowledge of Mendelssohn and received with gratitude by the adherents of the Berlin *Haskalah*, "made the Jews a test case for the validity of the ideas of the Enlightenment."[45]

The tension between *Einheit* and *Einerleiheit*—unity and sameness—emerged as a key issue facing the Berlin Jewish community in the 1780s and '90s. In the seventeen years that separated the publication of Dohm's treatise and that of the *Haskalah* writer Wolf Davidson, who appropriated Dohm's title, the tendency among Berlin Jews was toward radical acculturation and, increasingly, conversion to Christianity.[46] Davidson advocated a complete assimilation of Jews into Prussian society. As evidence of the potential for Jews to become active "contributors" to Prussian culture, he cited scores of Jewish professionals, thinkers, and artists who had already assumed such a role. Among these Jews, Davidson cited Sara Levy and Zippora Wulff as two women—"superb keyboardists"—whose contributions to music justified the full integration of Jews in Prussian society.[47]

Emotional Sympathy, the Metaphor of the Family, and Musical Practice

Mendelssohn's calls for a perpetual "unity in multiplicity" in the religious realm were complemented by his descriptions of precisely how such a united but diverse society should work. Individuals within this society would be bound together through their universal "sympathy"—an emotional resonance that they would share with one another, and that would, therefore, shape their relationships with one another.[48] The fine arts served Mendelssohn as a testing ground for such relationships, a testament to his deep engagement with aesthetic concerns. In numerous passages, he also employed the metaphor of the family to describe the interlocking components of his unity-in-multiplicity complex. As I will suggest further on, this family metaphor may serve as a springboard for reconsideration of the musical genre of the duet as cultivated within the circle of Sara Levy.

Mendelssohn's discussion of music in the eleventh of the "Letters on Sentiments" provides a first instance of this family metaphor at work. After noting the three sources of pleasure of which music was capable, Mendelssohn framed them using the metaphor of a family: "All these delights"—the appreciation of beauty, intellectual stimulation, and engagement with the senses—"*offer their hands to one another as sisters* [*schwesterlich*] and vie for our favor in competition with one another."[49] In proposing sisterhood as a model for the unification of beauty, intellectual perfection, and sensuous gratification, Mendelssohn proposed the family as a site for the perfection of the human mind and spirit. The same metaphorical family relationship, indeed, governed Enlightenment ideals of tolerance among people of different faiths. Among the most profound sources of this ideal was Gotthold Ephraim Lessing's *Nathan the Wise* (1779), whose titular character was apparently modeled after Mendelssohn. Each of the three princes—brothers—who own the three proverbial rings learns to "rival the others only in uncorrupted love, free from prejudice."[50] Each must recognize the limitations of his own perception of the divine, existing alongside his brothers in a perpetual and unresolvable state of diversity. Mendelssohn's suggestion that the family presented a formula for the complete intellectual and sensory experience enriches the fable embedded in Lessing's drama: the family relationship serves as a model for the peaceful and tolerant coexistence of people with varying perspectives. The family itself represents a "unity in multiplicity," with the individuals existing independently and yet bound to one another.

The family as a metaphor for society figured prominently in the writings of Mendelssohn and his contemporaries, and the fine arts represented a testing ground for the perfection of human relationships. Drawing heavily on Lessing's Aristotelian theories, Mendelssohn suggested a link between the emotions that may be stimulated by the arts and broader social theories in his "Rhapsodie," published as a supplement to the "Letters on Sentiments." In this work, Mendelssohn explored the essentially neo-Platonist idea of emotional sympathies. One person—for example, a character in a drama—experiencing an emotion stimulates a like emotion in the beholder. Mendelssohn proposed that the goal of all individuals was to experience a state of emotional and intellectual perfection, and the fine arts could be employed to help a beholder achieve this state. To those who say that this goal would produce nothing but selfish individuals, Mendelssohn responded, "Do I love my friend selfishly if I regard his well-being as my own, if I look upon everything good that crosses his path as if it had crossed my own path? *Do I act selfishly towards my fatherland* if I regard its prosperity as a part of my own happiness and seek to promote my own perfection in its perfection?"[51] The state, here, is represented by the father within a family, whose children must cultivate their own "happiness" and "perfection" alongside one another. And, returning to the metaphor of family bonds, Mendelssohn continued,

> Far from canceling the mutual interest of moral entities or even weakening it in the slightest, the basic principle of perfection is instead the source of

universal sympathy, of this brotherhood of spirits [*Verbrüderung der Geister*]—
if I may be allowed the expression—which engulfs and intertwines each
person's own interest and the common interest in such a way that they can
no longer be separated without destruction of all sides. . . . Human politics
strives for a goal which is attained to the highest possible degree in God's
wise and peaceful government, namely, the goal of having each member
advance what is best for the community by working on his own well-being.[52]

Having established earlier in his *Jerusalem* that an *Einheit in der Mannigfaltigkeit*
of religions represented the best means of advancing the interests of the state
and its subjects, Mendelssohn further articulated how "sympathy" would be
of help to all individuals in the state. Arguing against the right of a religious
community to be empowered to excommunicate, he explained that the sympathetic effects of coexistence with other human beings had the power to balance reason and the gratification of the senses. As he wrote,

In fact, the most essential purpose of religious society is mutual edification.
By the magic power of sympathy one wishes to transfer truth from the mind
to the heart; to vivify, by participation with others, the concepts of reason,
which at times are lifeless, into soaring sensations. When the heart clings too
strongly to sensual pleasures to listen to the voice of reason, when it is on the
verge of ensnaring reason itself, then let it be seized here with a tremor of
pious enthusiasm, kindled by the fire of devotion, and acquainted with joys
of a higher order which outweigh even in this life the joys of the senses.[53]

Thus even in articulating the need for separation of political power from a
religious community, Mendelssohn made the case for a sympathetic emotional,
sensory, and intellectual connection among all individuals—a connection
based in the model of the family. The fine arts offered a glimpse of this ideal
coexistence. The formulation of this concept, articulated in Mendelssohn's
"Rhapsodie," overlaps to a surprising degree with his rhetoric concerning
political theory in *Jerusalem,* as quoted above: "If an artist does not misuse the
arts of *poetry*, *painting*, and *sculpture* for some ignoble purpose, these arts show
us ethical rules in examples that are fictional and have been *beautified by the art,
examples which again animate knowledge; each dry truth is transformed into an ardent
and sensuous intuition.*"[54] Here, too, Mendelssohn's goal is for the sensuous, the
emotional, and the intellectual to complement and balance with one another.
It is the flourishing of a *Mannigfaltigkeit* within *Einheit*—modeled after that of
members of a family—that allows this balance to take hold.

Although historians once believed that women of the Enlightenment
read only novels, while men read more "serious" works, including philosophy, Natalie Naimark-Goldberg has shown that these literary barriers are a
latter-day construction. Some women, indeed, read philosophical works, while

others encountered philosophical ideas through summaries in journals or through discussion with well-read peers.[55] Steven Lowenstein has documented the involvement of elite Berlin families in supporting Mendelssohn's publications,[56] suggesting that the women as well as the men would have had easy access to those works. The Itzig daughters socialized with Mendelssohn's family and students,[57] and Sara's sister Fanny is known to have maintained a diary in which she wrote down maxims summarizing Mendelssohn's ideas, among other items of philosophical, literary, and artistic interest. In nineteenth-century accounts—admittedly unreliable[58]—Sara Levy was reported to have repeated the dictum from Mendelssohn's *Jerusalem* that if Judaism was the foundation of Christianity, then she should not be required to "break down the basement in order to live in the first floor."[59] This adage represents a clear articulation of the idea that Judaism and Christianity should be allowed to coexist in a perpetual state of *Mannigfaltigkeit,* and indeed, Sara stood apart from many others in her social circle because she never baptized.[60]

Although the precise textual or discursive means through which the Itzig daughters would have become familiar with Mendelssohn's ideas are unclear, their awareness of both his aesthetic and political ideas seems highly likely, for they themselves had much invested in those discussions. And Mendelssohn himself had an active presence within the musical world of Berlin in the 1750s through the early '80s, with his aesthetic theories becoming influential for some of the most important composers and musicians of the age.[61] There was, in the words of Anselm Gerhard, an "essential influence" between Mendelssohn's aesthetic theories and the musical practice of Enlightenment Berlin.[62] Mendelssohn's theories found strong resonance within the musical practices of his day.

With these connections between the theoretical and the practical as a point of departure, I will now synthesize the disparate parts of my argument. The musical genre of the duet was, in the view of Sulzer and Quantz, a manifestation of the principle of *Einheit in der Mannigfaltigkeit.* Quantz conceived of the duet broadly speaking as a pedagogical genre for use by amateurs or by teacher and student together, and keyboard duo was likewise a mode of music-making situated primarily within student-teacher and family relationships. Although Moses Mendelssohn never wrote about the musical duet in particular, he adopted the vocabulary of *Einheit in der Mannigfaltigkeit* in articulating both his aesthetic views and his religious and political theories—in particular, in his advocacy for religious pluralism within a state that allowed for the cultivation of the individual good as a component of the welfare of society as a whole. The family served as a model for the fashioning of relationships among people within such a society.

Sara Levy's extensive collection of duos, as well as her familiarity with the social issues of the Berlin Enlightenment, raises the possibility that she and others in her circle saw this musical genre as a social metaphor, as Moses Mendelssohn did. Duets for two like instruments enabled the players to articulate their family bonds within a tightly knitted familial and social circle, but also allowed for participation by a wide array of individuals, including both Jews and Christians, artists and intellectuals, philosophers and socialites. Through music, they engaged each other through the mind, the body, and the emotions. The matching bodily motions of the players would have produced like emotions, thoughts, and sensory reactions.[63] The genre of the duet forced players to enact their own balance of *Einheit* and *Mannigfaltigkeit*, asserting their individual identities even as they accommodated their partner. It represented an aesthetic model for the kind of tolerant society that Mendelssohn imagined.

Notes

1. See, for example, Steven Zohn's chapter in the present volume as well as Edward Klorman, *Mozart's Music of Friends: Social Interplay in the Chamber Works* (Cambridge: Cambridge University Press, 2016). General biographical information on Sara Levy and her family appears in Thekla Keuck, *Hofjuden und Kulturbürger: Die Geschichte der Familie Itzig in Berlin* (Göttingen: Vandenhoeck & Ruprecht, 2011).

2. "Beyde darinn vorkommende Stimmen Hauptstimmen sind, und keine über die andre herrscht; daß bald die eine, bald die andre eine Zeitlang sich allein hören läßt, hernach aber beyde zugleich, jede aber in ihrem besondern Gang. Hieraus entsteht in beyden Arten die Nothwendigkeit, daß das Duet fugenmäßig und völlig nach der Kunst des doppelten Contrapunkts gesetzt seyn müssen, damit beyde Melodien bey der Einheit des Charakters eine schöne Mannigfaltigkeit haben." Johann Georg Sulzer, *Allgemeine Theorie der schönen Künste in einzeln, nach alphabetischer Ordnung der Kunstwörter auf einander folgenden, Artikeln abgehandelt* (Leipzig: Weidmanns, Erben, & Reich, 1773), 1:377–78. Emphasis added.

3. "Fk." and "BR" are the two standard catalogues of works by Wilhelm Friedemann Bach. The Falck catalogue is in Martin Falck, "Thematisches Verzeichnis der Kompositionen Wilhelm Friedemann Bachs," in *Wilhelm Friedemann Bach: Sein Leben und seine Werke* (Leipzig: C. I. Kahnt, 1913). The BR (Bach-Repertorium II) catalogue, in preparation, is Peter Wollny, *Thematisch-systematisches Verzeichnis der Werke Wilhelm Friedemann Bachs*.

4. "so wie im Original, Primo und Secondo auf einem Bogen." "gutes weißes Papier, ich zahle gerne etwas mehr dafür." Quoted in Peter Wollny, *"Ein förmlicher Sebastian und Philipp Emanuel Bach-Kultus": Sara Levy und ihr musikalisches Wirken mit einer Dokumentensammlung zur musikalischen Familiengeschichte der Vorfahren von Felix Mendelssohn Bartholdy* (Wiesbaden: Breitkopf & Härtel, 2010), 39. "D-Bsa SA" is the library siglum for Germany: Sing-Akademie zu Berlin, Notenarchiv.

5. Wollny, *"Ein förmlicher Sebastian und Philipp Emanuel Bach-Kultus,"* 25–28.

6. On these arrangements including flute, see Rebecca Cypess, "Arrangement Practices in the Bach Tradition, Then and Now," in "Musical Interpretation Today," ed. Sezi Seskir and David Hyunsu Kim (unpublished manuscript, September 1, 2017).

7. Steven Zohn, *Music for a Mixed Taste: Style, Genre, and Meaning in Telemann's Instrumental Works* (Oxford: Oxford University Press, 2008), 460–61.

8. "Les imitations et les variétes des desseins étant plus sensibles dans le duo que dans toute autre pièce . . . les imitations doivent être très justes & regulières, dans quelque intervalle qu'elles se fassent. . . . Les deux parties y doivent participier également tour à tour, de façon que l'une semble toujours enlever le dessein à l'autre." Johann Joachim Quantz, *Sei duetti a due flauti traversi* (Berlin: Georg Ludwig Winter, 1759), ii.

9. Rebecca Cypess, "Keyboard Duo Arrangements in Eighteenth-Century Musical Life," *Eighteenth-Century Music* 14, no. 2 (2017): 183–214.

10. "Ce trio, ainsi que l'Apothéose de Corelli; & le livre complet de trios que j'espere donner au mois de Juillet prochain, peuvent s'exécuter à deux clavecins, ainsi que sur tous autres instrumens. Je les execute dans ma famille; & avec mes éléves, avec une réüssite tres heureuse, sçavoir, en joüant le premier dessus, & la basse sur un des clavecins: & le second, avec le même basse sur un autre à l'unisson." François Couperin, "Avis" to *Concert instrumental sous le titre d'Apothéose composé à la mémoire immortelle de l'incomparable Monsieur de Lully* (Paris: L'auteur and Le Sieur Boivin, 1725), n.p.

11. Jane Stevens, *The Bach Family and the Keyboard Concerto: The Evolution of a Genre* (Warren, MI: Harmonie Park, 2001), 48–49; Martin Falck, *Wilhelm Friedemann Bach: Sein Leben und seine Werk* (Leipzig: C. I. Kahnt, 1913), 62–63.

12. See Stevens, *The Bach Family and the Keyboard Concerto*, 49; and David Schulenberg, *The Music of Wilhelm Friedemann Bach* (Rochester, NY: University of Rochester Press, 2010), 87–89.

13. Peter Wollny, "Sara Levy and the Making of Musical Taste in Berlin," *Musical Quarterly* 77, no. 4 (1993): 658; and Wollny, *"Ein förmlicher Sebastian und Philipp Emanuel Bach-Kultus,"* 40–42.

14. "nicht gedruckt, und ziemlich schwer zu bekommen sind." *Allgemeine deutsche Bibliothek*, ed. Friedrich Nicolai (Berlin: Friedrich Nicolai, 1772), 17:239.

15. The surviving sources for the Concerto Fk. 10 are listed in the notes to Wilhelm Friedemann Bach, *Klaviermusik I: Sonaten und Konzert für Cembalo solo; Konzert für zwei Cembali*, ed. Peter Wollny. Gesammelte Werke, vol. 1 (Stuttgart: Carus, 2009).

16. Wollny, *"Ein förmlicher Sebastian und Philipp Emanuel Bach-Kultus,"* 40.

17. This manuscript is now held in the Österreichische Nationalbibliothek, A-Wn Mus.Hs.5008. For more on this source and its significance in the musical culture of Vienna in the late eighteenth century, see Christoph Wolff, *Mozart at the Gateway to His Fortune: Serving the Emperor, 1788–1791* (New York: W. W. Norton, 2012), 58–63. See also Dietrich Kilian's critical report on organ trios in the *Neue Bach Ausgabe*, series 4, vol. 7 (Kassel: Bärenreiter, 1988), 59.

18. A-Wn Mus.Hs.5008. See Kilian, critical report on organ trios, 59.

19. Quoted in Wollny, *"Ein förmlicher Sebastian und Philipp Emanuel Bach-Kultus,"* 22.

20. Sara Levy's score of the organ trios is in the Staatsbibliothek zu Berlin, D-B N Mus. Ms. 10486.

21. D-B N.Mus. SA 4.

22. Wollny, "Sara Levy and the Making of Musical Taste," 657–58; R. Larry Todd, *Mendelssohn: A Life in Music* (Oxford: Oxford University Press, 2003), 11.

23. Michael Latcham has explored these hybrid instruments, including those intended for two players, in several articles: see Michael Latcham, "Swirling from One Level of Affects to Another: The Expressive Clavier in Mozart's Time," *Early Music* 30, no. 4 (2002): 502–30; Michael Latcham, "Mozart and the Pianos of Johann Andreas Stein," *Galpin Society Journal* 51 (1998): 114–53; Michael Latcham, "The Apotheosis of Merlin," in *Musique ancienne—instruments et imagination: Actes de rencontres internationales* harmoniques, *Lausanne 2004. Music of the Past: Instruments and Imagination: Proceedings of the* Harmoniques *International Congress, Lausanne 2004,* ed. Michael Latcham (Bern: Peter Lang, 2006), 271–98; Michael Latcham, "Johann Andreas Stein and the Search for the Expressive *Clavier,*" in *Cordes et clavier au temps de Mozart. Bowed and Keyboard Instruments in the Age of Mozart,* ed. Thomas Steiner (Bern: Peter Lang, 2010), 133–216.

24. See Rebecca Cypess, "Timbre, Expression, and Combination Keyboard Instruments: Milchmeyer's Art of *Veränderung,*" *Keyboard Perspectives* 8 (2015): 43–69, and Cypess, "Keyboard-Duo Arrangements," 201–9.

25. This letter is transcribed in Wollny, *"Ein förmlicher Sebastian und Philipp Emanuel Bach-Kultus,"* 53–54.

26. I am grateful to Christoph Wolff for suggesting this instrumentation for the organ trios. See also Cypess, "Keyboard-Duo Arrangements," 207–9.

27. See Elias Sacks's contribution to this volume, as well as Willi Goetschel, *Spinoza's Modernity: Mendelssohn, Lessing, and Heine* (Madison: University of Wisconsin Press, 2004), 88. For more on the relevance of aesthetics in other political and intellectual pursuits, see Sorkin, *Moses Mendelssohn and the Religious Enlightenment,* especially ch. 5, "Psalms." Other studies of the ethical implications of Mendelssohn's aesthetics include Leah Hochman, *The Ugliness of Moses Mendelssohn: Aesthetics, Religion, and Morality in the Eighteenth Century* (New York: Routledge, 2014); and Carsten Zelle, "Verwöhnter Geschmack, schauervolles Ergötzen und theatralische Sittlichkeit: zum Verhältnis von Ethik und Ästhetik in Moses Mendelssohns ästhetischen Schriften," in *Musik und Ästhetik im Berlin Moses Mendelssohns,* 97–115.

28. As Daniel O. Dahlstrom has explained, this work was later included in the *Philosophische Schriften* of 1761, revised in 1771, and reissued in 1777 and 1783. See Moses Mendelssohn, *Philosophical Writings,* trans. with notes and introduction by Daniel O. Dahlstrom (Cambridge: Cambridge University Press, 1997), xxxvi–xxxvii.

29. Moses Mendelssohn, *Philosophische Schriften* (Carlsruhe: im Verlag der Schmiederischen Buchhandlung, 1761), 1:27. Translated in Moses Mendelssohn *Philosophical Writings,* 22. In this early work, Mendelssohn used

the term "Einheit" (unity), interchangeably with "Einerleiheit" (sameness); this is not the case in his later work on religion and politics—a point to which I shall return.

30. "Die Gleichheit, das Einerley im Mannigfaltigen ist ein Eigenthum der schönen Gegenstände. Sie müssen eine Ordnung oder sonst eine Vollkommenheit darbieten, die in die Sinne fällt, und zwar ohne Mühe in die Sinne fällt. Wenn wir eine Schönheit fühlen wollen, so wünchet unsre Seele mit Gemächlichkeit zu geniessen. Die Sinne sollen begeistert seyn, und von ihnen soll sich die Lust auf die müssige Vernunft ausbreiten." Mendelssohn, *Philosophische Schriften*, 1:28, trans. in Mendelssohn, *Philosophical Writings*, 22.

31. Alexander Altmann, *Moses Mendelssohn: A Biographical Study* (Tuscaloosa: University of Alabama Press, 1973), 57. On the implications of Sulzer's aesthetics for his views of ethics, see Matthew Riley, "Civilizing the Savage: Johann Georg Sulzer and the 'Aesthetic Force' of Music," *Journal of the Royal Musical Association* 127, no. 1 (2002): 1–22.

32. "Das Einerley im Mannifgaltigen, oder die Schönheit, die Einhelligkeit des Mannigfaltigen, oder die verständliche Vollkommenheit, und endlich der verbesserte Zustand unserer Leibesbeschaffenheit, oder die sinnliche Lust. Alle schönen Künste holen aus diesem heiligthume das Labsal, womit sie die nach Vergnügen dürstende Seele erfrischen." Moses Mendelssohn, *Philosophische Schriften*, 1:84–85; translated in Mendelssohn, *Philosophical Writings*, 48.

33. "Die Natur hat einen unermeßlichen Plan. Die Mannigfaltigkeit desselben erstreckt sich vom unendlich kleinen bix ins unendlick Grosse, und seine Einheit ist über alles Erstaunen hinweg. Die Schönheit der äusserlichen Formen überhaupt, ist nur ein sehr geringer Theil von ihren Absichten." Mendelssohn, *Philosophische Schriften*, 2:114, trans. in Mendelssohn, *Philosophical Writings*, 176.

34. See Hochman, *The Ugliness of Moses Mendelssohn*, 51–54.

35. Michah Gottlieb, "Mendelssohn's Metaphysical Defense of Religious Pluralism," *Journal of Religion* 86, no. 2 (2006): 205–25.

36. David Sorkin, *Moses Mendelssohn and the Religious Enlightenment* (Berkeley: University of California Press, 1996), 140.

37. Gottlieb, "Mendelssohn's Metaphysical Defense," 222–23.

38. See Altmann, *Moses Mendelssohn*, 194–263; Sorkin, *Moses Mendelssohn and the Religious Enlightenment*, 25–30; and Hochman, *The Ugliness of Moses Mendelssohn*, 132–35.

39. "Brüder! Ist es euch um wahre Gottseligkeit zu thun; so lasset uns keine Uebereinstimmung lügen, wo Mannigfaltigkeit offenbar Plan und Endzweck der Vorsehung ist." Moses Mendelssohn, *Jerusalem, oder über religiose Macht und Judentum* (Berlin: Friedrich Maurer, 1783), 138. Translated in Sorkin, *Moses Mendelssohn and the Religious Enlightenment*, 140 and in Gottlieb, "Mendelssohn's Metaphysical Defense of Enlightenment," 217.

40. Gottlieb, "Mendelssohn's Metaphysical Defense of Enlightenment," 218.

41. "In der vollkommensten Einheit ist eine unendliche Mannigfaltigkeit. . . . In allen Naturkräften zum Grunde liegt, ist Tendenz zur Harmonie des Mannigfaltigen, oder zur Vollkommenheit." Moses Mendelssohn, Letter to

Frhrn. Von Dalberg, September 5, 1777, printed in *Moses Mendelssohns gesammelte Schriften*, ed. G. B. Mendelssohn (Leipzig: Brochaus, 1844), 541.

42. "Die Glieder eines Staats haben mannigfaltigen Willen, mannigfaltige Kräfte.—In der Vereingung derselben zum allgemeinen Besten besteht die Vollkommenheit der Regierung. Aus den verschiedenen Nuancen, in welchen sich diese Mannigfaltigkeit und Einheit einander einschränken und abändern, entspringen die verschiedenen Regierungsformen." Moses Mendelssohn, "Ueber die Einrichtung einer Volkslehre: Nach den Begriffen des Verfassers über den Patriotismus," in Moses Mendelssohn, *Sammlung theils noch ungedruckter, theils in andern Schriften zerstreuter Aufsätze und Briefe von ihm, an und über ihn*, ed. J. Heinemann (Leipzig: G. Wolbrecht'sche Buchhandlung, 1831), 150–51. Translation adapted from the appendix to Moses Mendelssohn, *Jerusalem: A Treatise on Ecclesiastical Authority and Judaism*, trans. M. Samuels (London: Longman, Orme, Brown, & Longmans, 1838), 182–83.

43. "Ich kann es zugeben, daß die Juden sittlich verdorbner seyn mögen, als andere Nationen." Christian Wilhelm von Dohm, *Ueber die bürgerliche Verbesserung der Juden* (Berlin: Friedrich Nicolai, 1781), 34; translated in the appendix to Gotthold Ephraim Lessing, *Nathan the Wise*, trans. and ed. with introduction by Ronald Schechter (Boston: Bedford St. Martin's, 2004), 132.

44. "Der Jude ist noch mehr Mensch als Jude." Dohm, *Ueber die bürgerliche Verbesserung*, 28; trans. Schechter in *Nathan the Wise*, 132.

45. Shmuel Feiner, *The Jewish Enlightenment*, trans. Chaya Naor (Philadelphia: University of Pennsylvania Press, 2002), 121; see Feiner's discussion of Dohm, pp. 120–24.

46. See Natalie Naimark-Goldberg, *Jewish Women in Enlightenment Berlin* (Oxford: Littman Library of Jewish Civilization, 2013). For a more specific study of this radical tendency in Mendelssohn's daughter, see Susanne Hillman, "The Conversions of Dorothea Mendelssohn: Conviction or Convenience?" *German Studies Review* 29, no. 1 (2006): 127–44.

47. On the problems associated with the "contribution discourse" in Jewish historiography, see Moshe Rosman, *How Jewish Is Jewish History?* (Oxford: Littman Library of Jewish Civilization, 2007), 111–30; and Rebecca Cypess, "Music Historicism: Sara Levy and the Jewish Enlightenment," *Bach Perspectives* 12, ed. Robin Leaver (2018):129–51. On these women as "vehicles of emancipation," see Anselm Gerhard, "Einleitung," in *Musik und Ästhetik im Berlin Moses Mendelssohns*, 16–18.

48. An overview of "sympathy" in music of the seventeenth and eighteenth centuries is in Ruth HaCohen, "The Music of Sympathy in the Arts of the Baroque; or, the Use of Difference to Overcome Indifference," *Poetics Today* 22, no. 3 (2001): 607–50; see also Ruth HaCohen, *The Music Libel Against the Jews* (New Haven, CT: Yale University Press, 2011), ch. 2, "Rethinking and Enacting Sympathetic Worlds: The Eighteenth-Century Oratorical Legacies of Bach, Lessing, and Handel."

49. "Wir sind endlich so weit, daß wir eine dreyfache Quelle des Vergnügens entdeckt, und ihre verwirrten Grenzen auseinander gesetzt haben. . . . Göttliche Tonkunst! Du bist die einzige, die uns mit allen Arten von Vergnügen

überraschet! Welche süße Verwirrung von Vollkommenheit, sinnlicher Lust und Schönheit! Die Nachahmungen der menschlichen Leidenschaften; die künstliche Verbindung zwischen widersinnigen Uebellauten: Quellen der Vollkommenheit! Die leichten Verhältnisse in den Schwingungen; das Ebenmaß in den Beziehungen der Theile auf einander und auf das Ganze; die Beschäftigung der Geisteskräfte in Zweifeln, Vermuthen und Vorhersehen: Quellen der Schönheit! Die mit allen Saiten harmonische Spannung der nervigten Gefäße: eine Quelle der sinnlichen Lust! *Alle diese Ergößlichkeiten bieten sich schwesterlich die Hand und bewerden sich wetterfernd um unsere Gunst.*" Moses Mendelssohn, *Philosophische Schriften*, 1:84–85; translated in Mendelssohn, *Philosophical Writings*, 48. Emphasis added.

50. "Es eifre jeder seiner unbestochnen / Von Vorurteilen freien Liebe nach!" Gotthold Ephraim Lessing, *Nathan der Weise* (Germany: Wilhelm Goldmann Verlag, 1979), act 3, scene 7, trans. Schechter in Lessing, *Nathan the Wise*, 74. On the latent anti-Judaism in *Nathan der Weise*—Lessing's association with the principles of tolerance notwithstanding—see Martha B. Helfer, *The Word Unheard: Legacies of Anti-Semitism in German Literature and Culture* (Evanston, IL: Northwestern University Press, 2011), ch. 1, "Lessing and the Limits of Enlightenment," reproduced in the present volume.

51. "Liebe ich meinen Freund eigennützig, wenn ich sein Wohlseyn als das meinige betrachte, wenn ich alles Gute, das ihm wiederfährt, mit solchen Augen ansehe, als wenn es mire selbst wiederführe? Hendele ich eigensüchtig gegen mein Vaterland, wenn ich seinen Wohlstand als einen Theil meiner Glückseligkeit betrachte, und in seiner Vollkommenheit, die meinige zu befördern suche?" Mendelssohn, *Philosophische Schriften*, 2:53, trans. in Mendelssohn, "Rhapsody, or Additions to the Letters on Sentiments," in *Philosophical Writings*, 151. Emphasis added.

52. "Weit gefehlt, daß der Grundsatz der Vollkommenheit das gegenseitige Interesse moralischer Wesen aufheben, oder nu rim geringsten schwächen sollte; er ist vielmehr die Quelle der allgemeinen Sympathie, dieser Verbrüderung der Geister, wenn man mir diesen Ausdruck erlaubt, die ihr eigenes und gemeinsames Interesse dergestalt in einander verschlinget, daß sie ohne Zernichtung nicht mehr getrennet werden können. . . . In der weisen und eintrachtsvollen Regierung Gottes wird die Absicht im allerhöchsten Grade erreicht, nach welcher die menschliche Politik ringet, daß nehmlich jedes Mitglied das gemeinsame Beste befördere, indem es an seinem eigenen Wohlseyn arbeitet." Mendelssohn, *Philosophische Schriften*, 56; trans. in *Philosophical Writings*, 153.

53. "In der That, die wesentlichste Absicht religioser Gesellschaften ist gemeinschaftliche Erbauung. Man will durch die Zauberkraft der Sympathie, die Wahrheit aus dem Geiste in das Herz übertragen, die zuweilen todte Vernunsterkenntniß durch Theilnehmung zu hohen Empfindnissen beleben. Wenn das Herz allzusehr an sinnlichen Lüsten klebt, um der Vernunft Gehöhr zu geben; wenn es auf dem Punkt ist, die Vernunft selbst mit ins Garn zu locken; so werde e shier von Schauer der Gottseligkeit ergriffen, von Feuer der Andacht entflammt, und lerne Freuden höherer Art kennen, die auch

hieniden schon den sinnlichen Freuden die Wage halten." Mendelssohn, *Jerusalem*, 94; trans. in Mendelssohn, *Jerusalem, or On Religious Power and Judaism*, trans. Allan Arkush, with intro. and commentary by Alexander Altmann (Hanover, NH: Brandeis University Press and University Press of New England, 1983), 74. Emphasis added.

54. Mendelssohn, *Rhapsodie*, 167. Emphasis added.

55. Naimark-Goldberg, *Jewish Women in Enlightenment Berlin*, ch. 2, "Jewish Women and the Reading Public," especially pp. 95–99.

56. Steven M. Lowenstein, *The Berlin Jewish Community: Enlightenment, Family and Crisis, 1770–1830* (New York: Oxford University Press, 1994), 39–40.

57. See the numerous references to Samuel and Sara Levy in Sabattia Joseph Wolff's biographical sketch of Salomon Maimon, a one-time student of Mendelssohn, in Sabattia Joseph Wolff, *Maimoniana: Oder Rhapsodien zur Charakteristik Salomon Maimon's aus seinem Privatleben gesammelt* (Berlin: G. Hayn, 1813), 108–13.

58. On the unreliability of later accounts of the women of Sara Levy's circle, see Naimark-Goldberg, *Jewish Women in Enlightenment Berlin*, 188–92.

59. Nahida Remy, *The Jewish Woman*, trans. Louise Mannheimer with preface by Dr. Lazarus (Cincinnati, OH: C. J. Krehbiel, 1895), 200.

60. For more on Sara Levy's strong connection to Judaism, see Naimark-Goldberg's contribution to this volume.

61. On Mendelssohn's musical training and its implications for his theories of music, see Laurenz Lütteken, "Zwischen Ohr und Verstand: Moses Mendelssohn, Johann Philipp Kirnberger, und die Begründung des 'reinen Satzes' in der Musik," in *Musik und Ästhetik im Berlin Moses Mendelssohns*, 135–63.

62. Gerhard, "Einleitung," 20. Applications of Mendelssohn's aesthetic theories to the music of C. P. E. Bach may be found in Annette Richards, "An Enduring Monument: C. P. E. Bach and the Musical Sublime," in *C. P. E. Bach Studies*, ed. Annette Richards (Cambridge: Cambridge University Press, 2006), 169–71; and in Hartmut Grimm, "Moses Mendelssohns Beitrag zur Musikästhetik und Carl Philipp Emanuel Bachs Fantasie-Prinzip," in *Musik und Ästhetik im Berlin Moses Mendelssohns*, 187–216. See also Altmann, *Moses Mendelssohn*, 56–67.

63. On the perception by late-eighteenth-century theorists of *Einheit in der Mannigfaltigkeit* within the music of J. S. Bach, see Matthew Dirst, *Engaging Bach: The Keyboard Legacy from Marpurg to Mendelssohn* (Cambridge: Cambridge University Press, 2012), 20–30.

Chapter Nine

The Sociability of Salon Culture and Carl Philipp Emanuel Bach's Quartets

Steven Zohn

Even in late-eighteenth-century Berlin, where the music of Johann Sebastian Bach enjoyed a healthy afterlife through the advocacy of his sons and former pupils, the extensive cultivation of Bach-family works by the Itzig circle was remarkable. The "veritable Sebastian and Emanuel Bach cult" centered in the house of the royal banker Daniel Itzig from the 1770s was maintained above all by his daughter Sara Levy well into the nineteenth century.[1] A prominent keyboardist and *salonnière*, Levy studied with Wilhelm Friedemann Bach, corresponded with Carl Philipp Emanuel Bach, and evidently commissioned works from both. Her enthusiasm for music of the Bach family, alongside mid-century works by Berlin composers employed by King Frederick the Great and Princess Anna Amalia, has been considered evidence of a "conservative-enlightened musical taste" that gradually ossified over several decades.[2]

Levy's manuscript copies of music by Sebastian Bach include a representative sampling of keyboard and chamber works from across the composer's career—from the early Toccata in D Major, BWV 912, and the English and French Suites, to more mature works such as the organ trios, selections from the Well-Tempered Clavier, sonatas for violin or flute and obbligato keyboard, and keyboard concertos that she played in house concerts in her salon or performed publicly over several decades.[3] It should come as no surprise that this list includes compositions that Emanuel Bach considered to have aged particularly well. In 1774 he wrote to Johann Nikolaus Forkel that his father's violin and obbligato keyboard sonatas "still sound excellent and give me much joy, although they date back more than fifty years. They contain some *Adagii* that could not be written in a more singable manner today."[4] And as the presumed author of a comparison between his father and Handel published in 1788, Emanuel noted that the organ trios are "written in such a *galant* style that they still sound very good, and never grow old, but on the contrary will outlive all revolutions of fashion in music."[5] Nevertheless, Sebastian's music—especially the keyboard suites—could hardly have been seen as progressive during the last quarter of the eighteenth century. And so Levy's interest in it speaks mainly to the antiquarian side of her musical taste. In this she was hardly atypical among her peers, for Berlin salon culture was pluralistic in its consumption of literature and music from both past and present.[6] In fact, building collections of Bachiana and other old music, as both Levy and Princess Anna Amalia did, may even have been considered fashionable within the upper social strata of late-eighteenth-century Berlin.

This essay focuses on some of the most modern Bach-family works collected by Levy: Emanuel's three Quartets in A minor, D major, and G major for flute, viola, and keyboard, Wq. 93–95 / H. 537–39, which were composed in January 1788 and likely commissioned by the *salonnière*.[7] Levy owned autograph fair-copy scores of at least Wq. 94 and 95, which passed from her collection to Carl Friedrich Zelter and then to the Berlin *Sing-Akademie* (where they remain today), and it is probable that the lost autograph fair-copy score of Wq. 93 was once in her possession as well. Whether she would have played the quartets on harpsichord or fortepiano is a matter for speculation, since most of the works' sources designate the keyboard parts with generic terms ("Clavier" in Bach's scores and in Johann Heinrich Michel's scores owned by Joseph Haydn, "Cembalo" in other sources). But Zelter specified "Fortepiano" on the title to a composite manuscript that apparently once included the two autograph scores.[8] Although there are no concrete indications of who may have played the flute and viola parts, it has been suggested that Samuel Salomon Levy, whom Sara had married in 1783, was an amateur flutist.[9] Certainly the dozens of flute duos, trios, quartets, and concertos in the Levy collection suggest that the instrument was played by someone in the household, by a close family member, or by a frequent visitor to the salon. Likewise, there must have been at least two capable violists in Levy's circle, as witnessed by her ownership of the autograph manuscript of Wilhelm Friedemann Bach's viola duets, Fk. 60–62, works that she may have commissioned as well.[10]

Owing in part to their unique scoring—dispensing not only with a continuo part, but also with one for cello—Emanuel's quartets have long been placed among the composer's most stylistically progressive and anomalous instrumental works. Ernst Fritz Schmid, the quartets' first modern editor, saw in Wq. 94 a "complete breakthrough to the Viennese classical style."[11] He further considered the middle movements of Wq. 93 and 94 to anticipate Beethoven, found Mozartian harmony in the middle movement of Wq. 95, and characterized the finale of Wq. 94 as thoroughly Haydnesque.[12] Eugene Helm saw the quartets as marking Bach's turn to the Classical style, even adumbrating Beethoven's piano quartets.[13] For Hans-Günter Ottenberg, the quartets offer a link between C. P. E. Bach and Haydn, and he further detects in them an incipient Romanticism.[14]

If more recent commentators have tended to stress the quartets' individuality and independence from specific stylistic models, they too have felt obliged to invoke Bach's Viennese contemporaries, if only to downplay their potential influence on him. Friedhelm Krummacher stresses the novelty of Bach's forms while discounting any similarities with Haydn and Beethoven (as noted by Schmid and Ottenberg); Klaus G. Werner finds the quartets' surface features relatively conventional (that is, closely tied to Baroque tradition) when placed beside the music of Haydn and Mozart; Günther Wagner proposes that the quartets exhibit "an undeniable difference from contemporaneous Viennese classicism"; David Schulenberg suggests that "what sound to modern ears like echoes of [Haydn's and Mozart's music] are more likely borrowings from a more generic Classical style"; and Siegbert Rampe judges the quartets qualitatively comparable to the finest among Haydn's and Mozart's piano trios and string quartets, but notes that they are stylistically "unadulterated" examples of Bach's late idiom and "reveal Viennese influences with the utmost freedom."[15]

Each of these views bears witness, in its own way, to the quartets' strikingly modern aesthetic, one that indeed marks a break from Bach's previous instrumental works. This new orientation has much to do with how the three instruments relate to one another, their independence offset by intricate alliances that yield frequent textural and coloristic shifts and which, perhaps inevitably, invite comparison with conversation.[16] Thus Werner likens passages in the first movement of Wq. 93 to a "question–answer" dialogue that alternately suggests unity and disunity among the instruments.[17] And Christoph Wolff observes in the quartets "an evenly balanced instrumental discourse that permits the composer to engage in a lively, intense, and witty musical dialogue," a counterpart to the verbal conversations in Sara Levy's salon.[18]

Whether or not one hears the quartets as dialogic, it is above all their sociable orientation that marks them as exceptional within Bach's output. For they represent a shift away from an aesthetic of self-expression, encountered in much of his earlier music for instrumental ensemble, and toward one emphasizing collaboration between multiple instrumental personas. In this respect, it is significant that another work from Bach's last year, *C. P. E. Bachs Empfindungen*, Wq. 80 / H. 536 (a version of the Fantasia for Keyboard in F-sharp Minor, Wq. 67 / H. 300, to which the composer added a solo violin part and appended an Allegro from the earlier Sonata for Keyboard in B-flat Major, Wq. 65.45 / H. 212), represents an unusual cross between self-expression and sociability.[19] The quartets' sociable dynamic also recalls the conversational style of the sonatas and rondos Bach published in his last three collections of *Clavier-Sonaten und Freye Fantasien nebst einigen Rondos fürs Fortepiano für Kenner und Liebhaber*, Wq. 58–59 and 61 (1783, 1785, and 1787). In these works, frequent and unpredictable shifts between contrasting affects, topics, themes, registers, and dynamic levels can be heard as modeling a conversation between multiple characters, all given voice by a single player. To borrow W. Dean Sutcliffe's observation regarding the "human deportment" of late-eighteenth-century instrumental music generally, the discourse of the sonatas, rondos, and quartets is "one of constant qualification, of always conceding another point of view or mode of expression; it is relativistic rather than revelatory."[20]

The fact that Bach's quartets were designed to be played and heard in a salon setting—and a specific salon, at that—prompts the question of whether Levy's commission inspired him to adopt a communicative mode of expression mirroring that of his younger contemporaries. It also makes them especially inviting subjects for the kind of "sociable" analysis that I will undertake below. To be sure, few other chamber works of the time can be so closely associated with such a venue, one in which conversation was more of a central focus than in other performance settings. In this context it is worth recalling that Bach was himself a lively conversationalist, and that he often combined socializing with solo performances at the keyboard or other forms of music making. When Charles Burney visited Bach at his Hamburg home in October 1772, for example, he found the composer in the company of both family and friends ("three or four rational, and well-bred persons"). Bach played for Burney both before and after dinner.[21] Writing to Carl Gottlieb Bock in 1776, Johann Friedrich Reichardt reported that "Herr Kapellmeister Bach honors me with the warmest hospitality; tirelessly and with constant good humor he plays to me all sorts of pieces, composed at various stages during his life, every time I visit him. . . . Whenever I visit Herr Bach, he performs for me three, four, or even more of his sonatas."[22] Reichardt also recalled leading a rehearsal of Bach's string sinfonias Wq. 182/H. 657–62 (1773) during a sociable gathering at the home of the mathematician Johann Georg Büsch, a close acquaintance of the composer.[23] Yet despite the combination of socializing and music making on these occasions, and on earlier ones in Berlin when Bach performed his musical portraits of acquaintances, none featured the salon's particular mode of conversational discourse.[24] Before engaging with Bach's music directly, then, let us first consider how conversation related to other forms of sociable interaction, including music making, in late-eighteenth-century salons.

Music as Conversation, Conversation as Music

Conversation as a metaphor for the interaction of anthropomorphic personas in instrumental chamber music has had a long history, first coming to prominence during the last quarter of the eighteenth century with reference to the string quartet.[25] But as we have seen, quartets like Bach's—mixing string, wind, and keyboard instruments, with or without continuo accompaniment—have also been compared to conversation.[26] The metaphor's limitations have been pointed out by a number of writers, yet it remains useful, provided one acknowledges that a musical conversation necessarily differs from a verbal one in several important respects. For example, speakers normally take turns in order to avoid a cacophony of competing utterances, and they may depart entirely from the initial subject to follow multiple (and often open-ended) paths of inquiry. But in music it is usual for most, if not all, of the instruments to be "speaking" simultaneously, or for one instrument in particular (normally the first violin in a string quartet) to predominate for long stretches in a way that would seem inappropriate in a verbal context. Moreover, music tolerates only a limited amount of digression from the principal thematic material before it lays itself open to the charge of incoherence.[27]

Nowhere was the art of conversation cultivated with such enthusiasm and skill as at the eighteenth-century French salon, which in many ways served as a model for those in Germany and elsewhere.[28] This "social base of the Enlightenment Republic of Letters" consisted of a regular gathering in the home of a *salonnière*, or salon hostess.[29] According to French writers of the time, the pleasing conversations that were central to such gatherings should be reasonable and light without descending into frivolity, and any expressions of wit should be both subtle and inclusive of all participants.[30] A good conversationalist maintains the continuity of ideas and establishes a give-and-take allowing each conversationalist to shine in turn; one must be spontaneous, natural, and vivacious, but also know when to be silent. Poor conversationalists, on the other hand, tend to be inattentive or too studied in their responses, interrupt others (though some in France found this a virtue rather than a vice), speak at the same time as another, dominate the conversation, engage in pedantry, or show off.[31] It was the *salonnière* who took responsibility for stimulating conversation among her guests, maintaining an equitable exchange between them, and keeping their attention focused on the topic at hand. Thus, in the salon of Madame Geoffrin, "the reunion of all ranks, like that of all types of minds, prevented any one tone from dominating."[32] And minimizing distractions allowed a *salonnière* such as Madame Suzanne Curchod Necker to create "a serious discursive space" that fostered the development, exchange, and criticism of ideas.[33]

In this egalitarian dynamic, which applied equally to conversation and music making, differences in social status were said to be temporarily suspended. As one Viennese periodical reported of the city's salons, "music works the miracle here that is normally ascribed only to love: it makes all classes equal. Aristocrats, bourgeois, princes and their vassals sit beside each other at one desk and forget the disharmony of their class in the harmony of the tones."[34] Yet for some denizens of the salon, the social leveling effects of conversation and music were something less than miraculous. Sara Levy's socially marginal, outsider status as a Jewish woman in Berlin allowed her to bring together people who might not otherwise mix in such a highly stratified society, as Liliane Weissberg observes of Jewish hostesses in the city. But it was also her Jewishness that would have prevented her from visiting the homes of gentile guests. Levy's salon therefore "celebrated a social one-way street" that "provided a clearly circumscribed amusement as a parlor game, the rules of which had to be understood."[35]

The connection between conversation and music is perhaps most elegantly expressed by the French writer, political activist, and *salonnière* Baroness Anne Louise Germaine de Staël-Holstein (often referred to as Madame de Staël) in her celebrated study of German culture:

> The necessity of conversation is felt by all classes of people in France: speech is not there, as elsewhere, merely the means of communicating from one to another, ideas, sentiments, and transactions; but it is an instrument on which they are fond of playing, and which animates the spirits, like music among some people, and strong liquors among others. . . . When an argument tires, or a tale grows tedious, you are seized with I know not what impatience, similar to that which is experienced when a musician slackens the measure of an air.[36]

Madame de Staël might well have agreed with the proposition that music, among all the arts, is especially well suited to mirroring sociable interactions—but perhaps only with reference to the French language.[37] Having spent most of 1803/4 in Germany, she devotes the better part of two chapters ("Of the Spirit of Conversation" and "Of the German Language, in Its Effects upon the Spirit of Conversation") to demonstrating why its people are such poor conversationalists, for, among other things, they "never hear a word without drawing a consequence from it, and do not conceive that speech can be treated as a liberal art, which has no other end or consequence than the pleasure which men find in it."[38] One wonders how Madame de Staël would have regarded French conversations conducted at German salons, such as might have occurred under the guidance of Levy, who along with her sisters had a good command of the French language and culture so highly prized at the Berlin court of Frederick the Great.[39]

Revealing, if idealized, glimpses of sociability in late-eighteenth-century France are offered by paintings, engravings, and etchings from the period. Such images show various types of sociable interaction in the private architectural spaces known as salons, but whether they are also meant to depict the egalitarian gatherings named after these spaces, of the kind hosted by Levy, is

Figure 9.1. François-Nicolas-Barthélemy Dequevauviller, *L'assemblée au salon* (Paris: Dequevauviller, 1783), after a painting in gouache by Niklas Lafrensen the younger (also known as Nicolas Lavreince). New York, Metropolitan Museum of Art, 35.100.17, metmuseum.org/art/collection/search/382296.

unclear in the absence of a moderating *salonnière*. Several recreational activities are depicted in *L'assemblée au salon* (Gathering at a Salon), a 1783 etching by François-Nicolas-Barthélemy Dequevauviller after a painting by Nicolas Lavreince (fig. 9.1). Here a large neoclassical room is populated by six women and five men engaged in conversation (center), a game of dice (left), and a game of cards (right); playing as well are two dogs in the center of the room. Only a man who has just entered the room, behind the dice players and still holding his hat, and a seated woman reading a book by the window at far left strike solitary, contemplative poses rather than interactive ones.[40] We may be given to understand from this image that such diverse activities happen concurrently in salons, or perhaps we are instead seeing everything that might occur over the course of an afternoon.[41]

It is especially tempting to view images depicting the confluence of music making and conversation as telescoped representations of successive, rather than simultaneous, events. Thus in Michel-Barthélémy Ollivier's painting *Le thé à l'anglaise dans le salon des Quatre-Glaces, au Temple, avec toute la cour du prince de Conti* (English Tea in the Salon of the Four Mirrors at the Temple, with the Entire Court of the Prince of Conti), which commemorates a 1766 Parisian gathering, most of the guests are immersed in drinking tea, eating, conversing, and reading. Several of them also gaze at two musicians, the ten-year-old Wolfgang Amadeus Mozart seated at a harpsichord and the singer Pierre Jélyotte (now tuning his guitar), who are apparently about to perform. Barbara R. Hanning has cautioned against assuming that all the activities depicted by Ollivier occurred at once, especially since the conventions of genre painting allowed both a long timeline and multiple separate activities to be represented as a single moment.[42] Similarly, the 1774 engraving *Le concert* by Antoine Jean Duclos, after a 1763 drawing by Augustin de Saint-Aubin, shows a performance in a salon by a centrally positioned ensemble consisting of a singer, flutist, violinist, cellist, and harpsichordist. An idle oboe, violin, cello, double bass, and harp, as well as stacks of manuscript or printed music and unoccupied music desks, all promise further performances to come. But a majority of the numerous onlookers (if one may call them that) are conversing among themselves or otherwise gazing away from the musicians.[43] We may doubt, with Hanning, that real salon audiences could have been so oblivious to musical entertainments as the fictional ones depicted by Ollivier and Duclos. Yet it is important to consider that the discontinuous, "sociable nature of listening" often practiced by the eighteenth-century *beau monde* differed from the sort of absorbed listening that arose during the nineteenth century.[44]

Exceptional among musical salon images, though infrequently discussed by musicologists, is Dequevauviller's *L'assemblée au concert* (Gathering at a Concert, 1783–84), a companion to his *L'assemblée au salon* (fig. 9.2) Here conversation is actively halted during preparations for a musical performance in an oval, neoclassical music room framed on either side by statues of muses playing a lyre and lute, and graced above with garlands and putti, some of whom also play musical instruments. The symmetry of the architectural elements—two window-door pairs surrounding a central niche, all delineated by ten fluted ionic pilasters—is mirrored in the groupings of people and furniture: three sets of musicians at center flanked on the left by a conversational group and on the right by a table, screen, and chair. The musicians, including both men and women, are about to perform a composition apparently scored for voice, flute, two violins, and continuo of cello with harpsichord or fortepiano. On the right, a horn lying on the floor, a violin and bow on the table, and a cello leaning against the chair portend additional music making, as in *Le concert*. The flutist practices his part, one violinist plucks out a few notes while another is in conversation with the singer, and two men without instruments (curious onlookers?) inspect the music. Meanwhile, the keyboardist—perhaps the hostess, unless this is the singer, who is centrally positioned in front of the niche and repeats the shape of the eagle-topped vase behind her—is helping the cellist tune.[45] But the most dynamic figure in the image is a man standing behind the continuo team holding a directorial scroll of paper. He motions

Figure 9.2. François-Nicolas-Barthélemy Dequevauviller, *L'assemblée au concert* (Paris: Dequevauviller, ca. 1783–84), after a painting in gouache by Niklas Lafrensen the younger (also known as Nicolas Lavreince). Washington, Library of Congress, Music Division, Dayton C. Miller Collection, 219/Y, loc.gov/item/ miller.0219/.

with his free hand not at the musicians, but towards the conversational group, imploring them to be quiet as the performers ready themselves.[46] Thus in the moment captured here, music becomes the focal point of the gathering, taking precedence over conversation with a force that is absent in contemporaneous images.[47]

Returning to music itself, the explicit association in France between instrumental works and conversation goes at least as far back as Louis-Gabriel Guillemain's two sets of *Six sonates en quatuors, ou conversations galantes et amusantes* for flute, violin, viola da gamba, and continuo (Paris, 1743 and 1756). Rapid-fire shifts of themes, motives, textures, and tone colors in these works are easily compared to the contrapuntal exchange of ideas in a lively and pleasant discussion. This quality, together with the music's Italianate style and scoring, owes much to the eloquence of Georg Philipp Telemann's quartets, published in Paris between 1736 and 1760.[48] From the 1760s, a number of French publishers advertised as *quatuors dialoguées* or *quatuors concertants* string quartets by Haydn, Carl Joseph Toeschi, and others in which each instrument assumes thematic importance. This so-called *style dialogué* was still being celebrated by French writers after 1800, for like a pleasant conversation, it allowed each musical participant to share equally in the discourse without unduly taxing the listener.[49]

The idea of quartets as dialogues or conversations brings us back to the salon of Sara Levy, who owned at least seventy-nine such works in various scorings (though apparently not for two violins, viola, and cello). Earliest among these are Telemann's Quartet in G Major for flute, oboe, violin, and continuo, TWV 43:G6; the same composer's six *Quadri* (Hamburg, 1730) for flute, violin, viola da gamba or cello, and continuo; and Johann Joachim Quantz's six quartets for flute, violin, viola, and continuo, QV 4:8–13.[50] Such works undoubtedly influenced the Berlin composers Johann Gottlieb Graun, Johann Gottlieb Janitsch, and Christoph Schaffrath, all of whom are represented by quartets in the Levy collection. In fact, the scoring of Quantz's quartets, which substitutes viola for Telemann's viola da gamba or cello, predominates in Levy's repertory. Of the thirteen Graun works, all but one includes a part for flute, and eight follow Quantz's scoring.[51] Each of the forty-one Janitsch quartets—in which the principle of dialoguing among the melody instruments can take on an almost mechanized quality—includes one or more flute parts, and twenty-four are scored for flute, violin, viola, and continuo or give this scoring as an option; another four works are scored for flute, two violas, and continuo.[52] Both of the Schaffrath quartets are for flute, violin, viola, and continuo, and Levy also owned single quartets for this combination by Johann Christian Bach, Johann Adolf Hasse, and Toeschi.[53]

All of this suggests that when Emanuel Bach was commissioned to write quartets for Levy and her musical companions, he was instructed to supply parts for flute and viola, or else knew that this was a favorite combination at the salon. His inclusion of an obbligato keyboard part would seem to require less explanation, given Levy's prowess as a keyboardist, but it is noteworthy that two further quartets in her collection, by Leopold Hofmann and Johann Schobert, include obbligato keyboard parts as well.[54]

Sociability and Agency in C. P. E. Bach's Quartets

Recent studies of musical sociability have focused almost exclusively on the instrumental works of composers a generation or two younger than C. P. E. Bach, including his brother Johann Christian, Haydn, Ignaz Pleyel, Mozart, and Beethoven.[55] This emphasis reflects a view of the late eighteenth- and early nineteenth-century repertory as overtly communicative by nature, resulting in an international, listener-friendly style that is more socially attuned than music of earlier or later eras.[56] Just who is communicating—the players, the music, the composer, or some combination of these agents—depends on the listener's perspective, and is often subject to multiple interpretations. Attempting to clarify this social dynamic, Edward Klorman has coined the term "multiple agency" to describe the concept of "an encoded musical exchange in which each player assumes an individual character" engaging in spontaneous actions that are volitional and purposive.[57] This exchange between fictional, sentient personas may, but need not, resemble verbal discourse, and of course it depends on viewing the individual characters as capable of independent action. For Sutcliffe, however, it the inherent ambiguity of agency that allows late-eighteenth-century instrumental music to so effectively embody a sociable ideal.[58]

My intent in the following analysis is to demonstrate that C. P. E. Bach's quartets, and in particular the Quartet in D Major, Wq. 94, are sociable in similar ways to the music of his younger contemporaries, especially those in the Viennese orbit. I shall avoid pointing to specific musical models or emphasizing formal aspects, which have been the focus of most previous studies of these works, in favor of close, sociable readings of the work's first movement and of selected passages from the others. Although I treat the instruments as possessing agency, I happily let stand any ambiguities about their roles.

The first measure of the D-Major Quartet's opening Allegretto commands our attention with its implied forte dynamic level, tutti scoring, unison texture, and portentous dotted rhythm. (ex. 9.1). One could be forgiven for hearing this musical gesture as theatrical, like the loud chords of an opera orchestra hushing up the audience before the stage action commences, or the director in *L'assemblée au concert* cutting off chattering salon guests with an insistent hand gesture. The unusual placement of a tenuto marking on the first beat, countering the players' instincts to cut the quarter note a bit short, ensures a sustained and weighty sound associated with so-called heavy execution.[59] What follows in the second measure could scarcely be more different: loud turns to soft, long and dotted note values to shorter and even ones, detached articulation to legato, and unison scoring to homophony featuring flute supported by the viola's bassetto. The absence here of a true bass line contributes to a feeling of instability, as does the implied half-cadence. The flute's lyrical line is unabashedly vocal in conception, as if the orchestra's curtain-raising gesture has now given way to the opera's first aria. In sociable terms, we have heard what Sutcliffe calls a "gracious riposte": a vehement opening statement met by a contrasting gesture that strikes the listener as genial, polite, or conciliatory.[60] Such gentle responses often feature appoggiaturas, as here on the third beat of measure 2.[61]

A light-execution, decorated, and extended version of the opening gesture follows in measures 3–4, confirming the opening half-cadence and providing a counterweight to the first two measures as a unit.[62] When the flute reenters in measure 5, now in a higher tessitura, it attempts to lighten the discourse:

Example 9.1. Carl Philipp Emanuel Bach, Quartet in D Major for flute, viola, and keyboard, Wq. 94 / H. 538, mvt. 1, mm. 1–54. After *Quartets and Miscellaneous Chamber Music*, ed. Laura Buch, *Carl Philipp Emanuel Bach: The Complete Works*, series 2, volume 5 (Los Altos, CA: The Packhard Humanities Institute, 2016).

Example 9.1.—*(continued)*

Example 9.1.—*(continued)*

Example 9.1.—*(continued)*

Example 9.1.—*(continued)*

Example 9.1.—*(continued)*

Example 9.1.—(continued)

Example 9.1.—*(continued)*

Example 9.1.—*(continued)*

Example 9.1.—*(continued)*

Example 9.1.—*(concluded)*

breathless phrases featuring faster and more varied rhythms take the place of the earlier legato line, though the melodic arch of measures 1–2 is retained. The viola's bassetto now traces a descending octave progression—an accompanimental device conventionally associated with serious sentiments (think of the descending tetrachord of the Baroque lament tradition or the descending bass lines underlying many stately chaconnes), and thus lending a sense of affective or topical dissonance to this passage. Two more solos follow: a brief yet elegant filigree of right-hand figuration in the keyboard accompanied by the flute's sighing appoggiatura-suspensions, and another flute-bassetto riposte in which the flute speaks more purposefully through an angular descent spanning more than an octave, even if it again concludes with a collegial appoggiatura.

To this point, each change of texture, instrumentation, affect, and topic has occurred within a framework of two-measure phrases, suggesting a relatively polite and equitable exchange of ideas. But starting in measure 11, the give-and-take is simultaneously more urgent and less schematic owing to close imitations and phrases that are longer, irregular, and frequently elided. Brief rhythmic motives, starting with a dotted-trill figure (first brought up in measure 4), now assume quasi-thematic status, while the keyboard gradually emerges as *primus inter pares* and the flute's utterances become progressively less distinct from those of its companions. The keyboard's increasingly vehement statements begin in measure 13 with pretentious-sounding octaves that prompt mock-serious suspensions in the flute and viola. Things come to a head in measure 19, when the keyboard, aided by the viola, follows a three-fold statement of a dotted gesture in octaves by shouting out a dominant seventh chord (the loudest gesture heard so far), momentarily shocking the other instruments into the submissive role of accompanying its concerto-like figuration (mm. 20–24). Up until this passage,

Levy's keyboard had acted as musical *salonnière*, offering ample space for the others' interactions through its continuity and relative restraint.[63] But its newfound assertiveness, bringing to mind the accompanied keyboard sonata, allows it to dominate the transition to the second key area of what David Schulenberg aptly describes as a "through-composed sonata" form.[64]

The first six measures of this area offer a dominant restatement of the movement's opening. But the flute's second riposte (mm. 29–30) begins unaccompanied, suggesting either that it gets an exceptionally attentive reception or, less charitably, that its remark falls on deaf ears. Now the viola, which has spent much of the previous thirty measures nodding its head in agreement with the other instruments, suddenly speaks its mind in one of the movement's longest solo passages (mm. 31–34). "Who knew she had so much to say?," the other instruments think as they smirk at each other. This soliloquy may be heard as initiating the development, and in fact much of the material in the ensuing nineteen measures derives from the exposition. First, the viola's concluding appoggiatura in measure 34 is "spoken over" by the flute's rising dotted motive, supported by continuo chords in the keyboard. After the viola engages the flute in a second rising dotted motive (mm. 36–38), a switch in conversational partners sees the flute and keyboard exchange thirty-second note scalar figures. Flute and viola reunite when the keyboard claims the scalar figure for itself (mm. 40–41), restating the second dotted motive in fragmentary form with diminishing volume. This last exchange transforms what had been an assertive statement of fact into a gentle question or raised eyebrow (note the motive's derivation from and similar transformation in mm. 15–18). It is answered decisively by a descending dotted motive played in unison by flute and keyboard right hand—a rhetorical reversal of the ascending dotted motive heard earlier—and leading to the dotted-trill figure first heard in measures 4 and 11–12. When this alternation repeats in measures 45–48, it is extended by a quasi-canonic restatement in the flute and viola, a self-conscious display of learnedness that recalls their earlier suspension chains (m. 13).

Cascading keyboard runs lead to the retransition (mm. 50–52), where gentle questions become exasperated pleas on $\hat{5}$ and $\flat\hat{6}$. This prompts yet another gracious riposte from the flute, now sounding especially conciliatory, even cowed, in its high register and drooping appoggiaturas (two instead of the single one in m. 2). But there is an important difference from earlier ripostes, for the keyboard has joined the viola in providing a bassetto accompaniment. Moreover, both instruments offer their own gracious appoggiaturas, with the keyboard additionally mirroring the flute's line through an imitation in contrary motion. Has the flute finally swayed the other conversationalists toward its point of view? If so, then we may hear the recapitulation, beginning in measure 53, more as a retrospective summation than a restatement of the previous arguments.

Yet such summations are more closely associated with rhetorical orations than with the type of social interaction evoked here, which serves to reminds us that it was surely not Bach's intention to portray a conversation from start to finish entirely at the expense of formal conventions.[65] He had, in fact, already done precisely this back in 1749, in the first two movements of a programmatic trio sonata for two violins and continuo that he described as a "conversation between a Sanguineus and Melancholicus" (Wq. 161/1 / H. 579).[66] That simulating a verbal dialogue marked by extended conflict and eventual agreement required not only extreme contrasts of material between the violinist-speakers, but also through-composed forms—not to mention explanatory text keyed to no fewer than forty-three passages in the score— points up the limitations of this expressive musical language to suggest social interaction without a good measure of special pleading. No wonder, then, that this was an experiment Bach never repeated. A similar exploration of vocality in instrumental music, but taking a monologic rather than a dialogic approach, was undertaken by the poet Heinrich Wilhelm von Gerstenberg, who in 1767/68 wrote monologues by Hamlet (based on the famous soliloquy) and the dying Socrates and set them, recitative-style, to Bach's keyboard Fantasia in C Minor from the *18 Probestücke* of 1753 (Wq. 63/6 / H. 75).[67] In contrast to the trio and fantasia, the more communicative language of the D-Major Quartet can convey at least the broad outlines of sociable interaction without resorting to stylistic, formal, and generic distortions, as in the trio, or to a mixture of improvisatory and accompanied recitative styles, as in Gerstenberg's "analysis" of Bach's fantasia.

To return to the quartet, the Allegretto's recapitulation concludes with an exchange of the gently questioning motive that goes unanswered during a beat of silence (m. 76) before prompting a final, and especially dramatic, "shock" chord (vii°⁷/vi) that resolves via gracious appoggiaturas to B minor—a seeming tonal non sequitur that nevertheless links the first movement and the "very slow and held out" ("Sehr langsam und ausghalten") second one in G major by third relationships (I–vi–IV; ex. 9.2). There are sociable aspects to this second movement as well. The flute's initial $\hat{5}$–$\hat{1}$ scalar descent is repeated in different forms and at varying pitch levels throughout, functioning at times almost as a rondo refrain (see mm. 1–2, 3–4, 5–8, and 11–12 in ex. 9.3). This formal conceit, in combination with the halting effect of frequent phrase-ending pauses, encourages us to hear a desultory conversation filled with tentative statements and circular arguments. In measure 9, our keyboardist-*salonnière* attempts to move the still-sputtering conversation to more fruitful (if not more sociable)

Example 9.2. Carl Philipp Emanuel Bach, Quartet in D Major for flute, viola, and keyboard, Wq. 94 / H. 538, mvt. 1, measures 75–78. *Quartets and Miscellaneous Chamber Music*, ed. Laura Buch, *Carl Philipp Emanuel Bach: The Complete Works*, series 2, volume 5 (Los Altos, CA: The Packhard Humanities Institute, 2016).

ground by effecting a sudden, *sotto voce* shift to the parallel minor (if played on a fortepiano, the effect could be heightened by engaging the moderator). This understated remark, ending questioningly on v⁶, prompts a response in kind from the flute and viola (mm. 11–12), just as a whispered phrase is often spontaneously answered by another. Their further move toward the flat side (♭VI) suggests that this is an uncomfortable topic—the flute's fork-fingered notes (b♭', a♭', f') and the final e♭' are difficult to tune in this context—and so it is quickly abandoned in the following phrase, which restores the discussion to the sharp side, a *forte* dynamic, and a higher tessitura. Although this brief

Example 9.3. Carl Philipp Emanuel Bach, Quartet in D Major for flute, viola, and keyboard, Wq. 94 / H. 538, mvt. 2, mm. 1–16. *Quartets and Miscellaneous Chamber Music*, ed. Laura Buch, *Carl Philipp Emanuel Bach: The Complete Works*, series 2, volume 5 (Los Altos, CA: The Packhard Humanities Institute, 2016).

Example 9.3.—*(concluded)*

exchange between *salonnière* and guests seems quickly forgotten, the unexpected turn to a wistful Neapolitan harmony around the movement's midpoint (mm. 34–35) may be heard as a reminiscence.

We conclude with the most sociable moment in the quartet's finale. This comes during the development, where the keyboard creates a false-recapitulatory effect by prematurely introducing the main theme (albeit in the "wrong" key of B minor), as it does at the beginning of both halves of the movement and at the actual recapitulation. But when its initial two measures do not inspire the flute and viola to join in with the phrase's continuation (compare measures 1–4 with measures 84–86 in ex. 9.4), it falls silent, as if realizing that it has spoken out of turn. The keyboard offers a timid repetition, softly and in a higher register (mm. 87–89), whereupon it is finally answered (mm. 89–93). But this is not the hoped-for response: the step-like figuration in all parts properly follows the complete eight-measure theme, not just the first two measures, and here it rises instead of falls, as in all previous iterations (compare mm. 9–10). Stung by this rebuke, the keyboard is momentarily rendered speechless (mm. 93–94) before trying once more to force a recapitulation, now in E minor, with another soft statement of the theme's opening measures (mm. 94–96). Again, no luck, though the disapproving step figuration does at least fall (mm. 96–100). From here the conversationalists blithely move on toward the retransition and structural recapitulation, as if saying collectively, "Let's just forget this ever happened." The false-recapitulatory passage is undeniably Haydnesque in its capricious, disorienting effect, and perhaps this is one reason that the movement reminded Ernst Schmid so strongly of the composer. But we need not imagine Bach deliberately paying homage to Haydn's quartets, for this is the type of witticism that lets everyone in on the joke and allows the flow of ideas to be maintained—in other words, the kind of humor most compatible with polite conversation.[68]

Example 9.4a. Carl Philipp Emanuel Bach, Quartet in D major for flute, viola, and keyboard, Wq. 94 / H. 538, mvt. 3: (a) measures 1–14; (b) measures 80–102. *Quartets and Miscellaneous Chamber Music*, ed. Laura Buch, *Carl Philipp Emanuel Bach: The Complete Works*, series 2, volume 5 (Los Altos, CA: The Packhard Humanities Institute, 2016).

Example 9.4b.—*(continued)*

Example 9.4b.—*(concluded)*

   If Bach's other two quartets are less overtly communicative, they do
include moments when one or more instruments perform agential roles in
shaping the nature of their interactions. All three works may therefore be
seen as reflecting an aesthetic turn in his late style toward sociable expression, mirroring not only the culture of Sara Levy's salon, but also the discursive musical idiom of his younger contemporaries. In this respect, one might
draw a parallel with Sebastian Bach, who decades earlier had shown himself
willing and able to embrace the *galant* musical aesthetic then sweeping across
Europe, if only to a limited degree and initially with some reservation.[69] Such
a parallel may not have been lost on Levy and her guests, as they discussed
the different manifestations of musical expression encompassed by nearly a
century of Bach-family music.

Notes

My thanks to Annette Richards and W. Dean Sutcliffe for their valuable suggestions during the preparation of this essay.

1. Adolf Weissmann, *Berlin als Musikstadt: Geschichte der Oper und des Konzerts von 1740 bis 1911* (Berlin: Schuster & Loeffler, 1911), 36.

2. Peter Wollny, "Sara Levy and the Making of Musical Taste in Berlin," *Musical Quarterly* 77 no. 4 (1993): 659. On Levy's engagement with music of the Bach family, see also Peter Wollny, "'Ein förmlicher Sebastian und Philipp Emanuel Bach-Kultus': Sara Levy, geb. Itzig und ihr musikalisch-literarischer Salon," in *Musik und Ästhetik im Berlin Moses Mendelssohns*, ed. Anselm Gerhard (Tübingen: Niemeyer, 1999), 217–55; and Peter Wollny, *"Ein förmlicher Sebastian und Philipp Emanuel Bach-Kultus": Sara Levy und ihr musikalisches Wirken* (Wiesbaden: Breitkopf & Härtel, 2010).

3. See the list of works in Wollny, *"Ein förmlicher Sebastian und Philipp Emanuel Bach-Kultus,"* 69–71. The sources are described in greater detail in Wolfram Enßlin, ed., *Die Bach-Quellen der Sing-Akademie zu Berlin: Katalog*, 2 vols. (Hildesheim: Olms, 2006).

4. Letter of October 7, 1774. Translated in *The New Bach Reader A Life of Johann Sebastian Bach in Letters and Documents*, ed. Hans T. David and Arthur Mendel, revised and enlarged by Christoph Wolff (New York: W. W. Norton, 1998), 388.

5. David, Mendel, and Wolff, *The New Bach Reader*, 406.

6. Petra Wilhelmy-Dollinger, "Singen, Konzertieren, Diskutieren: Musikalische Aktivitäten in den Salons der 'Berliner Klassik,'" in *Urbane Musikkultur: Berlin um 1800*, ed. Eduard Mutschelknauss (Hanover: Wehrhahn, 2011), 143.

7. Bach considered the keyboard's right and left hands as providing two of the works' four instrumental lines; hence their designation as quartets ("Quartett" or "Quartetto" in the principal manuscript sources). The mistaken notion that Bach intended a cello to double the keyboard's left hand, as is common in keyboard trios, goes back to shortly after Bach's death and has been frequently noted in the literature on the quartets. The now generally accepted hypothesis that Levy commissioned the quartets was first advanced by Wollny, "Sara Levy and the Making of Musical Taste in Berlin," 658–59, and "'Ein förmlicher Sebastian und Philipp Emanuel Bach-Kultus,'" 230. Scores of Wq. 93 and 94 prepared by Johann Heinrich Michel, Bach's principal Hamburg copyist, and formerly in the possession of Joseph Haydn include dates following the last measure ("Mense Jan: 88" for Wq. 93 and "27. Jan: 88" for Wq. 94). These dates likely derive from Bach's lost "house" scores. On the sources and transmission of Bach's quartets, see Laura Buch, "Carl Philipp Emanuel Bach's Flute Quartets," in *Carl Philipp Emanuel Bach im Spannungsfeld zwischen Tradition und Aufbruch*, ed. Christine Blanken and Wolfram Enßlin (Hildesheim: Olms, 2016), 313–35; and Carl Philipp Emanuel Bach, *Quartets and Miscellaneous Chamber Music*, ed. Laura Buch, *Carl Philipp Emanuel Bach: The Complete Works*, series 2, volume 5 (Los Altos, CA: The Packhard Humanities Institute, 2016), xiii–xviii and 202–4. I am grateful to Buch for providing me with a prepublication copy of her article.

8. Buch, "Carl Philipp Emanuel Bach's Flute Quartets," 329, suggests that Bach's lost title page to the quartets would have specified the fortepiano, pointing to the other work that Levy commissioned from Bach in 1788, the Concerto in E-flat Major for harpsichord, fortepiano, and orchestra, Wq. 47 / H. 479, of which she owned a fair-copy score in the composer's hand. Ernst Fritz Schmid was apparently the first to suggest that Bach "thought in the first place of the piano" for his quartets. See Schmid's preface to Carl Philipp Emanuel Bach, *Quartett D-dur für Klavier, Flöte, Viola, Violoncello,* ed. Ernst Fritz Schmid (Kassel: Nagel, 1952), [3]. David Schulenberg also advocates for the fortepiano, based on the works' scoring without separate bass part, which "presupposes a stronger keyboard instrument than in Bach's trios, and it is harder here to imagine use of anything other than a piano." David Schulenberg, *The Music of Carl Philipp Emanuel Bach* (Rochester, NY: University of Rochester Press, 2014), 225.

9. Wollny, *"Ein förmlicher Sebastian und Philipp Emanuel Bach-Kultus,"* 28.

10. Wollny, "Sara Levy and the Making of Musical Taste in Berlin," 659, and "'Ein förmlicher Sebastian und Philipp Emanuel Bach-Kultus,'" 230. See the listings of these duets, and of a spurious trio for two flutes and viola, in Wollny, *"Ein förmlicher Sebastian und Philipp Emanuel Bach-Kultus,"* 73–74; and Enßlin, *Die Bach-Quellen,* volume 1, 321, 325–26, and 328–29.

11. Schmid, preface to Bach, *Quartett D-dur für Klavier,* [3].

12. Ernst Fritz Schmid, *Carl Philipp Emanuel Bach und seine Kammermusik* (Kassel: Bärenreiter, 1931), 143 and 147.

13. Eugene Helm, "Bach, Carl Philipp Emanuel," *New Grove Dictionary of Music and Musicians,* ed. Stanley Sadie (London: Macmillan, 1980), 1:853.

14. Hans-Günter Ottenberg, *C. P. E. Bach,* trans. Philip J. Whitmore (Oxford: Oxford University Press, 1987), 180 and 182. Ottenberg (61–62) also stresses the quartets' modernity in their "equalization and individualization of all four parts," comparing them in this respect to Haydn's opus 33 string quartets: "The texture of these works is no longer governed by older polyphonic concepts, but rather by the more recent techniques of thematic development and fragmentation."

15. Friedhelm Krummacher, "Kontinuität im Experiment: Die späten Quartette von Carl Philipp Emanuel Bach," in *Carl Philipp Emanuel Bach und die europäische Musikkultur des mittleren 18. Jahrhunderts,* ed. Hans Joachim Marx (Göttingen: Vandenhoeck & Ruprecht, 1990), 245–67; Klaus G. Werner, "Formeln und Kombinationen—Empfindungen und Individualisierungen: Zum Kopfsatz des Quartetts a-moll (Wq. 93, H. 537) von C. P. E. Bach," *Die Musikforschung* 46, no. 4 (1993): 388; Günther Wagner, "Vom Generalbass zum 'obligaten Akkompagnement': Stilistische Entwicklung im kammermusikalischen Werk Carl Philipp Emanuel Bachs," *Jahrbuch des Staatlichen Instituts für Musikforschung Preußischer Kulturbesitz* (1997): 107; Schulenberg, *The Music of Carl Philipp Emanuel Bach,* 225; Siegbert Rampe, *Carl Philipp Emanuel Bach und seine Zeit* (Laaber: Laaber, 2014), 440. Elsewhere, Schulenberg observes more broadly of Bach that his "brand of music-making could not occur in the Viennese Classical style, which, for all its genuinely comic and popular elements, takes its coherence and integration too seriously to attempt the types

of risks and disruptions that Bach routinely essayed in his instrumental works."
David Schulenberg, "Carl Philipp Emanuel Bach: A Tercentenary Assessment,"
Early Music 42, no. 3 (2014): 342.

16. The independence of the instruments marks these works as fundamentally different from the thirteen keyboard trios, really accompanied keyboard sonatas,
that Bach published in three sets between 1776 and 1778 (Wq. 89–91). In the
trios, the violin is subsidiary to the keyboard and the cello mostly doubles the
keyboard's left hand.

17. Werner, "Formeln und Kombinationen," 380. Werner views such exchanges as
primarily concerto-like, as if the instruments belong to a "concertino," but also
compares them to a rhetorical oration (389–90). Wagner, "Vom Generalbass
zum 'obligaten Akkompagnement,'" 100, similarly views the quartets as "disguised" concertos.

18. Christoph Wolff, "A Bach Cult in Late-Eighteenth-Century Berlin: Sara Levy's
Musical Salon," *Bulletin of the American Academy of Arts and Sciences* 58, no. 3
(2005): 30.

19. Sara Gross Ceballos, "Sympathizing with *C. P. E. Bachs Empfindungen*," *Journal
of Musicology* 34, no. 1 (2017): 1–31, offers a sociable reading of the piece from
the perspective of eighteenth-century notions of sympathy, finding that both
sections of the piece "reinforce and celebrate the role of the violin as a sympathetic, collaborative, and supportive reader and interpreter" (26).

20. W. Dean Sutcliffe, "The Shapes of Sociability in the Instrumental Music of the
Later Eighteenth Century," *Journal of the Royal Musical Association* 138, no. 1
(2013): 2 and 8.

21. Charles Burney, *The Present State of Music in Germany, The Netherlands, and
United Provinces*, 2nd edition (London: Becket, Robson, & Robinson, 1775), 2:
269–70.

22. Johann Friedrich Reichardt, *Briefe eines aufmerksamen Reisenden die Musik betreffend*, 2 vols. (Frankfurt am Main, 1774, 1776), 2:8, 10. Translated in Ottenberg,
C. P. E. Bach, 151.

23. Johann Friedrich Reichardt, "Autobiographie," *Allgemeine musikalische Zeitung*
16, no. 3 (January 12, 1814), column 29.

24. Concerning Bach's Berlin musical portraits, see especially Joshua S. Walden,
"Composing Character in Musical Portraits: Carl Philipp Emanuel Bach and
'L'Aly Rupalich,'" *Musical Quarterly* 91, nos. 3/4 (2008): 379–411.

25. For surveys of the metaphor's use, see Edward Klorman, *Mozart's
Music of Friends: Social Interplay in the Chamber Works* (Cambridge:
Cambridge University Press, 2016), chapter 2; and Hans-Joachim Bracht,
"Überlegungen zum Quartett-'Gespräch,'" *Archiv für Musikwissenschaft* 51,
no. 3 (1994): 169–89. The metaphor is extended to a typology (including
the lecture, polite conversation, debate, and conversation) in Mara Parker,
The String Quartet, 1750–1797: Four Types of Musical Conversation (Aldershot:
Ashgate, 2002).

26. See my own observations regarding Georg Philipp Telemann's quartets in
Steven Zohn, *Music for a Mixed Taste: Style, Genre, and Meaning in Telemann's
Instrumental Works* (New York: Oxford University Press, 2008), 240 and 454.

27. Concerning these and other complications with the conversation metaphor, see Gretchen Wheelock, "The 'Rhetorical Pause' and Metaphors of Conversation in Haydn's Quartets," in *Haydn & Das Streichquartett*, ed. Georg Feder and Walter Reicher (Tutzing: Schneider, 2003), 67–88; W. Dean Sutcliffe, "Haydn, Mozart and Their Contemporaries," in *The Cambridge Companion to the String Quartet*, ed. Robin Stowell (Cambridge: Cambridge University Press, 2003), 185–209; Mary Hunter, "'The Most Interesting Genre of Music': Performance, Sociability and Meaning in the Classical String Quartet, 1800–1830," *Nineteenth-Century Music Review* 9 (2012): 53–74; and Klorman, *Mozart's Music of Friends*, 113–27.

28. Several recent studies situate the Berlin salons within a more local context. See Ulrike Weckel, "A Lost Paradise of Female Culture? Some Critical Questions Regarding the Scholarship on Late Eighteenth- and Early Nineteenth-Century German Salons," *German History* 18, no. 3 (2000): 310–36; Barbara Hahn, *The Jewess Pallas Athena: This Too a Theory of Modernity*, trans. James McFarland (Princeton, NJ: Princeton University Press, 2005); and Natalie Naimark-Goldberg, *Jewish Women in Enlightenment Berlin* (Oxford: Littman Library of Jewish Civilization, 2013), 188–92.

29. Dena Goodman, *The Republic of Letters: A Cultural History of the French Enlightenment* (Ithaca, NY: Cornell University Press, 1994), 91.

30. French attitudes toward conversation are surveyed in Barbara Russano Hanning, "Conversation and Musical Style in the Late Eighteenth-Century Parisian Salon," *Eighteenth-Century Studies* 22, no. 4 (1989): 513–19. An overview of early modern conversation manuals and similar writings is provided by Peter Burke, *The Art of Conversation* (Cambridge: Polity, 1993), chapter 2. For an entertaining introduction to the ideologies of conversation, taking the form of an imaginary salon discussion between eighteenth-century writers as they listen to a Haydn sonata movement, see Elisabeth Le Guin, "A Visit to the Salon de Parnasse," in *Haydn and the Performance of Rhetoric*, ed. Tom Beghin and Sander M. Goldberg (Chicago: University of Chicago Press, 2007), 14–35.

31. The difference between polite conversation and pointless chattering is illustrated musically by two of Telemann's characteristic suite movements. "La conversation de la table" from TWV 50:21 is a gavotte *en rondeau* in which pairs of flutes and horns engage the strings in a civil dialogue, whereas the amusing "Galimatias en rondeau" (nonsensical talk) from TWV 55:e3 alternates between repetitive, comic banter and pretentious pronouncements. For discussions of these movements, see Zohn, *Music for a Mixed Taste*, 94–96 and 99–100.

32. Antoine-Léonard Thomas, "A la mémoire de Madame Geoffrin," in *Eloges de Mme Geoffrin, contemporaine de Madame Du Deffand*, ed. André Morellet (Paris: Nicolle, 1812), 89, cited in translation by Goodman, *The Republic of Letters*, 101.

33. Dena Goodman, "Seriousness of Purpose: Salonnières, Philosophes, and the Shaping of the Eighteenth-Century Salon," *Proceedings of the Annual Meeting of the Western Society for French History* 15 (1988): 116. On conversation as managed by women in late eighteenth-century British salons, see Jane Donawerth, *Conversational Rhetoric: The Rise and Fall of a Women's Tradition, 1600–1900* (Carbondale: Southern Illinois University Press, 2012), 41–52.

34. *Vaterländische Blätter für den oesterreichischen Kaiserstaat* 1, no. 17 (Vienna, 1808), 39. Quoted and translated in Mary Sue Morrow, *Concert Life in Haydn's Vienna: Aspects of a Developing Musical and Social Institution* (Stuyvesant, NY: Pendragon Press, 1989), 22. However, Morrow (25 and 32–33) expresses doubt that such class harmony was common at private Viennese concerts. Compare the report of the *Vaterländische Blätter* to Johann Conrad Wilhelm Petiscus, "Ueber Quartettmusik," *Allgemeine musikalische Zeitung* 12 (May 16, 1810), column 514: "Not only in big cities but also in small ones, even in villages, if there are friends of music who play string instruments, then they will find themselves playing quartets together. The magic of the music makes everyone equal, and in a friendly way binds together what rank and station would otherwise have divided forever." Quoted and translated in Hunter, "'The Most Interesting Genre of Music,'" 56.

35. Liliane Weissberg, "Literary Culture and Jewish Space around 1800: The Berlin Salons Revisited," in *Modern Jewish Literatures: Intersections and Boundaries*, ed. Sheila E. Jelen, Michael P. Kramer, and L. Scott Lerner (Philadelphia: University of Pennsylvania Press, 2011), 31–32.

36. Baroness Staël-Holstein, *De l'Allemagne / Germany*, 3 vols. (London: John Murray, 1813), 1:102 and 117 (English); 1:96 and 110 (French): "Dans toutes les classes, en France, on sent le besoin de causer: la parole n'y est pas seulement comme ailleurs un moyen de se comminquer ses idées, ses sentiments et ses affaires, mais c'est un instrument dont on aime à jouer et qui ranime les espirits, comme la musique chez quelques peuples, et les liqueurs fortes chez quelques autres. . . . Lorsqu'une discussion s'appesantit, lorsqu'un conte s'alonge, il vous prend je ne sais quelle impatience semblable à celle qu'on éprouve quand un musicien ralentit trop la mesure d'un air." The book, originally published in Paris in 1810 but immediately suppressed, was re-issued three years later in London in both French and (anonymous) English translation.

37. See Sutcliffe, "The Shapes of Sociability," 6.

38. Staël-Holstein, *Germany*, 1:105; *De l'Allemagne*, 1:99: ." . . car ils n'entendent pas un mot sans en tirer une conséquence, et ne conçoivent pas qu'on puisse traiter la parole en art libéral, qui n'a ni but ni résultat que le plaisir qu'on y trouve."

39. Wollny, "Sara Levy and the Making of Musical Taste in Berlin," 651. During the French occupation of Berlin in 1806/7, the Levy salon frequently hosted French military officers and administrators. Petra Wilhelmy, *Der Berliner Salon im 19. Jahrhundert (1780–1914)* (Berlin: de Gruyter, 1989), 96–97.

40. For a discussion of the etching's composition with respect to the physical space and furnishings, see Mimi Hellman, "Furniture, Sociability, and the Work of Leisure in Eighteenth-Century France," *Eighteenth-Century Studies* 32, no. 4 (1999): 420–21.

41. One late-eighteenth-century account of a Viennese salon supports the latter interpretation: when participants tire of conversing, they move on to a card game or listen to a young lady sing to her own accompaniment at the keyboard. [Joseph Richter], *Briefe eines Eipeldauers an seinen Herrn Vetter in Krakau*

über d'Wienstadt (Vienna: Rehm, 1794–97), 65–66. Quoted in Morrow, *Concert Life in Haydn's Vienna*, 4.

42. Barbara R. Hanning, "The Iconography of the Salon Concert: A Reappraisal," in *French Musical Thought, 1600–1800*, ed. Georgia Cowart (Ann Arbor: UMI Research Press, 1989), 129–48. The painting is available at commons.wikimedia.org/wiki/File:Le_Thé_à_l'anglaise.jpg.

43. See the discussion in Hanning, "Conversation and Musical Style," 525–28. The engraving is available at rijksmuseum.nl/en/collection/RP-P-194-58. Among earlier eighteenth-century images, Nicolas Lancret's ca. 1720 paintings *Concert in the Paris Home of Crozat* and *Concert in the Oval Salon of Pierre Crozat's House at Montmorency* (the latter available at dma.org/collection/artwork/nicolas-lancret/concert-oval-salon-pierre-crozats-chateau-montmorency) show at least some of the guests listening attentively to musicians. Lancret's paintings are discussed by Mary Tavener Holmes in the exhibition catalog *Watteau, Music, and Theater*, ed. Katherine Baetjer (New York: The Metropolitan Museum of Art; New Haven, CT: Yale University Press, 2009), 54–58.

44. William Weber, "Did People Listen in the 18th Century?," *Early Music* 25, no. 4 (1997): 688. Le Guin, "A Visit to the Salon de Parnasse," 23n17, expresses doubt "that eighteenth-century drawing room listening precluded speech. . . . The varieties of attentional possibility in a social situation far exceed any simple duality of listening *or* talking." On the shift to absorbed listening, with special reference to the string quartet, see Nancy November, "Theater Piece and *Cabinetstück*: Nineteenth-Century Visual Ideologies of the String Quartet," *Music in Art* 29, nos. 1/2 (2004): 135–50.

45. It is possible that one of these women is meant to represent the dedicatee of the etching, Louise Adélaïde de Bourbon (1757–1824), whose father was Louis Joseph de Bourbon (1736–1818), Prince of Condé from 1740. The Bourbon coat of arms is placed centrally in the lower margin (not shown).

46. The director's raised arm also appears to refer to a common gesture articulating social power through grace. Visual examples of this gesture are discussed in Richard Leppert, *The Sight of Sound: Music, Representation, and the History of the Body* (Berkeley: University of California Press, 1993), 77.

47. For Anne Leonard, *L'assemblée au concert* "signaled a new importance of music in the private realm. . . . Music has won the honor of being an object of attention in itself rather than a mere accompaniment to a social gathering." Anne Leonard, "Picturing Listening in the Late Nineteenth Century," *Art Bulletin* 89, no. 2 (2007): 267.

48. *Six quatuors* (1736–37; a reprint of the *Quadri*, published Hamburg, 1730), *Six quatuors ou trios* (1746–48; a reprint of the identically titled Hamburg publication of 1733), *Nouveaux quatuors* (1738; published during Telemann's visit to Paris), and *Quatrième livre de quatuors* (1752–60; a presumably unauthorized arrangement of much earlier works). The first and third collections share the scoring of Guillemain's quartets. For discussions of all four, see Zohn, *Music for a Mixed Taste*, 266–69, 413–17, 438–39, and 452–58. Slightly earlier, Joseph Bodin de Boismortier had published a set of *Six sonates à quatre parties différentes et également travaillées*, op. 34 (Paris, 1731) for three flutes, violins, or other

instruments with continuo, the collection's title notably stressing the parts' independence and equality, as if they are partners interacting in a discussion. Lost are Boismortier's *Six sonates de chambre en quatuor,* op. 55 (Paris, ca. 1734) for flute, violin, cello or viola da gamba, and continuo, the scoring of which suggests the influence of Telemann's *Quadri* or *Musique de table* (Hamburg, 1733).

49. Hanning, "Conversation and Musical Style," 524. The classic study of this repertory remains Janet M. Levy, "The *Quatuor Concertant* in Paris in the Latter Half of the Eighteenth Century" (PhD diss., Stanford University, 1971).

50. In a suggestive connection to the Parisian repertory discussed above, the title of "Concert" on the manuscript of TWV 43:G6 (D-B, SA 3584) was later supplemented with "Quatuor Concertanto" in red pencil. The *Quadri* manuscript copy is SA 3906 and the Quantz manuscripts are SA 2930–34 and 3509. For a discussion of Quantz's quartets, see Mary Oleskiewicz, "Quantz's 'Quatuors' and Other Works Newly Discovered," *Early Music* 31, no. 4 (2003): 484–504.

51. GraunWV Av:XIV:1–3, 5–13, and 16 (D-B, SA 3371 and 3374–85).

52. These works, identified on their title pages as belonging to opp. 1–7, include D-B, SA 3131, 3133–62, 3166, 3431–34, 3442, 3445–48, and 5175 (1). Concerning the five quartets including parts for viola da gamba, see Michael O'Loghlin, *Frederick the Great and his Musicians: The Viola da Gamba Music of the Berlin School* (Aldershot, UK: Ashgate, 2008), 176–89.

53. Schaffrath (D-B, SA 3537 and 3543, the latter initially attributed to Johann Philipp Kirnberger); Bach, WarB B 51 (SA 3346), published as op. 8, no. 1 (London, 1772); Hasse (SA 2234); and Toeschi, LeeT IV:2 (SA 2779). I am grateful to Rebecca Cypess for calling my attention to the Schaffrath, Hasse, and Toeschi quartets, as well as to the Schobert quartet mentioned below.

54. Johann Schobert, Quartet in E-flat Major for "Cembalo obligato," violin, viola, and cello (SA 4858), published as op. 7, no. 1 (Paris, 1764). Leopold Hofmann, Quartet (Divertimento) in D Major for "Cembalo Obligato," two flutes, and cello (SA 3545). Hofmann's work was advertised by Johann Gottlob Immanuel Breitkopf in Supplement V (1770) of his thematic catalog. See Barry S. Brook, ed., *The Breitkopf Thematic Catalogue: The Six Parts and Sixteen Supplements 1762–1787* (New York: Dover, 1966), 404.

55. See especially Wheelock, "The 'Rhetorical Pause'"; James L. Currie, "Waiting for the Viennese Classics," *Musical Quarterly* 90 (2008): 123–66; W. Dean Sutcliffe, "Before the Joke: Texture and Sociability in the Largo of Haydn's Op. 33, No. 2," *Journal of Musicological Research* 28, nos. 2–3 (2009): 92–118; Hunter, "'The Most Interesting Genre of Music'"; Sutcliffe, "The Shapes of Sociability"; and Klorman, *Mozart's Music of Friends.*

56. See the discussion in Sutcliffe, "Before the Joke," 93–99.

57. Klorman, *Mozart's Music of Friends,* 123 (quotation) and 127–55.

58. Sutcliffe, "The Shapes of Sociability," 10.

59. The question of whether music requires "heavy or light execution" ("schwere oder leichte Vortrag") is addressed at length in Daniel Gottlob Türk, *Klavierschule, oder Anweisung zum Klavierspielen für Lehrer und Lernende* (Leipzig: Türk, 1789; repr. Kassel: Bärenreiter, 1997), 35–5 (§35–51); trans. Raymond H.

Haggh as *School of Clavier Playing, or Instructions in Playing the Clavier for Teachers & Students* (Lincoln: University of Nebraska Press, 1982), 342–53.

60. Sutcliffe, "The Shapes of Sociability," 6–9.

61. In what could be considered an ironic commentary on this convention, the keyboard's opening statement in the finale of the Quartet in A Minor, Wq. 93 / H. 537, is answered by a series of imitative appoggiatura figures in the flute and viola.

62. Bach's performance direction under the first system of the score ("NB die geschwinden Noten nach den Punckten werden abgestoßen"; "NB the quick notes after the dots should be detached") serves to emphasize the heavy vs. light, slurred vs. detached contrasts in this passage.

63. For a meditation on the role of the *salonnière* as conversational and musical leader, see Le Guin, "A Visit to the Salon de Parnasse," 32–33.

64. Schulenberg, *The Music of Carl Philipp Emanuel Bach*, 225.

65. As Klorman observes of his analytical method, "the multiple-agency perspective is well suited for explaining individual moments within a composition, but these moments may not always cohere into a comprehensible, continuous plot." Klorman, *Mozart's Music of Friends*, 150.

66. Carl Philipp Emanuel Bach, *Zwey Trio* (Nuremberg: Schmid, 1751), "Vorbericht": "Es soll gleichsam ein Gespräch zwischen einem Sanguineus und Melancholicus vorstellen. . . ." On the literary and musical background of this particular musical conversation, see Richard Will, "When God Met the Sinner, and Other Dramatic Confrontations in Eighteenth-Century Instrumental Music," *Music & Letters* 78, no. 2 (1997): 176–85. See also discussions in Ottenberg, *C. P. E. Bach*, 58–60, and Schulenberg, *The Music of Carl Philipp Emanuel Bach*, 103–6.

67. On Bach's much-discussed "Hamlet" Fantasy, see especially Annette Richards, *The Free Fantasia and the Musical Picturesque* (Cambridge: Cambridge University Press, 2001), 95–100, and Tobias Plebuch, "Dark Fantasies and the Dawn of the Self: Gerstenberg's Monologues for C. P. E. Bach's C Minor Fantasia," in *C. P. E. Bach Studies*, ed. Annette Richards (Cambridge: Cambridge University Press, 2006), 25–66.

68. As Sutcliffe notes of humor in late-eighteenth-century music generally, "a self-conscious discursive style, full of qualification and relativism, will be apt to find the funny side of things. . . . The grand, forceful and brilliant are all liable to be undercut by the modest or the ordinary." Sutcliffe, "The Shapes of Sociability," 21.

69. The classic study of this aspect of Sebastian Bach's music is Robert L. Marshall, *The Music of Johann Sebastian Bach: The Sources, the Style, the Significance* (New York: Schirmer Books, 1989), ch. 2, "Bach the Progressive: Observations on His Later Works," 23–58.

Appendix

The *Salonnière* and the Diplomat

Letters from Sara Levy to Karl Gustav von Brinckmann

Barbara Hahn

Sara Levy's letters to Karl Gustav von Brinckmann (1764–1847) ended up in a castle in Southern Sweden. Trolle Ljungby, built in the Renaissance style, holds one of the most extensive turn-of-the-nineteenth-century private manuscript collections that have come down to us. In this private archive, hundreds of letters written by Jewish women in Berlin around 1800 survive. Brinckmann, who served as Swedish diplomat at the Prussian court, was acquainted with Rahel Levin, Henriette Mendelssohn, and Brendel Veit (later Dorothea Schlegel), Sara and Marianne Meyer, Henriette Herz, Friederike Liman, and Freude Fränkel, among many others.[1] And he was in close contact with the Itzig daughters. From Brinckmann's "Briefverzeichnisse," the almost obsessive lists of letters he had written and received, we know that he corresponded with five of the sisters: Vögele/Fanny von Arnstein, Zippora Wulff/Cäcilie von Eskeles, Sara Levy, Rebecca Ephraim, and Recha Itzig.[2] His affection even extended to women of the next generation: Henriette von Pereira-Arnstein, Lilla Salomon/Lea Mendelssohn Bartholdy, as well as her older sister Rebekka Salomon/Seligmann.

Karl Gustav von Brinckmann preserved all of the letters written by Berlin's Jewish women, who must in turn have received more than a thousand letters from the Swedish diplomat.[3] Unfortunately, only Rahel Levin handed his letters down to posterity; all the other letters were lost.[4] Only one-sided dialogues can be found in the Swedish castle. Only the women's voices have survived.

Like so many of her contemporaries, Sara Levy was engaged in extensive correspondences. From the letters she wrote to Brinckmann, we learn that she was in close contact with her older sisters Fanny von Arnstein and Cäcilie von Eskeles, both of whom lived in Vienna. With those who lived in Berlin, such as Bella Salomon, grandmother of Fanny Hensel and Felix Mendelssohn Bartholdy, and Hannah Fließ (at whose house the famous "Fließische Konzerte" took place), Sara Levy probably exchanged billets, short and often very sophisticated texts delivered by servants. When Henriette Mendelssohn first moved to Vienna and then to Paris where she worked as a governess in noble families, Sara Levy kept in close touch with her.[5]

We do not know how and when Sara Levy and Brinckmann first met. It was probably in the summer of 1796; the first time Brinckmann mentions her in his lists of correspondence is an entry dated July 29 of that year. A couple of months later, Sara Levy penned a rather long letter to her new friend, asking him for help. She appealed to Brinckmann on behalf of Charles Chrétien de la Jonchère, a French émigré from an old noble family, who could not remain in Berlin, probably for political reasons. On his way to Sweden, where he would later settle, de la Jonchère would need to spend a couple of weeks in Stralsund (Swedish at the time, now in Germany), waiting for a post boat to Stockholm. Sara Levy inquired as to whether Brinckmann might know of families in Stralsund who could invite the poor man to their house and "mellow moments of displeasure and unpleasant memories in entertainment."[6]

This letter was probably typical for Sara Levy. People in need seem to have turned to her. Peter Wollny's book on Levy's musical interests and activities presents letters written by Johanna Maria Bach, Carl Philipp Emanuel Bach's widow, and Johann Adam Hiller that show this social engagement very clearly.[7] Her letters and billets to Brinckmann, though, display the most interesting mixture of gestures and writing styles; they are funny and ironic, serious and yet almost whimsical. They reveal Sara Levy not only as a gifted musician but also as a talented writer.

For more than twenty years, from the summer of 1796 to the winter of 1819, she wrote to the Swedish diplomat. Below are four documents that allow Levy's literary voice to be heard—one in French, the *lingua franca* of European nobility before the French Revolution, and three in German, all with English translations.

Document One

The first letter traveled to Paris, where Brinckmann served as legation counselor to the Swedish ambassador, Erik Magnus Stael von Holstein, husband of the writer and novelist Germaine de Stael.

To Brinckmann in Paris. Berlin, July 3, 1798.[8]

You could easily consider me to be ungrateful, my dear Mr. von Brinkmann! if I did not take advantage of the very precious permission to write you, as you have so generously granted! It is not only that I would merely be ungrateful and you would lose nothing, because: were you to compare the likelihood that I would answer you to the possibility of winning the lottery: so it is, if you truly have been mistaken in your assumptions, the odds are not yet in your favor, but I would also be totally useless, and [one word missing] too little of our time, if I should not overcome my aversion and fear, and—now! You see, I'm sure!—Judge for yourself how much pleasure your letters give me if—in the hope (naturally) of your magnanimity—even I—

You surely understand me.—

I've learned that you have been informed of our current guests and have heard so many pleasant and kind things from Henriette[9] and I absolutely concur with you in singing her praises. It moves my heart when I tell you that in twelve days we will lose this beloved company and my good Wulff[10] from our circle, and I'm convinced you share in our sorrow, because you doubtless know how fine and happy we are together. I hope for my dear Wulff that after the strains she will be refreshed and replenished by a happy stay in Vienna, and to my sister Arnstein I wish the good fortune of well-being, with the great privilege to contribute to that of a much beloved sister.

In previous years I had the pleasure of finding you with my sister and niece, otherwise I would have occasionally maintained and obtained permission from you to benefit from your presence. Now that my sister Wulff has once again left the Lion [four letters undeciphered] Circle, I will move ardently and seriously toward writing, now that you have granted me the pleasure of receiving letters from you (have no fear, I am not saying we should exchange). While I am, of course, eager to answer my sister, the same joyful posture about her reply I cannot dispute, and who better than you, my good-willed friend! Charitable is he who does not quarrel about promptness or proper etiquette. Surely, you will write me often about how you fare with curiosities in all sorts of situations, and whether you have made further contacts in addition to those locally, because you must be pleased in the Humboldt household and with their many interesting guests at all times and occasions.[11] Well, enough about these and other provincial themes, how are you doing in Paris?—If you have learned anything about our quiet, simple Berlin, you learn of what I know, faithfully recounted. In three days we will have the *Geister* composed by Reichardt for the Huldigungs Celebration.[12] Whether this work that he joyfully put together will please our critical musical audience (lacking any ability of being critical) is yet to be seen! Farewell my dear Mr. von Brinkmann and remember well

Yours sincerely, Levy née Itzig

(Berlin den 3ten July 1798

Sie könnten mich leicht für undankbar halten, mein lieber H v Brinkmann! wenn ich nicht die mir sehr schätzbare Veranlaßung zu einer schriftlichen Unterhaltung mit Ihnen, die Sie mir sehr großmütiger Weise geben benutzte. Ich wäre undankbar nicht blos u Sie verlören dabey nichts, denn: wenn Sie auch scherzhafterweise die Wahrscheinlichkeit daß ich Ihnen antworten würde, mit der Möglichkeit das große Loos in der Lotterie zu gewinnen, verglichen: so ist wenn Sie Sich in Ihrer Voraussetzung nun würklich geirrt haben, der Vortheil noch nicht auf Ihrer Seite, aber ich wäre auch gar zu uneigennützig, u [one word undeciphered] zu wenig in der jetzigen Zeit, als daß ich nicht meine Abneigung u Furcht überwinden sollte, u———nun! Sie sehen es ja!———Urtheilen Sie also wie viel Vergnügen mir Ihre Briefe machen wenn— in der Hoffnung (freylich) auf Ihre Großmuth———ich sogar———

Sie verstehen mich schon.—

Daß Sie von der Anwesenheit unserer lieben Gäste benachrichtigt sind, u viel Gutes und Liebenswürdiges von Henriette gehört u gelesen haben werden überhebt mich nun, auch ihr Lob in das ich ganz mit einstimme, zu singen. Das wir diese lieben Menschen nun aber in 12 Tagen u unsere gute Wulff dazu aus unserem Kreise verlieren das sage ich Ihnen mit gerührtem Herzen, u bin überzeugt Theilnahme an unserem Schmerz zu finden, weil Sie es wohl wissen wie gut, u gern wir zusammen sind. Für meine liebe Wulff hoff' ich auf Erholung u Ersaz für manches Leiden von einem frohen Aufenthalt zu Wien u meiner trefflichen Schwester Arnstein gönne ich das Glück zum Wohl einer mit großem Recht vielgeliebten Schwester beyzutragen.

Wie ich nun aber hätte ich im vorigen Jahr nicht oft das Vergnügen gehabt, Sie bey meiner Schwester u meinen Nichten zu finden, wohl angelegentlich darauf gehalten, u bestanden hätte, das Sie mir den Vorzug Ihres Umganges gewährten, so werde ich nun wo meine Schwester W: sich wieder aus Ihrem Loewen [three letters undeciphered] kreise entfernt, recht sehnlich u ernstlich darauf antragen, daß Sie mir das Vergnügen Briefe von Ihnen zu erhalten (fürchten Sie nicht ich sage nicht, mit Ihnen zu wechseln) zuwenden. Meiner Schwester Gewandheit im Antworten geht mir freylich ab aber gleiche Empfänglichkeit zur Freude über Ihre Zuschrift laße ich mir nicht abstreiten, u wer gern wie Sie mein gutwilliger Freund! wohlthätig ist, der wird auch nicht um prompt u richtige Haftung nach Etikettenrecht hadern. Sie schreiben mir gewiß recht fleißig wie es Ihnen an dem an Merkwürdigkeiten aller Art reichsten Ort geht, u ob Sie neue Verbindungen außer den einheimischen gemacht haben. Denn im Hause der Humboldt's u ihrer intereßanten Gefährten müßten Sie sich zu allen Zeiten u an allen Orten gefallen. Also abstraction Faite, von dieser u anderen Landsmännischen Ressourcen, wie geht es Ihnen in Paris?—Wenn Ihnen dafür aus unserem einförmigen stillen Berlin etwas zu wißen gelegen ist: so erfahren Sie was mir davon bekannt wird, gewiß recht treulich. In 3 Tagen haben wir zur Huldigungsfeyer die Geister v. Reichardt in Music gesetzt. Ob diese seine Arbeit die er mit Lust gemacht unserem (ohne Kritik) critisier-enden musicalischem Publicum gefallen wird, steht dahin! Leben Sie wohl! lieber H v. Brinkmann u behalten Sie in gutem Andenken Ihre ergebene Levy geb: Itzig.)

Sara Levy waited a couple of months before she received a response to her letter. On December 5, 1798, Brinckmann found a convenient opportunity to expedite a package of letters back to Berlin. The list of recipients is revealing, as it shows how close Brinckmann was to the Jewish world of Berlin: Henriette Mendelssohn, Rahel Levin, and Brinckmann's banker, Joseph Michael Fränkel, each received two letters. The others were addressed to Brendel Veit, Henriette Herz, Markus Herz, Lilla Salomon, Rebekka Seligmann, and Sara Levy.[13]

Document Two

After two months in northern Germany,[14] Brinckmann returned to Berlin. Sara Levy again included him immediately in her circle of friends and family. On a Sunday in August 1801, she offered to take him to a "Meyerey," a dairy outside the Berlin city walls that her father once had bought and that now belonged to Bella Salomon, who used it as a summer retreat. The "residents" Brinckmann wished to meet were most likely Bella Salomon together with her daughters Lilla Salomon and Rebekka Seligmann.

To Brinckmann in Berlin. Berlin, August 16, 1801.

Yesterday you were swept away so suddenly that today I must try to make up for it.

Some weeks ago you expressed the desire to be accompanied to the residents of the Meyerey, outside of the Silesian Gate, and so I gladly offer to meet at 6 o'clock this evening if you are available.

You see how quickly I seek to use the first moment of need which your cir-cumstances allow. By this you may recognize at least the sort of worth I place on prioritizing your company, and it is not too demanding if I ask you from time to time to regard me as more than wholly underserving.

My heartfelt greetings to Mad. Yvon
Yours respectfully, Levy.

(Sie wurden mir gestern so schnell entzogen, daß ich's versuchen muß, mich heute zu entschädigen.

Vor einigen Wochen äußerten Sie das Verlangen daß ich Sie zu den Bewohnern der Meyerey vor dem schlesischen Thore führen möchte, u dazu erbiete ich mich mit Vergnügen für diesen Abend, halb 6 Uhr wenn es Ihnen so gelegen ist.

Sie sehen wie schnell ich die ersten Augenblicke von Muße, die Ihnen die Umstände gewähren, zu benutzen suche. Mögen Sie daraus wenigstens erkennen, welchen Werth ich in dem Vorzug Ihrer Gesellschaft theilhaft zu werden setze, u es nicht für zudringlich halten wenn ich Sie zuweilen bitte mich dann nicht ganz unwerth zu achten.

Meinen herzlichen Gruß an Mad. Yvon

Ihre ergebenste Levy.)

Brinckmann must have responded immediately, as his list of letters sent shows.

Document Three

Sara Levy never converted. But was she an observant Jew? It is difficult to say. The following billet, written on October 29, 1801, a Thursday, invites Brinckmann to dinner at her house on a Friday evening. This invitation opens the possibility that Brinckmann would have dined with the Levys at a traditional Jewish Sabbath meal, but we cannot know for certain. The limits and possibilities of interfaith sociability in the late eighteenth century were not static categories.

To Brinckmann in Berlin. Berlin, October 29, 1801.

It is with profound regret that I learned, subsequent to the last evening we had the pleasure of spending together, that a nasty fever has kept you in bed. Even though you weren't able to arrive in time for the meal itself, it was nevertheless consoling to see that the conversation you had with your neighbor seemed to be to your liking, really the only thing I regret is that I am not able to do anything about your current state of health. I hope it will not prevent you from keeping your promise to dine with us tomorrow as previously arranged. The esteemed honor and pleasure of seeing you is such that I can only implore you in the strongest terms possible to keep your promise.

I wish you the best of health and assure you of my most respectful sentiments.

My sister Arnstein wishes deeply to see you this evening and I as well, if it so pleases you.

S. L.

(C'est avec infiniment de regret que jai appris, qu'une vilaine fievre Vs arretait au lit, depuis la derniere Soirée que nous avons eu le plaisier de passer avec Vous. Vous ne pouretz en arr—[four letters undeciphered] le Souper, c'est ma consolation, jai vu au Surplus que la conversation que Vs avez eu avec Votre voisine a eté satisfaisante pour Vous, de sorte que je ne me fait d'autre reproche que celui de ne pas pouvoir Vous debarasser de Votre indisposition, qui cependant à ce que jespere sera assez discrete pour Vous permettre d'accomplir Votre promesse de diner avec nous demain, qui etait le jour que Vs aviez fixé, pour nous accorder l'honneur et le plaisier de Vs voir que je sais trop bien apprecier pour ne pas Vs solliciter bien vivement de remplir la promesse faite.

Je Vs souhaite la meilleure santé, et Vs assure des Sentiments les plus respectueux.

Ma soeur A: desire beaucoup Vs voir ce Soir, et moi de meme si cela plait.
S L.)

Document Four

Fanny von Arnstein spent the fall of 1801, together with her daughter Henriette von Pereira-Arnstein, in Berlin. In January of 1802, in the middle of a very cold winter, they traveled back to Vienna, accompanied by Cäcilie—who, after her divorce from Benjamin Isaac Wulff, had married the Viennese banker Bernhard von Eskeles—and Sara Levy. Cäcilie von Eskeles, forty-two at the time, was expecting her first child. A few months later, Sara Levy wrote this:

To Brinckmann in Berlin. Vienna, March 10, 1802.[15]

Do not be angry my dear Mr. von Brinckmann! if despite your encouragement, I have not yet written. But, I can do nothing else at the moment! And if I did not love you so, as I truly do, I wouldn't already be writing you today. It doesn't bother me at all that up to now you do not have in writing how much I care for you, if only I know it, and I will never sin against you so that I can honestly love you forever.—You can't imagine how fine I feel here, when I sit by my sister Eskeles who is lying in, or enjoy a cozy hour with our Jette,[16] even if you have never heard that people actually live here in the middle of nowhere. Both of the aforementioned creatures serve me well here and help to lighten some of the great burden I bear.

Something that contributed somewhat to my immense reluctance to write was the shame of my long journey over the mountain and down in the valley during which I came across absolutely no woman for you. I know well that your marriage with my sister Recha is impossible to surpass, but I advise you nevertheless to persist in it; in any case you will no longer be able to count on my friendship on this account. Because: the magical Jette is so excellent that you could not believe that I would have merely needed to interfere in order to select an attractive woman for you. Adorned, splendid, comely enough! But without all the glory, I wouldn't like to see her myself, certainly not. –

Attribute to it no lack of provision and participation, if I have not yet attended to the requested article und continue to expect a letter from me such a woman as you—deserve and I would wish for you! . . .

Concerning the little Eskeles, nothing is yet decided, and I almost doubt that the mother (who often sends her regards to you) may soon be inclined to choose a Cicisbeo for the Donzella. Supposedly the child already bristled against Italian habits in Trieste, and the mother immediately passed on her distaste for seaside resorts to the child.

What do you think of this? And of your ever most sincere Levy?

(Wien den 10ten Märtz 1802

Zürnen Sie nicht, lieber Herr von Brinckmann! wenn ich Ihnen der gütigen Aufmunterung ungeachtet, die Sie mir geben noch nicht geschrieben habe. Aber ich kann nun einmal nicht anders! Und hätte ich Sie nicht so lieb, wie ich Sie würklich liebe, ich schriebe Ihnen auch heute noch nicht. Es kümmert mich gar nicht, daß Sie's noch nicht schwarz auf weiß haben, daß ich Ihnen herzlich gut bin, wenn ich's nur weiß u ich mich niemals so gegen Sie versündige daß ich Sie ehrlicherweise immer fortlieben kann.—Wie wohl es mir hier geht, wenn ich bey meiner Schwester Eskeles Wochenbette sitze, oder mit unserer Jette ein trauliches Stündchen genieße, davon können Sie Sich einen Begriff machen, wenn Sie auch nie gehört haben, daß hier hinterm Ofen auch Leute wohnen.

Beyde ebengenannte Wesen thun mir gar wohl hier u helfen mir manche Last die die große Maße mir aufbürdet leichter tragen.

Was ein wenig dazubeygetragen hat, daß ich den Muth nicht fassen konnte Ihnen zu schreiben, war die Beschämung auf meiner so langen, weiten über Berg und Thal führenden Reise ganz und gar auf keine Frau für Sie gestoßen zu seyn. Ich weiß es wohl daß die Ehe mit meiner Schwester Recha Ihnen unmöglich genügen kann, aber ich rathe Ihnen doch noch eine Weile darin zu verharren; wenigstens können Sie auf meinen Beystand von hier aus nicht rechnen. Denn: das die Zauberjette hier so gut gerathen ist, muß Sie nicht glauben machen, daß ich nur so blos zuzugreifen hätte, um Ihnen eine schmucke Frau auszusuchen. Geschmückte, prächtige, stattliche genug! Aber ohne all die Herrlichkeit möcht' ich selbst sie kaum gern sehn, geschweige denn:——

Schreiben Sie's also ja keinem Mangel an Fürsorge u Theilnahme zu, wenn ich mit dem verlangten Artikel noch nicht aufgewartet habe, u erwarten Sie immer noch eher einen Brief von mir als eine Frau, wie Sie sie——verdiene und ich Sie Ihnen——wünsche! . . .

Wegen der kleinen Eskeles ist noch nichts beschloßen, u ich zweifle fast daß die Mutter (die sich Ihnen recht angelegenthlich empfiehlt) so bald geneigt seyn dürfte, zur Wahl eines Cicisbeo für die Donzella zu schreiten. Das Kind soll sich schon in Triest gegen die italienische Sitte gesträubt haben, u die Mutter hat der Abneigung des Kindes gegen die Seebäder sogleich nachgegeben.

Was halten Sie davon? Und von Ihrer treuergebensten Levy?)

This is a most pointed letter that "the most sincere Levy" wrote to her young friend. She pretends to be trying to find a wife for Brinckmann, a passionate bachelor who flirted with many women and never ever made a serious attempt at getting married. She calls him the husband of her sister Recha, who, like Brinckmann, never married. On her long journey from Berlin via Prague to Vienna, Sara Levy did not encounter any women suitable for her fastidious friend. The "Zauberjette," the magical Henriette, her niece, whom Brinckmann adored, was no longer available; she was about to marry Aaron Heinrich von Pereira-Arnstein. Cäcilie von Eskeles's newborn daughter Maria Anna, called Marianne, born on March 2, a Donzella, a young girl, doesn't need a Cicisbeo yet. The remark recalls one of the most famous of these ladies' men from the operatic stage, Cherubino in Wolfgang Amadeus Mozart's *Le Nozze de Figaro*, which Sara Levy, well versed in the musical repertoire of her time, would probably have known.

Sara Levy's aesthetic tastes went well beyond the world of music. In May 1804, she wrote to Brinckmann:

Accept my warmest gratitude for the collection of your beautiful poems you kindly forwarded, for which I can thank you for some very pleasant moments, and which I plan to read with true devotion. If later my garden would be stimulating for you, I may flatter myself that you personally would introduce me to more of these poems. You will find a warm reception and thankful heart in your most sincere Levy. Wednesday, May 2, [180]4.[17]

(Nehmen Sie meinen herzlichsten Dank für die mir gütig überschickte Sammlung Ihrer schönen Gedichte, denen ich schon einige sehr angenehme Augenblicke verdanke, u die ich mit wahrer Andacht lesen will. Wenn späterhin mein Garten wiederum einigen Reiz für Sie haben kann: so darf ich mir wohl schmeicheln daß Sie Selbst mich mit mehreren derselben werden bekannt machen wollen. Ein dafür empfängliches Gemüth u dankbares Herz finden Sie in Ihrer ergebensten Levy. Mittwoch den 2t Mai 4.)

And another:

In 1816, after a long interruption in their correspondence, she wrote to Brinckmann, who had returned to Sweden for good:

Wouldn't you like to see all the magnificent objects that our diligent Rauch crafts for Berlin here and in Italy? His works get a lot of praise and—truly! the statue of the highly adored queen is a great masterpiece that one likes to study.

(Wollen Sie nicht alle Herrlichkeiten die unser fleißiger Rauch hier u in Italien für Berlin fertigt sehen? Seine Arbeiten werden gar sehr gelobt, u warlich! ist die Statue der hochverehrten Königin ein hohes Meisterwerk, dem man sich gern zur Betrachtung hingiebt.)

Sara Levy probably was aware of the fact that Brinckmann had encountered the Prussian queen Luise in Königsberg, East Prussia, where the court found refuge after Napoleon's troops conquered Berlin in 1806. Christian Daniel Rauch's famous sarcophagus of Luise, featuring her as a sleeping beauty, created in Carrara and delivered to Berlin in 1815, might remind Levy's addressee of his conversations with the queen, who had passed away in 1809.

"Friendship" may be too grand a word to characterize Sara Levy's relationship with Karl Gustav von Brinckmann. Her letters rather form a stage on which a close-knit circle of family members appears, which she presented to her addressee. It was a world created by women. In the letters, Brinckmann is the only man who plays a role. Neither Salomon Levy nor Daniel Bernhard von Eskeles nor Nathan von Arnstein is ever mentioned. Even Henriette Pereira's husband Heinrich Aaron remains absent. Levy's letters introduce us to a world created by Jewish women who granted access to this precious space only to this Christian man. Brinckmann acknowledged this privileged position—and handed down their voices to posterity.

Notes

Many thanks to Renate Rüb who deciphered and transcribed Sara Levy's handwriting, sponsored by a grant from the *Stiftung Preußische Seehandlung* in Berlin. Andrea Weatherman helped with the translation of Sara Levy's letters. Michael Levine and Jim McFarland provided me with help and advice.

1. Some of these correspondences were quite extensive: The archive holds thirty-eight letters by Henriette Herz, sixty-two by Freude Fränkel (later Pobeheim), and twenty-eight by Henriette Mendelssohn.

2. A recent study by Thekla Keuck reconstructs the history of the Itzig family: Thekla Keuck, *Hofjuden und Kulturbürger: Die Geschichte der Familie Itzig in Berlin* (Göttingen: Vandenhoeck und Rupprecht, 2011).

3. Brinckmann's archive holds two letters by Fanny von Arnstein, two by Recha Itzig, twelve by Cäcilie Wulff / Eskeles, and sixteen by Sara Levy. Even more extensive were the correspondences with the Itzig granddaughters: forty-two letters by Henriette von Pereira-Arnstein and sixty-eight by Lilla Salomon, later Lea Mendelssohn Bartholdy.

4. Rahel Levin and Karl Gustav von Brinckmann exchanged more than 300 letters; the correspondence will be published as part of the *Edition Rahel Levin Varnhagen*, edited by Barbara Hahn and Ursula Isselstein (in preparation).

5. On April 17, 1819, Sara Levy writes to Brinckmann: "Do you still receive letters from Henriette Mendelssohn in Paris? In the first years of her absence from here we corresponded very frequently but now, the exchange of letters stopped for no apparent reasons. In former times this would have seemed impossible to me, even if predicted." (Erhalten Sie noch zuweilen von Henriette Mendelssohn aus Paris Briefe? In den ersten Jahren ihrer Abwesenheit v. hier, war ein sehr regelmäßiger Briefwechsel zwischen uns, u nun ist aber . . . ohne alle äußere Veranlaßung ein Stillstand u Stocken eingetreten, daß mir unmöglich geschienen hätte, wenn es mir früher vorausgesagt worden wäre.)

6. The passage, including the quoted sentence, reads in German: "Der Professor de la Jonchere aus Stockholm, um welchem ich Sie jüngst schon bat, Sich bey dem Baron Brentano zu verwenden, ist seit einigen Wochen hier, u sieht sich genöthigt unverzüglich nach Stockholm zurückzureisen, weil er hier nicht bestehn kann. Er geht von hier nach Stralsund, wo er aber wie man sagt, vielleicht—Wochen bis zum Abgang eines Packetbootes warten muß, in welcher Zeit er sich nun in einem ihm völlig unbekannten Orte, allein, verlaßen u hülflos finden wird. Dies ist eine sehr traurige Lage für einen ohnedies schon sehr unglücklichen Menschen, u um ihn diese zu erleichtern hab' ich Sie guter lieber H v. Brinkmann! bitten wollen ihn wenn Sie meinem Zeugniß einiges Gewicht geben, eine Adresse an einer Ihnen dort bekannten Familie zu geben, damit er während seines Aufenthaltes daselbst doch irgendwo eine Zuflucht habe, um Augenblicke von Unmuth u unglücklicher Erinnerung durch gesellige Unterhaltung zu mildern." The letter is dated December 26, 1796.

7. Peter Wollny, *"Ein förmlicher Sebastian und Philipp Emanuel Bach-Kultus": Sara Levy und ihr musikalisches Wirken* (Wiesbaden: Breitkopf & Härtel, 2010), 49–52.

8. According to Brinckmann's list of letters received, the letter arrived in Paris on July 17.
9. Henriette Pereira.
10. Zippora Wulff, later Cäcilie von Eskeles.
11. Caroline and Wilhelm von Humboldt had moved to Paris in the fall of 1797. As we know from Caroline von Humboldt's letters to Rahel Levin Varnhagen, Brinckmann spent many afternoons and evenings with the Humboldts.
12. Johann Friedrich Reichardt, *Die Geisterinsel, Singspiel in drei Akten von F. W. Gotter nach Shakespear's Sturm zur Huldigungsfeier Seiner Majestät des Königs von Preußen Friedrich Wilhelm III* (Berlin: Neue Berlinische Musikhandlung, 1799). The opera, based on Shakespeare's *The Tempest*, was first performed on July 6, 1798, in Berlin's National Theatre.
13. The entry in the list reads: "An Fränkel a part /An dens. ein Paket /An dens. einen älteren Brief / An Msl Levin Nr. 2 **/ An Msl. Mendelson Nr. 79 / An dieselbe Nr. 80 / Madame Veit / Prof. Hertz / Hofräthin Hertz / Msl Salomon / Mad. Levy Itzig / Mad. Seligman /Mle. Levin."
14. In a letter by Rahel Levin to Brinckmann, March 16, 1800, we learn that Brinckmann spent his time in Hamburg with acquaintances of Sara Levy's: "Yesterday, I told Madame Levy at the Itzigs' with whom you are spending your time in Hamburg. She seemed to be extraordinarily happy to hear it, I suppose they are also her friends." (Gestern erzählt' ich Mad. Lewy bei Itzigs, mit wem Sie in Hamburg leben, sie schien sich außerordentlich darüber zu freuen; ich schließe, es sind auch ihre Freunde.) *Rahel. Ein Buch des Andenkens für ihre Freunde*, ed. Barbara Hahn (Göttingen: Wallstein Verlag, 2011) 1:203.
15. According to Brinckmann's list of letters, the letter arrived in Berlin on March 17, 1802.
16. Henriette von Pereira-Arnstein.
17. Brinckmann had just published his second collection of poems, *Gedichte*, Erstes Bändchen (Berlin: J. D. Sander, 1804).

Bibliography

s.n. *Statuten des von Baruch Auerbach gegründeten jüdischen Waisen-Erziehungs-Instituts zu Berlin.* Berlin: Friedländer, 1839.

s.s.v.v. *Sammlung der Schriften und Gedichte welche auf die poetische Krönung der hochwohlgebohrnen Frauen, Frauen Christianen Marianen von Ziegler, gebohrnen Romanus, verfertiget worden.* Leipzig: Bernhard Christoph Breitkopf, 1734.

s.s.v.v. *Die vernünfftigen Tadlerinnen, erster Jahr-Theil.* Halle: Johann Adam Spörl, 1725.

Adler, Marcus. *Chronik der Gesellschaft zur Verbreitung der Handwerke und des Ackerbaues unter den Juden im preussischen Staate.* Berlin: R. Boll, 1899.

Ahlquist, Karen. "Men and Women of the Chorus: Music, Governance, and Social Models in Nineteenth-Century German-Speaking Europe." In *Chorus and Community*, edited by Karen Ahlquist, 265–92. Urbana: University of Illinois Press, 2006.

Altmann, Alexander. *Moses Mendelssohn: A Biographical Study.* Tuscaloosa: University of Alabama Press, 1973.

Applegate, Celia. *Bach in Berlin: Nation and Culture in Mendelssohn's Revival of the* St. Matthew Passion. Ithaca, NY: Cornell University Press, 2005.

Arendt, Hannah. *Rahel Varnhagen: Lebensgeschichte einer deutschen Jüdin aus der Romantik.* Munich: Piper, 1981.

———. *Rahel Varnhagen: The Life of a Jewess.* Edited by Liliane Weissberg. Translated by Richard and Clara Winston. Baltimore, MD: Johns Hopkins University Press, 1997.

Arkush, Allan. *Moses Mendelssohn and the Enlightenment.* Albany: SUNY Press, 1994.

Aspden, Suzanne. *The Rival Sirens: Performance and Identity on Handel's Operatic Stage.* Cambridge: Cambridge University Press, 2013.

Assaf, Simha. *Mekorot Le-toldot Ha-Ḥinukh Be-yisra'el.* Tel Aviv: Devir, 1954.

Atkins, Stuart. "The Parable of the Rings in Lessing's *Nathan.*" *Germanic Review* 26, no. 4 (1951): 259–67.

Auerbach, Baruch. *Eilfter [sic] Jahresbericht über die jüdische Waisen-Erziehungs-Anstalt für Mädchen zu Berlin.* Berlin: Friedländer 1854.

———, ed., *Gesänge und Gebete zur Todtenfeier, wie sie von den Zöglingen der jüdischen Gemeindeschule zu Berlin begangen wird,* 2nd ed. [Berlin]: Öhmigke, 1835.

———. *Geschichte des Baruch Auerbach'schen Waisenhauses für jüdische Knaben vom Tage der Stiftung bis zu seinem fünf und zwanzigjährigen Jubiläum.* Berlin: Friedländer, 1858.

———. *Ueber die gegenwärtige Einrichtung der jüdischen Gemeindeschule הרות דומלת zu Berlin.* Berlin: J. Lewent, 1832.

———. *Zwei und Zwanzigster Jahresbericht über die jüdische Waisen-Erziehungs-Anstalt für Knaben zu Berlin.* Berlin: Friedländer, 1855.

Bach, Johann Sebastian. *Johann Sebastian Bach: Neue Ausgabe sämtlicher Werke (Neue Bach-Ausgabe).* Leipzig and Kassel: Bärenreiter, 1954–2007.

Bach-Archiv, ed. *Bach-Dokumente.* Leipzig: VEB Deutscher Verlag für Musik and Kassel: Bärenreiter, 1963–present.

Baetjer, Katherine, ed. *Watteau, Music, and Theater.* New Haven, CT: Yale University Press, 2009.

Badt-Strauss, Bertha. *Jüdinnen.* Berlin: Joachim Goldstein, Jüdischer Buchverlag, 1937.

Balin, Carole. *"To Reveal Our Hearts": Jewish Women Writers in Tsarist Russia.* Cincinnati, OH: Hebrew Union College Press, 2000.

Barner, Wilfried. "Lessings *Die Juden* im Zusammenhang seines Frühwerks." In *Humanität und Dialog. Lessing und Mendelssohn in neuer Sicht,* edited by Ehrhard Bahr, Edward P. Harris, and Lawrence G. Lyon, 189–209. Detroit, MI: Wayne State University Press, 1982.

———. "Vorurteil, Emperie, Rettung. Der junge Lessing und die Juden." In *Juden und Judentum in der Literatur,* edited by Herbert A. Strauss and Christhard Hoffmann, 52–77. Munich: Deutscher Taschenbuch Verlag, 1985.

Becker-Cantarino, Barbara. "Die 'andere Akademie': Juden, Frauen und Berliner literarische Gesellschaften 1770–1806." In *Europäische Sozietätsbewegung und demokratische Tradition: Die europäischen Akademien der Frühen Neuzeit zwischen Frührenaissance und Spätaufklärung. Volume 2, 1478–1505,* edited by Klaus Garber and Heinz Wismann, 1478–1505. Tübingen: Niemeyer, 1996.

Beiser, Frederick. *Diotima's Children: German Aesthetic Rationalism from Leibniz to Lessing.* Oxford: Oxford University Press, 2009.

Belfer, Lauren. *And After the Fire.* New York: Harper Collins, 2016.

Bendavid, Lazarus. *Versuch einer Geschmackslehre.* Berlin: Belitz & Braun, 1799.

Berghahn, Klaus L. *Grenzen der Toleranz: Juden und Christen im Zeitalter der Aufklärung.* Cologne: Böhlau, 2000.

———. "On Friendship: The Beginnings of a Christian-Jewish Dialogue in the 18th Century." In *The German-Jewish Dialogue Reconsidered: A Symposium in Honor of George L. Mosse,* edited by Klaus L. Berghahn, 5–23. New York: Peter Lang, 1996.

Berkowitz, Joel, and Jeremy Dauber, eds. and trans. *Landmark Yiddish Plays: A Critical Anthology.* Albany: SUNY Press, 2006.

Bill, Oswald. "Die Liebesklage der Armida. Händels Kantate HWV 105 in Spiegel Bachscher Aufführungspraxis." In *Ausstellung aus Anlaß der Händel-Festspiele des Badischen Staatstheater Karlsruhe 1985,* 25–40. Karlsruhe: Badische Landisbibliothek & Badisches Staatstheater, 1985.

Blanken, Christine. "A Cantata-Text Cycle of 1728 from Nuremberg: a Preliminary Report on a Discovery relating to J. S. Bach's so-called 'Third Annual Cantata Cycle.'" *Understanding Bach* 10 (2015): 9–30.

———. "Ein wieder zugänglich gemachter Bestand alter Musikalien der Bach-Familie im Verlagsarchiv Breitkopf & Härtel." *Bach-Jahrbuch* 99 (2013): 79–128.

Blechschmidt, Eva Renate. *Die Amalien-Bibliothek. Musikbibliothek der Prinzessin Anna Amalia von Preußen (1723–1787).* Berliner Studien zur Musikwissenschaft 8. Berlin: Merseburger, 1965.

Bodian, Miriam. "The Jewish Entrepreneurs in Berlin and the 'Civil Improvement of the Jews' in the 1780s and 1790s" (Hebrew). *Zion* 49, no. 2 (1984): 159–84.

Borchard, Beatrix. "Zur Rolle der Instrumentalmusik im jüdischen Akkulturationsprozeß." *Menora Jahrbuch für deutsch-jüdische Geschichte*, 16 (1996): 171–202.

Botstein, Leon. "Mendelssohn, Werner, and the Jews: A Final Word." *Musical Quarterly* 83, no. 1 (1999): 45–50.

Böttiger, Karl August. *Literarische Zustände und Zeitgenossen*. Edited by K. W. Böttiger. 2 volumes. Leipzig: Brockhaus, 1838; reprinted Frankfurt am Main: Athenäum, 1972.

Bracht, Hans-Joachim. "Überlegungen zum Quartett-'Gespräch.'" *Archiv für Musikwissenschaft* 51, no. 3 (1994): 169–89.

Brady, Emily. *The Sublime in Modern Philosophy: Aesthetics, Ethics, and Nature*. Cambridge: Cambridge University Press, 2013.

Braiterman, Zachary. "The Emergence of Modern Religion: Moses Mendelssohn, Neoclassicism, and Ceremonial Aesthetics." In *German-Jewish Thought Between Religion and Politics: Festschrift in Honor of Paul Mendes-Flohr on the Occasion of His Seventieth Birthday*, edited by Christian Wiese and Martina Urban, 11–27. Berlin: de Gruyter, 2012.

Brann, Mordechai (Markus). "Aleh nidaf" (Hebrew). *Magazin für hebräische Literatur und Wissenschaft* 2 (1888): 435–36.

Breuer, Edward. *The Limits of Enlightenment: Jews, Germans, and the Eighteenth-Century Study of Scripture*. Cambridge, MA: Harvard University Press, 1996.

———. "Rabbinic Law and Spirituality in Mendelssohn's *Jerusalem*." *Jewish Quarterly Review* 86, no. 3–4 (1996): 299–321.

Brook, Barry S., ed. *The Breitkopf Thematic Catalogue: The Six Parts and Sixteen Supplements 1762–1787*. New York: Dover, 1966.

Buch, Laura. "Carl Philipp Emanuel Bach's Flute Quartets." In *Carl Philipp Emanuel Bach im Spannungsfeld zwischen Tradition und Aufbruch*, edited by Christine Blanken and Wolfram Enßlin, 313–35. Hildesheim: Olms, 2016.

Burke, Peter. *The Art of Conversation*. Cambridge: Polity, 1993.

Burney, Charles. *A General History of Music from the Earliest Ages to the Present Period*. London: s.n., 1776–89. Reprint, New York: Dover, 1957.

———. *The Present State of Music in German, The Netherlands, and United Provinces*. 2nd edition. London: Becket, Robson, & Robinson, 1775.

Carlebach, Julius. "The Forgotten Connection: Women and Jews in the Conflict between Enlightenment and Romanticism." *Yearbook of the Leo Baeck Institute* 24 (1979): 107–39.

Ceballos, Sara Gross. "Sympathizing with *C. P. E. Bachs Empfindungen*." *Journal of Musicology* 34, no. 1 (2017): 1–31.

Cohen, Hagit, and Stefan Litt. "Publication and Marketing in the Haskalah Republic" (Hebrew). In *The Library of the Haskalah: The Creation of a Modern Republic of Letters in Jewish Society in the German-Speaking Sphere*, edited by Shmuel Feiner, Zohar Shavit, Natalie Naimark-Goldberg, and Tal Kogman, 195–233. Tel Aviv: Am Oved, 2014.

Cohen, Tova, and Shmuel Feiner, eds. *Voice of a Hebrew Maiden: Women's Writings of the Nineteenth-Century Haskalah Movement* (Hebrew). Tel Aviv: Hakibbutz Hameuchad, 2006.

Conway, David. *Jewry in Music: Entry to the Profession from the Enlightenment to Richard Wagner.* Cambridge: Cambridge University Press, 2012.

Couperin, François. "Avis." In *Concert instrumental sous le titre d'Apothéose composé à la mémoire immortelle de l'incomparable Monsieur de Lully.* Paris: L'auteur and Le Sieur Boivin, 1725.

Currie, James L. "Waiting for the Viennese Classics." *Musical Quarterly* 90 (2008): 123–66.

Cypess, Rebecca. "Ancient Poetry, Modern Music, and the *Wechselgesang der Mirjam und Debora*: The Meanings of Song in the Itzig Circle." *Bach: Journal of the Riemenschneider Bach Institute* 47, no. 1 (2016): 21–65.

———. "Arrangement Practices in the Bach Tradition, Then and Now." In "Musical Interpretation Today," edited by Sezi Seskir and David Hyunsu Kim. Unpublished manuscript, September 1, 2017.

———. "Keyboard Duo Arrangements in Eighteenth-Century Musical Life." *Eighteenth-Century Music* 14, no. 2 (2017): 183–214.

———. "Music Historicism: Sara Levy and the Jewish Enlightenment." *Bach Perspectives* 12. Bach and the Counterpoint of Religion, edited by Robin Leaver (forthcoming).

———. "Timbre, Expression, and Combination Keyboard Instruments: Milchmeyer's Art of *Veränderung*." *Keyboard Perspectives* 8 (2015): 43–69.

David, Hans T., and Arthur Mendel. *The New Bach Reader: A Life of Johann Sebastian Bach in Letters and Documents.* Revised and enlarged by Christoph Wolff. New York: W. W. Norton, 1998.

Davidson, Cathy N., and Jessamyn Hatcher. "Introduction." In *No More Separate Spheres!*, edited by Cathy N. Davidson and Jessamyn Hatcher, 7–26. Durham, NC: Duke University Press, 2002.

[Davidson, Wolf.] *Briefe ueber Berlin.* Landau: Francini, 1798.

———. *Über die bürgerliche Verbesserung der Juden.* Berlin: Ernst Felisch, 1798.

Davies, Martin L. *Identity or History? Marcus Herz and the End of the Enlightenment.* Detroit, MI: Wayne State University Press, 1995.

De Dijn, Annelien. "The Politics of Enlightenment: From Peter Gay to Jonathan Israel." *Historical Journal* 55 (2012): 785–805.

Devrient, Eduard. *Meine Erinnerungen an Felix Mendelssohn-Bartholdy und seine Briefe an mich.* Leipzig: Weber, 1872.

Dick, Jutta, and Barbara Hahn. *Von einer Welt in die andere: Jüdinnen im 19. und 20. Jahrhundert.* Vienna: C. Brandstätter, 1993.

Dirst, Matthew. *Engaging Bach: The Keyboard Legacy from Marpurg to Mendelssohn.* Cambridge: Cambridge University Press, 2012.

Dohm, Christian Wilhelm von. *Ueber die bürgerliche Verbesserung der Juden.* Berlin: Nicolai, 1781.

Dollinger, Petra. "Die internationale Vernetzung der deutschen Salons (1750–1914)." In *Europa Ein Salon? Beiträge zur Internationalität des literarischen Salons,* edited by Roberto Simanowski, Horst Turk, and Thomas Schmidt, 40–65. Göttingen: Wallstein, 1999.

Donawerth, Jane. *Conversational Rhetoric: The Rise and Fall of a Women's Tradition, 1600–1900.* Carbondale: Southern Illinois University Press, 2012.

Drewitz, Ingeborg. *Berliner Salons: Gesellschaft und Literatur zwischen Aufklärung und Industriezeitalter.* Berlin: Haude & Spener, 1979.

Dubnow, Shimon. *History of the Jews.* Volume 4. Translated by Moshe Spiegel. South Brunswick, NJ: T. Yoseloff, 1971.

Dürr, Alfred. *The Cantatas of J. S. Bach.* Translated by Richard Jones. Oxford: Oxford University Press, 2005.

Eberspächer, Martina. "Wie Weihnachten deutsch wurde: Die Erfolgsgeschichte der modernen Weihnacht." In *Weihnukka: Geschichten von Weihnachten und Chanukka,* edited by Cilly Kugelmann, 33–39. Berlin: Nicolai, 2005.

Efron, John M. *German Jewry and the Allure of the Sephardic.* Princeton, NJ: Princeton University Press, 2016.

Ehrmann, Sabine. "Johann Sebastian Bachs Textdicterin Christine Mariane von Ziegler." *Beiträge zur Bach-Forschung* 9–10 (1991): 261–68.

Elbert, Monika M. "Introduction." In *Separate Spheres No More: Gender Convergence in American Literature 1830–1930,* edited by Monika M. Elbert, 1–25. Tuscaloosa: University of Alabama Press, 2000.

Eliav, Mordechai. *Jewish Education in Germany in the Period of Enlightenment and Emancipation* (Hebrew). Jerusalem: Jewish Agency, 1960.

Enßlin, Wolfram, ed. *Die Bach-Quellen der Sing-Akademie zu Berlin: Katalog.* 2 volumes. Hildesheim: Olms, 2006.

Erman, Wilhelm. *Paul Erman, ein Berliner Gelehrtenleben, 1764–1851.* Berlin: Mittler, 1927.

Erspamer, Peter R. *The Elusiveness of Tolerance: The "Jewish Question" from Lessing to the Napoleonic Wars.* Chapel Hill: University of North Carolina Press, 1997.

Euchel, Isaac. *Reb Henoch, oder: Woß tut me damit: Eine jüdische Komödie der Aufklärungszeit. Jidische schtudies* 11, edited by Marion Aptroot and Roland Gruschka. Hamburg: H. Buske, 2004.

———, ed. and trans. *Gebete der hochdeutschen und polnischen Juden.* Königsberg: Kanter, 1786.

Evans, Marshall Blakemore. *The Passion Play of Lucerne: An Historical and Critical Introduction.* New York: Modern Language Association of America, 1943.

Falck, Martin. *Wilhelm Friedemann Bach: Sein Leben und seine Werk.* Leipzig: C. I. Kahnt, 1913.

Faulstich, Bettina. *Die Musikaliensammlung der Familie von Voß. Ein Beitrag zur Berliner Musikgeschichte um 1800.* Catalogus Musicus. Kassel: Bärenreiter, 1997.

Feilchenfeldt, Konrad. "Die Anfänge des Kults um Rahel Varnhagen und seine Kritiker." In *Juden im Vormärz und in der Revolution von 1848,* edited by Walter Grab and Julius Schoeps, 214–32. Stuttgart: Burg, 1983.

———. "'Berlin Salon' und Briefkultur um 1800." *Der Deutschunterricht* 36 (1984): 77–99.

———. "Die Berliner Salons der Romantik." In *Rahel Levin Varnhagen: Die Wiederentdeckung einer Schriftstellerin,* edited by Barbara Hahn and Ursula Isselstein, *LiLi Beiheft* 14 (1987): 152–63.

Feiner, Shmuel. *The Jewish Enlightenment.* Translated by Chaya Naor. Philadelphia: University of Pennsylvania Press, 2004.

————. "The Modern Jewish Woman: A Test Case in the Relationship between Haskalah and Modernity" (Hebrew). In *Sexuality and the Family in History: Collected Essays*, edited by Israel Bartal and Isaiah Gafni, 253–303. Jerusalem: Zalman Shazar Center for Jewish History, 1998.

————. *The Origins of Jewish Secularization in Eighteenth-Century Europe.* Translated by Chaya Naor. Philadelphia: University of Pennsylvania Press, 2010.

————. "The Pseudo-Enlightenment and the Question of Jewish Modernization." *Jewish Social Studies* (new series) 3, no. 1 (1996): 62–86.

————and David Sorkin, eds. *New Perspectives on the Haskalah.* London: Littman Library of Jewish Civilization, 2001.

Fischer, Axel, and Matthias Kornemann, eds. *The Archive of the Sing-Akademie zu Berlin: Catalogue / Das Archiv der Sing-Akademie zu Berlin: Katalog.* Berlin: de Gruyter, 2010.

Fischer, Barbara, and Thomas C. Fox. "Lessing's Life and Work." In *A Companion to the Works of Gotthold Ephraim Lessing*, edited by Barbara Fischer and Thomas C. Fox, 13–39. Rochester, NY: Camden House, 2005.

Frenzel, Herbert A., and Elisabeth Frenzel. *Daten deutscher Dichtung. Chronologischer Abriß der deutschen Literaturgeschichte*, 2 vols., 22nd ed. Munich: Deutscher Taschenbuch Verlag, 1985.

Freudenthal, Gad. "Aaron Salomon Gumpertz, Gotthold Ephraim Lessing, and the First Call for an Improvement of the Civil Rights of Jews in Germany." *Association of Jewish Studies Review* 29, no. 2 (2005): 299–353.

Freudenthal, Gideon. *No Religion without Idolatry: Mendelssohn's Jewish Enlightenment.* Notre Dame. IN: University of Notre Dame Press, 2012.

Friedman, Philip. "Joseph Perl as an Educational Activist and His School in Tarnopol." *YIVO bleter* 31–32 (1948): 131–90.

Frühwald, Wolfgang. "Antijudaismus in der Zeit der deutschen Romantik." In *Conditio Judaica: Judentum, Antisemitismus und deutschsprachige Literatur vom 18. Jahrhundert bis zum Ersten Weltkrieg*, Part 2, edited by Hans Otto Horch and Horst Denkler, 72–91. Tübingen: Niemeyer, 1989.

Fürstenau, Moritz. *Zur Geschichte der Musik und des Theaters am Hofe zu Dresden.* Dresden: Rudolf Kuntze, 1861–62.

Garloff, Katja. "Sublimation and Its Discontents: Christian-Jewish Love in Lessing's *Nathan der Weise*." *Lessing Yearbook / Jahrbuch* 36 (2004/2005): 51–68.

Gaus, Detlef. *Geselligkeit und Gesellige: Bildung, Bürgertum und bildungsbürgerliche Kultur um 1800.* Stuttgart: J. B. Metzler, 1998.

Geck, Martin. *Die Wiederentdeckung der Matthäuspassion im 19. Jahrhundert.* Regensburg: Gustav Bosse Verlag, 1967.

Geiger, Ludwig, ed. *Briefwechsel des jungen Börne und der Henriette Herz.* Oldenburg: Schulzesche Hof-Buchhandlung und Hof-Buchdruckerei Rudolf Schwartz, 1905.

————. *Geschichte der Juden in Berlin. Festschrift zur zweiten Säkulär-Feier* (1871). Berlin: Arani, 1988.

Gerhard, Anselm. "Einleitung." In *Musik und Ästhetik im Berlin Moses Mendelssohns*, edited by Anselm Gerhard, 1–16. Wolfenbütteler Studien zur Aufklärung 25. Tübingen: Max Niemeyer Verlag, 1999.

Glöckner, Andreas. "Neuerkenntnisse zu J. S. Bachs Aufführungskalender zwischen 1729 und 1735." *Bach-Jahrbuch* 67 (1981): 66–75.

Goetschel, Willi. "Lessing and the Jews." In *A Companion to the Works of Gotthold Ephraim Lessing*, edited by Barbara Fischer and Thomas C. Fox, 185–208. Rochester, NY: Camden House, 2005.

———. *Spinoza's Modernity: Mendelssohn, Lessing, and Heine*. Madison: University of Wisconsin Press, 2004.

Goodman, Dena. *The Republic of Letters: A Cultural History of the French Enlightenment*. Ithaca, NY: Cornell University Press, 1994.

———. "Seriousness of Purpose: Salonnières, Philosophes, and the Shaping of the Eighteenth-Century Salon." *Proceedings of the Annual Meeting of the Western Society for French History* 15 (1988): 111–18.

Goodman, Katherine R. *Amazons and Apprentices: Women and the German Parnassus in the Early Enlightenment*. Columbia, SC: Camden House, 1999.

Goozé, Marjanne E. "Challenging Separate Spheres: Female *Bildung* in Eighteenth- and Nineteenth-Century Germany—An Introduction." In *Challenging Separate Spheres: Female* Bildung *in Late Eighteenth- and Nineteenth-Century Germany*, edited by Marjanne E. Goozé, 13–30. North American Studies in Nineteenth-Century German Literature. Oxford: Peter Lang, 2007.

———. "'Ja ja, ich bet' ihn an': Nineteenth-Century Women and Goethe." In *The Age of Goethe Today: Critical Reexamination and Literary Reflection*, edited by Gertrud Pickar and Sabine Cramer, 39–49. Munich: Fink, 1990.

———. "Mimicry and Influence: The French Connection and the Berlin Jewish Salon." In *Readers, Writers, Salonnières: Female Networks in Europe 1700–1900*, edited by Hilary Brown and Gillian Dow, 49–71. European Connections 31. Oxford: Peter Lang, 2011.

———. "Utopische Räume und idealisierte Geselligkeit: Die Rezeption des Berliner Salons im Vormärz." In *Romantik und Vormärz: Differenzen und Kontinuitäten*, edited by Wolfgang Bunzel, Peter Stein, and Florian Vaßen, 363–90. Forum Vormärz-Forschung. Vormärz-Studien 10. Bielefeld: Aisthesis, 2003.

———. "Wilhelm von Humboldt und die Judenemanzipation: Leistungen und Widersprüche." *Seminar* 48, no. 3 (2012): 317–32.

Gordon, Linda. *U.S. Women's History*. 2nd edition. Washington: American Historical Association, 1997.

Gottlieb, Michah. "Aesthetics and the Infinite: Moses Mendelssohn on the Poetics of Biblical Prophecy." In *New Directions in Jewish Philosophy*, edited by Aaron Hughes and Elliot Wolfson, 326–53. Bloomington: Indiana University Press, 2010.

———. "Mendelssohn's Metaphysical Defense of Religious Pluralism." *Journal of Religion* 86, no. 2 (April, 2006): 205–25.

Gradenwitz, Peter. *Literatur und Musik im geselligem Kreise: Geschmacksbildung, Gesprächsstoff und musikalische Unterhaltung in der bügerlichen Salongesellschaft*. Stuttgart: Franz Steiner, 1991.

Graetz, Heinrich. *History of the Jews*. Volume 5. Translated by Bella Löwy. Philadelphia, PA: The Jewish Publication Society of America, 1891–98.

———. *Volkstümliche Geschichte der Juden in drei Bänden*. 3 volumes. Leipzig: s.n., 1888.

Grattenauer, Karl Wilhelm. *Wider die Juden: Ein Wort der Warnung an alle unsere christliche Mitbürger.* Berlin: Schmidt, 1803.

Grimm, Hartmut. "Moses Mendelssohns Beitrag zur Musikästhetik und Carl Philipp Emanuel Bachs Fantasie-Prinzip." In *Musik und Ästhetik im Berlin Moses Mendelssohns,* edited by Anselm Gerhard, 187–216. Wolfenbütteler Studien zur Aufklärung 25. Tübingen: Max Niemeyer Verlag, 1999.

Großmann-Vendrey, Susanna. *Felix Mendelssohn Bartholdy und die Musik der Vergangenheit.* Regensburg: Bosse, 1969.

Guthke, Karl S. "Lessing und das Judentum. Rezeption. Dramatik und Kritik. Krypto-Spinozismus." In *Judentum im Zeitalter der Aufklärung, Wolfenbütteler Studien zur Aufklärung,* volume 4, edited by Günter Schulz, 229–71. Wolfenbüttel: Jacobi, 1977.

Habermas, Jürgen. *The Structural Transformation of the Public Sphere: An Inquiry into a Category of Bourgeois Society.* Translated by Thomas Burger. Cambridge, MA: MIT Press, 1991.

HaCohen, Ruth. *The Music Libel Against the Jews.* New Haven, CT: Yale University Press, 2011.

———. "The Music of Sympathy in the Arts of the Baroque; or, the Use of Difference to Overcome Indifference." *Poetics Today* 22, no. 3 (2001): 607–50.

Hahn, Barbara. "Häuser für die Musik: Akkulturation in Ton und Text um 1800." In *Fanny Hensel. Komponieren zwischen Öffentlichkeit und Privatheit. Symposionsbericht Berlin 1997,* edited by Beatrix Borchard and Monika Schwarz-Danuser, 3–26. Stuttgart: Metzler, 1999.

———. *The Jewess Pallas Athena: This Too a Theory of Modernity.* Translated by James McFarland. Princeton, NJ: Princeton University Press, 2005.

———. *Die Jüdin Pallas Athene: Auch eine Theorie der Moderne.* Berlin: Berliner Taschenbuch Verlag, 2002.

———. "Der Mythos vom Salon: 'Rahels Dachstube' als historische Fiktion." In *Salons der Romantik: Beiträge eines Wiepersdorfer Kolloquiums zu Theorie und Geschichte des Salons,* edited by Hartwig Schultz, 213–34. Berlin: de Gruyter, 1997.

Hammer, Reuven, translator. *Sifre: A Tannaitic Commentary on the Book of Deuteronomy.* New Haven, CT: Yale University Press, 1986.

Hanning, Barbara R. "Conversation and Musical Style in the Late Eighteenth-Century Parisian Salon." *Eighteenth-Century Studies* 22, no. 4 (1989): 513–19.

———. "The Iconography of the Salon Concert: A Reappraisal." In *French Musical Thought, 1600–1800,* edited by Georgia Cowart, 129–48. Ann Arbor: UMI Research Press, 1989.

Hargrave, Mary. *Some German Women and Their Salons.* London: T. Werner Laurie, 1912.

Head, Matthew. "'If the Pretty Little Hand Won't Stretch': Music for the Fair Sex in Eighteenth-Century Germany." *Journal of the American Musicological Society* 52, no. 2 (1999): 203–54.

Heine, Heinrich. *Buch der Lieder.* Hamburg: Hoffmann und Campe, 1827.

Heinrich, Gerda. "Die Berliner Salons in der literarischen Kommunikation zwischen 1790 und 1800. Ein Beitrag zur geschichtlichen Funktionsbestimmung." *Zeitschrift für Germanistik* 3, no. 2 (1993): 309–19.

Heinz, Härtl. "Romantischer Antisemitismus: Arnim und die 'Tischgesellschaft.'" *Weimarer Beiträge* 33, no. 7 (1987): 1159–73.

Helfer, Martha B. *The Word Unheard: Legacies of Anti-Semitism in German Literature and Culture.* Evanston, IL: Northwestern University Press, 2011.

Hellman, Mimi. "Furniture, Sociability, and the Work of Leisure in Eighteenth-Century France." *Eighteenth-Century Studies* 32, no. 4 (1999): 415–45.

Hendrie, Gerald. *Mendelssohn's Rediscovery of Bach.* London: Open University, 1971.

Herbst, Wolfgang. "Ein Vergleich zwischen Joh. Seb. Bach und Chr. Mariane v. Ziegler." *Musik und Kirche* 30 (1960): 248–55.

Herder, Johann Gottfried von. *Herders Werke.* Edited by Heinrich Düntzel. Berlin: Hempel, 1879.

Hertz, Deborah. *How Jews Became Germans: The History of Conversion and Assimilation in Berlin.* New Haven, CT: Yale University Press, 2007.

———. "Ihr offenes Haus—Amalia Beer und die Berliner Reform." *Kalonymos* 2, no. 1 (1999): 1–4.

———. *Jewish High Society in Old Regime Berlin.* New Haven, CT: Yale University Press, 1988.

Hertzberg, Arthur. *The French Enlightenment and the Jews.* New York: Columbia University Press, 1968.

Herz, Henriette. "Memoirs of a Jewish Girlhood." Translated by Marjanne E. Goozé with Jeannine Blackwell. In *Bitter Healing: German Women Writers from 1700 to 1830: An Anthology,* edited by Jeannine Blackwell and Susanne Zantop, 303–47. Lincoln: University of Nebraska Press, 1990.

———. *Henriette Herz. Ihr Leben und ihre Erinnerungen.* Edited by J. Fürst. Zweite, durchgesehene und vermehrte Auflage. Berlin: Besser, 1858.

———. *Henriette Herz: Ihr Leben und ihre Zeit.* Edited by Hans Landsberg. Weimar: Kiepenheuer, 1913.

———. "Jugenderinnerungen von Henriette Herz." Edited by Heinrich Hahn. *Mittheilungen aus dem Litteraturarchive in Berlin* 1 (1896): 139–84.

Herz, Markus. *Versuch über den Geschmack und die Ursachen seiner Verschiedenheiten.* Leipzig: Voss, 1776.

Hess, Jonathan M. *Germans, Jews and the Claims of Modernity.* New Haven, CT: Yale University Press, 2002.

Hesse, Carla. *The Other Enlightenment: How French Women Became Modern.* Princeton, NJ: Princeton University Press, 2001.

Heyden-Rynsch, Verena von der. *Europäische Salons: Höhepunkte einer versunkenen weiblichen Kultur.* Munich: Artemis & Winkler, 1992.

Hillman, Susanne. "The Conversions of Dorothea Mendelssohn: Conviction or Convenience?" *German Studies Review* 29, no. 1 (2006): 127–44.

Hochman, Leah. *The Ugliness of Moses Mendelssohn: Aesthetics, Religion, and Morality in the Eighteenth Century.* New York: Routledge, 2014.

Hoffmann, Klaus. "Alte und neue Überlegungen zu der Kantate 'Non sa che sia dolore' BWV 209." *Bach-Jahrbuch* 76 (1990): 7–25.

Horowitz, Elliott. "The Early Eighteenth Century Confronts the Beard: Kabbalah and Jewish Self-Fashioning." *Jewish History* 8, no. 1–2 (1994): 95–115.

Hübner, Maria. *Anna Magdalena Bach: Ein Leben in Dokumenten und Bildern*. Leipzig: Evangelische Verlagsanstalt, 2004.

Hunter, Mary. "'The Most Interesting Genre of Music': Performance, Sociability and Meaning in the Classical String Quartet, 1800–1830." *Nineteenth Century Music Review* 9 (2012): 53–74.

Isselstein, Ursula. "Die Titel der Dinge sind das Fürchterlichste! Rahel Levins Erster Salon." In *Salons der Romantik: Beiträge eines Wiepersdorfer Kolloquiums zu Theorie und Geschichte des Salons*, edited by Hartwig Schulz, 172–212. Berlin: de Gruyter, 1997.

Jacobson, Jacob. *Jüdische Trauungen in Berlin, 1759–1813*. Berlin: de Gruyter, 1968.

Jaenecke, Joachim. "Das Archiv der Sing-Akademie zu Berlin." *Fontes Artis Musicae* 51, nos. 3–4 (2004): 373–78.

Jastrow, Marcus. *A Dictionary of the Targumim, the Talmud Babli and Yerushalmi, and the Midrashic Literature*. 2 volumes. New York: Judaica Press, 1996.

Jones, Peter Ward. "Mendelssohn's Performances of the 'Matthäus-Passion': Considerations of the Documentary Evidence." *Music & Letters* 97 (2016): 409–64.

Jospe, Raphael. "The Superiority of Oral over Written Communication: Judah Halevi's *Kuzari* and Modern Jewish Thought." In *From Ancient Israel to Modern Judaism: Intellect in Quest of Understanding: Essays in Honor of Marvin Fox*, edited by Jacob Neusner, Ernest Frerichs, and Nahum Sarna. 4 volumes. 3:138–41. Atlanta, GA: Scholars Press, 1989.

Joyce, James. *Ulysses*. New York: Random House, 1990.

Kale, Steven. *French Salons: High Society and Political Sociability from the Old Regime to the Revolution of 1848*. Baltimore, MD: Johns Hopkins University Press, 2004.

Kant, Immanuel. *Anthropologie in pragmatischer Hinsicht* (1798). Edited by Wolfgang Becker. Stuttgart: Reclam, 1983.

———. *Critique of the Power of Judgment* (1790). Translated by J. H. Bernard. New York: Hafner, 1951.

Kaplan, Marion. *The Making of the Jewish Middle Class: Women, Family, and Identity in Imperial Germany*. Oxford: Oxford University Press, 1991.

Karp, Jonathan. "The Aesthetic Difference: Moses Mendelssohn's *Kohelet Musar* and the Inception of the Berlin Haskalah." In *Renewing the Past, Reconfiguring Jewish Culture: From al-Andalus to the Haskalah*, edited by Ross Brann and Adam Sutcliffe, 93–120. Philadelphia: University of Pennsylvania Press, 2003.

Katz, Jacob. *Masoret u-Mashber: Ha-Ḥevrah Ha-yehudit Be-motsa'ei Yemei Ha-benayim*. Jerusalem: Mossad Bialik, 1957–58.

———. *Out of the Ghetto: The Social Background of Jewish Emancipation, 1770–1870*. Cambridge, MA: Harvard University Press, 1973.

———. *Tradition and Crisis: Jewish Society at the End of the Middle Ages*. Translated by Bernard Dov Cooperman. New York: New York University Press, 1993.

Kerber, Linda K. "Separate Spheres, Female Worlds, Woman's Place: The Rhetoric of Women's History." In *No More Separate Spheres!*, edited by Cathy N. Davidson and Jessamyn Hatcher, 29–65. Durham, NC: Duke University Press, 2002.

Keuck, Thekla. *Hofjuden und Kulturbürger: Die Geschichte der Familie Itzig in Berlin*. Göttingen: Vandenhoeck & Ruprecht, 2011.

Klorman, Edward. *Mozart's Music of Friends: Social Interplay in the Chamber Works.* Cambridge: Cambridge University Press, 2016.

Kogman, Tal. "From Press to Manuscript: Leaflets in the Jewish Republic of Letters" (Hebrew). In *The Library of the Haskalah: The Creation of a Modern Republic of Letters in Jewish Society in the German-Speaking Sphere,* edited by Shmuel Feiner, Zohar Shavit, Natalie Naimark Goldberg, and Tal Kogman, 81–101. Tel Aviv: Am Oved, 2014.

———. *The Maskilim in the Sciences: Jewish Scientific Education in the German-Speaking Sphere in Modern Times* (Hebrew). Jerusalem: Magnes Press, 2013.

Konold, Wulf. *Felix Mendelssohn Bartholdy und seine Zeit.* Laaber: Laaber, 1984.

Kornemann, Matthias. "Zelter's Archive: Portrait of a Collector." In *The Archive of the Sing-Akademie zu Berlin: Catalogue / Das Archiv der Sing-Akademie zu Berlin: Katalog,* edited by Axel Fischer and Matthias Kornemann, 19–25. Berlin: de Gruyter, 2010.

Krochmalnik, Daniel. "Die Psalmen in Moses Mendelssohns Utopie des Judentums." In *Der Psalter in Judentum und Christentum,* edited by Erich Zenger, 235–67. Freiburg: Herder, 1998.

Krummacher, Friedhelm. "Kontinuität im Experiment: Die späten Quartette von Carl Philipp Emanuel Bach." In *Carl Philipp Emanuel Bach und die europäische Musikkultur des mittleren 18. Jahrhunderts,* edited by Hans Joachim Marx, 245–67. Göttingen: Vandenhoeck & Ruprecht, 1990.

Landes, Joan B. *Women and the Public Sphere in the Age of the French Revolution.* Ithaca, NY: Cornell University Press, 1988.

Latcham, Michael. "The Apotheosis of Merlin." In *Musique ancienne—instruments et imagination. Actes de rencontres internationales* harmoniques, *Lausanne 2004. Music of the Past: Instruments and Imagination: Proceedings of the* Harmoniques *International Congress, Lausanne 2004,* edited by Michael Latcham, 271–98. Bern: Peter Lang, 2006.

———. "Johann Andreas Stein and the Search for the Expressive *Clavier.*" In *Cordes et clavier au temps de Mozart. Bowed and Keyboard Instruments in the Age of Mozart,* edited by Thomas Steiner, 133–216. Bern: Peter Lang, 2010.

———. "Mozart and the Pianos of Johann Andreas Stein." *The Galpin Society Journal* 51 (1998): 114–53.

———. "Swirling from One Level of Affects to Another: The Expressive Clavier in Mozart's Time." *Early Music* 30, no. 4 (2002): 502–30.

Le Guin, Elisabeth. "A Visit to the Salon de Parnasse." In *Haydn and the Performance of Rhetoric,* edited by Tom Beghin and Sander M. Goldberg, 14–35. Chicago: University of Chicago Press, 2007.

Le Huray, Peter, and James Day, eds. *Music and Aesthetics in the Eighteenth and Early Nineteenth Centuries.* Cambridge: Cambridge University Press, 1981.

Lehmann, Klaus-Dieter, and Ingo Kolasa, eds. *Die Trophäenkommissionen der Roten Armee. Eine Dokumentensammlung zur Verschleppung von Büchern aus deutschen Bibliotheken.* Frankfurt/Main: Klostermann, 1996.

Leonard, Anne. "Picturing Listening in the Late Nineteenth Century." *The Art Bulletin* 89, no. 2 (2007): 266–86.

Leonard, Miriam. *Socrates and the Jews: Hellenism and Hebraism from Moses Mendelssohn to Sigmund Freud*. Chicago, IL: University of Chicago Press, 2012.

Leppert, Richard. *The Sight of Sound: Music, Representation, and the History of the Body*. Berkeley: University of California Press, 1993.

Lessing, Gotthold Ephraim. *Gotthold Ephraim Lessing: Werke und Briefe in zwölf Bänden*. Edited by Wilfried Barner. Frankfurt am Main: Deutscher Klassiker Verlag, 1985–2001.

———. *Nathan der Weise*. Germany: Wilhelm Goldmann Verlag, 1979.

———. *Nathan the Wise*. Translated and edited with introduction by Ronald Schechter. Boston: Bedford St. Martin's, 2004.

Levenson, Edward. "Moses Mendelssohn's Understanding of Logico-Grammatical and Literary Construction in the Pentateuch: A Study of His German Translation and Hebrew Commentary (the Bi'ur)." PhD diss., Brandeis University, 1972.

Leventhal, Robert S. "The Parable as Performance: Interpretation, Cultural Transmission and Political Strategy in Lessing's *Nathan der Weise*." *German Quarterly* 61, no. 4 (1988): 502–27.

Levinsohn, Isaac Baer. *Te'udah Beyisra'el: Kolel Gidrei ha-Torah veha-ḥokhmah*. Vilna-Horodno: Menachem Man & Simcha Zimel Publishers, 1828.

Levy, Janet M. "The *Quatuor Concertant* in Paris in the Latter Half of the Eighteenth Century." PhD diss., Stanford University, 1971.

Lewald, Fanny. *Meine Lebensgeschichte*. 3 volumes. Berlin: Janke, 1862.

Lifschitz, Avi. "A Natural yet Providential Tongue: Moses Mendelssohn on Hebrew as a Language of Action." In *Language as Bridge and Border: Linguistic, Cultural, and Political Constellations in 18th to 20th Century German-Jewish Thought*, edited by Sabine Sander, 31–50. Berlin: Hentrich & Hentrich, 2015.

Lohman, Uta and Ingrid Lohman, eds. *Chevrat Chinuch Nearim. Die jüdische Freischule in Berlin (1778–1825) im Umfeld preußischer Bildungspolitik und jüdischer Kultusreform. Eine Quellensammlung*. Münster: Waxmann, 2001.

Lougee, Carolyn C. *Le Paradis des femmes: Women, Salons, and Social Stratification in Seventeenth-Century France*. Princeton, NJ: Princeton University Press, 1976.

Lowenstein, Steven M. *The Berlin Jewish Community: Enlightenment, Family, and Crisis, 1770–1830*. New York: Oxford University Press, 1994.

———. "Court Jews, Tradition and Modernity." In *Hofjuden: Ökonomie und Interkulturalität die jüdische Wirtshaftselite im 18. Jahrhundert*, edited by Rotraud Ries and J. Friedrich Battenberg, 369–81. Hamburg: Christians Verlag, 2002.

———. "Jewish Upper Crust and Berlin Jewish Enlightenment: The Family of Daniel Itzig." In *From East and West: Jews in a Changing Europe, 1750–1870*, edited by Frances Malino and David Sorkin, 182–201. Oxford: Blackwell, 1990.

Lowth, Robert. *Lectures on the Sacred Poetry of the Hebrews*. Oxford, 1787.

Lund, Hannah Lotte. *Der Berliner "jüdische Salon" um 1800: Emanzipation in der Debatte*. Berlin: de Gruyter, 2012.

Lütteken, Laurenz. "Zwischen Ohr und Verstand: Moses Mendelssohn, Johann Philipp Kirnberger und die Begründung des 'reinen Satzes' in der Musik." In *Musik und Ästhetik im Berlin Moses Mendelssohns*, edited by Anselm Gerhard, 135–64. Wolfenbütteler Studien zur Aufklärung 25. Tübingen: Max Niemeyer Verlag, 1999.

Marissen, Michael. *Bach & God*. Oxford: Oxford University Press, 2016.

————. *Lutheranism, Anti-Judaism, and Bach's St. John Passion.* New York: Oxford University Press, 1998.

————. "Religious Aims in Mendelssohn's 1829 Berlin Sing-Akademie Performances of Bach's St. Matthew Passion." *Musical Quarterly* 77, no. 4 (1993): 718–26.

Marshall, Robert L. *The Music of Johann Sebastian Bach: The Sources, the Style, the Significance.* New York: Schirmer Books, 1989.

Marx, [Adolph Bernhard.] "Bekanntmachung." *Berliner allgemeine musikalische Zeitung* 6, no. 8 (February 21, 1829): 57.

————. "Bekanntmachung." *Berliner allgemeine musikalische Zeitung* 6, no. 9 (February 28, 1829): 65.

————. "Erster Bericht über die 'Passionsmusik nach dem Evangelisten Matthäus' von Johann Sebastian Bach." *Berliner allgemeine musikalische Zeitung* 6, no. 10 (March 7, 1829): 73–78.

————. "Zweiter Bericht über die Passionsmusik nach dem Evangelium Mattäi von Johann Sebastian Bach." *Berliner allgemeine musikalische Zeitung* 6, no. 11 (March 14, 1829): 79–83.

Marx, Hans Joachim. *Hallische Händel-Ausgabe,* vol. 3: Kantaten mit Instrumenten II. Kassel: Bärenreiter, 1995.

Maul, Michael and Peter Wollny. Introduction to *Weimarer Orgeltabulatur,* edited by Michael Maul and Peter Wollny. Kassel: Bärenreiter, 2007.

Meixner, Horst. "Berliner Salons als Ort Deutsch-Jüdischer Symbiose." In *Gegenseitige Einflüsse deutscher und jüdischer Kultur: Von der Epoche der Aufklärung bis zur Weimarer Republik.* Jahrbuch des Instituts für Deutsche Geschichte, Beiheft 4, edited by Walter Grab, 97–109. Tel Aviv: Tel Aviv University, 1982.

Melamed, Yitzhak. "Two Letters by Salomon Maimon on Fichte's Philosophy and on Kant's Anthropology and Mathematics." *International Yearbook of German Idealism* 9 (2011): 385–86.

Melton, James van Horn. *The Rise of the Public in Enlightenment Europe.* Cambridge: Cambridge University Press, 2001.

Mendelsohn, Ezra. "On the Jewish Presence in Nineteenth-Century European Musical Life." *Studies in Contemporary Jewry, An Annual: Modern Jews and Their Musical Agendas,* 9 (1993): 3–16.

Mendelssohn, Moses. "Betrachtungen über das Erhabene und das Naive in den schönen Wissenschaften." *Bibliothek der freyen Wissenschaften und der schönen Künste* 2, no. 1 (1758): 229–67.

————. *Gesammelte Schriften Jubiläumsausgabe.* Edited by Fritz Bamberger et al. 24 volumes. Stuttgart-Bad Canstatt: Frommann, 1971–.

————. *Jerusalem: A Treatise on Ecclesiastical Authority and Judaism.* Translated by M. Samuels. London: Longman, Orme, Brown, and Longmans, 1838.

————. *Jerusalem, oder über religiose Macht und Judentum.* Berlin: Friedrich Maurer, 1783.

————. *Jerusalem, or On Religious Power and Judaism.* Translated by Allan Arkush, with introduction and commentary by Alexander Altmann. Hanover, NH: Brandeis University Press and University Press of New England, 1983.

————. "Lowth, R.: De sacra poesi Hebraeorum. Oxford 1753: Rezension." *Bibliothek der schönen Wissenschaften und der freyen Künste* 1, no. 1 (1757): 122–55; and no. 2 (1757): 269–97.

————. *Moses Mendelssohns gesammelte Schriften.* Edited by G. B. Mendelssohn. Leipzig: Brochaus, 1844.

————. *Philosophical Writings.* Translated by Daniel O. Dahlstrom. Cambridge: Cambridge University Press, 1997.

————. *Philosophische Schriften.* Carlsruhe: im Verlag der Schmiederischen Buchhandlung, 1761.

————. *Die Psalmen, uebersetzt von Moses Mendelssohn.* Berlin: Friedrich Maurer, 1781.

————. *Sammlung theils noch ungedruckter, theils in andern Schriften zerstreuter Aufsätze und Briefe von ihm, an und über ihn.* Edited by J. Heinemann. Leipzig: G. Wolbrecht'sche Buchhandlung, 1831.

————. *Writings on Judaism, Christianity, and the Bible.* Translated by Allan Arkush, Curtis Bowman, and Elias Sacks. Edited by Michah Gottlieb. Waltham, MA: Brandeis University Press, 2011.

Merklinger, Philip M. *Philosophy, Theology, and Hegel's Berlin Philosophy of Religion, 1821–1827.* Albany: SUNY Press, 1993.

Meyer, Bertha. *Salon Sketches: Biographical Studies of Berlin Salons of the Emancipation.* New York: Bloch, 1938.

Meyer, Michael A. *The Origins of the Modern Jew: Jewish Identity and European Culture in Germany 1749–1824.* Detroit, MI: Wayne State University Press, 1967, reprint 1979.

Meyer, Michael A., Michael Brenner, Mordechai Breuer, and Michael Graetz, eds. *German-Jewish History in Modern Times, II: Emancipation and Acculturation, 1780–1871.* New York: Columbia University Press, 1997.

Miron, Dan. *A Traveler Disguised: A Study in the Rise of Modern Yiddish Fiction in the Nineteenth Century.* New York: Schocken Books, 1973.

Morrow, Mary Sue. *Concert Life in Haydn's Vienna: Aspects of a Developing Musical and Social Institution.* Stuyvesant, NY: Pendragon Press, 1989.

————. *German Music Criticism in the Late Eighteenth Century: Aesthetic Issues in Instrumental Music.* Cambridge: Cambridge University Press, 1997.

Mosse, George. *German Jews Beyond Judaism.* Bloomington: Indiana University Press, 1985.

Munk, Reiner, ed. *Moses Mendelssohn's Metaphysics and Aesthetics.* New York: Springer, 2011.

Naimark-Goldberg, Natalie. "The Entrance of Maskilim in Breslau into the German Literary Sphere" (Hebrew). In *The Library of the Haskalah: The Creation of a Modern Republic of Letters in Jewish Society in the German-Speaking Sphere,* edited by Shmuel Feiner, Zohar Shavit, Natalie Naimark-Goldberg, and Tal Kogman, 395–430. Tel Aviv: Am Oved, 2014.

————. "Entrepreneurs in the Library of the Haskalah: Editors and the Production of Maskilic Books" (Hebrew). In *The Library of the Haskalah: The Creation of a Modern Republic of Letters in Jewish Society in the German-Speaking Sphere,* edited by Shmuel Feiner, Zohar Shavit, Natalie Naimark-Goldberg, and Tal Kogman, 102–29. Tel Aviv: Am Oved, 2014.

————. *Jewish Women in Enlightenment Berlin.* Oxford: Littman Library of Jewish Civilization, 2013.

Neumann, Werner. "Das 'Bachische *Collegium musicum.*'" *Bach-Jahrbuch* 47 (1960): 5–27.

———, ed. *Sämtliche von Johann Sebastian Bach vertonete Texte.* Leipzig: VEB Deutscher Verlag für Musik, 1974.

Nicolai, Friedrich. *Beschreibung der Königlichen Residenzstädte Berlin und Potsdam und aller daselbst befindlicher Merkwürdigkeiten.* Berlin: Nicolai, 1779.

Nienhaus, Stefan. "Aufklärerische Emanzipation und romantischer Antisemitismus in Preußen im frühen neunzehnten Jahrhundert." *Studia theodisca* 2: (1995): 9–27.

Nietzsche, Friedrich. *The Portable Nietzsche.* Translated by Walter Kaufmann. New York: Viking Press, 1954.

Niggli, Arnold. *Faustina Bordoni-Hasse.* Leipzig: Breitkopf & Härtel, 1880.

Nisbett, Hugh Barr. *Lessing: Eine Biographie.* Translated by Karl S. Guthke. Munich: Beck, 2008.

November, Nancy. "Theater Piece and *Cabinetstück*: Nineteenth-Century Visual Ideologies of the String Quartet." *Music in Art* 29, nos. 1/2 (2004): 135–50.

Och, Gunnar. "'Eß- und Teetisch': Die Polemik gegen das akkulturierte Berliner Judentum im ausgehenden 18. und 19. Jahrhundert." In *Musik und Ästhetik im Berlin Moses Mendelssohns,* edited by Anselm Gerhard, 77–96. Wolfenbütteler Studien zur Aufklärung 25. Tübingen: Max Niemeyer, 1999.

———. *Imago judaica. Juden und Judentum im Spiegel der deutschen Literatur 1750–1812.* Würzburg: Königshausen & Neumann, 1995.

Odrich, Evelin and Peter Wollny, eds. *Die Briefentwürfe des Johann Elias Bach (1705–1755).* Leipziger Beiträge zur Bach-Forschung 3. Hildesheim: Olms, 2005.

Oleskiewicz, Mary. "Quantz's 'Quatuors' and Other Works Newly Discovered." *Early Music* 31, no. 4 (2003): 484–504.

O'Loghlin, Michael. *Frederick the Great and his Musicians: The Viola da Gamba Music of the Berlin School.* Aldershot: Ashgate, 2008.

Ottenberg, Hans-Günter. *C. P. E. Bach.* Translated by Philip J. Whitmore. Oxford: Oxford University Press, 1987.

Panwitz, Sebastian. "Die Berliner Vereine 1786–1815." In *Berliner Klassik. Eine Großstadtkultur um 1800 / Online-Dokumente* (Berlin-Brandenburgische Akademie des Wissenschaften, 2001 [http://www.berliner-klassik.de/forschung/dateien/panwitz_vereine.pdf]).

Panwitz, Sebastian and Ingo Schwarz, eds. *Alexander von Humboldt / Familie Mendelssohn, Briefwechsel.* Berlin: de Gruyter, 2011.

Parker, Mara. *The String Quartet, 1750–1797: Four Types of Musical Conversation.* Aldershot: Ashgate, 2002.

Parush, Iris. *Reading Jewish Women: Marginality and Modernization in Nineteenth-Century Eastern European Jewish Society.* Translated by Saadya Sternberg. Brandeis Series on Jewish Women, Tauber Institute for the Study of European Jewry series. Hanover, NH: Brandeis University Press, published by the University Press of New England, 2004.

Peters, Mark. *A Woman's Voice in Baroque Music: Mariane von Ziegler and J. S. Bach.* Aldershot: Ashgate, 2008.

[Petiscus, Johann Conrad Wilhelm.] "Ueber Quartettmusik." *Allgemeine musikalische Zeitung* 12 (May 16, 1810): columns 513–26.

Plebuch, Tobias. "Dark Fantasies and the Dawn of the Self: Gerstenberg's Monologues for C. P. E. Bach's C minor Fantasia." In *C. P. E. Bach Studies*, edited by Annette Richards, 25–66. Cambridge: Cambridge University Press, 2006.

Pohl, Nicole. "'Perfect Reciprocity': Salon Culture and Epistolary Conversations." *Women's Writing* 13, no. 1 (2006): 139–59.

Pollok, Anne. *Facetten des Menschen: Zur Anthropologie Moses Mendelssohns.* Hamburg: Meiner, 2010.

Quantz, Johann Joachim. Introduction to *Sei duetti a due flauti traversi.* Berlin: Georg Ludwig Winter, 1759.

Rasch, William. "Ideal Sociability: Friedrich Schleiermacher and the Ambivalence of Extrasocial Spaces." In *Gender in Transition: Discourse and Practice in German-Speaking Europe, 1750–1830*, edited by Ulrike Gleixner and Marion W. Gray, 319–39. Ann Arbor: University of Michigan Press, 2006.

Rampe, Siegbert. *Carl Philipp Emanuel Bach und seine Zeit.* Laaber: Laaber, 2014.

Reichardt, Johann Friedrich. "Autobiographie." *Allgemeine musikalische Zeitung* 15 (1813): 601–16, 633–42, 665–74; 16 (1814): 21–34.

———. *Briefe eines aufmerksamen Reisenden die Musik betreffend.* 2 volumes. Frankfurt am Main, 1774, 1776.

Remy, Nahida. *Das jüdische Weib.* 3rd edition. Leipzig: Verlag von G. Laudien, 1892.

———. *The Jewish Woman.* Translated by Louise Mannheimer with preface by Dr. Lazarus. Cincinnati, OH: C. J. Krehbiel, 1895.

Remy-Lazarus, Nahida Ruth. *Das jüdische Weib.* 4th edition. Berlin: Cronbach, 1922.

Richards, Annette. "Carl Philipp Emanuel Bach, Portraits, and the Physiognomy of Music History." *Journal of the American Musicological Society* 66, no. 2 (2013): 337–96.

———. "An Enduring Monument: C. P. E. Bach and the Musical Sublime." In *C. P. E. Bach Studies*, edited by Annette Richards, 149–72. Cambridge: Cambridge University Press, 2009.

———. *The Free Fantasia and the Musical Picturesque.* Cambridge: Cambridge University Press, 2001.

Richarz, Monika. "Der jüdische Weihnachtsbaum: Familie und Säkularisierung im deutschen Judentum des 19. Jahrhunderts." In *Und so zogen sie aus: Ein jeder bei seiner Familie und seinen Vaterhaus" (4. Moses 2, 34). Die vierte Joseph-Karlebach-Konferenz. Familie im Spannungsfeld zwischen Tradition und Moderne*, edited by Miriam Gillis-Carlebach and Barbara Vogel, 63–78. Hamburg: Dölling & Galitz, 2000.

[Richter], Jean Paul. *Jean Paul's Briefwechsel mit seinen Freunden Emanuel Osmund, Friedrich von Oertel und Paul Thieriot.* Munich: Fleischmann's Buchhandlung, 1865.

[Richter, Joseph]. *Briefe eines Eipeldauers an seinen Herrn Vetter in Krakau über d'Wienstadt.* Vienna: Rehm, 1794–97.

Richter, Simon. "The Ins and Outs of Intimacy: Gender, Epistolary Culture, and the Public Sphere." *German Quarterly* 69, no. 2 (1996), 111–24.

Riley, Matthew. "Civilizing the Savage: Johann Georg Sulzer and the 'Aesthetic Force' of Music." *Journal of the Royal Musical Association* 127, no. 1 (2002): 1–22.

Robertson, Ritchie. *The "Jewish Question" in German Literature, 1749–1939*. Oxford: Oxford University Press, 1999.

Rosman, Moshe. "The History of Jewish Women in Early Modern Poland: An Assessment." In *Polin: Studies in Polish-Jewry* 18: Jewish Women in Eastern Europe, edited by ChaeRan Freeze, Paula Hyman, and Antony Polonsky, 25–56. Oxford: Littman Library of Jewish Civilization, 2005.

———. *How Jewish Is Jewish History?* Oxford: Littman Library of Jewish Civilization, 2007.

———. "Law, Ethics, and the Needs of History: Mendelssohn, Krochmal, and Moral Philosophy." *Journal of Religious Ethics* 44, no. 2 (2016): 355–62.

———. *Moses Mendelssohn's Living Script: Philosophy, Practice, History, Judaism*. Bloomington: Indiana University Press, 2017.

Satanow, Isaac, ed. *Moreh Nevuchim*, volume 2. Berlin: Ḥevrat Ḥinuch Ne'arim, 1795.

———, ed. *Sefer Hag'darim*. Berlin: Ḥevrat Ḥinuch Ne'arim, 1798.

Schatz, Andrea. *Sprache in der Zerstreuung: Die Säkularisierung des Hebräischen im 18. Jahrhundert*. Göttingen: Vandenhoeck & Ruprecht, 2009.

Schilson, Arno. "Lessing and Theology." In *A Companion to the Works of Gotthold Ephraim Lessing*, edited by Barbara Fischer and Thomas C. Fox, 157–84. Rochester, NY: Camden House, 2005.

Schlegel, Friedrich. "Vom Wesen der Kritik" (1804). In *Kritische Friedrich Schlegel Ausgabe*, volume 3, *Charakteristiken und Kritiken II*, edited by Hans Eichner. Munich: Schöningh, 1975.

Schleiermacher, Friedrich Daniel Ernst. *Der christliche Glaube nach den Grundsätzen der evangelischen Kirche im Zusammenhange dargestellt*. Berlin, 1821–22, revised edition 1830–31.

———. *Friedrich Schleiermachers Briefwechsel mit seiner Braut*. Edited by Heinrich Meisner. Gotha: Klotz, 1919.

———. *Kritische Gesamtausgabe*. Part 1 (Schriften und Entwürfe). Edited by Günter Meckenstock. Berlin: de Gruyter, 2011.

———. *Kritische Gesamtausgabe*. Part 5 (Briefe). Edited by Andreas Arendt and Wolfgang Virmond. Berlin: de Gruyter, 1992.

Schletterer, Hans M. *Johann Friedrich Reichardt: Sein Leben und seine musikalische Thätigkeit*. Augsburg: J. A. Schlosser, 1865.

Schmölders, Claudia. "Einleitung." In *Die Kunst des Gesprächs: Texte zur Geschichte der europäischen Konversationstheorie*, edited by Claudia Schmölders, 9–68. Munich: DTV, 1979.

Schmid, Ernst Fritz. Preface to Carl Philipp Emanuel Bach, *Quartett D-dur für Klavier, Flöte, Viola, Violoncello*. Edited by Ernst Fritz Schmid. Kassel: Nagel, 1952.

———. *Carl Philipp Emanuel Bach und seine Kammermusik*. Kassel: Bärenreiter, 1931.

Scholl, Christian. "Normative Anschaulichkeit versus archäologische Pedanterie: Karl Friedrich Schinkels ästhetischer Philhellenismus." In *Graecomania*, edited by Gilbert Heß, Elena Agazzi, and Elisabeth Décultot, 85–98 Berlin: de Gruyter, 2009.

Scholz, Hannelore. "Geselligkeit als Utopie: Weiblicher Dialog in den Privatvorlesungen von A. W. Schlegel." In *Salons der Romantik: Beiträge eines Wiepersdorfer Kolloquiums zu Theorie und Geschichte des Salons*, edited by Hartwig Schultz, 135–46. Berlin: de Gruyter, 1997.

Schorch, Grit. *Moses Mendelssohns Sprachpolitik*. Berlin: de Gruyter, 2012.

Schulenberg, David. "Carl Philipp Emanuel Bach: A Tercentenary Assessment." *Early Music* 42, no. 3 (2014): 335–45.

———. *The Music of Carl Philipp Emanuel Bach*. Rochester, NY: University of Rochester Press, 2014.

———. *The Music of Wilhelm Friedemann Bach*. Rochester, NY: University of Rochester Press, 2010.

Schulte, Christoph. *Die jüdische Aufklärung*. Munich: C. H. Beck, 2002.

Schulze, Hans-Joachim. "Johann Friedrich Schweinitz, 'A Disciple of the Famous Herr Bach in Leipzig.'" In *About Bach*, edited by Gregory G. Butler, George B. Stauffer, and Mary Dalton Greer, 81–88. Urbana: University of Illinois Press, 2008.

———. "Neuerkenntnisse zu einigen Kantatentexten Bachs auf Grund neuer biographischer Daten." In *Bach-Interpretationen*, edited by Martin Geck, 22–28. Göttingen: Vandenhoeck & Ruprecht, 1969.

———. "Texte und Textdichter." In *Die Welt der Bach-Kantaten*, edited by Christoph Wolff, 109–25. Stuttgart: J. B. Metzler, 1996–99.

Schulze, Hans-Joachim and Christoph Wolff, eds. *Bach-Compendium*. Leipzig: Edition Peters, 1985–89.

Schumann, Robert. *Gesammelte Schriften über Musik und Musiker*. Edited by Martin Kreisig. Leipzig: Breitkopf & Härtel, 1914.

Schünemann, Georg. "Die Bachpflege der Berliner Singakademie." *Bach-Jahrbuch* 25 (1929): 138–71.

Schwenke, Paul. "Aus Wilhelm von Humboldts Studienjahren. Mit ungedruckten Briefen." *Deutsche Rundschau* 66 (1891): 228–51.

Scott, Joan Wallach. *Gender and the Politics of History*. New York: Columbia University Press, 1988.

Seibert, Peter. *Der literarische Salon: Literatur und Geselligkeit zwischen Aufklärung und Vormärz*. Stuttgart: Metzler, 1993.

Seidman, Naomi. *A Marriage Made in Heaven: The Sexual Politics of Hebrew and Yiddish*. Berkeley: University of California Press, 1997.

Sela, Yael. "The Voice of the Psalmist: On the Performative Role of Psalms in Moses Mendelssohn's *Jerusalem*." In *Psalms In and On Jerusalem*, edited by Ilana Pardes and Ophir Münz-Manor. Berlin: de Gruyter (forthcoming, 2018).

Sela-Teichler, Yael. "Music, Acculturation, and Haskalah between Berlin and Königsberg in the 1780s." *The Jewish Quarterly Review* 103, no. 3 (2013): 352–84.

Shapiro, Alexander H. "'Drama of an Infinitely Superior Nature': Handel's Early English Oratorios and the Religious Sublime." *Music & Letters* 74, no. 2 (1993): 215–45.

Shapiro, James. *Oberammergau: The Troubling Story of the World's Most Famous Passion Play*. New York: Pantheon Books, 2000.

Shavit, Yaacov. *Athens in Jerusalem: Classical Antiquity and Hellenism in the Making of the Modern Secular Jew*. Translated by Chaya Naor and Niki Werner. Oxford: Littman Library of Jewish Civilization, 1999.

Shavit, Zohar. "From Friedländer's Lesebuch to the Jewish Campe—The Beginning of Hebrew Children's Literature in Germany." *LBIYA* 33 (1988): 385–415.

Sheehan, Jonathan. *The Enlightenment Bible: Translation, Scholarship, Culture*. Princeton, NJ: Princeton University Press, 2005.

Simanowski, Roberto. "Einleitung: Der Salon als dreifache Vermittlungsinstanz." In *Europa—Ein Salon? Beiträge zur Internationalität des literarischen Salons*, edited by Roberto Simanowski, Horst Turk and Thomas Schmidt, 8–39. Göttingen: Wallstein, 1999.

Sinkoff, Nancy. "Haskalah." In *Europe 1450 to 1789: Encyclopedia of the Early Modern World*, edited by Jonathan Dewald, 3:141–43. New York: Charles Scribner's Sons, 2004.

———. *Out of the* Shtetl*: Making Jews Modern in the Polish Borderlands*. Brown Judaic Studies 336. Providence, RI: Brown University Press, 2004.

Smith, Ruth. *Handel's Oratorios and Eighteenth-Century Thought*. Cambridge: Cambridge University Press, 1995.

Sorkin, David. *Moses Mendelssohn and the Religious Enlightenment*. Berkeley: University of California Press, 1996.

———. *The Transformation of German Jewry, 1780–1840*. New York: Oxford University Press, 1987.

———. "Wilhelm von Humboldt: The Theory and Practice of Self-Formation (Bildung), 1791–1810." *Journal of the History of Ideas* 44 (1983): 55–73.

Spalding, Almut. *Elise Reimarus (1735–1805), The Muse of Hamburg: A Woman of the German Enlightenment*. Würzburg: Koenigshausen & Neumann, 2003.

Spiel, Hilde. *Fanny von Arnstein: A Daughter of the Enlightenment, 1758–1818*. Translated by Christine Shuttleworth. New York: St. Martin's Press and New Vessel Press, 1991.

Spitta, Philipp. "Mariane von Ziegler und Johann Sebastian Bach." In *Zur Musik. Sechzehn Aufsätze*. Berlin: Gebrüder Paetal, 1892; reprint Hildesheim: Georg Olms, 1976.

Sposato, Jeffrey S. *The Price of Assimilation: Felix Mendelssohn and the Nineteenth-Century Anti-Semitic Tradition*. Oxford: Oxford University Press, 2006.

Staël-Holstein, Baroness Anne Louise Germaine de. *De l'Allemagne / Germany*. 3 volumes. London: John Murray, 1813.

Statuten des von Baruch Auerbach gegründeten jüdischen Waisen-Erziehungs-Instituts zu Berlin. Berlin: D. Friedländer, 1839.

Stauffer, George B. "Bach and the Lure of the Big City." In *The Worlds of Johann Sebastian Bach*, edited by Raymond Erickson, 243–66. New York: Amadeus Press, 2009.

———. "Music for 'Cavaliers et Dames': Bach and the Repertoire of his Collegium Musicum." In *About Bach*, edited by Gregory G. Butler, George B. Stauffer, and Mary Dalton Greer, 135–56. Urbana, IL: University of Illinois Press, 2008.

———. "Leipzig: Cosmopolitan Trade Centre." In *Music and Society: The Late Baroque*, edited by George J. Buelow, 254–95. Englewood Cliffs, NJ: Prentice Hall, 1993.

Steinberg, Michael P. "Culture, Gender, and Music: A Forum on the Mendelssohn Family." *Musical Quarterly* 77, no. 4 (1993): 648–50.

———. "The Incidental Politics to Mendelssohn's *Antigone*." In *Mendelssohn and his World*, edited by R. Larry Todd, 137–57. Princeton, NJ: Princeton University Press, 1991.

———. *Listening to Reason: Culture, Subjectivity, and Nineteenth-Century Music*. Princeton, NJ: Princeton University Press, 2006.

———. "Mendelssohn and Judaism." In *The Cambridge Companion to Mendelssohn*, edited by Peter Mercer-Taylor, 26–41. Cambridge: Cambridge University Press, 2011.

———. "Mendelssohn's Music and German-Jewish Culture: An Intervention." *Musical Quarterly* 83, no. 1 (1999): 31–44.

Stevens, Jane. *The Bach Family and the Keyboard Concerto: The Evolution of a Genre*. Warren, MI: Harmonie Park, 2001.

Strauss, Jutta. "Aaron Halle-Wolfson: ein Leben in drei Sprachen." In *Musik und Ästhetik in Berlin Moses Mendelssohns*, edited by Anselm Gerhard, 57–76. Tübingen: Max Neimeyer Verlag, 1999.

Stern, Selma. "Die Entwicklung des jüdischen Frauentypus seit dem Mittelalter." *Der Morgen* (Berlin) 1 (1925): 496–516.

Sulzer, Johann Georg. *Allgemeine Theorie der schönen Künste in einzeln, nach alphabetischer Ordnung der Kunstwörter auf einander folgenden, Artikeln abgehandelt*. Leipzig: Weidmanns, Erben, & Reich, 1773.

Sutcliffe, Adam. "Can a Jew Be a Philosophe? Isaac de Pinto, Voltaire, and Jewish Participation in the European Enlightenment." *Jewish Social Studies* (new series) 6, no. 3 (2000): 31–51.

Sutcliffe, W. Dean. "Before the Joke: Texture and Sociability in the Largo of Haydn's Op. 33, No. 2." *Journal of Musicological Research* 28, nos. 2–3 (2009): 92–118.

———. "Haydn, Mozart and Their Contemporaries." In *The Cambridge Companion to the String Quartet*, edited by Robin Stowell, 185–209. Cambridge: Cambridge University Press, 2003.

———. "The Shapes of Sociability in the Instrumental Music of the Later Eighteenth Century." *Journal of the Royal Musical Association* 138, no. 1 (2013): 1–45.

Tewarson, Heidi Thomann. *Rahel Levin Varnhagen: The Life and Work of a German Jewish Intellectual*. Lincoln: University of Nebraska Press, 1998.

Thomas, Antoine-Leónard. "A la mémoire de Madame Geoffrin." In *Eloges de Mme Geoffrin, contemporaine de Madame Du Deffand*, edited by André Morellet, 77–100. Paris: Nicolle, 1812.

Todd, R. Larry. "Echoes of the St. Matthew Passion in the Music of Mendelssohn." In *Mendelssohn Essays*, edited by R. Larry Todd, 117–33. New York: Routledge, 2008.

———. *Mendelssohn: A Life in Music*. Oxford: Oxford University Press, 2003.

Tornius, Valerian. *The Salon: Its Rise and Fall: Pictures of Society through Five Centuries*. Translated by Anges Platt. London: Thornton Butterworth, 1929.

Tosi, Pier Francesco. *Observations on the Florid Song*. Translated by [John Ernst] Galliard. London: J. Wilcox, 1743.

———. *Opinioni de' cantori antichi e moderni*. Bologna, 1723.

Türk, Daniel Gottlob. *Klavierschule, oder Anweisung zum Klavierspielen für Lehrer und Lernende*. Leipzig: Türk, 1789; reprint Kassel: Bärenreiter, 1997.

———. *School of Clavier Playing, or Instructions in Playing the Clavier for Teachers & Students*. Translated by Raymond H. Haggh. Lincoln: University of Nebraska Press, 1982.

Unger, Friederike Helene. "Briefe einer reisenden Dame über Berlin," *Jahrbücher der preussischen Monarchie unter der Regierung Friedrich Wilhelms des Dritten* 2 (May, 1798): 17–33; (June 1798): 133–43; (July 1798): 287–302.

Valeur, Peter Svare. "Notes on Friendship: Moses Mendelssohn and Gotthold Ephraim Lessing." *Oxford German Studies* 45, no. 2 (2016): 142–56.

Van Elferen, Isabella. "'Ihr Augen weint!' Intersubjective Tears in the Sentimental Concert Hall." *Understanding Bach* 2 (2007): 77–94.

Varnhagen, Rahel. *Edition Rahel Levin Varnhagen*. Edited by Barbara Hahn and Ursula Isselstein. Munich: Beck Verlag, 1997–.

———. *Familienbriefe*. Edited by Renata Buzzo Màrgari Barovero. Munich: Beck Verlag, 2009.

———. *Rahel: Ein Buch des Andenkens für ihre Freunde*. 3 volumes. Berlin: Duncker & Humblot, 1834.

———. *Rahel: Ein Buch des Andenkens für ihre Freunde*. Edited by Barbara Hahn. 6 volumes. Göttingen: Wallstein Verlag, 2011.

Varnhagen, Rahel, and David Veit, *Briefwechsel zwischen Rahel und David Veit*, 2 vols. Leipzig: Brockhaus, 1861.

Visser, Henk. "Mendelssohn's Euclidean Treatise on Equal Temperament." In *Moses Mendelssohn's Metaphysics and Aesthetics*, edited by Reiner Munk, 83–104. New York: Springer, 2011.

Wagner, Günther. "Vom Generalbass zum 'obligaten Akkompagnement': Stilistische Entwicklung im kammermusikalischen Werk Carl Philipp Emanuel Bachs." *Jahrbuch des Staatlichen Instituts für Musikforschung Preußischer Kulturbesitz* (1997): 74–107.

Wahrig, Gerhard. *Deutsches Wörterbuch*. Munich: Bertelsman, 1991.

Walden, Joshua S. "Composing Character in Musical Portraits: Carl Philipp Emanuel Bach and 'L'Aly Rupalich.'" *Musical Quarterly* 91, nos. 3/4 (2008): 379–411.

Weber, William. "Did People Listen in the 18th Century?" *Early Music* 25, no. 4 (1997): 678–91.

Weckel, Ulrike. "A Lost Paradise of Female Culture? Some Critical Questions regarding the Scholarship on Late Eighteenth- and Early Nineteenth-Century German Salons." *German History* 18, no. 3 (2000): 310–36, 318.

Weder, Christine. "Ein manipulierter Versuch: Das Märchen vom Experiment in Lessings *Nathan* und die naturwissenschaftliche Methodenlehre der 'durch Fleiß hervorgebrachten Erfahrung.'" *Deutsche Vierteljahrsschrift für Literaturwissenschaft und Geistesgeschichte* 2 (2008): 237–61.

Weissberg, Liliane. "Bodies in Pain: Reflections on the Berlin Jewish Salon." In *The German-Jewish Dialogue Reconsidered: A Symposium in Honor of George L. Mosse*, edited by Klaus L. Berghahn, 61–65. New York: Peter Lang, 1996.

———. *Life as a Goddess: Henriette Herz Writes her Autobiography*. Braun Lectures in the History of the Jews of Prussia 6. Ramat Gan: Bar-Ilan University, 2001.

———. "Literary Culture and Jewish Space around 1800: The Berlin Salons Revisited." In *Modern Jewish Literatures: Intersections and Boundaries*, edited by Sheila E. Jelen, Michael P. Kramer, and L. Scott Lerner, 24–43. Philadelphia: University of Pennsylvania Press, 2011.

———. "Weibliche Körperschaften: Bild und Wort bei Henriette Herz." In *Von einer Welt in die andere: Jüdinnen im 19. und 20. Jahrhundert*, edited by Jutta Dick and Barbara Hahn, 71–92. Vienna: Christian Brandstätter, 1993.

Weissmann, Adolf. *Berlin als Musikstadt. Geschichte der Oper und des Konzerts von 1740 bis 1911*. Berlin: Schuster & Löffler, 1911.

Werner, Klaus G. "Formeln und Kombinationen—Empfindungen und Individualisierungen: Zum Kopfsatz des Quartetts a-moll (Wq. 93, H. 537) von C. P. E. Bach." *Die Musikforschung* 46, no. 4 (1993): 371–90.

Werses, Shmuel. "Inter-Lingual Tensions in the Maskilic Periodical '*Hame'asef* and Its Time in Germany." *Dappim: Research in Literature* 11 (1997–98): 29–69.

Wessely, Naftali Herz (Hartwig). *Divrei Shalom Ve'emet*. Berlin: Ḥevrat Ḥinuch Ne'arim, 1782.

———. *Shirei Tif'eret*, volume 2. Berlin: Ḥevrat Ḥinuch Ne'arim, 1791.

Wheelock, Gretchen. "The 'Rhetorical Pause' and Metaphors of Conversation in Haydn's Quartets." In *Haydn & Das Streichquartett*, edited by Georg Feder and Walter Reicher, 67–88. Tutzing: Schneider, 2003.

Wilhelmy, Petra. *Der Berliner Salon im 19. Jahrhundert (1780–1914)*. Berlin: de Gruyter, 1989.

Wilhelmy-Dollinger, Petra. "Emanzipation durch Geselligkeit: Die Salons jüdischer Frauen in Berlin zwischen 1780 und 1830." In *Bild und Selbstbild der Juden Berlins zwischen Aufklärung und Romantik*, edited by Marianne Awerbuch and Stefi Jersch-Wenzel, 121–38. Berlin: Colloquium, 1992.

———. "Singen, Konzertieren, Diskutieren: Musikalische Aktivitäten in den Salons der 'Berliner Klassik.'" In *Urbane Musikkultur: Berlin um 1800*, edited by Eduard Mutschelknauss, 149–69. Hanover: Wehrhahn, 2011.

Will, Richard. "When God Met the Sinner, and Other Dramatic Confrontations in Eighteenth-Century Instrumental Music." *Music & Letters* 78, no. 2 (1997): 175–209.

Wolff, Christoph. "A Bach Cult in Late-Eighteenth-Century Berlin: Sara Levy's Musical Salon." *Bulletin of the American Academy of Arts and Sciences* 58, no. 3 (2005): 26–39.

———. "The Bach Tradition among the Mendelssohn Ancestry." In *Mendelssohn, the Organ, and the Music of the Past: Constructing Historical Legacies*, edited by Jürgen Thym, 213–23. Rochester, NY: University of Rochester Press, 2014.

———. *Johann Sebastian Bach: The Learned Musician*. New York: W. W. Norton, 2000.

———. *Mozart at the Gateway to His Fortune: Serving the Emperor, 1788–1791*. New York: W. W. Norton, 2012.

———. "Mozart 1782, Fanny Arnstein und viermal Bach." *Mozart-Jahrbuch* 10 (2009): 141–49.

———. "Recovered in Kiev: Bach et al. A Preliminary Report on the Music Collection of the Berlin Sing-Akademie." *Notes*, 2nd series, 58, no. 2 (2001): 259–71.

Wolff, Sabbatia Joseph. *Maimoniana oder Rhapsodien zur Charakteristik Salomon Maimons.* Edited by Martin L. Davies and Christoph Schulte. Berlin: Hayn, 1813; reprinted Berlin: Parerga, 2003.

Wolfssohn, Aaron Halle. "Leichtsinn und Frömmelei: Ein Familien Gemälde in Drei Aufzügen." In *Lustspiele zur Unterhaltung beim Purim-Feste.* Volume 1, 33–111. Breslau: s.n., 1796.

Wollny, Peter. "'Ein förmlicher Sebastian und Philipp Emanuel Bach-Kultus': Sara Levy, geb. Itzig und ihr musikalisch-literarischer Salon." In *Musik und Ästhetik im Berlin Moses Mendelssohns,* edited by Anselm Gerhard, 217–55. Wolfenbütteler Studien zur Aufklärung 25. Tübingen: Max Niemeyer, 1999.

———. *"Ein förmlicher Sebastian und Philipp Emanuel Bach-Kultus": Sara Levy und ihr musikalisches Wirken, mit einer Dokumentensammlung zur musikalischen Familiengeschichte der Vorfahren von Felix Mendelssohn Bartholdy.* Wiesbaden: Breitkopf & Härtel, 2010.

———. Introduction and Critical Notes. In *Klaviermusik I: Sonaten und Konzert für Cembalo solo; Konzert für zwei Cembali,* by Wilhelm Friedemann Bach, edited by Peter Wollny. Gesammelte Werke, volume 1. Stuttgart: Carus, 2009.

———. "Neuerkenntnisse zu einigen Kopisten der 1730er Jahre." *Bach-Jahrbuch* 102 (2016): 73–78.

———. "Sara Levy and the Making of Musical Taste in Berlin." *Musical Quarterly* 77, no. 4 (1993): 651–88.

Woyke, Saskia Maria. *Faustina Bordoni: Biographie, Vokalprofil, Rezeption.* Frankfurt: Peter Lang, 2010.

———. "Faustina Bordoni-Hasse—eine Sängerinnenkarriere im 18. Jahrhundert." In *Göttinger Händel-Beiträge* 7, edited by Hans Joachim Marx, 218–57. Göttingen: Vandenhoeck & Ruprecht, 1998.

Zedler, Johann Heinrich. *Grosses vollständige Universal-Lexicon.* Halle: Johann Heinrich Zedler, 1732–54.

Zelle, Carsten. "Verwöhnter Geschmack, schauervolles Ergötzen und theatralische Sittlichkeit: zum Verhältnis von Ethik und Ästhetik in Moses Mendelssohns ästhetischen Schriften." In *Musik und Ästhetik im Berlin Moses Mendelssohns,* edited by Anselm Gerhard, 97–115. Tübingen: Max Niemeyer, 1999.

Zelter, Carl Friedrich. *Carl Friedrich Zelters Darstellungen seines Lebens.* Edited by Johann Wolfgang Schottlaender. Weimar: Verlag der Goethe-Gesellschaft, 1931.

Ziegler, Christiane Mariane von. *Moralische und vermischte Send-Schreiben.* Leipzig: Braun, 1731.

Zohn, Steven. *Music for a Mixed Taste: Style, Genre, and Meaning in Telemann's Instrumental Works.* Oxford: Oxford University Press, 2008.

Contributors

REBECCA CYPESS, an associate professor of music at the Mason Gross School of the Arts and a faculty affiliate of the Department of Jewish Studies at Rutgers University, specializes in the history, interpretation, and performance practices of music in the seventeenth and eighteenth centuries. Her first book, *Curious and Modern Inventions: Instrumental Music as Discovery in Galileo's Italy* (University of Chicago Press, 2016), was supported by a grant from the American Association of University Women. A harpsichordist and fortepianist, she is founder of The Raritan Players, which released the recording *In Sara Levy's Salon* (Acis Productions) in 2017.

MARJANNE E. GOOZÉ is an associate professor of German studies and affiliated faculty in women's studies at the University of Georgia, where she teaches and does research in the areas of modern German literature, Jewish-German writers, Holocaust narratives, Jewish *salonnières*, women's studies, and feminist theory and criticism. She is the editor of two books: *Challenging Separate Spheres: Female Bildung in Late Eighteenth- and Nineteenth-Century Germany* (Peter Lang, 2007) and *International Women's Writing: New Landscapes of Identity*, with Anne E. Brown (Greenwood Press, 1995).

BARBARA HAHN is Max Kade Foundation Chair in German Studies at Vanderbilt University. Her books include *The Jewess Pallas Athena: This Too A Theory of Modernity* (2005) and *Endlose Nacht: Träume im Jahrhundert der Gewalt* (2016). In 2011, she published Rahel Levin Varnhagen's "Buch des Andenkens für ihre Freunde." Together with Ursula Isselstein, she is the editor-in-chief of an edition of Rahel Levin Varnhagen's letters and notes (7 volumes) and, together with Hermann Kappelhoff, Ingeborg Nordmann, Patchen Markell, and Thomas Wild, of a critical edition of Hannah Arendt's work (digital and print).

MARTHA B. HELFER is a professor of German at Rutgers University. She is the author of *The Word Unheard: Legacies of Anti-Semitism in German Language and Culture* (Northwestern University Press, 2011; German translation *Das unerhörte Wort: Antisemitismus in Literatur und Kultur* [Wallstein, 2013]). Together with

William Collins Donahue, she is the co-founder of the German Jewish Studies Workshop and coeditor of the series *Nexus: Essays in German Jewish Studies* (Camden House).

Natalie Naimark-Goldberg is a research fellow at the Braun Chair for the History of the Jews in Prussia, Bar-Ilan University, and at the Leo Baeck Institute Jerusalem. A scholar of German Jewish history and women's history, she is the author of *Jewish Women in Enlightenment Berlin* (Oxford, 2013) and the editor of a forthcoming Hebrew edition of Bertha Pappenheim's writings.

Elias Sacks is an assistant professor of religious studies and Jewish studies at the University of Colorado, Boulder. He is the author of *Moses Mendelssohn's Living Script: Philosophy, Practice, History, Judaism* (Indiana University Press, 2017), and has published some of the first English translations of Mendelssohn's Hebrew writings. He has also written on Moses Maimonides, Baruch Spinoza, Nachman Krochmal, Hermann Cohen, Franz Rosenzweig, and Jacob Taubes.

Yael Sela chairs the program in musicology at the Open University of Israel. Her research is concerned with gender, patronage, and domestic musical culture in early modern England, and with aesthetics, especially music, in the Berlin Enlightenment and Haskalah. Her most recent publications are "The Voice of the Psalmist: On the Performative Role of Psalms in Moses Mendelssohn's *Jerusalem*," in *Psalms In and On Jerusalem*, edited by Ilana Pardes and Ophir Münz-Manor (de Gruyter, forthcoming, 2018), and "Music, Acculturation, and Haskalah between Berlin and Königsberg in the 1780s," *Jewish Quarterly Review* 103, no. 3 (2013).

Nancy Sinkoff is an associate professor of Jewish studies and history and director of the Center for European Studies at Rutgers University. A historian of modern European Jewry with a focus on the Jews of Poland, she published *Out of the Shtetl: Making Jews Modern in the Polish Borderlands* (Brown University Press, 2004). *From Left to Right: Lucy S. Dawidowicz, the New York Intellectuals, and the Politics of Jewish History* is forthcoming with Wayne State University Press. Her most recent publication is "'A Melancholy Offering Tendered with Esteem': Gershom Scholem and Lucy S. Dawidowicz on Nathan Birnbaum, an Unexpected Conversation," *Jewish Quarterly Review* 107, no. 3 (2017).

George B. Stauffer is the dean of the Mason Gross School of the Arts and Distinguished Professor of Music History at Rutgers University. He is known for his writings on Baroque music and the life and works of J. S. Bach, in particular. His latest publications include *Bach: The Mass in B Minor* (Yale University Press, 2003) and *The World of Baroque Music* (Indiana University Press, 2006).

CHRISTOPH WOLFF is Adams University Professor Emeritus at Harvard University, where he has taught historical musicology since 1976. He was director of the Leipzig Bach Archive from 2001 through 2013 and currently serves on the graduate faculty of the Juilliard School in New York.

STEVEN ZOHN is Laura H. Carnell Professor of Music History at Temple University. His research focuses on the music of Telemann and the Bach family, and he is also professionally active as a performer on historical flutes. His most recent publications include "Morality and the 'Fair-Sexing' of Telemann's Faithful Music Master" in *Consuming Music: Individuals, Institutions, Communities, 1730–1830*, ed. Emily Green and Catherine Mayes (University of Rochester Press, 2017); and "Telemann's *Musique de table* and the *Tafelmusik Tradition*," Oxford Handbooks Online (2016).

Index

Italicized page numbers denote figures or musical examples.